M000251264

Multiple Intelligences and Leadership

LEA's Organization and Management Series

Arthur Brief and James P. Walsh, Series Editors

Ashforth • Role Transitions in Organizational Life: An Identity-Based Perspective

Beach • Image Theory: Theoretical and Empirical Foundations

Darley/Messick/Tyler • Social Influences on Ethical Behavior in Organizations

Denison • Managing Organizational Change in Transition Economies

Earley/Gigson • New Perspectives on Transitional Work Teams

Garud/Karnoe • Path Dependence and Creation

Lant/Shapira • Organizational Cognition: Computation and Interpretation

Pearce • Organization and Management in the Embrace of Government

Riggio/Murphy/Pirozzolo • Multiple Intelligences and Leadership

Thompson/Levine/Messick • Shared Cognition in Organizations: The Management of Knowledge

Multiple Intelligences and Leadership

Edited by

Ronald E. Riggio
Director

Susan E. Murphy
Associate Director

Francis J. Pirozzolo
Leadership Scholar-in-Residence

The Kravis-de Roulet Leadership Conference
Kravis Leadership Institute
Claremont McKenna College

LAWRENCE ERLBAUM ASSOCIATES, PUBLISHERS
2002 Mahwah, New Jersey London

Lawrence Erlbaum Associates, Inc., Publishers
10 Industrial Avenue
Mahwah, New Jersey 07430

Cover design by Kathryn Houghtaling Lacey

Library of Congress Cataloging-in-Publication Data

Kravis-de Roulet Leadership Conference (9th : 1999 : Claremont McKenna College)
Multiple intelligences and leadership / Ronald E. Riggio, Susan E. Murphy, Francis J. Pirozzolo, editors.
p. cm. -- (LEA's organization and management series)
"The Kravis-de Roulet Leadership Conference [sponsored by the] Kravis Leadership Institute [held at the] Claremont McKenna College."
Includes bibliographical references and index.
ISBN 0-8058-3466-4 (alk. paper)
1. Leadership--Congresses. 2. Multiple intelligences--Congresses. I. Riggio, Ronald E. II. Murphy, Susan E. III. Pirozzolo, Francis J. IV. Title. V. Series.

HD57.7.K733 1999
658.4'092--dc21 2001023919

Books published by Lawrence Erlbaum Associates are printed on acid-free paper, and their bindings are chosen for strength and durability.

Printed in the United States of America
10 9 8 7 6 5 4 3 2

THE KRAVIS-DE ROULET LEADERSHIP CONFERENCE

The Kravis-de Roulet Leadership Conference is an annual event sponsored by the Kravis Leadership Institute and dedicated to the discussion, promotion, and celebration of leadership. The conference brings recognized leadership scholars and practitioners to the Claremont McKenna College campus to explore current research and exchange ideas about leadership and the development of future leaders. The Kravis-de Roulet Leadership Conference is made possible through generous endowments from the Vincent de Roulet family and from Henry R. Kravis. *Multiple Intelligences and Leadership* represents the proceedings of the 9th annual Kravis-de Roulet Leadership Conference, held at Claremont McKenna College on April 28, 1999.

THE KRAVIS LEADERSHIP INSTITUTE

The Kravis Leadership Institute plays an active role in the development of young leaders via educational programs, research and scholarship, and the development of technologies for enhancing leadership potential.

Contents

About the Authors

Ram Aditya is a professor of Industrial and Organizational Psychology at Louisiana Tech University. He has a Bachelor's degree in Physics and a Master's degree in Business Administration from the University of Madras, India. He received his Ph.D. in Social and Organizational Psychology from Temple University in 1997. Prior to entering the doctoral program in the U.S., he worked for over a decade as a management professional in various types of organizations in the corporate sector. Currently, besides teaching and research, he conducts supervisory and executive training programs for organizations. His diverse academic training reflects a strong interdisciplinary approach in his work. His research interests include social intelligence, artifacts in research, leadership and cross-cultural issues, and the application of core social abilities in management development and in organizational behavior.

Bernard M. Bass is Distinguished Professor of Management Emeritus and Founding Director of the Center for Leadership Studies at Binghamton University, State University of New York. Dr. Bass is the author of over 300 articles and 22 books concentrating on leadership, organizational behavior, and human resource management. Between 1952 and the present, he has been the principal investigator on numerous federal, state, and private foundation research grants. He was a founding editor of *Leadership Quarterly,* and he has consulted with and conducted training for many of the Fortune 500 firms, and has lectured or run training workshops in over 40 countries. Professor Bass is also a Senior Scientist for the Gallup Organization and a member of the Board of Governors of the Kravis Leadership Institute.

For the past 20 years, Professor Bass has focused much of his research on transformational leadership and management development. In 1994, he received the Society for Industrial/Organizational Psychology (SIOP) Award for Distinguished Scientific Contributions. In 1997, he was honored by the Society for Psychology in Management with the annual Lifetime Award for the Practice of Psychology in Management.

David R. Caruso is a management psychologist. He received his Ph.D. in Psychology from Case Western Reserve University and was a postdoctoral fellow in developmental psychology at Yale University. Dr. Caruso has both a consulting practice and an active research program. He consults with individuals and companies on career, management, and organization development issues. Dr. Caruso's research activities include the study of career-related personality traits, emotional intelligence in the work place, and the development of emotional intelligence in children.

Dr. Caruso has lectured on issues ranging from career development to emotional intelligence and has coauthored a number of scientific publications. Dr. Caruso has hands-on experience in small business, consulting, and corporate environments, having held positions in marketing, research and development, strategic planning, and product management.

Martin M. Chemers is the Dean of Social Sciences and Professor of Psychology at the University of California at Santa Cruz. Prior to this appointment he was the Henry R. Kravis Professor of Leadership and Organizational Psychology and Director of the Kravis Leadership Institute at Claremont McKenna College. He was previously on the faculties of the Universities of Illinois, Delaware, Washington, and Utah where he was chair of the Department of Psychology.

Since receiving his Ph.D. in Social Psychology from the University of Illinois in 1968, he has been an active researcher and has published seven books and many articles on leadership, culture, and organizational diversity. His popular, practitioner-oriented book *Improving Leadership Effectiveness: The Leader Match Concept* (written with Fred Fiedler) is widely used as a basis for leadership training. Dr. Chemers' books have been translated into German, Japanese, Swedish, Spanish, and Portuguese. His most recent book, *An Integrative Theory of Leadership,* was published in the fall of 1997. The Japanese edition was published in 1999.

Fred Fiedler is Professor of Psychology Emeritus at the University of Washington. After serving in the U.S. Army during World War II, Dr. Fiedler received his Ph.D. in 1949. Professor Fiedler's pioneering work on the contingency model of leadership in the 1950s and 1960s culminated in his book, *A Theory of Leadership Effectiveness* in 1967.

In recognition of Dr. Fiedler's many contributions to research on leadership, he has won The Ralph Stogdill Award for Outstanding Contribution to Leadership Research (1978), the Award for Distinguished Research Contributions to Military Psychology (1979), the 1996 Distinguished Scientific Contributions Award from the Society of Industrial/Organizational Psychology (SIOP), and the prestigious James McKeen Award in 1999 from the American Psychological Society. He is a Fellow of the American Psychological Association, and was listed as one of the most frequently cited psychologists. After amassing more than 200 publications over the years, Fred Fiedler continues to be an active and enthusiastic researcher.

Joyce Hogan is Senior Vice President of Hogan Assessment Systems, a corporation specializing in test publishing and assessment consulting. She is responsible for research and development of assessment products.

Dr. Hogan received her Ph.D. from the University of Maryland. From 1975 to 1982, she taught and was a research scientist at Johns Hopkins University. From 1982 to 1997, Dr. Hogan was Professor of Psychology at the University of Tulsa. She edited the book *Business and Industry Testing* and is currently the editor of the journal, *Human Performance.* Along with Robert Hogan, Joyce writes on leadership assessment with emphasis on effectiveness, multiple perspectives, and dysfunctional characteristics.

Robert Hogan is McFarlin Professor of Psychology at the University of Tulsa, and President of Hogan Assessment Systems, a test publishing and consulting firm in Tulsa, Oklahoma. Within Industrial Psychology, Dr. Hogan is recognized as having pioneered the use of personality tests for making decisions within organizations. He is also the author of three well-regarded personality inventories and supporting assessment materials.

Robert Hogan received his Ph.D. from the University of California at Berkeley, and was Professor of Psychology and Social Relations at Johns Hopkins University in Baltimore before moving to Tulsa. He is the author of more than 100 scholarly articles, chapters, and books, and he lectures extensively in the U.S., Europe, and Australia on a variety of topics related to psychology and business.

Robert J. House received his Ph.D. in Management from Ohio State University. He is currently the Joseph Frank Bernstein Professor of Organization Studies at the Wharton School of Business at the University of Pennsylvania. He has published approximately 100 articles in refereed journals and has coauthored six books. House cofounded *Leadership Quarterly* (with Bernard M. Bass and Henry L. Tosi, Jr.), and founded MESO, an organization devoted to the encouragement of the integration of micro and macro organizational behavior theory and research. He has received grants from the U.S. Department of Education and the National Science Foundation to support his ongoing research on crosscultural organizational practices and leader behavior.

His current research concerns the distribution and exercise of power in complex organizations, the nature and effect of exceptional leaders, the role of personality variables in organizational performance, and crosscultural organizational practices and leader behavior.

John (Jack) D. Mayer is Professor of Psychology at the University of New Hampshire. He is codeveloper, with Dr. Peter Salovey, of the theory of emotional intelligence (popularized in the best-selling book, *Emotional Intelligence,* by Daniel Goleman). Dr. Mayer's theoretical contributions include emotional intelligence and the development of a systems framework for understanding personality. His articles have appeared in numerous scientific journals and books, and he has served on the editorial boards of the *Journal of Personality,* the *Journal of Personality and Social Psychology,* and *Psychological Bulletin.* Dr. Mayer has lectured widely on emotional intelligence and on his systems approach to personality at colleges and universities, and in nonprofit, corporate, and government settings.

Susan E. Murphy is an Associate Professor of Psychology at Claremont McKenna College and Associate Director of the Kravis Leadership Institute. Among her research interests are investigating the contribution of personality characteristics and early leadership experiences in effective leadership, and the role of mentoring in career and leadership development. Immediately prior to joining Claremont McKenna College, Professor Murphy worked as a research scientist at Batelle Seattle Research Center where she designed and delivered leadership development programs for senior-level managers in a wide range of industries in the United States, and for the nuclear power industry in Japan. Much of this work focused on identifying the critical requirements for effective leadership and motivation of work groups based on assessment of current culture and future strategic objectives.

Lynn R. Offerman is Professor and Director of the Industrial and Organizational Psychology program at the George Washington University. She is the author of numerous articles on leadership, teams, and diversity issues. Among her research contributions, Dr. Offermann was senior co-editor of a special issue of the *American Psychologist* on cutting edge issues in organization psychology in 1990 that included future leadership issues. From 1993 to 1997, Dr. Offermann was involved with the Kellogg Leadership Studies Project, a funded effort to advance leadership for the next century, and she served as Convener of the Leadership and Followership focus group from 1996 to 1997. This involvement culminated in the publication of *The Balance of Leadership and Followership* in 1997, edited with Dr. Edwin Hollander. An active practitioner, she has worked with numerous public, private, multinational, and international organizations on executive development and coaching, team development, change management, and organizational development. Dr. Offermann currently serves on the Editorial Board of *Leadership Quarterly.*

Ly U. Phan is a doctoral student in the Industrial/Organizational Psychology program at the George Washington University. Her research interests include cultural diversity, 360-degree feedback, and leadership. She has worked with the World Bank Executive Development Program, and currently is employed by the Vandaveer Group. Ly received her B.A. from the University of St. Thomas in Houston, Texas.

Francis J. Pirozzolo is a Leadership Scholar-in-Residence at the Kravis Leadership Institute at Claremont McKenna College, and the president of the consulting firm, Competitive Advantage. Dr. Pirozzolo received his Ph.D. from the University of Rochester and was the Chief of Neuropsychology at Baylor College of Medicine, where he conducted research in neuropsychology, was the editor of the journal, *Developmental Neuropsychology,* and published in journals such as *Neurology, Brain and Language,* and *Science.* He has authored eleven books on the brain and behavior. For many years, Dr. Pirozzolo has also worked in the area of performance enhancement for professional and amateur athletes, and has worked with the New York Yankees and Houston Astros baseball organizations, with members of the U.S. Olympic teams, and with professional and college athletes across the country.

Ronald E. Riggio is the Henry R. Kravis Professor of Leadership and Organizational Psychology at Claremont McKenna College and Director of the Kravis Leadership Institute. His early research interests focused on the measurement of communication and social skills, with a particular emphasis on the communication of emotion, and the role of communication skills and emotion in charisma and charismatic leadership. He is the author of more than 40 journal articles in organizational psychology, social psychology, management, and education, as well as author or co-editor of several books, including *Assessment Centers: Research and Practice* (Select Press, 1997), and his textbook *Introduction to Industrial/ Organizational Psychology* (Prentice Hall, 2000), now in its third edition.

Prior to coming to Claremont McKenna College, Dr. Riggio was at California State University at Fullerton, where he helped develop the Student Outcome Assessment Center designed to identify the skills needed for success in business careers as well as predictors of leadership potential.

Peter J. Salovey is Professor of Psychology at Yale University. His research cuts across a variety of areas, including social/personality psychology, public health, and clinical and developmental psychology. Along with Jack Mayer, he is codeveloper of the theory of emotional intelligence. Much of his recent research has focused on the role of persuasion, message framing, and social influence in encouraging prevention and early detection behaviors relevant to HIV/AIDS and cancer.

Dr. Salovey has published over 135 articles and chapters in the scientific literature, and he is coauthor of a textbook, *Psychology: Being Human.* He edits the Guilford Press series on *Emotions and Social Behavior,* and was an associate editor of *Psychological Bulletin* and founding editor of *General Psychology Review.* Dr. Salovey was a recipient of a National Science Foundation Presidential Young Investigator Award, and he is presently a member of the NIMH Behavioral Science Task Force.

Robert J. Sternberg is IBM Professor of Psychology and Education in the Department of Psychology at Yale University. His interests in psychology cut across various areas. A fellow of ten divisions of the American Psychological Association, Sternberg has received two awards from APA—the Distinguished Scientific Award for an Early Career Contribution to Psychology, and the Boyd R. McCandless Young Scientist Award. He has won numerous awards from various other organizations, such as the Cattell Award of the Society of Multivariate Experimental Psychology, Distinguished Contribution Award of the National Association for Gifted Children, and the James McKeen Cattell Award of the American Psychological Society. Much of Sternberg's research investigates the application of his theories to teaching at all levels. Sternberg is also a fellow of the American Academy of Arts and Sciences, the American Association for the

Advancement of Science, and the American Psychological Society. He is past editor of the *Psychological Bulletin* and editor of *Contemporary Psychology.* Sternberg is most well-known for his triarchic theory of intelligence, triangular theory of love, theory of mental self-government, and investment theory of creativity (developed in collaboration with Todd Lubart). He also has proposed a new balance theory of wisdom and propulsion theory of creative contributions. Sternberg has authored over 800 articles, books, and book chapters, including *Beyond IQ, Cupid's Arrow, Metaphors of Mind, Defying the Crowd* (with Todd Lubart), *Thinking Styles, Successful Intelligence,* and *Love is a story.* He is also the author of *In Search of the Human Mind* and of *Pathways to Psychology,* two introductory psychology texts, as well as of *Cognitive Psychology,* a cognition text.

David G. Winter is Professor of Psychology at the University of Michigan. He received his Ph.D. in Social Psychology from Harvard in 1967, and has been on the faculties of Wesleyan University, Harvard, and MIT. Dr. Winters pioneered the development of techniques for measuring personalities of political leaders at a distance. As a major contributor to research in personality and leadership, Winters is the author of *Motivating Economic Achievement* (with D.C. McClelland, 1969), *The Power Motive* (1973), *A New Case for the Liberal Arts* (with D.C. McClelland and A.J. Stewart, 1981), and *Personality: Analysis and Interpretation of Lives* (1996), in addition to numerous journal articles and book chapters. Dr. Winter has examined topics such as personality, power, and authority; motivation and performance in presidential candidates; leader appeal; and the motivational profiles of leaders and followers. He is also interested in authoritarianism and gender roles.

Dr. Winter has received numerous awards and recognition for his scholarship, and has been very active in the development of the emerging field of Political Psychology.

Stephen Zaccaro is a Professor of Psychology at George Mason University. Dr. Zaccaro's research and teaching interests include social and organizational psychology, specifically in the areas of leadership, team problem solving, work attitudes, and occupational stress. His papers have appeared in the *Journal of Applied Psychology, Organizational Behavior and Human Decision Processes,* and *Personality and Social Psychology Bulletin.* He has co-edited a book titled *Occupational Stress and Organizational Effectiveness,* and is currently coauthoring a second book, tentatively titled, *The Thinking Body: Developing Creative Leaders for a Complex World.* Dr. Zaccaro has consulted with the U.S. Army on various issues related both to leadership development and team problem solving.

Series Foreword

The aim of this series is to publish scholarly works that will alter the direction of research in the organizational sciences. Riggio and his colleagues have written a book that is likely to do just that in regards to the study of leadership. The edited volume should serve to direct the renewed interest in the "trait approach" to leadership by providing thorough assessments of the highly provocative propositions that intelligence is multifaceted and that these facets are differentially related to leadership and effectiveness. These assessments are supplied by some of the most prominent researchers in the fields of leadership and intelligence. Moreover, the book editors, in carefully crafted introductory and concluding chapters, skillfully bring the divergent views evident in the book together. We suspect the book will become a must read for serious leadership scholars and will entice many in that group who have not been taken by the trait approach to view it with considerably more optimism.

Arthur Brief
James P. Walsh
Series Editors

1

Multiple Intelligences and Leadership: An Overview

Ronald E. Riggio
Kravis Leadership Institute
Claremont McKenna College

Questions of the role that intelligence plays in leadership are old ones. Are the smartest individuals most likely to obtain positions of leadership? Are bright leaders the most effective leaders? Is a high IQ a prerequisite for leaders? While high-level leaders in politics, business, and social movements certainly seem smart, and appear to be well above average in intelligence, skeptics note that there have been prominent leaders of average (and perhaps even below average) intelligence. Moreover, many of our greatest intellectual minds are in the sciences, research, and education, and they neither obtain nor even pursue positions of leadership. So, what *is* the connection between intelligence and leadership?

Scientific studies of the role of intelligence in leadership date back to the 1920s and 1930s. Much of this early research suggested that intelligence did indeed contribute to leadership. For example, leaders were found to be more intelligent than their followers, and intelligence was consistently correlated with perceptions of leadership (see Bass, 1990, and Lord, DeVader, & Alliger, 1986, for reviews). One obvious limitation to this approach, however, was that it did not take context or situational factors into account. Early on, for example, Hollingworth (1926) found that if a leader's intelligence was too much greater than that of followers, the followers did not identify with the leader, and this presumably detracted from the leader's effectiveness. So we might expect that the leader of a cutting-edge software development company should be reasonably intelligent—at least on par with some of the bright software engineers she or he oversees. In contrast, the on-field leader of a sports team might not require a particularly high IQ, especially if he or she is a talented athlete, experienced, and knowledgeable of the sport. Because of situational factors, we cannot assume that the relationship between intelligence and leadership is a straightforward one. Of course, many modern theories of leadership emphasize this interaction of leader characteristics (such as intelligence) and qualities of the leadership situation.

Another limitation of this early research on intelligence and leadership was the overemphasis on general academic intelligence. Most commonly, research on intelligence and leadership focused on traditional, IQ-based notions of intelligence, even though early scholars did note the importance of a broader conceptualization of intelligence. For instance, constructs such as "emotional maturity," "social insight," "tact," and "social skills/competence" were all believed to be associated with effective leadership by early researchers (Bass, 1990). This makes sense. Although some prominent and successful leaders may not be intellectual giants in the academic sense, these individuals have some sort of savvy—a kind of "street smarts" that makes them effective in their leadership roles. In many ways, these other constructs discussed by early leadership researchers parallel the multiple types of intelligence that are now capturing the attention of intelligence researchers, personality and social psychologists, and social scientists in general. For example, social insight and social skills are components of the domain of "social intelligence" (Marlowe, 1986; Riggio, Messamer, & Throckmorton, 1991). The notion of "tact" is reflected in Sternberg and Wagner's conceptualization of "practical intelligence" (Sternberg & Wagner, 1986; Wagner & Sternberg, 1985), and "emotional maturity" has transformed into Salovey and Mayer's notion of "emotional intelligence" (Mayer & Salovey, 1993; Salovey & Mayer, 1990). The chapters of this book explore each of these various types of intelligence.

Even the earliest intelligence researchers knew that there was more to intelligence than the mental abilities represented in traditional intelligence tests. For example, Edward Thorndike first defined social intelligence in 1920, and there were soon several attempts to measure the construct (Moss, Hunt, Omwake, & Ronning, 1927; R.L. Thorndike & Stein, 1937). Guilford (1967) was a long-time advocate of multiple facets of intelligence, and in the past two decades, Gardner (1983) and Sternberg (1985) have argued for specific, multiple domains of intelligence. Today, intelligence is being more broadly conceptualized and defined. What is surprising is that it is only recently that these broader notions of intelligence have been applied to the study of leadership. For a long time, any scholar or informed observer of leadership has known that great and effective leaders have had something more than mere IQ going for them.

The most recent explosion of interest in intelligence and leadership has been fueled by the success of Daniel Goleman's (1995) *Emotional Intelligence*. Even though the construct of "emotional intelligence" itself is only a decade old, the past few years have seen the terms EI or EQ (as opposed to IQ) become commonplace terms, and there has been a rush of books on the importance of emotional intelligence in the workplace (e.g., Cooper & Sawaff, 1997; Feldman, 1999; Goleman, 1998; Ryback, 1997; Weisinger, 1998). Despite the popularity of the emotional intelligence concept, research has only begun to explore its depths, and to try to understand its true relationship to leader effectiveness. Moreover, emotional intelligence is only one type of intelligence that plays a part in successful leadership. Social intelligence, practical intelligence, and creativity are other facets of the broader construct of intelligence that are implicated in good leadership.

The resurgence of interest in leadership and intelligence, and particularly the exploration of the role of multiple types or facets of intelligence in leader effectiveness, appears to be a reawakening of the "trait approach" to leadership (see chapter 3). However, rather than focusing on narrow conceptualizations of leader characteristics, traits such as social, emotional, or practical intelligence represent complex constellations of abilities. These multiple forms of intelligence are not only possessed by effective leaders, but they are the types of characteristics that may make leaders effective in a range of leadership situations because they involve abilities to adapt to a variety of social and interpersonal situations. While IQ has not been a particularly good predictor of effective leadership across situations, a combination of general/academic intelligence, social intelligence, emotional intelligence, and perhaps other domains of intelligence, may do a good job of predicting leadership effectiveness. We are only beginning to explore the connections between multiple forms of intelligence and leadership.

This volume brings together well-known researchers from the field of intelligence who are investigating the multiple domains of intelligence, and renowned leadership scholars who are exploring the role that multiple intelligences play in effective leadership. In many ways, these two fields—intelligence and leadership—have been moving along parallel lines. While intelligence researchers were working to broaden the rather narrow existing emphasis on verbal and academic-based cognitive abilities, leadership researchers realized that while it was important for a leader to be smart, there was much more to "intelligent" leadership than simply IQ.

The first section looks at the multiple domains of intelligence—practical intelligence, social intelligence, emotional intelligence, and other domains. Robert J. Sternberg sets the stage with a discussion of what he calls "successful intelligence." According to Sternberg, successful intelligence is a fusion of traditional notions of analytical intelligence, practical intelligence, and creativity. An important theme, however, is that leaders are successful by recognizing and capitalizing on their strengths and compensating for their weaknesses.

Stephen J. Zaccaro next emphasizes the crucial role of social intelligence in organizational leadership. According to Zaccaro, there are two key components of social intelligence: the ability to perceive and interpret social situations, and behavioral flexibility or adaptability. Evidence suggests that the importance of social intelligence for effective leadership increases as one moves higher in the organizational hierarchy, where the complexity of social situations likewise increases.

David R. Caruso, John D. Mayer, and Peter Salovey present an overview of their recent ability model of emotional intelligence, and explore the role that emotional intelligence plays in effective leadership. According to these authors, emotional intelligence underlies a leader's "people" or "relationship" skills. Caruso, et al. apply their model of emotional intelligence to leadership in work organizations and discuss why organizations should consider emotional intelligence in the selection and development of leaders and managers.

Joyce Hogan and Robert Hogan further expand the multiple domains of intelligence with their concept of "sociopolitical intelligence."According to the Hogans, sociopolitical intelligence involves the possession of social skills and how critical they are for leader effectiveness in today's relationship-oriented, team-based organizations. Drawing on research examining the connections between personality constructs (such as empathy) and leader effectiveness, the Hogans have developed measures of sociopolitical intelligence and examined its role in leadership success and failure.

Chapters in the second section of this book call on renowned leadership scholars to explore the relationships between established leadership theories and multiple domains of intelligence. Fred E. Fiedler explores the role that situational factors play in influencing the leader's deployment of intellectual resources. According to Fiedler, leaders may possess intelligence, but it may not be utilized effectively due to situational factors. Fiedler reminds us that effective leadership is a complex interaction of the leader's characteristics, the leader's experience, and elements of the situation. Simply possessing multiple domains of intelligence is not enough if a leader cannot use these resources effectively.

Bernard M. Bass explores how three types of intelligence—cognitive intelligence, social intelligence, and emotional intelligence—contribute to transformational leadership. Bass's thesis is that truly exceptional leaders, those we call "transformational," must possess multiple types of intelligence. Social and emotional intelligence are particularly important because these contribute to the transformational leader's ability to inspire and build relationships with followers.

David G. Winter explores the motivational dimensions of leadership, suggesting that the leaders' motives influence the utilization of multiple intelligences. Winter looks at the motivational profiles of political leaders and explores relationships between motives, intelligence, and leader effectiveness. Winter uses contemporary examples such as Clinton's presidency to examine how motivation and multiple intelligences interconnect.

Martin M. Chemers recently presented an integrative theory of leadership (Chemers, 1997) that provides a unifying framework for the study of effective leadership. He further extends this work by exploring how multiple domains of intelligence contribute to leadership effectiveness. Chemers also shows how possession of multiple intelligences contributes to a crucial component of effective leaders, what he calls "leadership efficacy."

The final section moves us from the theoretical to the applied, and explores how multiple intelligences play a role in effective leadership in conditions of stress, in multicultural work environments, and in the international environment. Drawing on a social cognitive approach to leadership, Susan E. Murphy begins by reporting research that demonstrates the roles that social and emotional intelligence play in leader self-regulation and efficacy when under stressful circumstances.

Lynn R. Offermann and Ly U. Phan address the issue of the increasing diversity of the workforce with the concept of "cultural intelligence." According to Offermann and Phan, cultural intelligence is a form of meta-intelligence that allows leaders to function effectively in a variety of cultures.

Ram N. Aditya and Robert J. House further explore this multicultural focus by examining how social intelligence plays a role in cross-national leadership using data from the Global Leadership and Organizational Behavior Effectiveness (GLOBE) research program. Aditya and House find that elements of social intelligence, as represented by the construct of interpersonal acumen, play an important part in cross-cultural leadership effectiveness.

Finally, Francis J. Pirozzolo and I conclude by noting common themes presented throughout the volume, determining what this collection of research tells us about multiple intelligences and leadership, and exploring the implications that research on multiple intelligences has for leadership selection, training, and development. Although we conclude that we are only beginning to understand the concept of multiple intelligences, and only starting to explore its relationship to leadership, we firmly believe that this line of research can be readily applied to the selection, training, and developing of future leaders.

REFERENCES

Bass, B. M. (1990). *Bass & Stogdill's handbook of leadership: Theory, research, and managerial applications.* (3rd ed.). New York: Free Press.

Chemers, Martin M. (1997). *An Integrative Theory of Leadership*. Mahwah, NJ: Lawrence Erlbaum Associates.

Cooper, R. K., & Sawaff, A. (1997). *EQ: Emotional intelligence in leadership and organizations.* New York: Grosset/Putnam.

Feldman, D. A. (1999). *The handbook of emotionally intelligent leadership: Inspiring others to achieve results.* New York: Leadership Performance Solutions.

Gardner, H. (1983). *Frames of mind: The theory of multiple intelligences.* New York: Basic Books.

Goleman, D. (1995). *Emotional intelligence: Why it can matter more than IQ.* New York: Bantam.

Goleman, D. (1998). *Working with emotional intelligence.* New York: Bantam.

Guilford, J. P. (1967). *The nature of human intelligence.* New York: McGraw-Hill.

Hollingworth, L. S. (1926). *Gifted children.* New York: Macmillan.

Lord, R. G., DeVader, C. L., & Alliger, G. M. (1986). A meta-analysis of the relation between personality traits and leadership perceptions: An application of validity generalization procedures. *Journal of Applied Psychology, 71*, 402–410.

Marlowe, H. A. (1986). Social intelligence: Evidence for multidimensionality and construct independence. *Journal of Educational Psychology, 78*, 52–58.

Mayer, J. D., & Salovey, P. (1993). The intelligence of emotional intelligence. *Intelligence, 17*, 433–442.

Moss, F. A., Hunt, T., Omwake, K. T., & Ronning, M. M. (1927). *Social intelligence test*. Washington, DC: George Washington University.

Riggio, R. E., Messamer, J., & Throckmorton, B. (1991). Social and academic intelligence: Conceptually distinct but overlapping constructs. *Personality and Individual Differences, 12*, 695–702.

Ryback, D. (1997). *Putting emotional intelligence to work: Successful leadership is more than IQ*. Oxford: Butterworth-Heinemann.

Salovey, P., & Mayer, J. D. (1990). Emotional intelligence. *Imagination, Cognition, and Personality, 9*, 185–211.

Sternberg, R. J. (1985). *Beyond IQ: A triarchic theory of human intelligence*. Cambridge: Cambridge University Press.

Sternberg, R. J., & Wagner, R. K. (1986). *Practical intelligence: Nature and origins of competence in the everyday world*. Cambridge: Cambridge University Press.

Thorndike, E. L. (1920). Intelligence and its uses. *Harper's Magazine, 140*, 227–235.

Thorndike, R. L., & Stein, S. (1937). An evaluation of the attempts to measure social intelligence. *Psychological Bulletin, 34*, 275–285.

Wagner, R. K., & Sternberg, R. J. (1985). Practical intelligence in real-world pursuits: The role of tacit knowledge. *Journal of Personality and Social Psychology, 48*, 436–458.

Weisinger, H. (1998). *Emotional intelligence at work*. San Francisco, CA: Jossey-Bass.

I

Multiple Domains of Intelligence

2

Successful Intelligence: A New Approach to Leadership

Robert J. Sternberg
Yale University

SUCCESSFUL INTELLIGENCE AND LEADERSHIP

What distinguishes successful leaders from the rest? No doubt there are many attributes, but intelligence certainly would seem to be one of them—but is it?

The intelligence-based approach to leadership has not been a strikingly successful one. On the one hand, intelligence as conventionally measured seems to have some predictive value. On the other hand, its predictive value is not terribly high (see Sternberg, et al. 2000). The predictive value of intelligence for leadership also may vary across situations. Fiedler and Link (1994), for example, have suggested that intelligence predicts leadership success under conditions of low stress but not under conditions of high stress, where experience becomes more important.

The modest and elusive correlations between intelligence and leadership may result not from the inadequacy of intelligence as a predictor of leadership, but of the particular operationalization that has been used to measure intelligence. In other words, the predictive value of intelligence may have been flagged in various studies because these studies examined and measured aspects of intelligence that, however effective they may be in predicting academic and certain other kinds of performance, are not effective predictors of leadership performance.

THE THEORY OF SUCCESSFUL INTELLIGENCE

Conventional conceptions of intelligence deal almost exclusively with the analytical aspect of intelligence, but a full conception of intelligence comprises other aspects as well.

Successful intelligence is the ability to achieve success by one's own standards, given one's sociocultural context. Note that in this definition, there is no single criterion of success that serves as a standard for all people. Rather people define their own criteria of success. The criteria must be within some context of life, however. Success is always within a sociocultural context: Those who abandon it do so at their peril. Thus an ax murderer may achieve success by his or her own standards, but may pay for it with his or her life. Of course, there are societies that themselves seem to violate universal laws (e.g., Nazi Germany), but it is beyond the scope of this chapter to deal with these issues (but see Sternberg, 1998). In short, though, when referring to *intelligence,* I am referring to *successful intelligence,* the kind that is most relevant for understanding leadership success.

According to the theory of successful intelligence (Sternberg, 1997), people achieve success by recognizing and capitalizing on their strengths and by recognizing and either correcting or compensating for their weaknesses. In other words, there is no small and delimited set of abilities (e.g., general intelligence in Spearman's [1904] theory or eight multiple intelligences in Gardner's [1983, 1999] theory) that can adequately predict who will be successful and who will not be. People find their own, idiographic patterns of strengths and weaknesses, and develop patterns of capitalization, correction, and compensation that enable them either to achieve their goals or not. Thus, in this essay, when I discuss successful leaders, I will be discussing ones who have understood their own strengths and weaknesses and, to a large extent, made the most of them. Those who do not do so—the Richard Nixons (who cannot conquer their morbid distrust of others) and the Joseph Stalins (who, in their monomaniacal need for absolute power, destroy so many others and become notorious and infamous rather than respected and famous)—pay the price and so, unfortunately, do the people whom they lead.

Intelligence as traditionally defined refers to adaptation to the environment (see e.g., Sternberg & Detterman, 1986). In addition, successful intelligence involves not just adaptation to environments, but a balance among adaptation to environments, shaping of environments, and selection of environments. In particular, adaptation involves changing oneself to suit the environment; shaping involves changing the environment (including people in it) to suit oneself; and selection involves finding a new environment. Leadership is largely a shaping function, although inevitably it involves compromises calling for a balance of adaptation with shaping. Thus, while conventional intelligence emphasizes adaptation, successful intelligence as applied to leadership emphasizes shaping. It is not so much about figuring out how to succeed within a set of rules as it is about establishing a set of rules to guide others.

Finally, successful intelligence further involves a balance in the use of analytical, practical, and creative abilities. Analytical or traditional abilities are involved in analyzing and evaluating existing ideas and systems, usually at a somewhat abstract level. People can be effective analytically in an academic setting and largely not be able to apply their skills to practical settings. People can also be effective in practical settings but be largely unable to apply their skills to abstract and academic settings. This essay focuses on the roles of practical and creative abilities in leadership because these are the two kinds of abilities that have been the most ignored in the literature relating intelligence to leadership skill. Each kind of ability and its relation to leadership will be discussed in turn.

LEADERSHIP AND PRACTICAL INTELLIGENCE

Practical intelligence is that aspect of successful intelligence that is relevant to adaptation, shaping, and selection in everyday life. There are a number of different ways of measuring practical intelligence (see reviews in Sternberg, et al. 2000; Sternberg & Wagner, 1986; Wagner, 2000), but the one described here involves the measurement of tacit knowledge (Polanyi, 1966; Sternberg, Wagner, Williams, & Horvath, 1995; Wagner & Sternberg, 1985). *Tacit knowledge* refers to what one needs to know to succeed in a given environment, and is knowledge that is typically not explicitly taught and often not even verbalized.

Tacit knowledge has a number of characteristics, but the five main ones are that it is (a) generally acquired on one's own, (b) usually unspoken and often implicit, (c) procedural in nature, (d) not readily articulated, and (e) directly related to practical goals that people value. Tacit knowledge is not the same as job knowledge that may be well articulated, which includes formal knowledge such as how to fill out complex tax forms or to operate a lathe. It also is not equivalent to general intelligence. Most importantly, it is not sufficient for effective leadership performance. In discussing tacit knowledge, I am making no claim that it is the story about leadership. Rather, it is one important part of that story.

We represent tacit knowledge in the form of a production system. A production system is nothing more than a sequence of if–then statements, which can be elaborated by conjunctions, disjunctions, or justifications (*because* statements). For example, in a study of military leadership (Hedlund, et al. 2000), we found one simple production system to be the following:

IF one of your units does an outstanding job in accomplishing a mission,
AND

IF you observed things that needed to be correct to improve their future performance,

THEN tell them they did a good job and hold the suggestions for improvement for a later time,

BECAUSE soldiers need time to enjoy, for a little while, the positive feelings of accomplishment.

Background Research

The background for our research on the role of tacit knowledge in leadership goes back to studies we have done on the role of tacit knowledge in management. In this research (summarized in Sternberg, et al. 2000; Sternberg, Wagner, & Okagaki, 1993; Sternberg & Wagner, 1993; Sternberg, Wagner, Williams, & Horvath, 1995), we created tacit knowledge inventories that consisted of several work-related problems along with 5 to 20 options for solving each problem. Respondents were asked to rate the quality of each option for addressing the situation. These inventories, which may be viewed as situational-judgment tests, are then scored in one of three ways: (a) by correlating responses with an index of group membership (e.g., expert, novice) with superior groups' responses scored as preferred; (b) by using professional "rules of thumb" available in published works; or (c) by computing a difference score or correlation between responses and an expert profile. The third method generally has proved to be the most satisfactory in terms of maximizing reliability and validity.

Those filling out the inventory respond on a Likert scale that ranges from 1 (extremely bad option) to 7 (extremely good option). Table 2.1 shows an item from the Tacit Knowledge Inventory for Managers (Wagner & Sternberg, 1991).

In a variety of such studies, conducted with managers, sales people, academic psychologists, elementary school teachers, college students, and people from many other occupations, both in the United States and in Spain (Grigorenko, Gil, Jarvin, & Sternberg, 2000), we have found that (a) tacit knowledge scores increase on average with experience, although it appears to be learning from experience rather than experience itself that matters; (b) tacit knowledge scores typically are uncorrelated with scores on tests of general ability, although occasionally they show significant positive correlations (see Wagner, et. al., 1999) or even significant negative correlations (see Grigorenko & Sternberg, in press); (c) tacit knowledge scores are uncorrelated with scores on tests of multiple abilities, such as the Armed Services Vocational Aptitude Battery (ASVAB-Eddy, 1988); (d) tacit knowledge scores are uncorrelated with scores on tests of personality and cognitive styles; (e) tacit knowledge scores correlate among themselves, both within and across occupations (see Wagner, 1987; Wagner & Sternberg, 1985); (f) tacit knowledge scores predict real-world criteria of success on the job as well as or better than does IQ; (g) tacit knowledge scores predict job-related criteria incrementally over cognitive, personality, and cognitive styles measures; and (h) in entry-level occupations, the tacit knowledge that leads to success in the United States is remarkably similar to that which leads to success elsewhere (e.g., in Spain).

TABLE 2.1
Example Item From the Tacit Knowledge Inventory for Managers

An employee who reports to one of your subordinates has asked to talk with you about waste, poor management practices, and possible violations of both company policy and the law on the part of your subordinate. You have been in your present position only a year, but in that time you have had no indications of trouble about the subordinate in question. Neither you nor your company has an "open door" policy, so it is expected that employees should take their concerns to immediate supervisors before bringing the matter to the attention of anyone else. The employee who wishes to meet with you has not discussed this matter with her supervisor because of its delicate nature.

Rate the quality of the following things that you are considering doing in this situation on a 1-to-7 point scale:

_____ Refuse to meet with the employee unless the individual first discusses the matter with your subordinate.
_____ Meet with the employee and then with your subordinate to get both sides of the story.
_____ Meet with the employee and then investigate the allegations if an investigation appears warranted before talking with your subordinate.
_____ Find out more information about the employee, if you can, before making any decisions.

The tacit knowledge measures we have used in the past have been oriented to measuring adaptation—the person's ability to conform to the demands of the environment. Will they work in predicting leadership success?

There are differing accounts of the relationship between adaptive and shaping skills, and between management and leadership skills. As pointed out by Sternberg, et al. (2000), two alternative positions have emerged concerning the relationship between leadership and management.

According to the first position, management and leadership are qualitatively different concepts. Often the distinction is made between managers and leaders rather than between management and leadership. For example, Zaleznik (1977) proposed that managers and leaders are different types of people in terms of their motivation, personal history, thoughts, and behaviors. Managers are problem solvers who create goals in order to maintain the stability of the organization. Leaders are visionaries who inspire workers to take part in their own and the organization's development and change. Bennis and Nanus (1985) also proposed that leaders and managers differ qualitatively in their perspectives and willingness to implement change. Managers have a narrow perspective that is more concerned with mastering routines to ensure the efficiency of daily operations. Leaders, in contrast, have a broad perspective that allows them to assess the organization's needs, envision the future, and implement change. Kotter (1987) made a distinction between leadership and management in terms of the processes involved rather than the personalities of individuals. Management tends to be a formal, scientific, and present-oriented process, while leadership tends to be an informal, flexible, inspirational, and future-oriented process.

There are others, however, who view leadership and management as overlapping processes that fulfill the functions or expectations of an organizational role. Mintzberg (1975), for example, suggested that one of the functions of the manager's role is to be a leader. According to this perspective, the term *manager* is a role label, while *leader* is a role function. Leadership is a process associated with the function of a leader. Both Yukl (1989) and Lau and Shani (1992) suggested that the functions associated with supervisory positions in organizations require the incumbent to be both a leader and a manager. Supervisors must practice both leadership and management in order to fill role requirements. Bass (1990) similarly suggested that leaders must manage and managers must lead. These researchers take the position that the terms leader and manager are largely interchangeable.

The Tacit Knowledge for Military Leadership Research

We addressed this issue and the general issue of the effectiveness of the practical-intelligence/tacit knowledge approach to leadership in a study that examined the effectiveness in military leadership as predicted by tacit knowledge (Hedlund, et al., in press). In this study that was done over a 6-year period, we (a) conducted interviews to generate examples of tacit knowledge through leadership stories, (b) coded stories to extract leadership lessons, (c) selected representative and relevant tacit knowledge items, and (d) expanded the material into leadership scenarios with multiple response options.

Here is an example of an item from one of three forms—that for platoon commanders (the other two forms are for company and battalion commanders, respectively) of the Tacit Knowledge Inventory for Military Leaders (TKML – Williams, et al. 1996), with response options rated on a 1 (extremely bad) to 9 (extremely good) Likert scale:

"You are a platoon leader, and one day your driver has a motivational problem while out in the field. He starts mouthing off to you while standing on top of the turret in front of the rest of the platoon. Everyone in the platoon is listening to what he's saying about you, and it is extremely negative and harsh. What should you do?"

___ Speak to your company commander about the problem.
___ In front of the platoon, order your driver to do an unpleasant task as punishment for his insubordination.
___ Pull him aside and read him his rights: really chew his butt.
___ Go to the PSG and tell him to take care of this problem.
___ Order your driver to be quiet and get back to his job.
___ Pull him aside and tell him to come speak to you in one hour.

Construct validation of the TKML involved five main measures: (a) the Tacit Knowledge Inventory for Military Leaders (TKML), (b) the Tacit Knowledge Inventory for Managers (TKIM)(Wagner & Sternberg, 1991); (c) the Concept Mastery Test (CMT)(Terman, 1950), a difficult test of crystallized abilities (Cattell, 1971; Horn, 1994) containing synonyms, antonyms, and verbal analogies; (d) amount of experience (as measured by months on the job); and (e) a Leadership Effectiveness Survey (LES).

The Leadership Effectiveness Survey was a new instrument created for our study. It was administered as a 360-degree assessment instrument, meaning that subordinates, peers, and superiors were asked to fill it out. Here is a sample item:

"Think about your battalion commander. Compared to all battalion commanders you have known, how effective is your battalion commander, overall, as a leader? Please circle the number under the statement that best corresponds to your rating."

In our study, we recruited 368 platoon commanders, 163 company commanders, and 31 battalion commanders. Each commander received a version of the Tacit Knowledge Inventory for Military Leaders. The platoon leader version had 15 scenarios with an alpha reliability of .69; the company leader version had 18 scenarios with an alpha reliability of .76; and the battalion leader version had 11 scenarios with an alpha reliability of .66.

Effectiveness was rated for platoon leaders by 2 peers and 1 superior. No subordinates were available to provide ratings. For company leaders, 2 subordinates, 3 peers, and 1 superior provided ratings. For battalion leaders, 3 subordinates, no peers, and 1 superior provided ratings. Peers were not used at this level because they generally were largely unaware of what each other was doing.

Our results are described fully in Hedlund, et al. (2000, see also Sternberg, et al. 2000), but the main results are summarized here. They indicate that the TKML Inventory was relatively effective.

First, at all three levels, TKML (leadership) scores did not correlate significantly with number of months in the current job. This correlation is perhaps not so meaningful, however, first, because officers do not necessarily stay in jobs for very long, and second, because staying at a given level of command often is not an auspicious sign. Second, higher TKML (leadership) scores were correlated with higher LES (criterion) scores at all three levels, although the levels varied with source of rater and type of rating. Correlations with superior ratings at the platoon level were significant, with a median of .17. Correlations with peer ratings at the company level were significant, with a median of .19. One (of three) correlations with superior ratings was significant at the battalion level (.42). Third, TKML scores correlated trivially to moderately with TKIM (management) and CMT (verbal ability) scores. These correlations were .36 at the platoon level, .32 at the company level, but –.06 at the battalion level. Fourth, TKIM (management) scores correlated with LES ratings only for ratings of subordinates at the battalion level (median of .24). Finally, TKML (leadership) scores explained rated leadership effectiveness significantly beyond CMT (verbal ability) and TKIM (management) scores at the platoon and company levels when such prediction was assessed with hierarchical regression. Increments in proportions of variance accounted for overall were .04 (β = .15) at the platoon level and .10 at the company level (β = .27). (Comparable figures were not assessed for battalion commanders due to the small number of battalion commanders in the sample.)

Thus, the tacit knowledge approach has been successful in predicting at least one aspect of leadership success in the military. Practical intelligence, therefore, is important not only for adaptation to existing environments, but also for shaping of such environments to transform them. How much transformation of environments do military leaders engage in? To what extent is what they do creative? In order to address this question, the issue of creativity and leadership needs to be addressed.

LEADERSHIP AND CREATIVE INTELLIGENCE

Leaders need not only to adapt to be practical in their roles as leaders, but to shape and thus to be creative as well. They need to formulate a vision of where to lead. Creative intelligence can help them in this regard.

Background Research

Much of our research on creativity has been guided by an investment theory of creativity (Sternberg & Lubart, 1991, 1995, 1996). The basic idea of this theory is that creative individuals are like good investors: they buy low and sell high, but in the world of ideas. In other words, they generate ideas that are analogous to stocks with low price-earnings ratios—initially such ideas are unpopular. Then the creative individuals convince other people of the value of their ideas, metaphorically boosting the value of their stock. Finally, they move on to their next unpopular idea.

Research motivated by the investment theory has shown that creativity is largely domain-specific and that it correlates, at best, only modestly with conventional analytical abilities. In particular, we had participants write creative short stories (using, for example, titles such as "Beyond the Edge" or "The Octopus's Sneakers,"), draw creative pictures (with themes such as "The Beginning of Time" or "Earth From an Insect's Point of View"), produce creative advertisements (such as for a new brand of door knob or for the Internal Revenue Service), or solve quasiscientific problems requiring creative thinking (such as how we might detect extraterrestrial aliens among us seeking to escape detection).

The investment model proved to be useful for understanding creativity, but left certain questions unanswered. For example, not all creative individuals "defy the crowd," as the investment theory would suggest. Some individuals seem to lead without actually being defiant. Where do they fit in?

The Propulsion Theory

I recently have proposed what I refer to as a propulsion theory of creative contributions (Sternberg, 1999), which examines the different kinds of creative leadership individuals (or collectivities) can assert. The main idea is that creative leadership is not of a single kind, but actually is of seven different kinds.

The theory is based upon a spatial model in which one imagines a landscape—whether of science, business, literature, music, art, or whatever—in a high-dimensional, multidimensional space. The field in which one works occupies a certain, perhaps irregularly formed, region within that space. The creative leader is attempting to move the field in some direction and at some length. What are the kinds of movements within the space that the creative leader can attempt to have followers make?

The panels of Fig. 2.1 summarize the seven kinds of creative leadership and are referred to in the following discussion (Sternberg, 1999).

Contributions That Leave the Field Where It Is

Type 1: Replication. Replication is illustrated in Panel a of Fig. 2.1. It is the limiting (and arguably trivial) case of creative leadership. Replications help solidify the current state of a field. The goal is not to move a field forward so much as to establish that it really is where it is supposed to be. Thus, in science, if a finding is surprising, then a replication can help establish that the finding is a serious one. In business, a replication typically is an attempt to copy a successful business, for example, by setting up a competitive franchise based largely upon the principles of the first franchise. If the replication fails, then contributors in the field need to question whether they are where they have supposed or perhaps have hoped themselves to be. In art or literature, replications essentially show that a style of work can be applied not just to a single artwork or literary work, but to other works as well.

Replications are limiting cases in that they in some sense seem, on their face, to offer little that is new in terms of the creative contributions that are considered in this taxonomy of contributions. Yet replications are important because they can help either to establish the validity or invalidity of contributions, or the utility or lack of utility of approaches, that have been offered. In business, replications are often what keep prices down and innovation up because they force the original innovator to innovate still further to keep ahead of the replicator.

Although work designed to yield exact replications and conceptual replications (where the generality of a finding or kind of product is assessed by trying to replicate it under circumstances somewhat different from those that originally

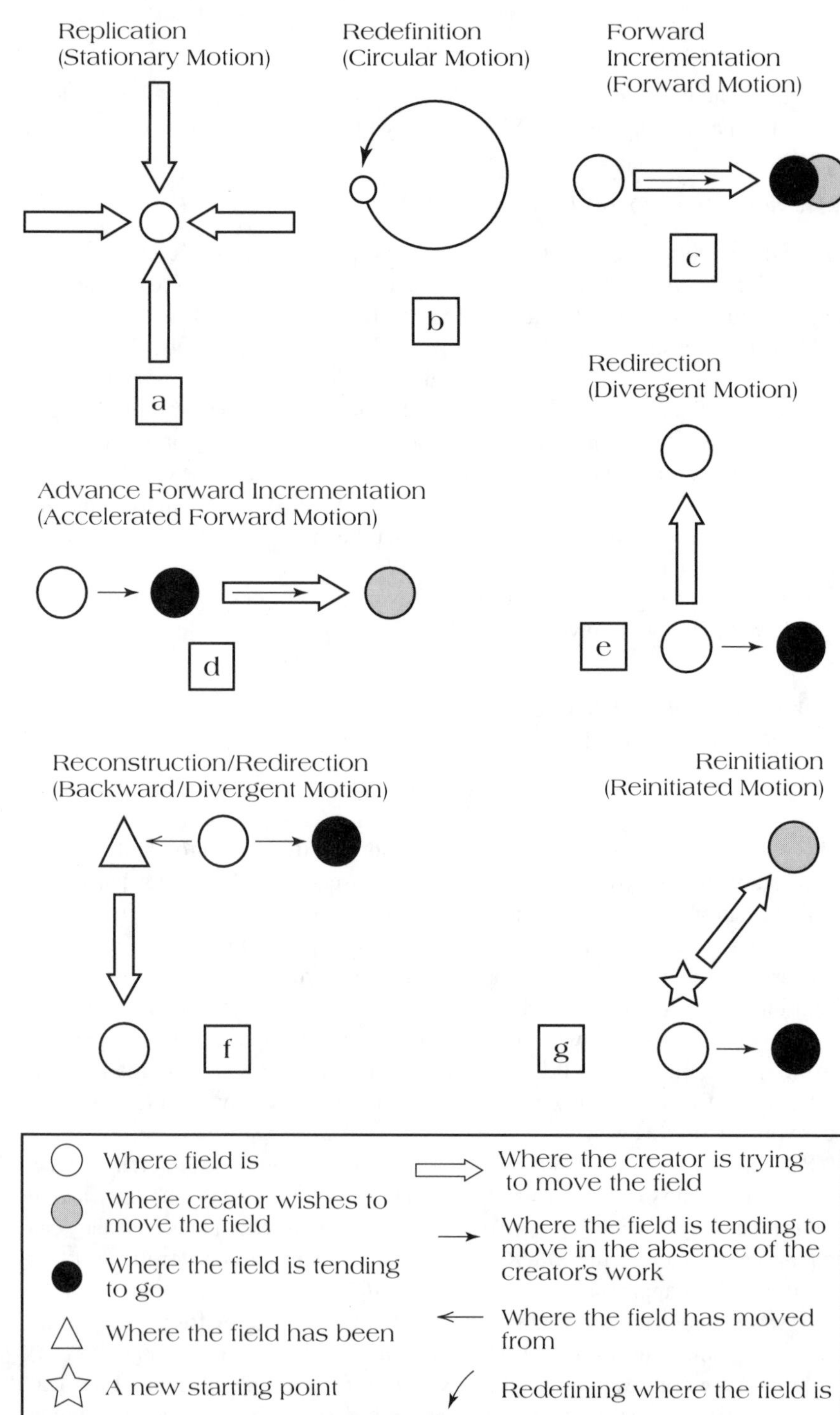

Replication
(Stationary Motion)
a
Redefinition
(Circular Motion)
b
Forward
Incrementation
(Forward Motion)
c
Redirection
(Divergent Motion)
Advance Forward Incrementation
(Accelerated Forward Motion)
d
e
Reconstruction/Redirection
(Backward/Divergent Motion)
Reinitiation
(Reinitiated Motion)
f
g
Where field is
Where creator wishes to move the field
Where the field is tending to go
Where the field has been
A new starting point
Where the creator is trying to move the field
Where the field is tending to move in the absence of the creator's work
Where the field has moved from
Redefining where the field is

gave rise to it) is about as unglamorous as any kind of work can be, replications are necessary for the development of a field. Without replications the field would be (and probably often is) very susceptible to Type 1 errors (false alarms). In science, replications help ensure the solidity of the base of empirical findings on which future researchers build. In the arts and letters, replications help ensure that an approach is robust and can generate a number and variety of works. For example, many artists imitated Monet's impressionistic techniques, and although they added nothing new to his techniques, they showed the robustness of the techniques for producing artworks.

Perhaps the crucial insight for the contributor is to know when there is a need for replication in the first place. In science, this need is associated with findings that are surprising or that seem at face value to be sufficiently dubious that either their existence or their generality needs to be demonstrated. In the arts and letters, this need is associated with techniques that may seem to be limited only to a single artwork or artist, or literary work or writer.

Type 2: Redefinition. Redefinition is illustrated in Panel b of Fig. 2.1. Redefinition, like replication, involves little or even no change of where a field is. What redefinition involves is a change in perception as to where that is. It is analogous to the realization of a navigator that a vehicle the navigator had thought to be in one place is really in another place. The place does not change, but the definition of where that place is does change. Similarly, a redefinition in a conceptual space leads people to realize that the field is not where they had thought. Work of this type is judged to be creative to the extent that the redefinition of the field is different from the earlier definition (novelty) and to the extent that the redefinition is judged to be plausible or correct (quality).

An example of a redefinition is provided by the work of Thomson (1939), who reinterpreted the work of Spearman (1904, 1927). Spearman was the English psychologist who invented factor analysis and who used this technique to argue that underlying all tests of mental abilities is a general factor, which he labeled *g*. Spearman's analysis had a powerful effect on the field and even continues to have

FIG. 2.1 Types of Creativity

(a) Replication helps solidify the current state of a field.

(b) Redefinition involves a change in perception as to where the field is.

(c) Incrementation occurs when a piece of work takes the field where it is and moves it forward from that point in the space of contributions in the direction work is already going.

(d) Advance incrementation occurs when an idea is "ahead of its time."

(e) Redirection involves taking the field where it is at a given time but attempting to move it in a new direction.

(f) Reconstruction involves moving the field backward to a point it previously was at but then moving in a direction different from that it has moved in.

(g) Reinitiation occurs when a contributor suggests that a field or subfield has reached an undesirable point or has exhausted itself moving in the direction that it is moving. The contributor suggests moving in a different direction from a different point in the multidimensional space of contributions.

such an effect today, with many theorists still believing in the existence and importance of the general factor (e.g., Brand, 1996; Carroll, 1993; Horn, 1994; Jensen, 1998).

Spearman believed his work to show that a single mental entity was responsible for interesting and consequential individual differences in performance on mental tests. Spearman (1927) suggested that this entity was mental energy. Thomson (1939) proposed that although Spearman was correct in asserting a general factor underlying mental tests, he was incorrect in his interpretation of it. According to Thomson, the general factor actually represented the workings of multitudinous "bonds." These bonds were all those mental processes that were common to performance on all mental tests. Thus, because all such tests require people to understand the instructions, read the terms of the problems, provide a response, and so forth, there might be many different sources of individual differences shared across these tests. They might appear via factor analysis to be a single entity, but in fact they are multifarious. Thus, Thomson proposed to change not the empirical status of work on intelligence, but how its empirical status was conceptualized. He argued that the field was not where Spearman and others thought it to be.

Redefinitions occur all the time in the world of business. For example, a company that formerly might have seen itself as being in the telephone business (e.g., AT&T) may come to realize that, at minimum, it is in the telecommunications business—that its business can no longer be limited to telephone service. A company that saw itself as being in the computer business may see itself as being in the information systems business. Today there is no viable computer business without taking into account the Internet. Businesses that do not adequately redefine themselves almost inevitably run the risk of extinction, much as would an enterprise that defined itself as in the business of selling horses and buggies. Leadership thus can be in redefining a present situation.

Redefinition is also important in military leadership. As the Cold War came to an end, it became apparent that the military needed to redefine its mission. But how? There was talk of a peace dividend, but such talk did not last long, at least not seriously. The military needed to prepare for a very different kind of world and a very different kind of war, as events in Kuwait and Serbia were to show. Intelligence agencies have faced a similar challenge.

Contributions That Move the Field Forward in the Direction It Is Going

Type 3: Forward incrementation. This type of creative contribution is illustrated in Panel c of Fig. 2.1. It probably represents the most common type of creative contribution. It occurs when a piece of work takes the field where it is and leads it forward from that point in the space of contributions in the direction work is already going. Work of this type is judged to be creative to the extent that it seems to move the field forward from where it is and to the extent that the movement appears to yield useful outcomes.

Hunt, Frost, and Lunneborg (1973) proposed that intelligence could be studied by investigators examining individual differences in cognitive performance on the kinds of tasks cognitive psychologists study in their laboratories. A few years later, Hunt, Lunneborg, and Lewis (1975) published an incrementation study that extended the range of tasks that could be studied using this paradigm, and suggested that certain ones of these tasks were particularly useful for studying individual differences in verbal ability. The second study was an incrementation study, building on a paradigm that Hunt and his colleagues had already established. The study provided a fairly substantial increment in both increasing the range of tasks and in focusing in particular on verbal ability.

Incrementation occurs in all fields. Elaborations on Impressionism by the minor Impressionists introduced new techniques but basically drew on the techniques introduced by Monet, Renoir, and others. The hard-boiled detective story pioneered by Dashiell Hammett and Raymond Chandler has been elaborated upon by countless writers, some of them moving the genre forward in major ways, such as Ross MacDonald, who introduced identity confusions as a major theme in his work. But MacDonald's work and that of others has its roots in the paradigm introduced by Hammett and Chandler (creator of Philip Marlowe).

Most business leadership, like most scientific leadership, is a story of forward incrementation—a new cereal is introduced, a new kind of cosmetic enters the marketplace, a new microchip is introduced that is an evolutionary development over the last one. Such forward incrementations are needed to keep a business competitive in a rapidly changing world, but they do not fundamentally alter the nature of the enterprise or, typically, of the competitive landscape.

Type 4: Advance forward incrementation. This kind of creative contribution is illustrated in Panel d of Fig. 2.1. Advance forward incrementation occurs when an idea is "ahead of its time." The field is moving in a certain direction but has not yet reached a given point ahead. Someone has an idea that emanates from that point not yet reached. The person pursues the idea and produces a work. Often the value of the work is not recognized at the time because the field has not yet reached the point where the contribution of the work can be adequately understood, and the leadership it provides, valued.

Royer (1971) published an article that was an information-processing analysis of the digit-symbol task on the Wechsler Adult Intelligence Scale (WAIS). In the article, Royer showed how information-processing analysis could be used to decompose performance on the task and understand the elementary information processes underlying performance on it. Royer's work foreshadowed the later work of Hunt (Hunt, Frost, & Lunneborg, 1973; Hunt, Lunneborg, & Lewis, 1975) and especially of Sternberg (1977, 1983), but his work went largely (although not completely) unnoticed. There could be any number of reasons for this phenomenon, but one of the reasons is likely to have been that the field was not quite ready for Royer's contribution. The field and possibly even Royer himself did not fully recognize the value of the approach Royer was taking.

Advance forward incrementations can occur in any field. Demosthenes, in proposing ideas similar to that of the contemporary idea of the atom, was way ahead of his time. Ignaz Semmelweis proposed the idea of bacteria contaminating the hands of doctors and was so scoffed at that eventually he was driven insane. Often it is only later that the value of such works is appreciated.

Advance forward incrementations are common in business. The Xerox Star System is one example. It was a great idea, but was so ahead of its time that Xerox did not quite know what to do with it. Apple did, and largely got credit for an idea almost identical to the one Xerox engineers had had a number of years earlier. Fax machines were introduced into the marketplace many years ago, but it is not until recently that they really came into their own. The list of innovations that were ahead of their time is endless, and often people who could have been leaders lost their leadership roles when they were unable to persuade people of the value of their ideas. Because people do not always see the value of exceptional innovations, often the most innovative products are not the ones that sell the best, as many manufacturers have found out too late (Norman, 1998).

Contributions That Move the Field in a New Direction

Type 5: Redirection. Redirection is illustrated in Panel e of Fig. 2.1. Redirection involves taking the field where it is at a given time, and attempting to lead it in a new direction. Work of this kind is creative to the extent that it leads a field in a new direction (novelty) and to the extent that this direction is seen as desirable (quality).

The pioneering Hunt, Frost, and Lunneborg (1973) article mentioned earlier suggested that researchers of intelligence use cognitive-psychological paradigms in order to study intelligence. The basic idea was to correlate scores on cognitive tasks with scores on psychometric tests. Sternberg (1977) used cognitive techniques as a starting point, but suggested that research move in a direction different from that suggested by Hunt. In particular, he suggested that complex cognitive tasks (such as analogies and classifications) be used instead of simple cognitive tasks (such as lexical access), and that the goal should be to decompose information processing on these tasks into its elementary information-processing components. Sternberg argued that Hunt was right in suggesting the use of cognitive tasks, but wrong in suggesting the use of very simple ones, which he believed involved only fairly low levels of intelligent thought. Sternberg was thus suggesting a redirection in the kind of cognitive work Hunt had initiated.

Beethoven's work can also be viewed as a redirection from the classical style of music that had been employed so successfully by Haydn, Mozart, and others. Beethoven used many of the same classical forms as had his predecessors, but he also showed that a greater level of emotionality could be introduced into the music without sacrificing the classical forms.

In business, some innovations bring a kind of product leadership that is revolutionary rather than evolutionary. Apple's home computers were of this nature. They created a new market on the basis of existing computer technology. DVD reproductions are doing the same as they slowly replace the much less effective VCR, which themselves replaced the more effective Betamax system. A redirection in business essentially creates a new kind of business by leading people from where they are, but in a new direction.

Type 6: Reconstruction and redirection. This type of creative contribution is illustrated in Panel f of Fig. 2.1. In using reconstruction and redirection, an individual suggests that the field should move *backwards* to a point it previously was at but then should move in a direction different from that it has moved in. In other words, the individual suggests that at some time in the past, the field went off track. The individual suggests the point at which this occurred and how the field should have moved forward from that point. The work is judged as creative to the extent that the individual is judged as correctly recognizing that the field has gone off-track (quality) and to the extent that the new direction suggested from the past is viewed as a useful direction for the field to pursue.

In the early part of the century, intelligence tests seemed to have potential for helping society understand why certain groups rose to the top of the society and other groups fell to the bottom of that society (see Carroll, 1982; Ceci, 1996; Gould, 1981). This often thinly disguised social Darwinism was based on the notion that those groups with more adaptive skills, on average, should and did in fact tend to have more success in adapting to the demands of the social structure of the society. In contrast, those groups with fewer adaptive skills, on average, did and should fall to the bottom. This kind of thinking became unpopular in the early part of the latter half of the century. Environment came to be seen as much more important than it had seemed before (Kamin, 1974; Lewontin, 1982). As a result, intelligence test scores were no longer being looked at as a cause of group differences, but rather, as an effect.

This balance was upset when Herrnstein and Murray (1994) argued that the older views were most likely correct in many respects. It is plausible, they argued, to believe that group differences in IQ are, in fact, due to genetic factors, and that these group differences result in social mobility. Herrnstein and Murray further suggested that what they considered a humane social policy could be constructed on the basis of these alleged facts. Many people who were secretly more comfortable with the older views or who were ready to be persuaded of these views found the Herrnstein-Murray arguments convincing.

Some literary scholars are now suggesting that literary criticism, too, has gone off track—that the kind of deconstructionism introduced by Derrida (1992) and others has produced a literary nihilism that has resulted in a degeneration of the field of literary criticism. These individuals, such as Bloom (1994), suggest that literary scholars return to their earlier tradition of finding meaning in literary works rather than asserting that virtually any meaning can be read into any literary work.

This kind of leadership is common in our educational system. An innovation is tried; it either fails or never is adequately tested; and then educational leaders call for a return to the good old ways—the three Rs. It also occasionally succeeds in business, as when old products are brought back, but in a more attractive form, such as hoola hoops, yo-yos, toy guns, and other products that keep coming back, but in new and supposedly more attractive forms.

Type 7: Reinitiation. This type of creative contribution is illustrated in Panel g of Fig. 2.1. In reinitiation, a contributor suggests that a field or subfield has reached an undesirable point or has exhausted itself moving in the direction it is moving. But rather than suggesting that the field or subfield move in a different direction from where it is (as in redirection), the contributor suggests moving in a different direction from a different point in the multidimensional space of contributions. In effect, the contributor is suggesting people question their assumptions and "start over" from a point that most likely makes different assumptions.

Spearman's (1904, 1927) emphasis on general ability was not shared by all investigators. For example, Thurstone (1938), Guilford (1967), and many other theorists suggested that intelligence comprises multiple abilities and that any general factor obtained in factor analyses was likely to be, at best, unimportant, and at worst, epiphenomenal. In all cases, intelligence was accepted as a unitary construct: What differed were investigators' views on how, if at all, the unitary construct should be divided up.

Gardner (1983, 1999), however, suggested that all these investigators had been wrong in one key respect: They had conceptualized intelligence as a unitary entity, however many abilities it may comprise. Gardner suggested that instead we think in terms of multiple intelligences, with each intelligence representing not just a separate ability, but a separate modular system of information processing distinct from all other such systems. Thus, the idea was that verbal and quantitative skills represented not just separate abilities within a single system of abilities, but separate systems of abilities altogether. Gardner further suggested that conventional paper-and-pencil tests of intelligence measure intellectual skills in a relatively trivial way, and that a continuation of research based on such tasks would be largely pointless. In making his suggestions, Gardner was attempting to reinitiate the field, starting it off at a new point and suggesting to lead it in a direction different from the one in which it had been moving.

Revolutionary works tend to be reinitiations. In the field of linguistics, Chomsky's (1965) transformational grammar changed the way many linguists looked at language. And of course Einstein revolutionized physics. Reinitiations can apply to entire fields, as in the case of Einstein, or to smaller subfields.

In each case, however, the creators are arguing for a fresh approach to creative work.

Reinitiations are very difficult to pull off in the business world, because they require moving not only a firm but also the firm's customers. Many young people decide to become entrepreneurs rather than executives in established businesses because they believe that they can pull off the kinds of reinitiations that conventional businesses never would allow. The first Internet businesses, such as Internet bookseller Amazon.com, were reinitiations, revolutionizing what it means for a customer to do business with a company.

CONCLUSION

One of several approaches to the study of leadership has emphasized intelligence as it is traditionally defined. This approach has met with limited success, in part because the relationships are modest and in part because they are not even consistently positive (Fiedler, 1995). My goal and that of my collaborators has been to investigate a broader approach to understanding the relationship between intelligence and leadership, an approach that examines the roles of practical and creative intelligence as well as of analytical intelligence. This approach does not deny or attempt to negate the role of intelligence, as traditionally defined, in leadership. Rather, it argues that a more comprehensive view of leadership might better take into account more of the range of what leaders actually do. In particular, leaders need not only analyze existing situations, but also need to have a vision of where to lead people (creative intelligence) and of how to get them there to convince them that this is indeed where they need to go (practical intelligence). Our theory and research suggest that practical and creative aspects of intelligence indeed can play an important role in understanding leadership and in predicting who will be an effective leader. Ultimately, this theory and research also may serve as a basis for training the leaders of tomorrow in how best to exercise leadership roles.

AUTHOR NOTES

Preparation of this chapter was supported in part by Contract MDA903-92-K from the U.S. Army Research Institute and in part by Grant R206R000001 from the Office of Educational Research and Improvement, U.S. Department of Education. I am grateful to my collaborators in the tacit knowledge for military leadership study (W. M. Bullis, M. Dennis, G. B. Forsythe, E. L. Grigorenko, J. Hedlund, J. A. Horvath, S. Snook, R. K. Wagner, W. M. Williams) for their joint contributions to this tacit knowledge work.

REFERENCES

Bass, B. M. (1990). *Bass and Stogdill's handbook of leadership: Theory, research, and managerial applications*. New York: The Free Press.

Bennis, W., & Nanus, B. (1985). *Leaders: The strategies for taking charge.* New York: Harper and Row.

Bloom, H. (1994). *The Western canon: The books and school of the ages.* New York: Harcourt Brace.

Brand, C. (1996). *The* g *factor: General intelligence and its implications.* Chichester, England: Wiley.

Carroll, J. B. (1982). The measurement of intelligence. In R. J. Sternberg (ed.), *Handbook of human intelligence* (pp. 29–120). New York: Cambridge University Press.

Carroll, J. B. (1993). *Human cognitive abilities: A survey of factor-analytic studies*. New York: Cambridge University Press.

Cattell, R. B. (1971). *Abilities: Their structure, growth and action.* Boston: Houghton Mifflin.

Ceci, S. J. (1996). *On intelligence . . . more or less* (expanded ed.). Cambridge, MA: Harvard University Press.

Chomsky, N. (1965). *Aspects of the theory of syntax.* Cambridge, MA: MIT Press.

Derrida, J. (1992). *Acts of literature.* (D. Attridge, Ed.). New York: Routledge.

Eddy, A. S. (1988). *The relationship between the Tacit Knowledge Inventory for Managers and the Armed Services Vocational Aptitude Battery.* Unpublished master's thesis, St. Mary's University, San Antonio, TX.

Fiedler, F. E. (1995). Cognitive resources and leadership performance. *Applied psychology: An international review, 44,* 5–28.

Fiedler, F. E. & Link, T. G. (1994). Leader intelligence, interpersonal stress, and task performance. In R. J. Sternberg & R. K. Wagner (eds.). *Mind in context: Interactionist perspectives on human intelligence* (pp. 152–167). New York: Cambridge University Press.

Gardner, H. (1983). *Frames of mind: The theory of multiple intelligences.* New York: Basic.

Gardner, H. (1999). Are there additional intelligences? The case for naturalist, spiritual, and existential intelligences. In J. Kane (ed.), *Education, information, and transformation* (pp. 111–131). Upper Saddle River, NJ: Prentice Hall.

Gould, S. J. (1981). *The mismeasure of man.* New York: Norton.

Grigorenko, E. L., Gil, G., Jarvin, L. & Sternberg, R. J. (2000). *Toward a validation of aspects of the theory of successful intelligence*. Manuscript submitted for publication.

Grigorenko, E. L. & Sternberg, R. J. (in press). Analytical, creative, and practical intelligence as predictors of self-reported adaptive functioning: A case study in Russia. *Intelligence.*

Guilford, J. P. (1967). *The nature of human intelligence*. New York: McGraw-Hill.

Hedlund, J., Forsythe, G. B., Horvath, J., Williams, W. M., Snook, S., Dennis, M., Sternberg, R. J. (2001). *Practical intelligence: The role of tacit knowledge in understanding leadership.* Manuscript submitted for publication.

Herrnstein, R. J., & Murray, C. (1994). *The bell curve.* New York: Free Press.

Horn, J. L. (1994). Theory of fluid and crystallized intelligence. In R. J. Sternberg (ed.), *The encyclopedia of human intelligence (Vol. 1)* (pp. 443–451). New York: Macmillan.

Hunt, E., Frost, N., & Lunneborg, C. (1973). Individual differences in cognition: A new approach to intelligence. In G. Bower (ed.), *The psychology of learning and motivation* (Vol. 7, pp. 87–122). New York: Academic Press.

Hunt, E. B., Lunneborg, C., & Lewis, J. (1975). What does it mean to be high verbal? *Cognitive Psychology*, *7*, 194–227.

Jensen, A. R. (1998). *The g factor: The science of mental ability*. Westport, CT: Praeger/Greenwood.

Kamin, L. (1974). *The science and politics of IQ*. Hillsdale, NJ: Lawrence Erlbaum Associates.

Kotter, J. (1987). *The leadership factor.* New York: Free Press.

Lau, J. & Shani, A. (1992). *Behavior in organizations: An experimental approach* (5th ed.). Homewood, IL: Irwin.

Lewontin, R. (1982). *Human diversity*. New York: Freeman.

Mintzberg, H. (1975). The manager's job: Folklore and fact. *Harvard Business Review, 4,* 49–61.

Norman, D. A. (1998). *The invisible computer: Why good products can fail, the personal computer is so complex, and information appliances are the solution*. Cambridge, MA: The MIT Press.

Polanyi, M. (1966). *The tacit dimensions*. Garden City, NY: Doubleday.

Royer, F. L. (1971). Information processing of visual figures in the digit symbol substitution task. *Journal of Experimental Psychology, 87,* 335–42.

Spearman, C. (1904). 'General intelligence,' objectively determined and measured. *American Journal of Psychology, 15,* 201–293.

Spearman, C. (1927). *The abilities of man*. London: Macmillan.

Sternberg, R. J. (1977). *Intelligence, information processing, and analogical reasoning: The componential analysis of human abilities*. Hillsdale, NJ: Lawrence Erlbaum Associates.

Sternberg, R. J. (1983). Components of human intelligence. *Cognition, 15,* 1–48.

Sternberg, R. J. (1997). *Successful intelligence*. New York: Plume.

Sternberg, R. J. (1998). A balance theory of wisdom. *Review of General Psychology, 2,* 347–365.

Sternberg, R. J. (1999). A propulsion model of types of creative contributions. *Review of General Psychology, 3,* 83–100.

Sternberg, R. J., & Detterman, D. K. (1986). *What is intelligence?* Norwood, NJ: Ablex Publishing Corporation.

Sternberg, R. J., Forsythe, G. B., Hedlund, J., Horvath, J., Snook, S., Williams, W.M., Wagner, R. K., & Grigorenko, E. L. (2000). *Practical intelligence in everyday life*. New York: Cambridge University Press.

Sternberg, R. J., & Lubart, T. I. (1991(8), April). Creating creative minds. *Phi Delta Kappan*, 608–614.

Sternberg, R. J., & Lubart, T. I. (1995). *Defying the crowd: Cultivating creativity in a culture of conformity*. New York: Free Press.

Sternberg, R. J., & Lubart, T. I. (1996). Investing in creativity. *American Psychologist, 51*, 677–688.

Sternberg, R. J., & Wagner, R. K. (Eds.). (1986). *Practical intelligence: Nature and origins of competence in the everyday world.* New York: Cambridge University Press.

Sternberg, R. J., & Wagner, R. K. (1993). The geocentric view of intelligence and job performance is wrong. *Current Directions in Psychological Science, 2,* 1–4.

Sternberg, R. J., Wagner, R. K., & Okagaki, L. (1993). Practical intelligence: The nature and role of tacit knowledge in work and at school. In H. Reese & J. Puckett (eds.), *Advances in lifespan development* (pp. 205–227). Hillsdale, NJ: Lawrence Erlbaum Associates.

Sternberg, R. J., Wagner, R. K., Williams, W. M., & Horvath, J. A. (1995). Testing common sense. *American Psychologist, 50,* 912–927.

Terman, L. M. (1950). *Concept Mastery Test*. New York: The Psychological Corporation.

Thomson, G. H. (1939). *The factorial analysis of human ability.* London: University of London Press.

Thurstone, L. L. (1938). *Primary mental abilities*. Chicago, IL: University of Chicago Press.

Wagner, R. K. (1987). Tacit knowledge in everyday intelligent behavior. *Journal of Personality and Social Psychology*, *52*, 1236–47.

Wagner, R. K. (2000). Practical intelligence. In R. J. Sternberg (ed.), *Handbook of human intelligence* (pp. 380–395). New York, NY: Cambridge University Press.

Wagner, R. K., & Sternberg, R. J. (1985). Practical intelligence in real-world pursuits: The role of tacit knowledge. *Journal of Personality and Social Psychology*, *49*, 436–458.

Wagner, R. K., & Sternberg, R. J. (1991). *Tacit knowledge inventory for managers*. San Antonio, TX: Psychological Corporation.

Wagner, R. K., Sujan, H., Sujan, M., Rashotte, C. A., & Sternberg, R. J. (1999). Tacit knowledge in sales. In R. J. Sternberg & J. A. Horvath (eds.), *Tacit knowledge in professional practice* (pp. 155–182). Mahwah, NJ: Lawrence Erlbaum Associates.

Williams, W. M., Horvath, J. A., Bullis, R. C., Forsythe, G. B., & Sternberg, R.J. (1996). *Tacit knowledge for military leadership inventories: Platoon leader, company commander, and battalion commander levels*. Alexandria, Virginia: U.S. Army Research Institute for the Behavioral and Social Sciences.

Yukl, G. (1989). Managerial leadership: A review of theory and research. *Journal of Management, 15,* 251–289.

Zaleznik, A. (1977). Managers and leaders: Are they different? *Harvard Business Review, 55,* 67–78.

3

Organizational Leadership and Social Intelligence

Stephen J. Zaccaro
George Mason University

UNDERSTANDING ORGANIZATIONAL LEADERSHIP

Leadership is inherently a social phenomenon. It resides in the actions of an individual or set of individuals who endeavor to move a collective along a goal path. The problems that are encountered along this path that must be solved by leaders often emerge from the social dynamics occurring within the collective, and between the collective and its embedding environment. Thus, organizational leadership typically requires leader role incumbents to generate solutions that (a) accommodate multiple social constituencies both within and outside of the organization, and (b) account for often conflicting social demands and requirements. Further, leaders sometimes need to implement these solutions by convincing initially skeptical superiors, peers, and subordinates of a solution's viability and by coordinating the activities of multiple organizational groups that are involved in the solution. Finally, effective leader problem solving requires that solution implementation be monitored through feedback from these various social groups. The inherent social embeddedness of organizational leadership means fundamentally that leader effectiveness is defined by how well leaders navigate through social dilemmas when generating problem solutions and implementing them within complex organizational dynamics.

Understanding organizational leadership requires that we examine closely this quality of social embeddedness and its implications for defining the characteristics of individuals who acquire leadership roles. The accurate specification of these characteristics also contributes to the construction of effective leader assessment, selection, training, and development systems. In this chapter, I define a set of personal characteristics that contribute to the effectiveness of individuals in organizational leadership roles. These qualities, grounded in the fact of leader social embeddedness and the need for leaders to solve problems in complex social domains, are grouped under the label *social intelligence.* They reflect competencies in accurately perceiving organizational problem requirements and selecting appropriate organizational and behavioral responses (Kenny & Zaccaro, 1983; Zaccaro, Foti, & Kenny, 1991; Zaccaro, Gilbert, Thor, & Mumford, 1991). Further, socially intelligent leaders are able to vary their responses in accordance with dynamic situational demands. The competencies stemming from high social intelligence are vital both for the interpretation of social problems and for the subsequent generation and implementation of effective solutions (Mumford, Zaccaro, Harding, Fleishman, & Reiter-Palmon, 1993).

A perspective of leadership that is grounded in the personal qualities of role incumbents invariably recalls the trait or, more characteristically, an individual difference approach to leadership. Many researchers consider such an approach roundly discredited in the history of leadership research. However, over the past several years, the individual difference approach to leadership has gained renewed vigor (House & Aditya, 1999; House & Baetz, 1979; Lord, De Vader & Alliger, 1986; Mumford, et al. 1993; Zaccaro, Foti, & Kenny, 1991; Zaccaro, Gilbert, et al. 1991). This resurgence can be attributed to a number of factors. First, unlike earlier approaches, current individual difference models follow from conceptual models of leadership that emphasize integrated contributions of multiple personal characteristics (Jacobs & Jaques, 1987, 1990, 1991; House, Spangler, & Woycke, 1991; Mumford, et al. 1993; Zaccaro, et al. 1996; Zaccaro, et al. 1997). Second, while prior trait approaches emphasized qualities that suggested behavioral invariance across organizational situations, more current models offer dispositional variables that foster behavioral variance and situational responsiveness (Hooijberg & Quinn, 1992; Zaccaro, Gilbert, et al. 1991). Third, advances in research methodology and statistical analysis have mitigated conclusions of low support for leader trait models from earlier reviews of the trait literature (Barnlund, 1962; Mann, 1959; Stogdill, 1948) and provided stronger evidence (Kenny & Zaccaro, 1983; Lord, et al. 1986; Zaccaro, Foti, & Kenny, 1991). Finally, there has been a sustained focus in leadership research on the assessment, selection, and development of leaders, all grounded in identifying key leader attributes that contribute to organizational effectiveness (Bray, Campbell, & Grant, 1974, Howard & Bray, 1988; Mumford, et al. 1993; Ritchie, 1994).

Each of these points has been reflected in recent research identifying social intelligence as an important leadership quality. For example, models of organizational leadership by Mumford, et al. (1993) and Zaccaro (1996, 1999) argue that as individuals ascend the organizational hierarchy, leadership performance requirements become more socially complex, increasing the importance of key social competencies for leader effectiveness. Further, Zaccaro (1996, 1999) presented a model of these competencies that emphasized their integrative contributions to leader flexibility. Evidence for some of these competencies were provided by Zaccaro, Foti, and Kenny (1991), who utilized an experimental design where group members and tasks were rotated to produce different group situations. This study demonstrated that the same individuals tended to emerge as leaders across these different situations, and that leadership scores were correlated with scores on measures of social capabilities. Finally, recent research on leader assessment, selection, and development has focused on the identification of social capacities that are linked to leader effectiveness at different organizational levels (Ritchie, 1994; Zaccaro, Zazanis, Diana, & Gilbert, 1994). Taken together, this body of research points to the importance of social intelligence and other social capabilities as key determinants of leader emergence and leader effectiveness in organizations.

This chapter examines some of these points and elaborates on them in greater detail, following recent empirical and conceptual studies of social intelligence and leadership. It derives from an earlier paper by Zaccaro, Gilbert, et al. (1991) that presented a definition of social intelligence and its components; this paper also linked these components to effective organizational leadership. This chapter expands the arguments from Zaccaro, Gilbert, et al. (1991) by presenting a broader conceptualization of social intelligence, and associating its components to leader performance requirements at different organizational levels. In the next section, I present a hierarchical model of organizational leadership requirements. Then, I define social intelligence and its components, and relate them to the performance of leaders at various levels of the organization. In the final section, I present some recent empirical findings supporting the link between social intelligence and organizational leadership.

THE NATURE OF ORGANIZATIONAL LEADERSHIP

A Functional Perspective

The specification of requisite leader characteristics should follow from a well-developed and integrated conceptual framework of leadership. Accordingly, Mumford, Zaccaro, and Fleishman developed a model that was grounded in a functional approach to leadership (Fleishman, Mumford, Zaccaro, Levin, Korotkin, & Hein, 1991; Mumford & Connelly, 1991, Mumford, et al. 1993; Zaccaro, Gilbert, et al. 1991; Zaccaro, et al. 1996; Zaccaro, et al. 1997; cf. Hackman & Walton, 1986). A central premise of this research is that effective organizational leadership involves complex social problem solving in which leaders identify key issues relevant to organizational goal attainment and generate solutions or approaches that address these issues. A critical distinction here is that leaders at upper organizational levels have significant discretion regarding the selection and application of actions to resolve organizational problems (Hunt, Osborn, & Martin, 1981; Jacobs & Jaques, 1987).

A functional approach to leadership emphasizes the problem-solving role of organizational leaders. As Hackman and Walton (1986, p.75) point out:

> The key assertion in the functional approach to leadership is that "[the leader's] main job is to do, or get done, whatever is not being adequately handled for group needs" (McGrath, 1962, p. 5). If a leader manages, by whatever means, to ensure that all functions critical to both task accomplishment and group maintenance are adequately taken care of, then the leader has done his or her job well.

Viewed in terms of boundary-role requirements, the effective leader is responsible for guiding adaptation and maintaining performance in the face of changing internal and external pressures. However, while the content of functional leadership roles varies substantially, the hierarchical nature of organizational systems imposes some common themes. As one ascends the organizational hierarchy, the environment typically becomes more complex. Upper-level leaders must consider the needs of multiple subsystems and integrate system actions with the needs of other social institutions (Katz & Kahn, 1978). This complexity involves changes in time frame, influence strategies, and interactional style (Jaques, 1978, 1986, 1989, 1990). It is difficult to force change on large subsystems and other social institutions. Thus, goals and policies must be negotiated with conflicting, but relevant, constituencies. Further, potential problems and opportunities must be anticipated and actions initiated over a significant period of time to ensure subsequent adaptation in organizational systems that often change slowly. Finally, the exercise of influence becomes more abstract, stressing long-term policies and outcomes as opposed to immediate, concrete interactions.

These observations bring to fore a common theme apparent in all leadership roles: Despite changes in complexity, any individual in a boundary-role position is expected to act to maintain and enhance group performance in a dynamic environment. The issues to be dealt with may range from a truculent subordinate to whether the company should invest in a new technology. In all cases, however, the leader must search for goals and paths to goal attainment that will enhance group performance and subsequent adaptation. Thus, a leader's performance is a function of whether he or she has been able to identify, construct, and follow viable paths in a volatile social environment; that is, the development and implementation of solutions to organizational problems is a key component of leader performance and effective leadership.

Organizational Stratification of Leadership Requirements

A key point here is the stratification of leader responsibilities. After reviewing the existing literature, Zaccaro (1999, 2001) developed a model of organizational leadership that specified both the common and different performance requirements leaders needed to address at different levels in the organization. Figure 3.1 presents this model. Five general premises that have received substantial empirical support from analyses of leadership work provide the bases for this model. These are (Zaccaro 2001, p. 284):

- Leader performance requirements can be described in terms of three distinct levels in organizational space.
- All organizational leaders engage in direction setting (e.g., goal setting, planning, strategy making, envisioning) for their constituent units. Such direction setting incorporates an increasingly longer time frame at higher organizational levels.
- All organizational leaders engage in boundary-spanning activities, linking their constituent units with their environments. At lower organizational levels, this environment is the broader organization. At upper levels, boundary spanning and environmental analysis occurs, increasing within the organization's external environment.
- All organizational leaders are responsible for operational maintenance and coordination within the organization. At upper levels, operational influence becomes increasingly indirect.
- As leaders ascend the organizational hierarchy, the degree of informational and social complexity becomes greater in their operating environment.

The leader performance requirements model in Fig. 3.1 specifies two qualitative shifts in requirements. The lowest level is *the production level.* This involves direct leadership of single organizational units. Leaders at this level define and translate short-term unit tasks and goals consistent with objectives that are established at higher levels. Problems confronting the leader are fairly concrete and reflect a short time frame (Jacobs & Jaques, 1987). They typically concern the resolution of immediate conflicts, crises, and emergencies that can impede production (Baehr, 1992; Paolillo, 1981). Several studies have demonstrated that leadership at this level involves more direct, face-to-face supervision of subordinates, including the training, motivation, and structuring of their work (Hemphill, 1959; Kraut, Pedigo, McKenna, & Dunnette, 1989; Mahoney, Jerdee, & Carroll, 1965; Pavett & Lau, 1983, Tornow & Pinto, 1976).

At the next level, *the organizational level,* leadership becomes increasingly more indirect. Leaders at this level manage multiple units, or subsystems of the organization, each of which has its own supervisor (Jacobs & Jaques, 1987). As Hemphill (1959) noted, "Supervision of work usually does not appear as a

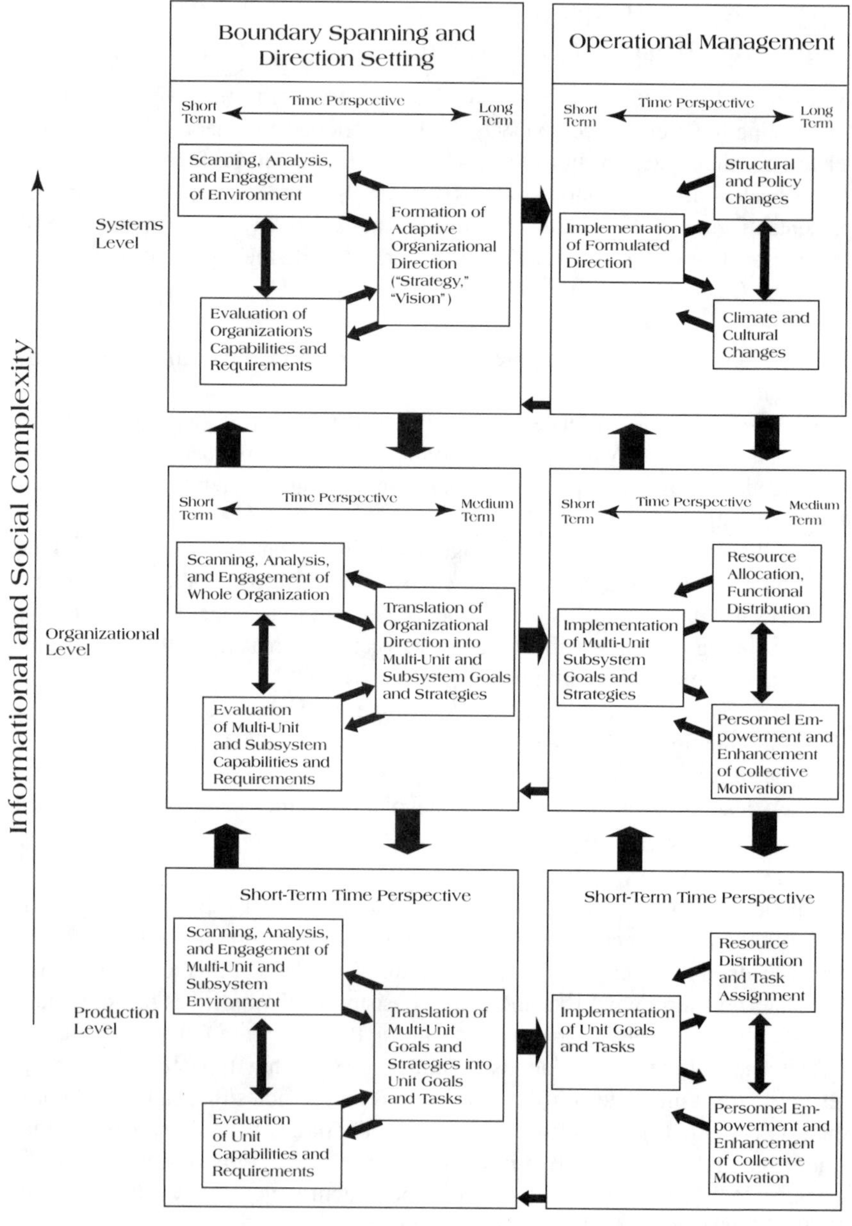

FIG. 3.1 Organizational leadership performance requirements. *Source: Reprinted from S. J. Zaccaro, Social Complexity, and the Competencies Required for Effective Leadership. In J. G. Hunt, G. Dodge, and L. Wong,* Out-of-the-Box leadership: Transforming the Twenty-first Century Army and other Top-Performing Organizations, *p. 142 Copyright 1999, with permission from Elsevier Science.*

characteristic of upper-management work" (p. 57). Problems at this level are more complex, they have multiple components, but they are still fairly well defined. The time horizon for these problems is longer than for lower-level managers. One of the central roles of middle managers is to translate the even longer-term perspectives, strategies, and objectives established at top organizational levels into concrete, short-term objectives for first-line managers. They also need to allocate organizational resources among functional units in line with organizational objectives. Along this line, several studies have demonstrated that the major task for managers at this level is the coordination of multiple organizational units. For example, Tornow and Pinto (1976) reported that middle management jobs were characterized more than other positions by the "coordination of other organizational units and personnel." They defined this factor as typical of a position incumbent who "coordinates the efforts of others over whom he/she exercises no direct control, handles conflicts or disagreements when necessary, and works in an environment where he/she must cut across existing organizational boundaries" (p. 414).

They found that this factor was substantially less characteristic of lower or upper level leadership positions than of middle managers. Other empirical evidence for this difference was offered by Alexander (1979), Baehr (1992), Kraut, et al. (1989), and Pavett and Lau (1983).

At *the systems level,* incorporating executive-level leadership, the leader is managing the organization as a whole. Typically, this occurs within the context of a very complex environment. Thus, this level of management is characterized more than others by external boundary-spanning activities (managers at lower levels are spanning the boundaries of their units or subsystems within the internal organizational environment). Executive leaders are required to scan and analyze the organization's environment to determine the nature of changes in that environment, the requirements for the organization in order for it to adapt to changes, and the resources available to the organization to meet these requirements.

Katz and Kahn (1978) suggested that environmental scanning by senior leaders also includes a sensitivity to opportunities in the environment for organizational growth and development. Zaccaro, Gilbert, et al. (1991) called this a search for environmental affordances and prescribed it as a key leadership ability. These scanning activities are combined with an analysis of organizational capabilities and requirements to determine (a) the needs of the organization with respect to environment resources and change, and (b) the kinds of opportunities in the environment to which the organization can be most responsive. Thus, environmental scanning both influences and is influenced by organizational evaluation and analysis. Finally, part of executive boundary spanning includes attempts by top leaders to influence and change the environmental conditions within which the organization must operate. Effective executives are not passive recipients of environmental contingencies; instead, they seek to engage the environment and shape these contingencies.

The time frame of systems leadership planning and action includes a long-term perspective, although the extent of this time horizon is debated by several executive leadership theorists. While Jacobs and Jaques (1987) argued that top executives operate within a 20–50 year time frame, Mintzberg (1994) suggested that long-term planning and reflection is dysfunctional. Empirical studies suggest that executive planning horizons probably stretch 5 to 10 years into future. For example, Lucas and Markessini (1993) reported planning time spans of 5–7 years for Army general officers. Markessini, Lucas, Chandler, and Jacobs (1994) found planning time frames of approximately 8.5 years in civilian military executives. Similar findings in military samples were reported by Jacobs and Jaques (1990) and Rigby and Harris (1987). Kotter (1982a,b) found that the typical planning agenda for his organizational managers included a 5 to 20 year horizon. Judge and Spitzfaden (1995) reported time spans of 5 to 8.5 years in eight businesses. However, they also found that the *diversity* of time spans in a company's strategic portfolio was more important than the *length* of executive time horizon. That is, executive leaders have multiple projects, some with immediate implications, others with very distant time frames. Note, that this combination of projects is not the same as long-term projects decomposed into short-term objectives. Instead, the executive leader typically has several ongoing and often indirectly related projects that reflect a range of time horizons. Thus, the model in Fig. 3.1 indicates that time perspectives for top executives will vary from short-term to long-term.

Long time span horizons and diversity among strategic plans means that organizational problems at the systems level become increasingly ill defined. Ill-defined problems are those for which the starting parameters, the permissible solutions, and the solution goals are ambiguous and unspecified (Holyoak, 1984). Accordingly, executive leaders confronting such problems need to construct their parameters, search for acceptable solution paths, and specify a goal state that may not generate universal consensus among organizational stakeholders regarding its appropriateness. Further, many of these problems will have elements that are substantially unfamiliar to even the most knowledgeable executive, and they will often require the generation of novel frames of reference and solutions (Mumford, et al. 1993). These problem characteristics contribute to the complexity of leadership at higher organizational levels.

Several empirical studies document the qualitative shift in leader performance requirements from middle to executive organizational levels. For example, Tornow and Pinto (1976) found that long-range thinking and planning was perhaps the most significant aspect of upper-level managerial positions; moreover, these functions were rated as one of the least important aspects of middle- and lower-level positions. Similar conclusions were offered by Baehr (1992), Hemphill (1959), and Mahoney, et al. (1965). The external boundary-spanning aspects of executive (versus lower-level) work has been demonstrated by Kraut, et al. (1989), who found that activities related to monitoring the business environment display a sharp increase in emphasis from the middle- to executive-level leadership. Hambrick (1981) found that environmental-scanning activities were significantly correlated with hierarchical level in colleges and insurance firms (but not in hospitals). Taken together, these data indicate substantially greater emphasis on long-term planning and boundary-spanning activities at the executive level than at other organizational levels.

Informational and Social Complexity

As leaders move to higher levels in an organization, the operating environment and the performance requirements of a leader increase commensurately. Leaders face increasingly greater demands for information processing, as well as social demands. There is great complexity in the assimilation of information, in the cognitive structures needed to fully integrate diverse organizational stimuli, and in the problems faced by executive leaders (Campbell, 1988; Schroder, Driver, & Streufert, 1967). The different internal and external stakeholders to whom the executive is beholden, as well as the range of dynamic environmental forces and influences (e.g., economic, political, legal, technological; Hall, 1991; Katz & Kahn, 1978) acting on the organization, virtually guarantee that top organizational executives will have to generate, attend to, and choose from multiple solution paths. Further, the diversity within and between constituencies as well as the fluid character of most organizational environments create multiple outcome possibilities, conflicting or interconnected solution paths, and ambiguous associations between defined solution paths and organizational outcomes. These characteristics of executive work result in higher information-processing demands and hence greater complexity (Campbell, 1988).

Greater social complexity results because executives must supervise and coordinate the activities of different departments and subsystems within the organization, with each subsystem presenting the leader with different and often conflicting demands, goals, and agendas. In developing an overall organizational direction, the executive needs to consider and reconcile the requirements engendered by each of these organizational subsystems. The socially complex dimension of this process is that executives then need to persuade various organizational constituents and stakeholders to accept their reconciliation of their demands. In order to successfully implement an organizational vision, executive leaders must fundamentally change the social dynamics of the organization. This requires far greater social negotiation skills than leaders at lower organizational levels where organizational complexity and social demands are far less.

SOCIAL CAPACITIES AND LEADER EFFECTIVENESS

The high levels of social complexity characterizing the operating environment of organizational leaders argue for social capacities as critical leadership competencies. Further, leader effectiveness at successively higher organizational levels requires more complex forms of these capacities. Production-level leadership involves boundary spanning across a small unit environment, translation of well-defined goals and strategies into individual and unit tasks, and face-to-face supervision of individuals and small units. Key social capacities at this level are those that foster accurate perception and interpretation of social cues in a well-structured environment, identification of individual and group dynamics that may hinder problem solving, implementation of solutions in a small group setting, and the selection of appropriate interpersonal responses to subordinate and small group contingencies.

These capacities become more complex for middle-level or organizational leaders who are responsible for operating in a multi-unit environment. They need to perceive and interpret social cues in a more ambiguous environment. They also need to develop and implement problem solutions while accounting for the dynamics and contingencies of multiple organizational units. At the systems level, these capacities become still more complex as leaders become responsible for working with a greater variety of external and internal stakeholders. They also need to identify and interpret cues in a broader, more complex environment, as well as manage the organization as a whole. Thus, they require the most complex level of social perception and behavioral response capacities.

The social capacities described in this section encompass two general sets of abilities: those related to social reasoning competencies, and those related to social interactional or relational competencies. These sets reflect broader conceptualizations of the basic components of social intelligence that have been defined by many theorists. Definitions of social intelligence have generally stressed two key aspects—social understanding and situationally appropriate behavior. For example, in a pioneering work in this area, Thorndike (1920) defined social intelligence as "the ability to understand men and women, boys and girls—to act wisely in human relations" (p. 228). Similar definitions were proposed by Moss and Hunt (1927), Strang (1930), Thorndike and Stein (1937), and Vernon (1933). More recently, Marlowe (1986) indicated social intelligence to be the "ability to understand the feelings, thoughts, and behaviors of persons, including oneself, in interpersonal situations and to act appropriately upon that understanding" (p. 52). Reflecting a more goal-oriented approach, Ford and Tisak (1983; p. 197) defined social intelligence as "one's ability to accomplish relevant objectives in specific social settings."

These definitions depict social intelligence as a set of attributes that enable highly intelligent individuals to: (a) perceive and accurately interpret the intricacies of any social situation; (b) derive and select the appropriate behavioral responses that are likely to lead to success for oneself and for others to whom one is beholden, and finally; (c) enact the selected social responses. Thus, social intelligence reflects an ability to successfully engage in fundamentally four cognitive and behavioral processes—*social awareness, social acumen, response selection,* and *response enactment.* Zaccaro, Gilbert, et al. (1991) defined competencies in accomplishing the first two processes as social perceptiveness; they defined competencies in accomplishing the latter, response-oriented processes as behavioral flexibility.

A key point here is that socially intelligent behavior incorporates both social reasoning and relational competencies. Zaccaro, Gilbert, et al. (1991) argued that to be effective, relational competencies and their behavioral manifestations must be applied in accordance with situational cues and requirements. This suggests that relational competencies are necessary, but not sufficient for effective leadership; what is also necessary are social reasoning abilities. A number of theorists have noted the failure of intellectually gifted individuals as leaders because they lack competencies related to the ability to perceive appropriate social situational contingencies (Boyatzis, 1982; Bureau of Public Personnel Administration, 1930; House & Baetz, 1979; Moss, 1931). Therefore, successful leadership requires a set of social reasoning abilities that promotes effective perception, judgment, and diagnosis of social demands, needs, and requirements, as well as a set of relational competencies that promotes situational responsiveness, effective management of social diversity, and social persuasiveness (Bass, 1990; Bray, 1982; Howard & Bray, 1988; Yukl, 1989; Yukl & Van Fleet, 1992; Zaccaro, Gilbert, et al. 1991).

Social Reasoning Competencies

Social perceptiveness. As noted, the basis for effective social reasoning is *social perceptiveness,* which refers to a capacity to be insightful regarding the needs, goals, demands, and problems of multiple organizational constituencies (Zaccaro, Gilbert, et al. 1991). Leader social perceptiveness does not just involve recognizing the needs and problems of individual followers (e.g., Bass, 1990, pp. 117–120), but extends to relations among followers, organizational units, and between a leader's organization and other organizations. In addition, social insightfulness of successful leaders also includes a recognition of the needs and goals of whole organizations and sensitivity to opportunities in the external environment that can advance organizational goals. For example, insightful leaders are quicker in perceiving and understanding how new laws, regulatory changes, or changes in a particular consumer market can be exploited for organizational gain. These processes follow from competency in *system perceptiveness.*

Zaccaro, Gilbert, et al. (1991) argued that social perception abilities have three foci: (1) acquiring and interpreting information about events that may hinder organizational progress; (2) understanding personnel dynamics that may interfere with implementation of planned problem solutions; and (3) the acquisition and interpretation of social information regarding opportunities for organizational growth. These three foci of social reasoning have in common the acquisition and utilization of social information. Leaders are acquiring information about emerging exigencies, solution impediments, and organizational growth opportunities, and using such information in their short- and long-term problem-solving activities.

It should be noted that social perceptiveness reflects abilities in two fundamental processes. The first is an ability for social awareness, or being able to identify social cues that are relevant to organizational problem solving; socially intelligent behavior obviously cannot proceed if leaders are unable to even perceive important social contingencies. However, this social awareness ability is not enough. Many individuals can become cognizant of something important in their social environments, but lack the competencies to accurately interpret or infer the meaning of such information. Thus, a second ability underlying social perceptiveness is social acumen, a quickness in understanding the meaning of social dynamics for organizational problem solving. Social awareness and social acumen are separate competencies; just as individuals may be aware of social cues, but not be able to interpret them, they may also be able to understand social dynamics but be insensitive to the actual occurrence. It is highly likely, though, that leaders possessing one of these abilities will also possess the other. However, measures of social intelligence that strive to assess social perception abilities will need to be constructed to reflect ability in both social awareness and social acumen.

Social knowledge structures. Successful social perception depends on the cognitive frames that individuals can apply to social information. Zaccaro, Gilbert, et al. (1991) noted that leaders with high social intelligence have richly organized social knowledge structures that encode information about organizational personnel, situations, and episodes, as well as rules and procedures that guide the utilization of such information (Cantor & Kihlstrom, 1987). The application of a leader's social reasoning skills is facilitated by elaborate cognitive models of the social dynamics in organizations (Zaccaro, Marks, O'Connor-Boes, & Costanza, 1995). When the categories that make up these mental models are sufficiently detailed, they enable leaders to attend not only to similarities among social elements, but also to the differences and distinct nuances among similar elements. Such skill allows the leader to develop a more fine-tuned understanding of organizational dynamics that leads to more effective social problem solving.

Metacognitive reasoning. A leader's social reasoning abilities also include competencies in metacognitive thinking. Perhaps the most common definition of metacognition is one's "knowledge and cognition about cognitive phenomena" (Flavell, 1979, p. 906; see also Brown, 1978; Davidson, Deuser, & Sternberg, 1994; Halpern, 1984; Jausovec, 1994a, 1994b; Nelson, 1992; Osman & Hannafin, 1992). Garafalo and Lester (1985, p. 164) distinguish between cognition and metacognition by noting that "cognition is involved in doing, whereas metacognition is involved in choosing and planning what to do and monitoring what is being done" (see Artzt and Armour-Thomas (1992) for an operationalization of this distinction). Several theorists have emphasized the critical role of metacognitive abilities in complex problem solving (Brown, 1978; Davidson, Deuser, & Sternberg, 1994; Gagné, 1985; Geiwitz, 1993; Sternberg, 1985). Here, metacognitive processes are defined as executive functions that control the application and operation of cognitive abilities and skills when confronting organizational problems.

Complex problem solving involves four basic processes. The first process is defining the nature of the problem to be solved. This includes the awareness that a problem exists, the identification and definition of the problem, and the construction of its parameters. Here, problem solvers may use an array of cognitive abilities such as verbal and written comprehension, memory skills, and inductive and deductive reasoning (Fleishman 1975; Fleishman & Quaintance, 1984) to interpret information regarding the nature of a particular problem. The second process is specifying the most appropriate solution paths. This specification may proceed from the application of convergent thinking, divergent thinking, or logical reasoning skills to information derived from the construction and representation of the problem. The third and fourth processes refer respectively to the implementation of the chosen solution and to the monitoring and evaluation of the solution and its consequences. As noted earlier in this chapter, because leaders implement solutions within complex social environments, they need to apply a variety of cognitive and social competencies that promote solution implementation and the acquisition of information needed for effective monitoring and evaluation.

These four processes are grounded in high-level cognitive abilities. Metacognitive thinking refers not to these abilities themselves, but rather to the awareness and regulation of their application in understanding a problem, specifying a solution, and implementing and evaluating best-fitting strategies. That is, for each of the aforementioned processes, metacognitive problem-solving skills reflect an expertise in knowing what cognitive abilities are applicable, in particular, problem domains and in evaluating the products of their application. For example, regarding problem definition or construction, cognitive reasoning skills (e.g., deductive reasoning) are used to generate a particular understanding of a problem from available information. The addition of metacognitive skills help the problem solver to evaluate the constructed problem both in terms of the processes that led to its derivation and of its fit to the extant problem domain (e.g., "Is this the 'correct' or best way to construct this problem?"). The value of metacognitive skills then is to facilitate flexibility in creative problem solving, particularly in how information is used and in the selection of solution strategies that correspond to different types of problems (Davidson, et al. 1994; Jausovec, 1994b).

Metacognitive thinking contributes to a leader's social reasoning abilities by regulating their application in social problem solving. They help leaders evaluate their own social perception processes and the interpretations they apply to acquired social information. Such metacognitive thinking abilities also facilitate a leader's understanding of how other organizational constituencies perceive his or her own leadership actions. This form of metacognition has been called "metaperception," and can be defined as the awareness and understanding one has of how others perceive and evaluate oneself (Shechtman & Kenny, 1994). Accuracy in metaperception is important for leaders to gauge their own legitimacy in terms of how much support they may have in problem-solving efforts. There has been little research in how metaperceptual skills contribute to socially intelligent behavior or to effective leadership. Thus, this is a fruitful area for future investigations of leader social reasoning competencies.

Relational Competencies

Relational competencies include a constellation of capacities and skills that facilitate complex interactions with organizational subordinates, peers, and superiors. These competencies include *behavioral flexibility, negotiation skills, conflict management, persuasion, and social influence skills.*

Behavioral flexibility. Complex social problem solving requires behavioral flexibility if a leader is to respond appropriately to a myriad of organizational scenarios (Bray, 1982; Howard & Bray, 1988; Zaccaro, Gilbert, et al. 1991). Zaccaro, Gilbert, et al. (1991) argued that such behavioral flexibility is linked to social knowledge structures, termed episode concepts (Cantor & Kihlstrom, 1987; Forgas, 1982), event schemata (Fiske & Taylor, 1991), or scripts (Abelson, 1981; Gioia & Poole, 1984; Schank & Abelson, 1977), that encode a wide range of appropriate leadership responses to the multiple problem scenarios that can occur in organizational domains. In essence, to behave flexibly, leaders need a large response repertoire and the ability to select the correct response for particular situational demands. A large repertoire is reflected in the number of different social knowledge structures encoded by an individual (Cantor & Kihlstrom, 1987; Zaccaro, Gilbert, et al. 1991). Selecting appropriate actions in response to situational problem elements is driven primarily from action rules (Abelson, 1981) that guide the implementation or actualization of a script.

Components of executive flexibility. The notion of flexibility as a key leader attribute has become a prominent theme in research on executive leadership. For example, Quinn's Competing Values Framework (Hart & Quinn, 1993; Hooijberg & Quinn, 1992; Quinn, 1984, 1988) argued that conflicting values and therefore opposing behavioral requirements are inherent in the nature of organizational senior leadership. Indeed, Denison, Hooijberg, and Quinn (1995) defined effective leadership as "the ability to perform the multiple roles and behaviors that circumscribe the requisite variety implied by an organizational or environmental context" (p. 526). Therefore, leader effectiveness entails the mastery of sometimes competing behavior patterns. Quinn and his colleagues called the display of this mastery *behavioral complexity.*

Hooijberg and Quinn (1992) argued that effective leaders will enact a greater variety of different roles than ineffective leaders. Also, effective leaders will balance these roles such that one role is not emphasized disproportionately. The enactment of multiple roles requires significant skill by the leader because many leadership roles can have countervailing ones. Thus, for example, leaders need to be innovative and adaptive with respect to the organization's operating environment, while at the same time maintaining stability and structure within the organization. Also, they must develop their subordinates by creating a nurturing environment, while also being task-focused and structuring in order to complete production goals in a timely manner. Thus, behavioral complexity is defined as the skillful balancing of multiple leadership roles in accordance with organizational requirements.

Hooijberg (1996) extended these notions by specifying two dimensions of behavioral complexity: *behavioral repertoire* and *behavioral differentiation.* Behavioral repertoire refers to the variety of behaviors an executive can enact in response to situational demands. The broader the manager's repertoire, the more effective the manager can be across diverse organizational contexts. Further, as social complexity within organizations increases, the more necessary is a wide behavioral repertoire.

Hooijberg (1996) noted that the extent of a manager's repertoire was necessary but not sufficient for effectiveness. Managers and executives also needed the ability to apply appropriate responses to particular situations. Hooijberg defined this ability as behavioral differentiation. He noted that "the concept of behavioral differentiation refers to the ability of managers to perform the leadership functions they have in their behavioral repertoire differently (more adaptively, more flexibly, more appropriately, more individualized, and situation specific) depending on the organizational situation" (p. 922).

The display of behavioral complexity in complex organizational domains, particularly at the executive level, is likely to be grounded in a number of different personal attributes. Zaccaro, Gilbert, et al. (1991) argued that behavioral flexibility follows from the aforementioned social reasoning skills that provide the foundation for a leader's ability to make appropriate responses across diverse social situations. This suggests that behavioral flexibility depends in part on skill in differentiating and integrating social domain knowledge, i.e., on integrative cognitive complexity.

Streufert and Swezey (1986) contrasted hierarchical integrative complexity from flexible integrative complexity in terms of the structure of cognition. Hierarchical complexity reflected fixed relationships among conceptual elements in a cognitive space, while flexible complexity resulted in dynamic and fluid relationships among conceptual elements that varied according to changes in environmental stimuli. Streufert and Swezey noted that "where flexible integration can be responsive to anticipated changes in the environment that would require reconceptualizations of event relationships, hierarchical integration cannot" (p. 17). For this reason, managers who exhibit flexible integrative complexity are hypothesized to be better executives than those who display hierarchical integrative complexity, particularly in a fluid and complex environment.

Flexibility also requires, however, that leaders display openness and tolerance in the face of social uncertainty and ambiguity. This quality, defined in terms of openness to experience, has been recognized as a major personality dimension distinguishing individuals (McCrae & Costa, 1987, 1990). Further, behavioral flexibility can become behavioral vacillation under conditions of uncertainty unless individuals possess a degree of self-discipline that force closure on a behavioral action, even when social cues do not point clearly to an appropriate response set. These observations have led several researchers to argue that flexibility, and related personal qualities (e.g., adaptability, openness) are important executive personality characteristics (Howard & Bray, 1988; Miller & Toulouse, 1986; Mumford, et al. 1993).

These various perspectives suggest that executive flexibility emerges from an integrated constellation of cognitive, social, and dispositional qualities. Effective executive leadership emerges in part from the joint influence of these qualities. In other words, these characteristics are not considered additive or independent in their influence on executive leadership. For example, integrative complexity allows the leader to develop the elaborate response models required in complex social domains; however, behavioral flexibility reflects the mechanism of translating leader thought and reflection to appropriate leader action across diverse organizational scenarios. Boal and Whitehead (1992) described individuals who are high on both of these dimensions as "informed flexibles" who have "both a wide array of cognitive maps with which to interpret the situation and a wide array of behavioral responses" (p. 239). Their approach, however, assumes an independence between these two qualities. The integrated model emphasizes their interdependence in terms of successful executive leadership.

Both cognitive and behavioral flexibility are facilitated by a disposition-based flexibility. Because individuals who can be characterized as high in this quality are more oriented toward adaptiveness instead of rigidity in dynamic social domains, they are more likely to be behaviorally flexible. Likewise, conceptual capacity and the constructions of elaborate frames of reference (see Jacobs & Jaques, 1987, 1990, 1991) necessitate a degree of openness and curiosity on the part of the executive leader. Without this quality, and a high tolerance for ambiguity, such leaders could not cope with the dynamic and complex environment they need to model.

Effective organizational leadership, particularly at the organizational level, lies at the nexus of behavioral flexibility, flexible integrative complexity, and dispositional factors that promote flexibility. Effective leadership in turbulent or dynamic organizational environments likely requires all forms of flexibility. Behavioral flexibility will not be displayed unless leaders also possess the disposition to be flexible, as well as the conceptual skills to develop and distinguish among different situationally appropriate response scripts. Therefore, research on executive leadership that assesses only one form of flexibility will present an incomplete or possibly misdirected picture of executive leadership.

Social influence skills. There is little doubt that successful executive leaders require skills in negotiation, conflict management, and persuasion (Thomas & Schmidt, 1976). Four of the ten managerial roles proposed by Mintzberg (1973) reflect the leader either as a representative of an organizational unit or responsible for resolving intraunit differences. Likert's linch-pin model of organizations emphasizes leaders as representatives of organizational subunits, while also part of more encompassing "organizational families" where negotiation and coordination occur to minimize organizational conflict (Likert, 1961, 1967). Katz and Kahn (1978) cite conflict resolution as one of three key functions of leadership across organizational levels and groups. Given the criticality of these leadership activities, social competencies such as negotiation skill, persuasion, and conflict management become important determinants of leader effectiveness (Bass, 1990; Morse & Wagner, 1978; Yukl & Van Fleet, 1992).

Negotiation and conflict management skills involve the ability to apply any and all appropriate tactics as well as the ability to discern which strategy is most likely to succeed in a given situation (Bass, 1990; Lewicki & Sheppard, 1985). For example, research by Sheppard (1984) and Kabanoff (1985) suggests that effective leaders cannot rely on a single negotiation or conflict management approach, but must have the skill to apply widely different approaches, and it is important to fit the appropriate strategy to a particular situation.

Leaders often utilize persuasion and other social influence skills, particularly when implementing an unpopular solution or course of action. Theories of charismatic and inspirational leadership rely heavily on the exercise of such skills to articulate a vision that is contrary to the status quo (Bass, 1985, 1990; House, 1977), and they use persuasion to convince followers of the power and correctness of their vision (Bass, 1985; Conger & Kanungo, 1987, 1988; House, 1977; House & Shamir, 1993). Persuasion skills likely play a critical part in both the practice and maintenance of a leadership role. Moreover, skills in the use of persuasion likely become more important in higher levels of organizational leadership (Jaques, et al. 1986).

Rational persuasion is just one of several social influence tactics required of leaders. Yukl and Van Fleet (1992) identified 10 social influence tactics, ranging from the use of threats and coercion to legitimating tactics and coalition formation to inspirational appeals and rational persuasion from surveys of managerial behaviors and critical incidents. They also noted that successful leader influence results most often when rational persuasion is combined with inspirational appeals, social exchanges, or subordinate consultations. As with conflict management strategies, the selection of influence tactics depends very much on such situational contingencies as the target of the influence (e.g., subordinates, peers, or supervisors), the goal of influence (e.g., passive versus active commitment), the time available, and the nature and strength of opposing constituencies. Thus, again, successful social influence by the leader requires the mastery of a range of skills and the ability to select and apply them to the appropriate situation.

Several researchers have suggested that another key interactional competency for leaders is the display of consideration and caring for subordinates. Using factorial analyses of leadership behavior, Fleishman (1953) identifies consideration as a key leadership dimension, characterized by caring for subordinate well being, knowing their needs, and being able to respond effectively within organizational constraints. Most importantly, the fact that such leaders focused on the development and mentoring of their subordinates is supported by theories of transformational leadership in which the enabling and empowerment of subordinates is critical to leadership success (Bass, 1985, 1990; Burns, 1978). Thus, such success will be conditioned by such interactional skills as coaching and empathy.

SOCIAL INTELLIGENCE AND LEADERSHIP: EMPIRICAL EVIDENCE

Several empirical studies have affirmed social reasoning and relational competencies as important leadership qualities. Early research provided mixed results. For example, some researchers have found that leaders score higher on measures of social accuracy and insight than nonleaders (Bell & Hall, 1954; Chowdhry & Newcomb, 1952; Fleishman & Salter, 1963; Stogdill, 1948), while others report no significant differences (Campbell, 1955; Hites & Campbell, 1950). Bass (1990) argued that a leader's social insight was enhanced by such situational circumstances as the organizational relevance of the qualities being perceived (Chowdhry & Newcomb, 1952), the familiarity of organizational members to the leader, and the degree of actual (rather than assumed) similarity between the leader and other organizational members. All of these factors are likely to contribute to the quality and complexity of a leader's social knowledge structures, which in turn facilitate the utility of social reasoning skills in organizational domains (Cantor & Kihlstrom, 1987; Zaccaro, Gilbert, et al. 1991). Issue relevance, familiarity, and similarity provide the leader with a wealth of information that can be applied to the diagnosis of organizational scenarios. That is, these factors promote the system perception skills of the leader.

Along these lines, Gilbert and Zaccaro (1995) examined social intelligence, social knowledge structures and career achievement in army officers ranging in rank from second lieutenant to colonel. These officers were also asked to generate solutions to a variety of problem domains that were typical of upper organizational military leaders. They found that officers who scored high on measures of social intelligence had more principle-based and elaborated social knowledge structures than officers who displayed lower social intelligence. Higher-ranking officers were also more attuned to environmental opportunities (or affordances) that existed in the various problem scenarios. Gilbert and Zaccaro also reported that systems perceptiveness, but not interpersonal perception skills, contributed significantly to the prediction of rank and career achievement, even after accounting for officer intelligence and creative thinking skills. That is, higher-ranking military officers displayed more systems perception and behavioral flexibility skills than lower ranking officers, and these skills predicted career success. Similar data were reported by Howard and Bray (1988). They found that skills in the perception of social cues were significantly associated with attained managerial level 8 and 20 years into a manager's career.

Several studies have provided evidence for social behavioral flexibility as a leader quality. Zaccaro, Foti, and Kenny (1991) found that individuals who received high leadership scores appeared to be those who were able to vary the frequency of certain leadership behaviors in accordance with changing situation requirements. Research on "self-monitoring," which has been operationalized as a form of social behavioral flexibility and response appropriateness (see Snyder, 1974, 1979), has consistently reported positive correlations between ratings of self-monitoring and leadership status (Dobbins, Long, Dedrick, & Clemons, 1990; Ellis, 1988; Ellis, Adamson, Deszca, & Cawsay, 1988; Garland & Beard, 1979; Zaccaro, et al. 1991).

Ritchie (1994) examined 24 individual characteristics, including behavioral flexibility, as part of an assessment of senior management potential. In his sample of 115 managers, approximately half had attained a level of middle- to upper-level management seven years after initial assessment. Ritchie found that behavioral flexibility was one of the top three correlates of attained level. Ritchie also completed a cluster analysis of managers and derived three clusters: "stars," "overachievers," and "plateaued." Thirty-eight percent of the stars, 16% of the overachievers, and none of the plateaued managers were promoted to upper-level management positions. Stars achieved higher ratings of behavioral flexibility than overachievers who scored higher than the plateaued group.

Hooijberg (1996) investigated the association between his two dimensions of behavioral complexity—behavioral repertoire and behavioral differentiation—and managerial effectiveness, assessed through ratings from a manager's subordinates, peers, and supervisors. Behavioral repertoire was measured by ratings from the manager's subordinates, peers, and supervisors of how often he or she displayed a number of leadership functions. Behavioral differentiation was assessed through the variance in behavioral ratings across subordinates, peers, and supervisors. The data were collected from 282 middle managers in an automotive company, and 252 managers in a public utility company. Hooijberg found in both samples that the extent of a manager's behavioral repertoire was positively associated with effectiveness ratings from the manager's role set. However, the results for behavioral differentiation ratings were mixed—they were positively associated only with the effectiveness ratings by supervisors and only in the automotive sample. In fact, behavioral differentiation was negatively associated with subordinate ratings of effectiveness. Hooijberg suggested that while supervisors may interpret response variation by their subordinate managers as consistent with the demands of the situation, a behaviorally differentiated manager's subordinates may interpret the same variation as inconsistency in behavior and therefore perceive their manager more negatively.

Other studies have provided evidence for social influence capacities as key leader attributes. Boyatzis (1982) used a critical incidence methodology (Flanagan, 1951) to compare effective and ineffective managers at different levels and to identify the particular traits and abilities associated with leader success. He found that effective managers display abilities in developing coalitions and organizational networks, persuading and gaining the cooperation of others, conflict management and resolution, and managing and facilitating team processes. McCall and Lombardo (1983) reported from interviews with executives and middle-level managers that those who tended to fail (or "derail") were perceived in part as weak in interpersonal skill, particularly social sensitivity.

Taken together, these studies demonstrate significant empirical support for the importance of capacities associated with social intelligence for effective organizational leadership. Further research is necessary to validate the proposed relationships among particular social intelligence abilities, the display of certain leadership patterns, and indexes of organizational effectiveness. Such research would be an important foundation for the development of effective assessment tools to measure social intelligence. It would also contribute to the construction of programs and interventions designed to develop social reasoning and relational capacities in rising organizational leaders.

CONCLUSION

This chapter examines the importance of social intelligence for effective organizational leadership. It defines several competencies that are associated with high levels of social intelligence and describes how these competencies promote leadership. A central argument in this paper is that the increasing level of social complexity that exists at ascending organizational levels also enhances the importance of social intelligence as a key leader attribute. Therefore such competencies as behavioral flexibility, conflict management, persuasion, and social reasoning skills become more important for executive leaders.

In essence, the social reasoning and relational competencies described in this chapter allow organizational leaders to interact, solve problems, and thus be in control of a diversity of complex and dynamic social domains. These attributes contribute to both cross-situational and situationally specific aspects of leadership. Accordingly, they inform us about how leaders contribute to organizational effectiveness. As further research on social intelligence accumulates, particularly in the areas of leader assessment, development, and selection, we will gain some valuable insights and tools to foster intelligent organizational leadership.

AUTHOR NOTES

Parts of this chapter were adapted, with permission, from Zaccaro 1999 and 2001. This research was funded under DoD Contract No. DASW01-98-K-005 P00002 by the U.S. Army Research Institute for the Behavioral and Social Sciences. The views, opinions, and/or findings contained in this report are those of the author and should not be construed as an official Department of the Army position, policy, or decision.

REFERENCES

Abelson, R. (1981). Psychological status of the script concept. *American Psychologist, 36,* 715–729.

Alexander, L. D. (1979). The effect level in the hierarchy and functional area have on the extent Mintzberg's roles are required by managerial jobs. *Proceedings, Academy of Management,* Atlanta, GA, 186–189.

Artzt, A. F., & Armour-Thomas, E. (1992). Development of a cognitive-metacognitive framework for protocol analysis of mathematical problem solving in small groups. *Cognition and Instruction, 9,* 137–175.

Baehr, M. E. (1992). *Predicting success in higher level positions: A guide to the system for testing and evaluation of potential.* New York: Quorum.

Barnlund, D. C. (1962). Consistency of emergent leadership in groups with changing tasks and members. *Speech Monographs, 29,* 45–52.

Bass, B. M. (1985). *Leadership and performance beyond expectations.* New York: Free Press.

Bass, B. M. (1990). *Bass & Stogdill's handbook of leadership: Theory, research, and managerial applications* (3rd ed.). New York: Free Press.

Bell, G. B., & Hall, H. G. (1954). The relationship between leadership and empathy. *Journal of Abnormal and Social Psychology, 49,* 156–157.

Boal, K. B., & Whitehead, C. J. (1992). A critique and extension of the Stratified Systems Theory perspective. In R. L. Phillips & J. G. Hunt (eds.), *Strategic leadership: A multi-organizational perspective.* Westport, CT: Quorum Books.

Boyatzis, R. R. (1982). *The competent manager: A model for effective performance.* New York: Wiley.

Bray, D. W. (1982). The assessment center and the study of lives. *American Psychologist, 37,* 180–189.

Bray, D. W., Campbell, R. J., & Grant, D. L. (1974). *Formative years in business: A long-term AT&T study of managerial lives.* New York: John Wiley.

Brown, A. L. (1978). Knowing when, where, and how to remember: The problem of metacognition. In R. Glaser (ed.), *Advances in instructional psychology.* New York: Halsted Press.

Bureau of Public Personnel Administration, (1930). Partially standardized tests of social intelligence. *Public Personnel Studies, 8,* 73–79.

Burns, J. M. (1978). *Leadership.* New York: Harper & Row.

Campbell, D. J. (1988). Task complexity: A review and analysis. *Academy of Management Review, 13,* 40–52.

Campbell, D. T. (1955). An error in some demonstrations of the superior social perceptiveness of leaders. *Journal of Abnormal and Social Psychology, 51,* 694–695.

Chowdhry, K., & Newcomb, T. M. (1952). The relative abilities of leaders and nonleaders to estimate opinions of their own groups. *Journal of Abnormal and Social Psychology, 47,* 51–57.

Cantor, N., & Kihlstrom, J. F. (1987). *Personality and social intelligence.* Englewood Cliffs, NJ: Prentice Hall.

Conger, J. A., & Kanungo, R. N. (1987). Towards a behavioral theory of charismatic leadership in organizational settings. *Academy of Management Review, 12,* 637–647.

Conger, J. A., & Kanungo, R. N. (eds.), (1988). *Charismatic leadership: The elusive factor in organizational effectiveness.* San Francisco, CA: Jossey-Bass.

Davidson, J. E., Deuser, R., & Sternberg, R. J. (1994). The role of metacognition in problem solving. In J. Metcalf & A. P. Shimamura, *Metacognition: Knowing about knowing.* Cambridge, MA: The MIT Press.

Denison, D. R., Hooijberg, R., & Quinn, R. E. (1995). Paradox and performance: Toward a theory of behavioral complexity in managerial leadership. *Organization Science, 6,* 524–540.

Dobbins, G. H., Long, W. S., Dedrick, E. J., & Clemons, T. C. (1990). The role of self-monitoring and gender on leader emergence: A laboratory and field study. *Journal of Management, 16* (3), 493–502.

Ellis, R. J. (1988). Self-monitoring and leadership emergence in groups. *Personality and Social Psychology Bulletin, 14,* 681–693.

Ellis, R. J., Adamson, R. S., Deszca, G., & Cawsay, T. F. (1988). Self-monitoring and leadership emergence. *Small Group Behavior, 19*(3), 312–324.

Fiske, S. T., & Taylor, S. E. (1991). *Social cognition,* (2nd ed.). New York: McGraw-Hill, Inc.

Flanagan, J. C. (1951). Defining the requirements of an executive's job. *Personnel, 28,* 28–35.

Flavell, J. H. (1979). Metacognition and cognitive monitoring: A new area of cognitive-developmental inquiry. *American Psychologist, 34,* 906–911.

Fleishman, E. A. (1953). The description of supervisory behavior. *Journal of Applied Psychology, 37,* 1–6.

Fleishman, E. A. (1975). Toward a taxonomy of human performance. *American Psychologist, 30,* 1127–1149.

Fleishman, E. A., Mumford, M. D., Zaccaro, S. J., Levin, K. Y., Korotkin, & Hein, M. B. (1991). Taxonomic efforts in the description of leader behavior: A synthesis and functional interpretation. *Leadership Quarterly, 2,* 245–287

Fleishman, E. A., & Quaintance M. K. (1984). *Taxonomies of human performance: The description of human tasks.* Orlando, FL: Academic Press.

Fleishman, E. A., & Salter, J. A. (1963). Relation between the leader's behavior and his empathy toward subordinates. *Journal of Industrial Psychology, 1,* 79–84.

Ford, M. E., & Tisak, M. S. (1983). A further search for social intelligence. *Journal of Educational Psychology, 75*(2), 196–206.

Forgas, J. P. (1982). Episode cognition: Internal representations of interaction routines. *Advances in Experimental Social Psychology, 15,* 59–101.

Gagné, R. M. (1985). *The conditions of learning and theory of instruction.* Philadelphia, PA: Holt, Rinehart, & Winston.

Garafolo, J., & Lester, F. K. (1985). Metacognition, cognitive monitoring, and mathematical performance. *Journal for Research in Mathematics Education, 16,* 163–176.

Garland, H., & Beard, J. F. (1979). Relationship between self-monitoring and leader emergence across two task situations. *Journal of Applied Psychology, 64,* 72–76.

Geiwitz, J. (1993). *A conceptual model of metacognitive skills* (ARI Tech. Rep. 51–1, Contract No. MDA903-93-C-0109). Alexandria, VA: U.S. Army Research Institute for the Behavioral and Social Sciences.

Gilbert, J. A., & Zaccaro, S. J. (1995). *Social intelligence and organizational leadership.* Presented at the 103th annual meeting of the American Psychological Association. New York, August, 1995.

Giola, D. A., & Poole, P. P. (1984). Scripts in organizational behavior. *Academy of Management Review, 9,* 449–459.

Hackman, J. R., & Walton, R. E. (1986). Leading groups in organizations. In P. S. Goodman & Associates (eds.), *Designing effective work groups.* San Francisco, CA: Jossey-Bass.

Hall, R. H. (1991). *Organizations: Structures, processes and outcomes* (5th ed.). Englewood Cliffs, NJ: Prentice Hall.

Halpern, D. F. (1984). *Thought and knowledge: An introduction to critical thinking.* Hillsdale, N.J.: Lawrence Erlbaum Associates.

Hambrick, D. C. (1981). Specialization of environmental scanning activities among upper-level executives. *Journal of Management Studies, 18,* 299–320.

Hart, S. L., & Quinn, R. E. (1993). Roles executives play: CEOs, behavioral complexity, and firm performance. *Human Relations, 46,* 543–574.

Hemphill, J. K. (1959). Job descriptions for executives. *Harvard Business Review, 37,* 55–67.

Hites, R.W., & Campbell, D. T. (1950). A test of the ability of fraternity leaders to estimate group opinion. *Journal of Social Psychology, 32,* 95–100.

Holyoak, K. J. (1984). Mental models in problem solving. In J. R. Anderson & K. M. Kosslyn (eds.), *Tutorials in learning and memory* (pp. 193–210). New York: Freeman.

Hooijberg, R. (1996). A multidirectional approach toward leadership: An extension of the concept of behavioral complexity. *Human Relations, 49,* 917–946.

Hooijberg, R., & Quinn, R. E. (1992). Behavioral complexity and the development of effective managers. In R. L. Phillips & J. G. Hunt (eds.), *Strategic leadership: A multiorganizational perspective.* Westport, CT: Quorum Books.

House, R. J. (1997). A 1976 theory of charismatic leadership. In J. G. Hunt & L. Larson (eds.), *Leadership: The cutting edge.* Carbondale, IL: Southern Illinois University Press.

House, R. J., & Aditya, R. (1999). *The social scientific study of leadership: Quo vadis?* Unpublished manuscript.

House, R. J., & Baetz, M. L. (1979). Leadership: Some empirical generalizations and new research directions. *Research in Organizations Behavior, 1,* 341–423.

House, R. J., & Shamir (1993). Toward the integration of transformational, charismatic, and visionary leadership theories. In M. Chemer & R. Ayman (eds.). *Leadership theory and research: Perspectives and directions.* New York: Academic Press.

House, R. J., Spangler, W. D., & Woycke, J. (1991). Personality and charisma in the U.S. presidency: A psychological theory of leader effectiveness. *Administrative Science Quarterly, 36,* 364–396.

Howard, A. & Bray, D. (1988). *Managerial lives in transition: Advancing age and changing times.* New York: Guilford Press.

Hunt, J. G., Osborn, R. N., & Martin, H. J. (1981). *A multiple influence model of leadership* (ARI Tech. Rep. 520). Alexandria, VA: U.S. Army Research Institute for the Behavioral and Social Sciences.

Jacobs, T. O., & Jaques, E. (1987). Leadership in complex systems. In J. A. Zeidner (ed.), *Human productivity enhancement (Vol. 2, Organizations, personnel, and decision making).* (pp. 7–65). New York: Praeger.

Jacobs, T. O., & Jaques, E. (1990). Military executive leadership. In K. E. Clark and M. B. Clark (eds.), *Measures of leadership.* Greensboro: Center for Creative Leadership.

Jacobs, T. O., & Jaques, E. (1991). Executive leadership. In R. Gal and D. Mangelsdorf (eds.), *Handbook of military psychology.* Chichester, U.K.: Wiley and Sons.

Jaques, E. (1978). *A general theory of bureaucracy.* Exeter, NH: Heinemann.

Jaques, E. (1986). The development of intellectual capability: A discussion of Stratified Systems Theory. *Journal of Applied Behavioral Science, 22,* 361–384.

Jaques, E. (1989). *Requisite organization.* Arlington, VA: Cason Hall.

Jaques, E. (1990). Task complexity. In G. H. Pollack (ed.), *Creativity and work* (pp. 43–80). Madison, CT: International Universities Press.

Jaques, E., Clement, S. D., Rigby, C., & Jacobs, T. O. (1986). *Senior leadership requirements at the executive level* (Res. Rep. 1420). Alexandria, VA: U.S. Army Research Institute for the Behavioral and Social Sciences.

Jausovec, N. (1994a). *Flexible thinking: An explanation for individual differences in ability.* Cresskill, NJ: Hampton Press.

Jausovec, N. (1994b). Metacognition in creative problem solving. In M. A. Runco (ed.). *Problem finding, problem solving, and creativity.* Norwood, NJ: Ablex.

Judge, W. Q., & Spitzfaden, M. (1995). The management of strategic time horizons within biotechnology firms. *Journal of Management Inquiry, 4,* 179–196.

Kabanoff, B. (1985). Potential influence structures as sources of interpersonal conflict in groups and organizations. *Organizational Behavior and Human Decision Processes, 36,* 113–141.

Katz, D., & Kahn, R. L. (1966, 1978). *The social psychology of organizations.* New York: Wiley.

Kenny, D. A., & Zaccaro, S. J. (1983). An estimate of variance due to traits in leadership. *Journal of Applied Psychology, 68,* 678–685.

Kotter, J. P. (1982a). *The general managers.* New York: Free Press.

Kotter, J. P. (1982b). What effective general managers really do. *Harvard Business Review, 60*(6), 156–167.

Kraut, A. I., Pedigo, P. R., McKenna, D. D., & Dunnette, M. D. (1989). The role of the manager: What's really important in different management jobs. *Academy of Management Executive, 3,* 286–293.

Lewicki, R. J., & Sheppard, B. H. (1985). Choosing how to intervene: Factors affecting the use of process and outcome control in third party dispute resolution. *Journal of Occupational Behavior, 6,* 49–64.

Likert, R. (1961). *New patterns of management.* New York: McGraw-Hill.

Likert, R. (1967). *The human organization.* New York: McGraw-Hill.

Lord, R. G., De Vader, C. L., & Alliger, G. M. (1986). A meta-analysis of the relation between personality traits and leadership perceptions: An application of validity generalization procedures. *Journal of Applied Psychology, 71,* 402–410.

Lucas, K. W., & Markessini, J. (1993). *Senior leadership in a changing world order: Requisite skills for U.S. Army one- and two-star generals* (ARI Tech. Rep. No. 976). Alexandria, VA: U.S. Army Research Institute for the Behavioral and Social Sciences.

Mahoney, T. A., Jerdee, T. H., & Carroll, S. I. (1965). The job(s) of management. *Industrial Relations, 4,* 97–110.

Mann, R. D. (1959). A review of the relationships between personality and performance in small groups. *Psychological Bulletin, 56,* 241–270.

Markessini, J., Lucas, K. W., Chandler, & Jacobs, T. O. (1994). *Executive leadership: Requisite skills and developmental processes for the U.S. Army's civilian executives* (ARI Res. Note 94-26). Alexandria, VA: U.S. Army Research Institute for the Behavioral and Social Sciences.

Marlowe, H. A., Jr., (1986). Social intelligence: Evidence for multidimensionality and construct independence. *Journal of Educational Psychology, 78*(1), 52–58.

McCall, M. W., Jr., & Lombardo, M. M. (1983). *Off the track: Why and how successful executives get derailed.* (Technical Report. No. 21). Greensboro, NC: Center for Creative Leadership.

McCrae, R. R., & Costa, P. T., Jr. (1987). Validation of the five-factor model of personality across instruments and observers. *Journal of Personality and Social Psychology, 52,* 81–90.

McCrae, R. R., & Costa, P. T., Jr. (1990). *Personality in adulthood.* New York: Guilford Press.

McGrath, J. E. (1962). *Leadership behavior: Some requirements for leadership training.* Washington, D.C.: U.S. Civil Service Commission.

Miller, D., & Toulouse, J. M. (1986). Chief executive personality and corporate strategy and structure in small firms. *Management Science, 32,* 1389–1409.

Mintzberg, H. (1973). *The nature of managerial work.* New York: Harper & Row.

Mintzberg, H. (1994). *The rise and fall of strategic planning.* New York: Free Press.

Morse, J. J., & Wagner, F. R. (1978). Measuring the process of managerial effectiveness. *Academy of Management Journal, 21,* 23–35.

Moss, F. A. (1931). Preliminary report of a study of social intelligence and executive ability. *Public Personnel Studies, 9,* 2–9.

Moss, F. A., & Hunt, T. (1927). Are you socially intelligent? *Scientific American, 137,* 108–110.

Mumford, M. D. (1986). Leadership in the organizational context: Conceptual approach and its application. *Journal of Applied Social Psychology, 16,* 212–226.

Mumford, M. D., & Connelly, M. S. (1991). Leaders as creators: Leader performance and problem solving in ill-defined domains. *Leadership Quarterly, 2,* 289–316.

Mumford, M. D., Zaccaro, S. J., Harding, F. D., Fleishman, E. A., & Reiter-Palmon, R. (1993). *Cognitive and temperament predictors of executive ability: Principles for developing leadership capacity.* Alexandria, VA: U.S. Army Research Institute for the Behavioral and Social Sciences.

Nelson, T. O. (1992). Introduction to conceptual and methodological issues: Forward. In T. O. Nelson (ed.), *Metacognition: Core readings.* Boston, MA: Allyn and Bacon.

Osman, M. E., & Hannafin, M. J. (1992). Metacognitive research and theory: Analysis and implications for instructional design. *Educational Technology Research and Development, 40,* 83–99.

Paolillo, J. G. (1981). Managers' self-assessments of managerial roles: The influence of hierarchical level. *Journal of Management, 7,* 43–52.

Pavett, C. M., & Lau, A. W. (1983). Managerial work: The influence of hierarchical level and functional specialty. *Academy of Management Journal, 26,* 170–177.

Quinn, R. E. (1984). Applying the competing values approach to leadership: Towards an integrative framework. In J. G. Hunt, D. Hosking, C. A. Schriesheim, & R. Stewart (eds.), *Leaders and managers: International perspectives on managerial behavior and leadership.* New York: Pergamon.

Quinn, R. E. (1988). *Beyond rational management: Mastering paradoxes and competing demands of high performance.* San Francisco, CA: Jossey Bass.

Rigby, C. K., & Harris, P. (1987). *Program management offices: Structural modeling through applications of stratified systems theory* (ARI Tech. Rep. 736). Alexandria, VA: U.S. Army Research Institute for the Behavioral and Social Sciences.

Ritchie, R. J. (1994). Using the assessment center method to predict senior management potential. Special issue: Issues in the assessment of managerial and executive leadership. *Consulting Psychology Journal: Practice and Research, 46,* 16–23.

Schank, R., & Abelson, R. (1977). *Scripts, plans, goals, and understanding.* Hillsdale, NJ: Lawrence Erlbaum Associates.

Schechtman, Z., & Kenny, D. A. (1994). Metaperception accuracy: An Israeli study. *Basic and Applied Social Psychology, 15,* 451–465.

Schroder, H. M., Driver, S., & Streufert, S. (1967). *The measurement of four systems of personality structure varying in level of abstractness: Sentence completion method* (ONR Tech. Rep. No. 11). Princeton, NJ: Princeton University.

Sheppard, B. H. (1984). Third party conflict intervention: A procedural framework. In B. M. Staw & L. L. Cummings (eds.), *Research in organizational behavior* (Vol. 6, pp. 141–190). Greenwich, CT: JAI Press.

Snyder, M. (1974). The self-monitoring of expressive behavior. *Journal of Personality and Social Psychology, 30,* 526–537.

Snyder, M. (1979). Self-monitoring processes. In L. Berkowitz (eds.), *Advances in experimental social psychology, 12,* (pp. 86–128). New York: Academic Press.

Sternberg, R. J. (1985). Implicit theories of intelligence, creativity, and wisdom. *Journal of Personality and Social Psychology, 49,* 606–627.

Stogdill, R. M. (1948). Personal factors associated with leadership: A survey of the literature. *Journal of Psychology, 25,* 35–71.

Strang, R. (1930). Measures of social Intelligence. *American Journal of Sociology, 37,* 263–269.

Streufert, S., & Swezey, R. W. (1986). *Complexity, managers, and organizations.* Orlando, FL: Academic Press.

Thomas, K. W. (1992). Conflict and negotiation processes in organizations. In M. D. Dunnette & L. M. Hough (eds.), *Handbook of industrial and organizational psychology* (Vol. 3). Palo Alto, CA: Consulting Psychologists Press.

Thomas, K. W., & Schmidt, W. H. (1976). A survey of managerial interests with respect to conflict. *Academy of Management Journal, 19,* 315–318.

Thorndike, E. L. (1920). Intelligence and its use. *Harper's Magazine, 140,* 227–235.

Thorndike, R. L., & Stein, S. (1937). An evaluation of the attempts to measure social intelligence. *Psychological Bulletin, 23,* 275–285.

Tornow, W. W., & Pinto, P. R. (1976). The development of a managerial job taxonomy: A system for describing, classifying, and evaluating executive positions. *Journal of Applied Psychology, 61,* 410–418.

Vernon, P. E. (1933). Some characteristics of the good judge of personality. *Journal of Social Psychology, 4,* 42–57.

Yukl, G. A. (1989). Managerial leadership: A review of theory and research. *Journal of Management, 15,* 251–289.

Yukl, G. A. (1994). *Leadership in organizations* (3rd ed.). Englewood Cliffs, NJ: Prentice Hall.

Yukl, G. A., & Van Fleet, D. D. (1992). Theory and research on leadership in organizations. In M. Dunnette & L. Hough (eds.), *Handbook of industrial and organizational psychology* (Vol. 3). Palo Alto, CA: Consulting Psychologists Press.

Zaccaro, S. J. (1996). *Models and theories of executive leadership: A conceptual/empirical review and integration.* Alexandria, VA: U.S. Army Research Institute for the Behavioral and Social Sciences.

Zaccaro, S. J. (1999). Social complexity and the competencies required for effective military leadership. In J. G. Hunt, G. E. Dodge, & L. Wong (eds.), *Out-of-the-box leadership: Transforming the twenty-first-Century Army and other top-performing organizations.* Stamford, CT: JAI Press.

Zaccaro, S. J. (2001). The nature of executive leadership: A conceptual and empirical analysis of success. Washington D.C.: American Psychological Association.

Zaccaro, S. J., Foti, R. J., & Kenny, D. A. (1991). Self-monitoring and trait-based variance in leadership: An investigation of leader flexibility across multiple group situations. *Journal of Applied Psychology, 76*(2), 308–315.

Zaccaro, S. J., Gilbert, J. A., Thor, K. K., & Mumford, M. D. (1991). Leadership and social intelligence: Linking social perceptiveness to behavioral flexibility. *Leadership Quarterly, 2,* 317–347.

Zaccaro, S. J., Marks, M., O'Connor-Boes, J., & Costanza, D. (1995). *The nature and assessment of leader mental models* (Tech. Rep. 95–3). Bethesda, MD: Management Research Institute.

Zaccaro, S. J., Mumford, M. D., Marks, M. A., Connelly, M. S., Threlfall, K. V., Gilbert, J. A., & Fleishman, E. A. (1996). *Cognitive and temperament determinants of Army leadership.* Alexandria, VA: U.S. Army Research Institute for the Behavioral and Social Sciences.

Zaccaro, S. J., White, L., Kilcullen, R., Parker, C. W., Williams, D., & O'Connor-Boes, J. (1997). *Cognitive and temperament predictors of Army civilian leadership.* Alexandria, VA: U.S. Army Research Institute for the Behavioral and Social Sciences.

Zaccaro, S. J., Zazanis, M. M., Diana, M., & Gilbert, J. A. (1994). *Investigation of a background data measure of social intelligence* (Tech. Rep. No. 1024). Alexandria, VA: U.S. Army Research Institute for the Behavioral and Social Sciences.

4

Emotional Intelligence and Emotional Leadership

David R. Caruso
Work-Life Strategies

John D. Mayer
University of New Hampshire

Peter Salovey
Yale University

INTRODUCING MODELS OF EMOTIONAL INTELLIGENCE

Phil Watkins[1] was the president of a division of a large paper brokerage firm. A paper broker buys paper from a paper mill, and then sells it to a manufacturer or printer. It's a risky business, with paper-thin margins, as it were, but it can also be a profitable one. The paper business is also one of the last vestiges of old-fashioned salesmanship, the kind where expense accounts sometimes include customer entertainment at "gentlemen's clubs," complete with a huge bar tab. Watkins had been in the business for almost 20 years and was thinking about getting out. He felt that he didn't fit in. "I'm not a sales guy, I'm not a financial guy, I just fell into this business when I was a kid," he once said.

Watkins did not seem to fit the mold. For one thing, he believed that his company could do good business by being tough but ethical in their dealings with customers and suppliers. In terms of personal interactions, Watkins sometimes was blindsided by others and their behavior. As a result, he was often taken advantage of by coworkers. He bent over backwards to rescue employees, one of whom was siphoning business to his personal account, and another who

[1]Names and details of the cases have been altered to protect the identity of clients.

complained that he needed his bonus just to make his house payments, but who at the same time, wasn't even making his minimum sales commission. The CEO was just as bad, and Watkins had to manage his own business as well as take care of the CEO and clean up after him. The business in general was profitable, so Watkins was not in danger of losing his job.

Is Watkins an effective leader? By most objective financial yardsticks, the answer is certainly "yes." By some subjective ratings of effectiveness, the answer would be mixed. Colleagues and employees enjoyed working with him, but Watkins had several serious, unresolved management issues. In addition, Watkins was not happy in his role. He had the potential to be an effective leader, but he had not gotten there and perhaps never would. In this chapter we attempt to discover the reasons for Watkins' successes and difficulties by addressing the role of emotional intelligence in leadership effectiveness.

There are two broad approaches to emotional intelligence: an ability approach (that views emotional intelligence as a set of cognitive abilities) and a mixed approach (that combines abilities and a broad range of personality traits). We examine each of these models, and apply the models to our analysis of Watkins. (For further discussion of competing models of emotional intelligence, see Mayer, Salovey, & Caruso, 2000.)

Ability Model of Emotional Intelligence

Is Watkins emotionally intelligent if we examine his leadership skills using an ability model? According to Mayer and Salovey's (1997) four-branch model of emotional intelligence, emotional intelligence is the ability to perceive emotions, to access and generate emotions to assist thought, to understand emotions and emotional knowledge, and to regulate emotions reflectively to promote emotional and intellectual growth. This revised model was based upon the first sustained academic development of the concept (Mayer, DiPaolo, & Salovey, 1990; Salovey & Mayer, 1990). Table 4.1 presents an analysis of Watkins on the four branches from Mayer and Salovey's ability model (1997), and on all 25 competencies drawn from a mixed model of emotional intelligence (Goleman, 1998a).

The first branch of the ability model is *Identifying Emotions*. This branch includes a number of skills such as the ability to identify feelings, to express emotions accurately, and to differentiate between real and phony emotional expressions. Is Watkins good at Identifying Emotions?[2] Watkins is capable of accurately identifying and expressing emotion, as he often makes insightful observations about his staff. He knows how others are feeling, and he can read the emotions of his staff, customers, and suppliers with great accuracy. He does this,

[2]While emotional intelligence ability testing is the best way to determine whether a person is emotionally intelligent, we will utilize Watkins' case study to illustrate important principles about these models.

TABLE 4.1
Evaluation of Phil Watkins on Ability and Mixed Models of Emotional Intelligence

Ability Model of Emotional Intelligence

Ability	*Level*	*Analysis*
Perceiving Identify emotions in thoughts Identify emotions in other people Express emotions accurately Discriminate between accurate and inaccurate feelings	High	He attended to emotions, but especially those of his staff. Sometimes, he misreads his own emotions.
Using Prioritize thinking by directing attention Generate emotions to assist judgment Mood swings change perspective Emotional states encourage problem solving	High	Very able to generate and use emotions to think creatively and make decisions.
Understanding Label and recognize relations among emotions Interpret meanings emotions convey Understanding complex feelings Recognize emotional transitions	Average	Although he understood some of the basics of emotions, he often misunderstood people's motives.
Managing Stay open to feelings Engage/detach from an emotion Reflectively monitor emotions	High/ Average	He was a master at managing emotions. Never defensive or closed off, he could put aside the blinding passions and make informed decisions, except when angry.

Mixed Model of Emotional Intelligence

Competency	*Level*	*Analysis*
Self-Awareness		
Emotional awareness	High	He had a rich inner life, although some of his self-perceptions were innaccurate, and was confident in only a few areas.
Accurate self-assessment	Average	
Self-confidence	Low	
Self-Regulation		
Self-control	Average	He was a man of his word, and promoted innovation in the workplace. However, he was not especially adaptable, being set in some of his ways.
Trustworthiness	Very High	
Conscientiousness	High	
Adaptability	Average	
Innovation	High	

(Continued)

Table 4.1
(Continued)

Mixed Model of Emotional Intelligence

Competency	*Level*	*Analysis*
Motivation		
Achievement	Low	He worked hard when he was at the office but he was not ambitious, and in fact, was looking for an exit strategy. He did enjoy generating enthusiasm and new ideas.
Commitment	Low	
Initiative	High	
Optimism	High	
Empathy		
Understanding others	Low	He misread people while at the same time believing in his people's potential. He cared about customers' needs, was happy working in a white-male environment but was politically naïve.
Developing others	High	
Service orientation	High	
Diversity	Average	
Political awareness	Low	
Social Skills		
Influence	High	He was unaware of just how good he was. He avoided direct conflict, but managed situations effectively. Watkins wanted things to change in the organization and was motivated to build a sense of team
Communication	High	
Conflict management	Average	
Leadership	High	
Change catalyst	High	
Building bonds	High	
Collaboration/cooperation	High	
Team capabilities	High	

in part, by carefully attending to their emotions. His recognition of his own emotions was sometimes inaccurate, as he would often claim to be feeling calm toward an employee when it was obvious to everyone else that he was angry with that person. Watkins appears to be skilled in some areas of Identifying Emotions.

The second branch of the ability model is *Using Emotions*. Using Emotions includes the ability to use emotions to redirect attention to important events, to generate emotions that facilitate decision making, to use mood swings as a means to consider multiple points of view, and to use different emotions to encourage different approaches to problem solving (for instance, to use a happy mood to assist in generating creative, new ideas). We know that Watkins motivates others and is fairly innovative. He harnesses certain moods and uses them to come up with new ideas. Watkins was known to be able to generate great excitement during sales conferences, and grab the attention of his senior staff at weekly staff meetings. Watkins' ability to Use Emotions is high.

The third branch is *Understanding Emotions*. This is the ability to understand complex emotions and emotional "chains," how emotions transition from one stage to another, the ability to recognize the causes of emotions, and the ability to understand relationships among emotions. Watkins' ability to Understand Emotions is not as high as is his ability to Identify or Use Emotions. Watkins appears to be somewhat blind to the true nature of some of his employees. This, if anything, was Watkins' fatal flaw: He often misunderstood what others' feelings would lead to. He did not seem to understand that the salesman who missed his quota would get angry with Watkins for setting his quota too high in the first place. This was not a problem of accurate assessment of emotions. Rather, it was a problem of being naive and too trusting, perhaps. Watkins did not dig deep enough into his people, and he was often unable to determine how they would react. The less scrupulous employees played off of Watkins' naiveté about people and took advantage of him and the company.

The fourth branch of the ability model is *Managing Emotions*. Managing Emotions includes the ability to stay aware of one's emotions, even those that are unpleasant, the ability to determine whether an emotion is clear or typical, and the ability to solve emotion-laden problems without necessarily suppressing negative emotions. Watkins manages emotions fairly effectively: He does not react blindly but integrates his emotions into his actions. Watkins assists his people in a constructive way when they are upset about a deal gone bad. Usually, when things go wrong, Watkins doesn't "think about it tomorrow," like Scarlett O'Hara; instead, he deals with the situation immediately for maximal effectiveness. But Watkins sometimes avoids confrontations that involve anger. This style causes him to live with pent-up frustration, and key people in his organization never get the feedback they need to do their jobs well.

What does the ability approach to emotional intelligence tell us about Watkins' leadership? We see that Watkins is an effective leader because he is able to harness his emotions to build a team, motivate his staff, and integrate his emotions into his planning and decision making. Frustration and anger were also managing him, and this caused him to be less effective and much less happy in his role. Watkins' career dissatisfaction may stem from his lack of understanding the motives of his staff, and the unpleasant performance surprises this entails. Viewing Watkins in this way, we can conclude that he has a few obstacles to becoming a highly effective leader, but the seeds of excellence are also apparent in his emotional intelligence profile. The ability model is deep and focused on emotion. Although it was not intended as a theory of leadership, it has much to offer leadership theory. Its value lies in the new insights it offers into the competencies of leadership, which have not previously been examined.

Mixed Model of Emotional Intelligence

Mixed models of emotional intelligence are based upon the ability model (see, for instance, Goleman, 1995) but add other psychological attributes. Goleman's initial approach to emotional intelligence included five components: knowing one's emotions, managing emotions, motivating yourself, recognizing emotions in other people, and, handling relationships (largely derived from Salovey & Mayer, 1990). There are other mixed models of emotional intelligence as well, most notably, that of Bar-On (Bar-On, 1997). Bar-On's model includes five broad categories: intrapersonal skills, interpersonal skills, adaptability, stress management, and general mood.

Goleman's ideas on emotional intelligence (1998a) were expanded to include 25 competencies grouped into the same five basic categories (although the labels changed): Self-Awareness (emotional awareness, accurate self-assessment, self-confidence); Self-Regulation (self-control, trustworthiness, conscientiousness, adaptability, innovation); Motivation (achievement, commitment, initiative, optimism); Empathy (understanding others, developing others, service orientation, diversity, political awareness); and Social Skills (influence, communication, conflict management, leadership, change catalyst, building bonds, collaboration/cooperation, team capabilities). In a way, he has combined in the same model both emotional abilities and the product of those abilities.

According to Goleman (1998a), to be emotionally intelligent Watkins would have to have many of these 25 competencies, presumably all at a high, or high enough, level. We'll examine a few of these. Watkins has a rich, inner life and is emotionally self-aware (the matching competency is Emotional Awareness). However, his self-perceptions were sometimes inaccurate (Accurate Self-assessment), and he was confident in just a few areas of his work life (either Accurate Self-assessment or Self-confidence). Watkins was a trusting and trustworthy leader, and colleagues could always count on him (Trustworthiness). While he was president of the division, he was not particularly ambitious (Achievement). He worked hard (Conscientiousness), but lacked the motivation to go to the next level, and retirement beckoned (Commitment). Part of Watkins' effectiveness was due to his high level of optimism (Optimism), something that he was not aware of, but that his staff perceived. He misread people and their motives much of the time (Understanding Others), but he believed in his people and tried to get them to do their best (Developing Others). He wanted to serve his customers and meet their needs (Service Orientation). Politically, Watkins was very naive, and didn't seem to know how things really worked (Political Awareness). Watkins was a communicator (Influence or Communication), and was invested in change (Change Agent, or Innovation). He spent a lot of time and energy in forming friendly relationships with his staff (Building Bonds), and was reasonably good at managing many types of emotional situations (Self-control, or Understanding Others).

What does this mixed approach to emotional intelligence tell us about Watkins? We see Watkins as a complex individual, and understand some of the reasons for his effectiveness. But the bottom line is unclear, because the list is so long. This is a wonderful list of things for a leader to aspire to, but where should one even begin? This analysis would likely predict that Watkins would fail in his role as a leader, or that he would not be a star performer. We will revisit Watkins at the conclusion of this chapter, and discover whether he makes it or not.

EVALUATING MODELS OF EMOTIONAL INTELLIGENCE

Let us consider the case study and the two approaches to emotional intelligence in greater detail.

The Strengths of the Ability Model

The ability model of emotional intelligence is focused on how emotions can facilitate thinking and adaptive behavior. It has to do with how people think, decide, plan, and create. Second, the ability model of emotional intelligence is skill-based. Emotional intelligence is considered a special class of mental attributes, either cognitive capacities parallel but separate from traits (e.g., McCrae & Costa, 1996), or as a distinct class of traits referred to as ability or cognitive traits (e.g., Cattell & Warburton, 1967, p. 10; Mayer, 1995, pp. 859–864). The model does not focus on personality traits or dispositions per se, except as a product of having these underlying skills. Similarly, emotional intelligence conceived of as an ability can be measured using objective, ability-based measures. Third, the ability model has been empirically validated. The four branches of emotional intelligence have been shown to be separable, but also related to a single construct (Mayer, Caruso, & Salovey, 1999). Most importantly, the ability model of emotional intelligence has utility in that it offers new insights to our understanding and prediction of effective leadership.

The Limitations of the Ability Model

The ability model, as presented in its academic context, is not a complete theory of workplace management (and does not claim to be). It is a model of a type of intelligence, and therefore, it is intended to coexist with, supplement, and clarify existing models of leadership—not replace them. Second, although data do support the model itself, and there are examples of what it predicts, the ability model of emotional intelligence is too new to have extensive empirical data in support of its predictive validity. Third, because of the depth of the model (and because it does not include products of emotional intelligence as part of the model), it is not likely to achieve the level of prediction that popular models of emotional intelligence boast, although we believe it will make significant contributions to our understanding of leadership.

The Strengths of the Mixed Model

There are several strengths of the mixed model and several reasons for its popularity. First, the mixed model includes a multitude of traits, and it is grand in its scope. Many traits have face validity as well: Few would argue that leadership, encouraging diversity, or team capabilities, for instance, are not important skills in the workplace. Second, the list of traits in the mixed model resonates with leaders, as well as human resource (HR) professionals. The model covers most of the present-day thinking on effectiveness, including traits such as service orientation, diversity, political awareness, and being a change catalyst. It is an amalgamation of many of the standard competency models put together by HR professionals every day. Third, the model claims to have tremendous predictive validity, accounting for up to 80% of the variance in life outcomes (Goleman, 1995).

The Limitations of the Mixed Model

It appears that the traits included in mixed models are essentially captured by the five-factor model of personality (Digman, 1990) as well as much of the existing trait research on leadership (see, for instance, Hogan, Curphy, & Hogan, 1994). For instance, Yukl's (1981) 14 leadership behaviors are remarkably similar to mixed models of emotional intelligence: planning and organizing, clarifying, informing, monitoring, consulting, recognizing, networking, rewarding, mentoring, delegating, team building and conflict resolution, problem solving, supporting, and motivating.

Another difficulty is that Goleman's revised (1998a) approach appears to be unclear in its grouping of competencies. For instance, the Empathy category includes Service Orientation, Diversity, and Political Awareness. In addition, the emotional competencies include not just traits or skills, but outcomes. Building Bonds, Commitment, or Political Awareness, for instance, appear to be more the product of emotional intelligence as opposed to a skill or a trait. Similarly, it is difficult to determine how some traits differ from one another, such as Influence and Communication.

Some researchers (i.e., Davies, Stankov, & Roberts, 1998) believe that emotional intelligence defined as a mixed model does not exist as a construct separable from other aspects of personality. These authors collected data on a diverse set of instruments purporting to measure emotional intelligence. They based their approach on both an early scientific definition of emotional intelligence (Salovey & Mayer, 1990) and Goleman's (1995) approach, as well as a mixture of early self-report and ability measures. They concluded that "little remains of emotional intelligence," as the measures were either unreliable or failed to load on nonpersonality trait factors. That is, measures of emotional intelligence drawn from the mixed model were better described using standard personality measures and traits. The one exception to this conclusion was for the early ability scales that came to make up one of our current scales (emotional perception).

How Should Emotional Intelligence Be Defined?

A mixed model approach to emotional intelligence offers little that is new to leadership theorists and practitioners. As noted above, existing theories of leadership and personality models already describe the traits included in the mixed approach. An ability model of emotional intelligence offers something new: a means to understand how leaders manage their own emotions, and that of others, to get results. We next examine the relationship of emotional intelligence to leadership functions.

EMOTIONAL INTELLIGENCE AND THEORIES OF LEADERSHIP

What Leaders Do

If we wish to examine leadership–emotional intelligence relationships, then we must first understand what it is that leaders do. We generally blur the distinction between management and leadership, although there are critical differences (e.g., Hersey & Blanchard, 1988; Kotter, 1990). Management is focused on specific functions or activities: planning, motivating staff, decision making, facilitating creative thinking, and social effectiveness (Yukl, Wall, & Lepsinger, 1990). Leadership is the influencing of others in order to achieve a goal. Emotional intelligence can facilitate these functions, but the successful leader will require more than just emotional intelligence in order to carry these out. We next examine ways in which emotional intelligence can assist these leadership functions.

Why Leaders Need to Be Able to Identify Emotions

The ability to identify emotions allows leaders to be aware of their own feelings and emotions. This ability also allows the leader to accurately identify the emotions of the group and of individual followers, to express emotions accurately, and to differentiate between honest and phony emotional expressions.

Greater self-awareness does indeed influence managerial performance. High-performing managers' self-ratings were more congruent with their direct reports' ratings than were average-performing managers (Church, 1997). Manager self-awareness (MSA) was viewed in this study as leading to greater management performance, and self-monitoring was positively related to MSA.

Why Leaders Need to Be Able to Use Emotions

Using Emotions allows leaders to understand and motivate others by making emotions available, engage in multiple perspectives that can help planning, and engage in activities facilitated by emotions (e.g., detail work when feeling neutral or down, or creative brainstorming activities when feeling happy). Leaders high on Using Emotions may be able to encourage open-minded decision making, planning, and idea generation by considering multiple points of view. Leaders can generate enthusiasm for a project and energize, direct, and motivate the group, and themselves.

That leadership comprises, in part, the utilization of emotions, then emotional intelligence may indeed be an important component of effective leadership. In fact, leadership has been defined along these lines: "Leadership, which embraces the emotional side of directing organizations, pumps life and meaning into management structures, bringing them to full life" (Barach & Eckhardt, 1996, p. 4). Certain forms of effective leadership may also involve the spreading of emotions among the group, a phenomenon known as emotional contagion (Barsade & Gibson, 1998). *Emotional contagion* can enhance group cooperation and reduce group conflict (Barsade, 1999). In addition, positive affect, and teams with homogenous positive affect, have a beneficial influence on team relationships (Barsade, et al. 1999).

Similarly, effective leadership directly involves the use of emotion, often through symbolic management. In symbolic management, the manager uses symbols—stories, rituals, myths, fables—to rouse and motivate staff to guide them toward achievement of a shared vision. Symbolic management depends on an emotional or intuitive "buy-in" from the followers: "Symbolic management is effective because it draws on the qualities of the heart and of the head—and, at times, it entirely bypasses the latter for the former" (Ashforth & Humphreys, 1995, p. 111).

Why Leaders Need to Be Able to Understand Emotions

Understanding Emotions includes the ability to recognize relationships between emotions, determine the meaning that emotions convey, understand complex feelings, and recognize how emotions change from one state to another. Understanding Emotions is the ability that provides a leader with the information on what makes people tick. This is the ability that also provides the leader with an understanding of other people's points of view. When trait-based, and other, leadership models talk about the human aspect of leadership, they often refer to social skills, people skills, or human relationship skills without clearly defining them. They talk about managing people, communication, influence, and other skills, but often, these terms are not operationalized to a sufficient enough extent to measure them and study them closely.

There are, of course, exceptions, but we believe that the skills of emotional intelligence might provide some insight into these heretofore slippery skills of leadership. For example, Hersey and Blanchard (1988) list the three skills of a manager as consisting of technical, human, and conceptual. They define human skills as the "ability and judgment in working with and through people, including an understanding of motivation and an application of effective leadership" (p. 7). They cite an American Management Association study that claimed that the ability to "get along with people" was "more vital than intelligence, decisiveness, knowledge, or job skills" (p. 8).

Communication has been studied as a factor in successful leadership. Research on leader–member exchange has suggested that the relationship between a leader and his or her subordinates is predictive of important outcomes (Gerstner & Day, 1997). Emotional intelligence may enhance our understanding of such exchanges.

Why Leaders Need to Be Able to Manage Emotions

Managing Emotions allows leaders to handle the stress of two quarters of disappointing sales, or not to fear a new competitive product introduction so that the disappointment or fear either paralyzes them or causes them to make poor decisions. An emotionally intelligent response to problem solving is viewed as being emotion-focused, wherein you use the emotions created by the situation to diagnose and solve the underlying problem (Mayer & Salovey, 1993). For instance, Weiss and Cropanzano (1996) indicate that a more effective coping strategy deals directly with the emotions while a less effective coping strategy deals with the emotion itself, rather than its causes, through techniques such as denial.[3] These authors add that problem-focused coping is usually the more productive alternative, but that there are times when a denial strategy may be a better way to get a specific task accomplished, at least in the short run, a position with which we agree.

One of the goals of effective leadership is to create and enhance individual and group relationships. Relationship formation has been studied by Kahn (1993), who views work relationships as emotional attachments. These attachments bind workers to each other, with these attachments created in a caregiving-care receiving environment. Kahn discusses eight dimensions of caregiving that form anchoring relationships at work, such as empathy, support, compassion, and

[3]We do not use their terms here since they use them in a different way than we do.

consistency. Emotions, and emotional skills, play an integral role in the everyday life of leaders.

George (1995) suggests that managerial mood, specifically positive mood, increases employee work performance. It is likely that emotional intelligence, specifically the ability to regulate one's own and other's emotions, is one of the skills that allow leaders to maintain such beneficial moods. Similarly, charisma, the regulation of the emotions of team members by its leader (Friedman, Riggio, & Casella, 1988; Wasielewski, 1985), appears to require the ability to enhance pleasant emotions and de-emphasize unpleasant emotions in others. Charismatic leadership, a form of transformational leadership (Bass, 1985, 1997; Bass, Avolio, & Goodheim, 1987), may also have its roots in Managing Emotions (Ashkanasy & Tse, 1998).

Emotional Intelligence and Leadership Traits

In order to understand better how this global ability—emotional intelligence—plays a role in effective leadership, we will also examine how it relates to other traits believed to be important to leadership. Trait models of leadership examine specific personality attributes thought to underlie leadership (e.g., Bass, 1985, 1997; Fiedler, 1967; Hogan, Curphy, & Hogan, 1994; Sternberg, 1997; Stogdill, 1974). Hundreds of traits have been examined, such as intelligence, extroversion, dominance, masculinity, adjustment (Lord, et al. 1986); drive, motivation, honesty, self-confidence, cognitive ability, knowledge of the business (Kirkpatrick & Locke, 1991); self-confidence, sociability, ambition, perseverance, and height (Porter, Lawler, & Hackman, 1975).

In a comprehensive review of leadership traits (Bass, 1981), three groups of traits were listed as being contributors to leadership effectiveness: intelligence (such as judgment, knowledge, decisiveness); personality (adaptability, alertness, creativity, personal integrity, self-confidence, emotional control, independence); and abilities (cooperativeness, popularity, sociability, social participation, tact). In fact, this comprehensive trait model appears to have a great deal of overlap with Goleman's (1998a) mixed approach.

More recently, Hogan and his colleagues (Hogan, Curphy, & Hogan, 1994) reviewed the extensive literature on leadership traits and concluded that the data could best be understood using the Big Five approach to personality. According to their analysis, leaders are high in surgency (dominance and sociability), emotional stability, and conscientiousness, as well as intellectance (or Openness). Hogan recommends selecting personality predictors based on job analyses and that the personality traits should be chosen from a select group of traits. He further believes that leaders should be screened for "dark side" traits using criteria from the DSM (Axis II personality disorders such as Narcissistic or Borderline Personality Disorder) and observer ratings. Hogan notes that personality traits "often lead to correlations in the .20 to .40 range; observer's ratings lead to correlations in the .30 to .60 range" (p. 501) for leadership potential.

Emotional intelligence, from an ability perspective, offers a distinctive and unique approach to an understanding of leadership, and supplements such a list of traits. Emotional intelligence may be a new trait to consider, along with these other central traits that predict leadership excellence. Emotional intelligence may also provide a means to operationalize these traits better.

APPLYING EMOTIONAL INTELLIGENCE TO LEADERS: HOW ABILITY MODELS OF EMOTIONAL INTELLIGENCE CAN ASSIST LEADERSHIP PRACTITIONERS AND RESEARCHERS

We believe that an ability-based model of emotional intelligence provides HR professionals with the conceptual approach and the specific tools they need to enhance organization effectiveness. Although leaders and senior executives are often loathe to discuss soft skills, and reject ambiguous claims and terms regarding people skills or personality traits, they may be more likely to embrace an ability-based approach to leadership. In this section, we discuss ways in which emotional intelligence theory can help HR professionals and leadership researchers to develop, test, and utilize skill-based models of leadership.

Measurement

Ability-based models of emotional intelligence require performance measures to assess emotional intelligence. That is, if emotional intelligence is conceptualized as a set of skills or abilities, then it is imperative to measure emotional intelligence using ability-based, or performance, measures rather than self-report measures. The data indicate that emotional intelligence—conceived of as an *ability*—can be reliably measured, and has divergent and convergent validity (see, for instance, Mayer, DiPaolo, & Salovey, 1990; Mayer & Geher, 1996; Mayer, Caruso, & Salovey, 1999).

The Multifactor Emotional Intelligence Scale (MEIS) is an ability-based test (Mayer, Salovey, & Caruso, 1997).[4] Initial research with these scales suggests that they are internally consistent, have adequate content validity and construct validity. The scales have interesting relationships with important real-life criteria, such as how one was parented and lifestyle behaviors (Mayer, Caruso, & Salovey, 1999).

Ability measures of emotional intelligence directly measure emotional skills. For instance, on one subtest of the MEIS that measures Identifying Emotions, the

[4]The best way to measure the traits in a mixed model is through the standard personality inventories (e.g., NEO Personality Inventory, Costa & McCrae, 1992).

test taker views a face and then reports the amount of specific emotional content in it using a five-point scale. A subtest that measures Managing Emotions presents the test taker with an emotional problem, such as how to cheer up a sad person, and asks the test taker to rate the effectiveness of various alternatives (such as "eating a big meal" or "taking a walk alone").

Using the MEIS in Team Leadership Research

Rice (1999) suggests that emotional intelligence plays a role in effective team leadership and team performance, but that it does not play a role in all aspects of such performance. These results, although preliminary, provide a useful model for leadership researchers interested in emotional intelligence.

Rice administered a short form of the MEIS to 164 people (159 of whom were women), in 26 teams, led by 11 team leaders. The teams were part of a processing facility at a large insurance company. The two department managers of these teams rated the team leaders and each team on six variables: customer service, accuracy of claims processing, productivity, commitment to continuous improvement, team leader overall performance, and team overall performance. Department managers then ranked the 11 leaders and 26 teams in terms of their overall effectiveness. An emotional intelligence score was computed for each of the 11 leaders, and an average team emotional intelligence score was also computed.[5]

Although team emotional intelligence did not significantly correlate with the department manager's rankings, there was a significant relationship between customer service and team emotional intelligence (r = .46). There was also a significant relationship between the emotional intelligence of the team and the manager-ranked effectiveness of the team leader (r = .34). Lastly, the team leader's emotional intelligence correlated .54 with the manager's ranking of the team leader's effectiveness.

This study, the first of its kind using an ability approach to emotional intelligence, indicates that emotional intelligence plays a role in team performance, but that the role is a complex one.

Competency Models

We believe that competency models of leadership and specific careers should address the role of emotional intelligence. However, emotional intelligence is not always an important component of leadership, nor is it always a key factor for many different careers.

Competency models of leadership, when addressing the role of emotional intelligence, must explicitly (a) analyze the nature of the leadership position; (b) state the model of emotional intelligence being employed; (c) list the specific emotional

[5]Team leader correlations are based upon a sample of 11 leaders, and team correlations are based on a sample of 26 teams.

skills included in the competency model; and, (d) demonstrate that the emotional skills are relevant to a critical aspect of the leadership position. It will no longer suffice to say that a leadership position requires a high level of emotional intelligence: one must also specify the competencies or skills.

Selection

Should emotional intelligence be used to select leaders? In some ways it already is, through the use of behavioral interviewing, and by judging leadership candidates as to whether they are competent to lead teams and organizations. However, we feel that ability-based measures of emotional intelligence may add to the selection process in a unique way, with a unique contribution to decision making. Assessment of emotional intelligence will need to be tied tightly to the competency model or job analysis for a specific position, which in turn, will explicitly list the specific emotional intelligence skills.

Senior executives are often loath to submit to psychological assessment, and many are uncomfortable discussing their inner emotional lives. They feel that their privacy is being invaded, and that the questions have little to do with the job itself.[6] We don't expect that senior executives will embrace emotional intelligence testing as part of pre-employment screening, but we have found that they have a greater acceptance of emotional intelligence tests than they do other measures (e.g., personality inventories). For instance, a subscale of the MEIS requires the examinee to indicate the presence or absence of a set of emotions in photos of people. Certainly, most senior executives will realize that the ability to "read" people is an important management skill, and will be more likely to accept the use of such an assessment tool.

Gender

The role of gender in leadership selection and development should include a discussion of emotional intelligence. Our data indicate that women score somewhat higher on measures of emotional intelligence than do men (Mayer, Caruso, & Salovey, 1999; Mayer & Geher, 1996). Extensive reviews of the data on leadership and gender indicate that women leaders are devalued in comparison to their male counterparts, but especially when women employ a stereotypical male leadership style, namely an autocratic as opposed to democratic, style (Eagly, Makhijani, & Klonsky, 1992). If emotional intelligence plays a role in effective leadership, and if women as a group are higher in emotional intelligence than are men, then we need to realize that women possess a critical leadership skill. Emotional intelligence, conceived of as an ability, also allows us to get away from "soft" or stereotypically feminine ways of describing leaders who are good with people and reason well

[6]Although they studied entry-level job applicants, Rosse, Miller, & Stecher (1994) found that personality tests were viewed as overly intrusive in the selection process, while personality tests in combination with ability measures had no such negative impact on applicants' perceptions.

with and about emotions. We do not need to steer clear of discussions of emotional skills in the workplace for fear that such discussions will center on "touchy-feely" skills. Emotionally intelligent female leaders can be viewed as being more intelligent than they are "emotional," and we need to consider the skills of emotional intelligence as objective, hard skills.

Training and Development

Can emotional intelligence be taught? Mixed models of emotional intelligence posit that these are emotional competencies, and as such, can be learned, although little support is offered. In fact, if we look at the literature on emotional stability while techniques to reduce anxiety and depression certainly exist, one has to wonder whether this and other traits can be learned or trained easily.[7]

We prefer to speak of teaching emotional knowledge and skills, and we believe that people can acquire emotional knowledge and emotional skills. For instance, it is relatively straightforward to teach an executive how to recognize emotional signals in others, especially nonverbal emotional signals. Executive coaching programs are designed to enhance managers' emotional and social skills. Anecdotal evidence from executive coaching programs indicates that emotional knowledge can be taught, and that doing so sometimes can have dramatic impact on a leader and an organization. These results also suggest that emotional intelligence is important in leadership effectiveness. For the most part, effective coaching programs will combine formal instruction in emotions, as well as hands-on instruction through the use of role playing and similar methods.

Keeping Things in Perspective

Emotional intelligence, like a winning smile, helps. The lack of emotional intelligence though does not always spell doom and disaster. Recently, one of the authors was involved in an executive coaching case in which a department head was asked to work on her interpersonal skills. She would frequently engage in very inappropriate behavior (she dealt with very tough personalities, and could curse fluently in four languages), to the point where turnover in her area, production and distribution, was much higher than in any other department in the company. Exit interviews uniformly blamed her leadership style as the reason the employee was quitting. Coaching included detailed career assessment (including the MEIS), which indicated that the production manager lacked even the basic skills of emotional intelligence. Her awareness of her own, and others', emotions was almost nil. She was moody and unable to generate enthusiasm or interest in her employees. She did not understand why employees would get upset with her. She seemed unable to manage her emotions, often selecting the most ineffectual of responses to handle emotional situations.

[7]Emotional stability is sometimes referred to as neuroticism, and consists of traits such as anxiety and depression. It is one of the traits previously noted to be important in leadership effectiveness.

Yet, her employer will not fire her, nor will she be demoted. The reason is simple: she gets things done, and she accomplishes a mission-critical task for her company. Although she burns through lower-level employees, she and her boss view these employees as expendable resources. If she could bolster her emotional skills, she would be a more effective leader, the company would save money, and production would run more efficiently. But she, and they, are willing to make this trade-off.

If she does not have emotional intelligence, she does possess a quality that is critical to her success: She knows the ropes. Her tacit knowledge is exceedingly high, and this knowledge is her power, providing her with the means to do her job, and achieve her goals. Indeed, Wagner and Sternberg (1985) examined the importance of practical intelligence in management effectiveness, and found that knowledge about how to manage your career and yourself in practical contexts is an important correlate of job performance.

Many other skills are required to be an effective leader. For instance, the management skills of the next generation of leaders have been hypothesized to include five components (Allred, Snow, & Miles, 1996). These components are a knowledge-based technical specialty (such as accounting or chemistry); cross-functional and international experience; collaborative leadership (leading a project team or being a team member); self-management skills (such as career planning and continuous learning); and personal traits (which include flexibility, integrity, and trustworthiness). Emotional intelligence plays a role in some of these areas, of course, but not in all areas. Therefore, we urge leadership researchers and practitioners to include other skills in their model, including intellectual ability, practical intelligence, tacit knowledge, and functional skills.[8]

CONCLUSION

We opened this chapter with the story of the reluctant leader, Phil Watkins. There is more to this story. Watkins participated in an in-depth, one-on-one, executive coaching program. As part of the program, he took the MEIS, an ability test of emotional intelligence. His results were intriguing: He scored above the 90th percentile on most of the subtests. However, he was low on a few subtests. One was Perspectives, a measure of the ability to understand emotions to reason about people. Watkins sometimes was blindsided by others and their behavior, and as a result, he sometimes was taken advantage of by coworkers. He was also lower on one subtest of Managing Emotions. Watkins' anger and frustration often greatly interfered with his decision making. His coaching focused on learning to understand other people better, and to form accurate judgments about his coworkers, even though he was their colleague, and in some cases, their friend. Watkins was also assisted in not repressing his negative emotions, but instead, utilizing them to approach his staff and provide them with negative but constructive feedback. Much of the coaching

[8]Proponents of the mixed approach also indicate that "IQ" and technical skills are still important in leadership effectiveness (Goleman, 1998b).

involved working through the mechanics of staff interactions, and getting Watkins to develop and practice new emotion-management behaviors. Watkins was able to develop his ability in these areas and to grow more comfortable with his role. Within one year, Watkins ousted the CEO, who was believed to be engaging in a host of unethical business practices. Profits were off significantly as well when Watkins took the reigns. Although he bent over backwards to rescue a few key employees, he grew to realize that they would not change, and would, in one case, continue to siphon off business. Watkins made several personnel changes, revised sales compensation, and instituted stricter financial controls. By the following year, the company posted greatly improved financial results—gross revenue was lower, but profit margins and the bottom line were vastly improved. Just as striking, in a company-wide climate survey, employees rated the company much higher than average, and were generally very satisfied with their work. A multirater assessment of Watkins resulted in well above-average ratings on 20 of the 21 individual leadership scales (only the Thrifty scale was below average, meaning that Watkins was somewhat extravagant). He was seen as caring, credible, persuasive, and enterprising. Just as important, Watkins' own feelings about his work had a dramatic turnaround: He grew to love his job. In Watkins' case, emotional intelligence did make a difference, and diagnosis and coaching tied to an ability model had significant, positive results.

We believe that emotional intelligence is an important theoretical concept that can contribute positively to the literature on leadership. We have stated a clear preference for an ability model, but mixed models are very appealing. Such models have excited the imagination of the public at large and human resource professionals in particular. These models have given new respectability to the discussion of emotions in the workplace, and in that way, they have proven to be of immense value.

Such enthusiasm is important, because leaders of today are still being chosen for their functional expertise.[9] If leaders do lack emotional intelligence, they may be unmoved by calls for greater understanding of emotions in the workplace. We suggest that HR practitioners and leadership researchers focus on the ability model because it offers a unique and valuable perspective on leadership. The ability approach will also avoid the problem of the CEO realizing that they are footing the bill—and sometimes a large bill—for selection and training that still talks about "people skills." However, the mere mention that emotions can be intelligent may grab the attention of bottom-line oriented, technically focused leaders.

Lastly, we believe that organizations, teams, and individuals all stand to benefit from choosing leaders who are high in emotional intelligence, and by developing the skills of less emotionally intelligent leaders.

---

[9]In a survey of Fortune 500 general managers (Martell & Carroll, 1994), functional skills (e.g., technical expertise) were rated as more important than management skills for marketing, R&D, and production top management. The article noted that "a manager must be highly proficient in his or her functional area to be an effective leader" (p. 86).

AUTHOR NOTES

We would like to thank Alan Harris, President of Harris-McCully Associates, Inc., where David Caruso is Vice President of Assessment. In that role, he has been given the opportunity of working with many emotionally intelligent senior executives. We are grateful to Neal Ashkanasy, Sigal Barsade, and Cheryl Rice for providing us with their work on emotional intelligence and leadership.

REFERENCES

Allred, B. B., Snow, C. C., & Miles, R. E. (1996). Characteristics of managerial careers in the 21st century. *Academy of Management Review, 10*, 17–27.

Ashkanasy, N. M., & Tse, B. (1998). Transformational leadership as management of emotion: A conceptual review. Presented at *The First Conference on Emotions and Organizational Life*. San Diego, CA.

Ashforth, B. E., & Humphreys, R. H. (1995). Emotion in the workplace: A re-appraisal. *Human Relations, 48*, 97–125.

Barach, J. A., & Eckhardt, D. R. (1996). *Leadership and the job of the executive*. Westport, CT: Quorum Books.

Bar-On, R. (1997). *Bar-On Emotional Quotient Inventory: A measure of emotional intelligence*. Toronto, ON: Multi-Health Systems, Inc.

Barsade, S. G. (1999). The ripple effect: Emotional contagion in groups. *Manuscript submitted for publication.*

Barsade, S. G., & Gibson, D. E. (1998). Group emotion: A view from top and bottom. *Research on managing groups and teams (Vol. 1)*, 81–102. Westport, CT: JAI Press.

Barsade, S. G., Ward, A. J., Turner, J. D. F., & Sonnenfeld, J. A. (1999). To your heart's content: The influence of affective diversity in top management teams. *Manuscript submitted for publication.*

Bass, B. M. (1981) *Stogdill's handbook of leadership (2nd Rev.)*. New York: Free Press.

Bass, B. M. (1985). *Leadership and performance beyond expectations*. New York: Free Press.

Bass, B. M. (1997). Does the transactional-transformational leadership paradigm transcend organizational and national boundaries? *American Psychologist, 52*, 130–139.

Bass, B. M., Avolio, B. J., & Goodheim, L. (1987). Biography and the assessment of transformational leadership at the world class level. *Journal of Management, 13*, 7–20.

Cattell, R. B., & Warburton, F. W. (1967). *Objective personality and motivation tests*. Urbana: University of Illinois Press.

Church, A. H. (1997). Managerial self-awareness in high-performing individuals in organizations. *Journal of Applied Psychology, 82*, 281–292.

Costa, P. T., & McCrae, R. R. (1992). *NEOPI-R Professional Manual.* Odessa, FU Psychological Assessment Resources.

Davies, M., Stankov, L., & Roberts, R. D. (1998). Emotional intelligence: In search of an elusive construct. *Journal of Personality and Social Psychology, 75*, 989–1015.

Digman, J. M. (1990). Personality structure: Emergence of the five-factor model. In *Annual Review of Psychology* (Vol. 41, pp. 417– 440). Palo Alto, CA: Annual Reviews.

Eagly, A. H., Makhijani, M. G., & Klonsky, B. G. (1992). Gender and the evaluation of leaders: A meta-analysis. *Psychological Bulletin, 111*, 3–22.

Fiedler, F. E. (1967). *A theory of leadership effectiveness*. New York: McGraw-Hill.

Friedman, H. S., Riggio, R. E., & Casella, D. F. (1988). Nonverbal skill, personal charisma, and initial attraction. *Personality and Social Psychology Bulletin, 14*, 203–211.

George, J. M. (1995). Leader positive mood and group performance: The case of customer service. *Journal of Applied Social Psychology, 25*, 778–794.

Gerstner, C. R., & Day, D. V. (1997). Meta-analytic review of leader-member exchange theory: Correlates and construct issues. *Journal of Applied Psychology, 82*, 827–844.

Goleman, D. (1995). *Emotional intelligence*. New York: Bantam.

Goleman, D. (1998a). *Working with emotional intelligence*. New York: Bantam.

Goleman, D. (1998b). What makes a good leader? *Harvard Business Review, November-December*, 93–102.

Hersey, P., & Blanchard, K. H. (1988). *Management of organizational behavior*. Englewood Cliffs, NJ: Prentice Hall.

Hogan, R., Curphy, G. J., & Hogan, J. (1994). What we know about leadership. *American Psychologist, 49*, 493–504.

Kahn, W. A. (1993). Caring for the caregivers: Patterns of organizational care giving. *Administrative Science Quarterly, 38*, 539–563.

Kirkpatrick, S. A., & Locke, E. A. (1991). Leadership: Traits do matter. *The Executive, 5*, 48–60.

Kotter, J. P. (1990). *A force for change: How leadership differs from management*. New York: Free Press.

Lord, R. G., DeVader, C. L., & Alliger, G. M. (1986). A meta-analysis of the relation between personality traits and leadership perceptions: An application of validity generalization procedures. *Journal of Applied Psychology, 71*, 402–410.

Martell, K., & Carroll, S. (1994). Stress the functional skills when hiring top managers. *HR Magazine*, July, 85–87.

Mayer, J. D. (1995). A framework for the classification of personality components. *Journal of Personality, 63*, 819–879.

Mayer, J. D., Caruso, D. R., & Salovey, P. (1999). Emotional intelligence meets traditional standards for an intelligence. *Intelligence*, 27, 267–298.

Mayer, J. D., DiPaolo, M. T., & Salovey, P. (1990). Perceiving affective content in ambiguous visual stimuli: A component of emotional intelligence. *Journal of Personality Assessment, 54*, 772–781.

Mayer, J. D., & Geher, G. (1996). Emotional intelligence and the identification of emotion. *Intelligence, 22*, 89–113.

Mayer, J. D., & Salovey, P. (1993). The intelligence of emotional intelligence. *Intelligence, 17*, 433–442.

Mayer, J. D. & Salovey, P. (1997). What is emotional intelligence? In P. Salovey & D. Sluyter (eds). *Emotional development and emotional intelligence: Implications for educators* (pp. 3–31). New York: Basic Books.

Mayer, J. D., Salovey, P., & Caruso, D. R. (1997). *The Multifactor Emotional Intelligence Scale (MEIS)*. Simsbury, CT: www.EmotionalIQ.com.

Mayer, J. D., Salovey, P., & Caruso, D. R. (2000). Models of emotional intelligence. In R. J. Sternberg (ed.). *The handbook of intelligence* (pp. 396–420). New York: Cambridge University Press.

McCrae, R. R., & Costa, P. T. (1996). Toward a new generation of personality theories: Theoretical contexts for the five-factor model. In J. S. Wiggins (ed.). *The five-factor model of personality*. New York: Guilford.

Porter, L. W., Lawler, E. E., & Hackman, J. R. (1975). *Behavior in organizations*. New York: McGraw-Hill.

Rice, C. L. (1999). *A quantitative study of emotional intelligence and its impact on team performance*. Unpublished master's thesis, Pepperdine University.

Rosse, J. G., Miller, J. L., & Stecher, M. D. (1994). A field study of job applicants' reactions to personality and cognitive ability testing. *Journal of Applied Psychology, 79*, 987–992.

Salovey, P., & Mayer, J. D. (1990). Emotional intelligence. *Imagination, Cognition, and Personality, 9*, 185–211.

Sternberg, R. J. (1997). *Successful intelligence*. New York: Plume.

Stogdill, R. M. (1974). *Handbook of leadership*. New York: Free Press.

Wagner, R. K., & Sternberg, R. J. (1985). Practical intelligence in real-world pursuits: The role of tacit knowledge. *Journal of Personality and Social Psychology, 49*, 436–458.

Wasielewski, P. L. (1985). The emotional basis of charisma. *Symbolic Interaction, 8*, 207–222.

Weiss, H. A., & Cropanzano, R. (1996). Affective events theory: A theoretical discussion of the structure, causes, and consequences of affective experiences at work. In B. M. Staw & L. L. Cummings (eds.), *Research in organizational behavior* (Vol. 18), 1–74.

Yukl, G. A. (1981). *Leadership in organizations*. Englewood Cliffs, NJ: Prentice Hall.

Yukl, G. A., Wall, S., & Lepsinger, R. (1990). Preliminary report on the validation of the management practices survey. In K. E. Clark & M. B. Clark (Eds.), *Measures of leadership* (pp. 223–238). West Orange, NJ: Leadership Library of America.

5

Leadership and Sociopolitical Intelligence

Joyce Hogan and Robert Hogan
Hogan Assessment Systems

WHAT IS LEADERSHIP?

Although leadership is probably the most extensively studied topic in the social, behavioral, and management sciences, there is still little consensus regarding the essential features of effective leadership. Part of the problem comes from a lack of attention to conceptual issues of three kinds. First, the term is rarely defined, or defined explicitly. This means that the subsequent research uses a wide variety of ad hoc criteria to define leadership, and the resulting literature is inconclusive. Thus, as of today, there is virtually no consensus regarding the characteristics of effective leadership other than to note that it somehow depends on the "situation." Second, most discussions never link leadership to a larger conception of human nature. This was not true earlier on; for example, Argyris, McGregor, and Herzberg in the 1960s criticized existing management practices on the basis of their (very similar) ideas about human motivation. They believed that the most powerful human motive is a need to grow, develop, and expand one's talents, that standard management practices infantilize employees, and that employees react in predictable ways in order to preserve their basic humanity. And third, academic research rarely links leadership to the performance of larger organizational units—thus, for most academic theories of leadership, a person can be a leader even though his or her organization fails.

A Personality-Based Definition of Leadership

Our model links leadership to personality on the one hand, and to organizational effectiveness on the other, and it can be described in the following way. Starting with personality, consider two well-established generalizations from anthropology and sociology. First, people evolved as social animals and they always live in groups. There are people who prefer to live alone, but they are special, and often schizophrenic—the defining characteristic of schizophrenia is social anhedonia, a condition in which social contact is not reinforcing. Second, every group has a status hierarchy with some people at the bottom, some in the middle, some at the top, and everyone knows who is where. These status hierarchies are ubiquitous in family, social, and work groups, and their inevitability is not adventitious.

These two generalizations allow us to make some informed speculations about human motivation. For example, there must be a reason for the fact that people always live in groups—namely, in a deep biological way, people must need attention, approval, and positive social contact; in the same way, they will try to avoid criticism, shunning, and rejection (Baumeister & Leary, 1995). In addition, there must be a reason why every human group has a status hierarchy. Again, in a deep biological way, people must need power, the control of resources, and the ability to bend others to their will; similarly, they must find the loss of status and control deeply disturbing (Kelvin & Jarrett, 1985). Why are these motives so potent? Because they are directly related to fitness. Evolutionary biology is all about fitness, and a person's fitness is defined by the number of his or her offspring who survive to maturity. Other things being equal, persons who are well liked and who control important resources will have more surviving children than people who are despised and poor.

Social life largely concerns negotiating for acceptance and status—we refer to this as trying to get along and trying to get ahead. We negotiate for acceptance and status during social interaction, and social interaction is an exchange process; after every social performance we gain or lose a little bit of respect and a little bit of power, and we are only as good as our last performance. There are conflicts built into the search for acceptance and status. Getting along with others requires that we agree with them and conform to their wishes. Getting ahead requires that we outperform others, which will be contrary to their wishes. People who are congenial tend not to be terribly successful, and people who are terribly successful must be prepared for others to dislike them—people will forgive you anything except your success.

Personality concerns both the general themes in human affairs and individual differences. Thus, some people are more successful at getting along than others, and some people are more successful at getting ahead than others, and these differences will be particularly obvious in work groups and occupational settings. In our view, the agenda for psychological assessment concerns measuring individual differences in peoples' potential for getting along and getting ahead.

We have been talking about personality without defining it. The word personality has two distinct but related definitions. On the one hand, there is personality from the actor's perspective—this is my view of me and your view of you. Over the years, there has been little progress in the study of personality from the actor's perspective, largely because it is studied using the self-reports of actors, which are inherently self-enhancing and hard to verify. Personality from the actor's perspective is, however, endlessly fascinating—everyone wants to know what they, and others, are really like—and it can be loosely summarized in terms of a person's goals, values, and aspirations, which we call "identity."

In contrast with the actor's perspective, there is personality from the observer's perspective—this is your view of me and my view of you. This aspect of personality is easy to study, it can be studied using observer ratings and evaluations, and is the same thing as a person's reputation. There are four points to be noted about reputation. First, since Allport's (1938) textbook, personality psychology has ignored reputation, and that was a mistake. People care deeply about their reputations, to the point that they will kill to maintain them. Despite the psychological importance of reputations, there are individual differences in peoples' ability to manage them, and the ability to manage one's reputation is related to the ability to get along and get ahead. Second, because the best predictor of future performance is past performance, and because reputations summarize past performance, reputations are good predictors of future performance. Third, the so-called Five-Factor Model of personality (Wiggins, 1996) is based on factor analyses of observer descriptions and therefore is a taxonomy of the elements of reputation. Thus, we have a good understanding of the structure of personality defined as reputation. The Five-Factor Model tells us that we think about and evaluate others in terms of their (1) self-confidence, (2) reliability and dependability, (3) social assertiveness, (4) warmth and charm, and (5) wit and imagination. And finally, a person's reputation is a summary of the accounting process that goes on after every interaction, i.e., reputations tell us at a glance about the amount of acceptance and status people enjoy in their community. Thus, we should take reputations very seriously.

We think about ourselves in terms of our identities, we think about others in terms of their reputations. What is the relationship between identity and reputation? They are only modestly related, in correlational terms, perhaps r = .36 (Connolly & Viswesveran, 1997). But social skill seems to be indexed by this correlation—the more social skill, the higher the correlation. That is, in the process of managing their reputations, socially skilled people pay attention to how they are being evaluated, and their self-appraisals resemble observer evaluations. Individual differences in the ability to manage one's reputation is a skill that has major consequences for life outcomes and is obviously related to concepts like social skill and social intelligence.

What does all of this have to do with leadership? The links between personality and leadership can be summarized in terms of three points. First, personality arises from and feeds back into social interaction; we have a personality vis-à-vis other people. In the same way, leadership arises out of and feeds back into group process; leadership can only be defined vis-à-vis a group of "followers." Moreover, it is probably best defined in terms of reputation, based on a person's actions and accomplishments as observed by others over time. Second, implicit leadership theory tells us that there is a specific kind of reputation that goes with successful leadership; namely good leaders are seen by others as trustworthy, competent, decisive, and having a clear plan, vision, or agenda (cf. Kouzes & Posner, 1987). Conversely, people who are seen as untrustworthy, incompetent, indecisive, or lacking vision are not seen as leaders, regardless of their official or nominal status in a group. Third, everyone wants acceptance and status, but some people are better at acquiring it than others. Leaders are, almost by definition, the well-liked, high-status people in a group. Social skill is the capacity to negotiate successfully for acceptance and status, and is therefore essential to leadership.

Leadership involves recruiting, motivating, coaching, and guiding an effective team, and social skills crucially enable this process. A team is a group of people who work toward a common goal, and who feel some commitment to the other members of the team and to the team goal. Thus, when team building is successful—when the process of leadership is successful—the self-interested search for power on the part of individual team members is substantially, if not entirely, suppressed. And the effectiveness of a team must be defined in relation to other teams engaged in the same activity. This means that a team can't be high performing (and an organization can't be effective) per se; it can only be high performing (or effective) in comparison with other competing groups (or organizations). Once again, then, the ultimate test of leadership is team performance.

Leadership and Group Performance

The preceding discussion concerns the links between leadership and personality. We turn now to the links between leadership and group performance. All the relevant data indicate that humans evolved as social animals, but people often forget that, in the ancestral environment of adaptation, human groups were in competition with one another. They competed for territory, food, shelter, and other vital resources, and the winning groups perpetrated substantial atrocities on the losing groups, pretty much as they do today. In this context, leadership must have influenced a group's ability to compete successfully. This is so because, once again, leadership involves persuading people to set aside their selfish tendencies and pursue a goal that promotes the welfare of the group as a whole. But most importantly, in this context the test of leadership is how well a group performs as compared with the other groups with which it is in competition, because, once again, poor performance can lead to extinction.

These considerations prompt three further observations. First, leadership is probably as important for the survival of groups and organizations today as it ever was—ask the suffering citizens of Serbia, Iraq, North Korea, or Angola. Second, the fundamental dynamic in human groups is the individual pursuit of power, and a (perhaps the) fundamental task of leadership is to persuade people to stop behaving selfishly and pursue the larger group agenda, at least for a while. Left to their own devices, people will follow selfish agendas, and the groups to which they belong become vulnerable to groups that are better organized. The Celts who lived in ancient Gaul (Spain and France) were as courageous and warlike as the Romans, but they lacked a comparable talent for social organization, and were easily conquered. Finally, some people are better at building a team than others; those who are better at it possess some distinctive characteristics as seen by others; and at some level most people understand what these characteristics are—in our terms, they are integrity, competence, decisiveness, and a sense of strategic direction, the characteristics identified by implicit leadership theory.

SOCIOPOLITICAL INTELLIGENCE: THE "G" FACTOR IN THE SOCIAL PROCESS

Certain characteristics typify effective leadership. From the observer's perspective, these are integrity, competence, decisiveness, and strategic vision. At the level of the individual, we think there is a "g" factor in leadership, it is generalized role-taking ability as originally described by George Herbert Mead (1934), and it is the core of social skill and the ability to build and maintain a team.

Generalized role-taking ability has two components: disposition and skill. The dispositional component concerns trying to put oneself in another person's place and trying to think about how that person sees the world—including how that person sees you. The ability component concerns the accuracy of the judgment once you have put yourself in another person's place—did you correctly evaluate the other person's perspective? In our view, there are substantial individual differences in generalized role-taking ability, they can be measured, they are associated with social skill, and therefore with leadership. For the sake of the present discussion we would like to call generalized role-taking ability "Sociopolitical Intelligence" or "SPIQ."

SPIQ enables leadership because it is the key to social skill and thus to the ability to build a team. Our earlier research (J. Hogan & Lock, 1997) indicates that social skill includes the following components: accurately reading interpersonal cues, accurately communicating intended meanings, conveying trustworthiness, building and maintaining relationships with others, and being a rewarding person to deal with. What evidence do we have that SPIQ in fact enables leadership? Hogan (1969) asked trained observers to rate two groups of people for the following characteristics:

1. Is socially perceptive of a wide range of interpersonal cues.
2. Seems to be aware of the impression he or she makes on others.
3. Is skilled in social techniques of imaginative play, pretending, and humor.
4. Has insight into own motives and behavior.
5. Evaluates the motivations of others in interpreting situations.

Hogan then identified a set of items on the California Psychological Inventory (CPI; Gough, 1987) that distinguished persons with high ratings from persons with low ratings for these five characteristics. The items were combined into a scale, and persons with high scores on this measure, called the CPI Empathy scale, are perceptive, insightful, and socially astute (cf. Hogan, 1969) i.e., they have SPIQ. Do they also have talent for leadership? Six lines of research support the notion that SPIQ is related to managerial performance, and we know of no studies that contradict the notion.

First, Conway (1999) factor-analyzed ratings for 2,000 managers on Benchmarks, a 360-degree management appraisal device developed at the Center for Creative Leadership. He found five factors as follows: (1) Social skill, defined by tact, flexibility, and the ability to put others at ease; (2) Decisiveness, defined by a willingness to take charge and to confront problems; (3) Team orientation, defined by trying to accomplish work through the efforts of others as opposed to doing it oneself; (4) Strategic thinking, defined by the ability to learn fast, think strategically, make good decisions, and solve problems; and (5) Leadership, defined as the ability to recruit, motivate, and delegate. The CPI Empathy scale was the best predictor of ratings for the Social Skill and Leadership factors, with correlations above .30. Why was it uncorrelated with the other three factors? Probably because those can be learned, based on experience.

Second, we developed a proxy for the CPI Empathy scale on the Hogan Personality Inventory (HPI; Hogan & Hogan, 1995), an inventory of normal personality based on the Five-Factor Model (Wiggins, 1996) and validated on working adults. In a sample of 25 managers from a large retail firm in the Midwest, this HPI-based measure of the CPI Empathy scale, i.e., SPIQ, had the following correlations with the following criteria, which were based on supervisors' ratings: Leadership .52; Management Skills .53; Administrative Skills .73; Technical Skills .45; and Communication Skills .66. Thus, persons with high scores for SPIQ had higher ratings for every aspect of corporate leadership in this small sample (J. Hogan & Holland, 1998).

Third, J. Hogan and Ross (1998) found that the HPI-based measure of SPIQ, in a sample of 140 managers in the energy business, correlated .65 with supervisors' ratings of the overall effectiveness. They interpret these data as showing that managers with high scores for SPIQ are rewarding to work with, concerned about the well-being of their staff, calm under pressure, and reliably in a good mood.

Fourth, Church (1997) devised an indirect measure of SPIQ by comparing managers' self-ratings of their performance with subordinates' ratings of their performance. He defined two groups of managers, taken from five organizations; the first group was regarded by their organizations as high potential, and the second group was regarded as average potential. The self-assessments of the high potential group were significantly closer to their subordinates' assessments of their performance than the self-assessments of the average potential group. The congruence between self- and subordinates' assessments is an index of SPIQ as we have defined it, and it is clearly related to effectiveness.

Fifth, in a conceptual replication of Church's findings, Shipper and Dillard studied a sample of 1,035 middle managers in "a large, nontraditional, high technology firm." Each manager described himself or herself using the Survey of Management Practices (Wilson & Wilson, 1991), and then was described by four subordinates on the same rating form. Shipper and Dillard identified four sets of managers: (1) new managers who were evaluated as being in the bottom 20% of their cohort; (2) new managers evaluated as being in the top 20% of their cohort; (3) midlevel managers evaluated as being in the bottom 20% of their cohort; (4) midlevel managers evaluated as being in the top 20% of their cohort. Consistent with Church's (1997) findings, the self-ratings of the high performing new and midlevel managers more closely agreed with subordinate ratings than the self-ratings of the low performing new and middle managers. Even more interesting is the fact that, among the low performing managers—all of whom were all about to derail—a portion of them recovered so that, four years later, they were highly regarded. The self-ratings of the recovered managers from both groups were significantly more accurate (more closely agreed with subordinates' ratings of them) than the self-ratings of the managers who derailed. SPIQ predicts both success and failure in this research.

Finally, although many academics may doubt our claim that SPIQ enables leadership, few would dispute the view that poor social skill undermines leadership, and the evidence clearly supports this view. Studies of managerial derailment (e.g., Leslie & Van Velsor, 1995; Lombardo & McCauley, 1988; Lombardo, Ruderman, & McCauley, 1987; McCall & Lombardo, 1983; Morrison, White, & Van Velsor, 1987), all conclude that when managers fail, they do so primarily because they are unable to understand other peoples' perspectives. This inability makes them "insensitive to others," unable to build a team, and consequently, unable to get their work done because they have to accomplish their work through the efforts of others. In the process of social interaction, the two key variables underlying every evaluation are trust and liking. Being insensitive causes others either not to trust or not to like the potential leader, or perhaps both at the same time. People who are not trusted or not liked will have trouble building a team.

Being unable to understand the perspectives of others is the definition of low SPIQ. SPIQ is normally distributed, and people often end up in management for political reasons rather than their demonstrated talent for leadership; consequently, many managers have low SPIQ; not surprisingly, the failure rate of major managers is quite high (the best estimate is 50%, cf. DeVries, 1992). The reason they fail, in our judgment, is because they lack SPIQ.

Personality and Leadership Style

We can illustrate how personality influences leadership style and how that style affects subordinates using three personality configurations: the dependent, the narcissistic, and the avoidant personality disorders. Hogan, Curphy, and Hogan (1992) suggest that the standard DSM–IV, Axis 2 personality disorders provide a preliminary taxonomy of factors leading to managerial derailment and our discussion elaborates that point. Our evidence for the description of these three types of leaders comes from subordinates' evaluations (cf. Hogan & Hogan, 1997) as well as our cumulative experience in management development. The following describes three midlevel managers who we know quite well. The discussion is somewhat anecdotal, but interested readers can take it as proposing hypotheses to be tested in future research.

The dependent personality shows up frequently in middle managers, and is characterized by a strong desire to be a good team player and please authority figures. From the perspective of their superiors, they are highly reliable (trustworthy) because they keep their bosses informed and always ask permission. They are appointed into middle management because their superiors know that they can be trusted to follow the party line; they are also trusted by their subordinates because they follow company policy and go by the book. On the other hand, they are disliked by their subordinates because they won't represent them, and willingly pass on any order or directive from a superior regardless of how it might affect staff morale. Here is an example taken from a university we know (and we have many such examples from all kinds of organizations). The president of the university appointed a dean who then chose a loyal faculty person to be associate dean. Soon afterwards the president was fired for sexual misconduct and the dean found another job. The president's last act before leaving was to promote the associate dean. As his first official act, the newly appointed dean raised faculty teaching loads, thinking this would endear him to the Board of Trustees. We asked him why he would do such an unpopular thing, given that he needed all the faculty support he could get. The dean, a well-educated student of political theory, replied: "Machiavelli says to commit your atrocities early!" Machiavelli provided a rationale for what this man wanted to do—curry favor with superiors, regardless of the effects of his actions on his subordinates.

Narcissism is also a common syndrome in managers (cf. Hogan, Raskin, & Fazzini, 1990). Narcissists are characterized by a grandiose sense of self-importance, an obsession with success and power, and a belief that they are unique and special people to whom others naturally owe respect. Narcissists often seem charming and self-confident and they tend to gravitate toward leadership positions because they feel entitled to the role. Unfortunately, they also need constant admiration, they are exploitative, they ignore the needs and feelings of others, and they are easily threatened by or become envious of others, including their subordinates. Narcissists expect others to comply with their requests without justifying or defending them. When things go right, they want credit for success; when thing go wrong, they blame others. Because of their insensitivity, insecurity, and preoccupation with their own success, narcissistic leaders are unable to acknowledge their subordinates' achievements, and may even take credit for them. To maintain positive relations with narcissistic leaders, subordinates must constantly feed their grandiosity; narcissists don't trust people who refuse to flatter them. Furthermore, subordinates must be constantly vigilant to please them; thus, subordinates must deal with a leader who not only demands respect and admiration, but also is a potential rival and competitor, which creates a climate of insecurity that demoralizes and threatens them. All of this explains why narcissistic leaders are unable to develop normal relationships with their constituency and therefore are unable to build a team.

A third syndrome common among derailed or incompetent managers is the avoidant personality disorder. Such people seem overtly self-confident, but cautious, detached, somewhat introverted, and tend to avoid interactions with new people in new places. They are also rule abiding, and they carefully support organizational rules, values, and procedures, making them popular with their superiors. Others describe them as steady, unassuming, cautious, and moderate. At their best, avoidant leaders seem "virtuous"; at their worst they are seen as indecisive, irrational, conforming, and somewhat authoritarian. They go about their duties in a low-key fashion, preferring to implement—but never challenge—policies set by their seniors; they are extremely reluctant to define new goals for the group or change existing systems and values. Despite their seeming self-confidence, they are deeply concerned about not making mistakes and not being criticized—they are primarily motivated by a fear of failure.

In contrast with the narcissist, the avoidant leader's sensitivity to the group's norms and strong belief in proper social behavior creates confidence that he or she will attend to the group's expectations. On the other hand, because they fear being criticized, they tend toward overcontrol and lack creativity in solving problems. They will also have trouble creating or acting on change. In contrast with the narcissist, they will maintain a civil ambience in the workplace, but they won't pressure subordinates for improved performance.

Such people are primarily oriented toward what they don't want to happen: they don't want change, they don't want to try new techniques, they don't want to make changes, they don't want to rock the boat, they don't want problems with their superiors, and they don't want their subordinates to cause them any problems. They create a climate of unassertive conformity that maintains the status quo. And they obviously will not be effective advocates for their teams when dealing with senior people; rather they will pass on unchallenged, absurd, and ridiculous requests from senior people, not understanding that loyalty must go both ways. Subordinates must be careful not to threaten them, and they are most easily threatened when they must do something unusual or not covered by existing rules and procedures. The bad news is that if subordinates want procedures to change, they will have to design the change themselves; the good news is that their leader will rarely challenge them or question their failure to follow the chain of command. They can, however, expect that their innovative effort will be met with passive resistance and no follow through.

These three personality types are deficient in SPIQ, but so are many people in senior positions in corporate America. Consider the leadership of American Airlines, which staggers from one seemingly avoidable labor dispute to another. Consider the leadership of the U.S. Postal Service where, in a workforce of 800,000, there are 150,000 labor grievances currently on file. Consider the major American railroads, where employees are considered "overhead" and labor disputes are endless. In our view, many of the problems encountered by these organizations are self-inflicted, caused by management's failure to consider how their actions are or will be perceived by their employees.

The Construct Validity of SPIQ

SPIQ turns out to predict indexes of leadership effectiveness in every case where it has been studied, so the link between SPIQ and leadership seems clear. What more specifically is SPIQ? Correlations between the CPI Empathy scale and the HPI (Hogan & Hogan, 1995) shows that SPIQ is related to Intellectance—imagination, creativity, and strategic thinking, Ambition—the desire to get ahead, and Sociability—the desire to get along. The 11 scales of the Hogan Development Survey (HDS; Hogan & Hogan, 1997) map the key DSM-IV, Axis 2 personality disorders, and these scales are associated with poor performance as a manager. Correlations between these scales and the HPI-based measure of SPIQ are as follows: Excitable (Borderline) –.47; Skeptical (Paranoid) –.76; Cautious (Avoidant) –.74; Reserved (Schizoid) –.17; Leisurely (Passive-Aggressive) –.04; Bold (Narcissism) –.49; Mischievous (Psychopathic) –.40; Colorful (Histrionic) .36; Imaginative (Schizotypal) .23; Diligent (Obsessive-Compulsive) .07; Dutiful (Dependent) .04. Six of these 11 scales, which are known to predict managerial derailment, are substantially and negatively correlated with an index of SPIQ, three are essentially uncorrelated, and histrionic and schizotypal tendencies, both related to being publicly entertaining, are positively correlated.

Parenthetically, we can ask what is the best way to measure SPIQ? There are only two choices: (a) with psychometric procedures, e.g., standardized tests and measures, or (b) with simulations, e.g., assessment center exercises. Our view is that certain deeply flawed individuals—e.g., paranoids, narcissists, and psychopaths—typically perform well in simulations, and their lack of SPIQ will go undetected. However, they will be reliably identified using psychometric methods. The problem is that simulations are one-item tests. For a simulation to be truly valid, it should be run 50 or 60 times, including times when the candidate and the evaluators are tired, bored, hung over, or ill. In this way scores on the simulation will begin to approximate the validity of scores on standardized measures. There are also substantial differences in the costs of the two methods; psychometric procedures can be used at a fraction of the cost of simulations.

The Multiple Determinants of Leader Effectiveness

We agree with Gardner (1995), Goleman (1995), and Sternberg (1985)—although we believe we said it first (cf. Hogan, 1980)—that there is more to occupational performance than IQ. We differ from these writers in two ways. First, we have a measure of that something more—SPIQ—and we actually have data to support its validity. Second, we think there is more to occupational performance than SPIQ; we think about it in terms of three measurement domains that we refer to as the bright side, the dark side, and the inside, and we believe that high level performance at anything requires the appropriate combination of all three, in conjunction with SPIQ.

The bright side concerns the characteristics that we see in other people during an interview or an assessment center activity. These are the sort of overt competencies that are assessed by measures of normal personality such as the CPI and the HPI. SPIQ is a bright side characteristic, and it clearly enables leadership. Successful performance in any occupation depends on the appropriate set of bright side characteristics.

Nonetheless, in a population with the appropriate bright side competencies, a substantial number of people (e.g., 60% of executives) will fail, because leadership also depends on the absence of disabling dark side tendencies. These dark side tendencies often coexist with an attractive bright side, which is why the managers get hired in the first place. The Hogan Development Survey (HDS; Hogan & Hogan, 1997) is an inventory of the standard DSM–IV, Axis 2 personality disorders; there are 11 of these, and they range from the borderline to the dependent personality. They are easily recognized in flawed public figures. Lyndon B. Johnson's ego, his overwhelming sense of entitlement, and his inability to learn from his mistakes suggests a narcissistic personality. Richard Nixon's sense of being an outsider, persecuted for his lack of Ivy League credentials, and his desire to retaliate (recall the enemies list?) suggests a paranoid personality. Bill Clinton's compulsive need to be on stage, admired, and well-liked, his indecisiveness, and his lack of concern for truth telling suggests histrionic tendencies. Moreover, these narcissistic, paranoid, and histrionic tendencies derailed these modern American presidents, just as they derail a substantial number of executives each year (cf. Charan & Colvin, 1999).

And finally, SPIQ predicts social skill, not worldly ambition, and leadership depends on having the appropriate motives. Motives and values are independent of personality, or at least seem to operate at a different level. Many people with attractive bright sides and benign dark sides still make poor leaders because they have the wrong values. We assess motives and values with the Motives, Values, and Preferences Inventory (MVPI, Hogan & Hogan, 1996). The MVPI covers 10 motivational syndromes (Aesthetic to Traditional) identified by the major theorists over the past 100 years. We have evaluated a large number of managers with the MVPI and we find that a combination of high Altruism and Power, and low Recognition—e.g., socialized power motives in McClelland's terms—is associated with effective performance. Conversely, managers who are primarily motivated by money or security are disliked by their subordinates and are unable to build a team.

CONCLUSION

We are now back to where we started. In our view, consequential social interaction largely concerns efforts to get along and get ahead. Individual differences in social skill or SPIQ are associated (empirically) with individual differences in the amount of acceptance and status that a person enjoys. Emergent leaders, as opposed to appointed leaders, are the well-liked, high-status people in their groups. Therefore, individual differences in SPIQ should predict individual differences in leadership potential. And they do. Conversely, persons who occupy leadership positions but lack SPIQ are at risk for derailment and this conclusion is also nicely supported in the empirical literature. Finally, leadership is not about the characteristics of individuals; it concerns getting others to pursue a common team goal and it concerns the ability to build and maintain a team that can outperform the competition.

In summary, we argued that leadership is a function of personality—leaders are people who excel at the process of getting along and getting ahead. We also argued that leadership is most appropriately evaluated in terms of team performance. And finally, we argued that SPIQ, which is the core of social skill, enables leadership because the key task of leadership is to recruit, maintain, and guide a team, processes that depend on social skill. We then provided data showing that a measure of individual differences in SPIQ is related to a variety of indexes of leadership effectiveness.

REFERENCES

Baumeister, R. F., & Leary, M. R. (1995). The need to belong: Desire for interpersonal attachments as a fundamental human motivation. *Psychological Bulletin*, 117, 497–529.

Charan, R., & Colvin, G. (1999). Why CEOs fail. *Fortune*, June 21, 69–78.

Church, A. H. (1997). Managerial self-awareness in high-performing individuals in organizations. *Journal of Applied Psychology, 82*, 281–292.

Connolly, J., & Viswesveran, V. (1997). The convergent validity between self and observer ratings of personality: A meta-analysis. Society for Industrial and Organizational Psychology. San Diego, CA.

Conway, J. M. (1999). Distinguishing contextual performance from task performance for managerial jobs. *Journal of Applied Psychology, 84(1)*, 3–13.

DeVries, D. L. (1992). Executive selection: Advances but no progress. *Issues & Observations*, 12, 1–5.

Gardner, H. (1995). *Leading minds*. New York: Basic Books.

Goleman, D. (1995). *Emotional intelligence*. New York: Bantam.

Gough, H. G. (1987). *California Psychological Inventory administrator's guide*. Palo Alto, CA: Consulting Psychologists Press.

Hogan, J. & Hogan, R. (1996). *Motives, values, preferences manual.* Tulsa, OK: Hogan Assessment Systems.

Hogan, J., & Lock, J. (1997). Interpersonal skills at work. Paper presented at the annual meeting of SIOP.

Hogan, J., & Ross, R. (1998). Validity of the Hogan Personality Inventory for identifying effective retail managers. Tulsa, OK: Hogan Assessment Systems.

Hogan, J. & Holland, B. (1998). Validity of the Hogan Personality Inventory for identifying effective petroleum resources managers. Tulsa, OK: Hogan Assessment Systems.

Hogan, R. (1969). Development of an empathy scale. *Journal of Consulting and Clinical Psychology, 33*, 307–316.

Hogan, R. (1980). The gifted adolescent. In J. Adelson (ed.), *Handbook of Adolescent Psychology*. New York: Wiley.

Hogan, R., Curphy, G., & Hogan, J. (1992).

Hogan, R., & Hogan, J. (1995). *Hogan Personality Inventory manual* (2nd ed.). Tulsa, OK: Hogan Assessment Systems.

Hogan R., & Hogan, J. (1997). *Hogan Development Survey manual*. Tulsa, OK: Hogan Assessment Systems.

Hogan, R., Raskin, R., & Fazzini, D. (1990). The dark side of charisma. In K. E. Clark & M. B. Clark (eds.), *Measures of leadership*. (pp. 171–184). West Orange, NJ: Leadership Library of America.

Kelvin, P., & Jarrett, J. (1985). *The social psychological effects of unemployment*. Cambridge: Cambridge University Press.

Kouzes, J. M., & Posner, B. Z. (1987). *The leadership challenge*. San Francisco: Jossey-Bass.

Leslie, J. B. & Van Velsor, E. (1995). *A look at derailment today*. Technical Report No. 169. Greensboro, NC: Center for Creative Leadership.

Lombardo, M. M., & McCauley, C. D. (1988). *The dynamics of management derailment*. Technical Report No. 34. Greensboro, NC: Center for Creative Leadership.

Lombardo, M. M., Ruderman, M. N., & McCauley, C. D. (1987). Explanations of success and derailment in upper-level management positions. *Journal of Business and Psychology, 2,* 199–216.

McCall, M. W., Jr., & Lombardo, M. M. (1983). *Off the track: Why and how successful executives get derailed* (Technical Report No. 21). Greensboro, NC: Center for Creative Leadership.

Mead, G. H. (1934). *Mind, self, and society*. Chicago: University of Chicago Press.

Morrison, A. M., White, R. & Van Velsor, E. (1987). *Breaking the glass ceiling: Can women make it to the top of America's largest corporations?* Reading, MA: Addison-Wesley.

Shipper, F. & Dillard, J. (1994). Academy of Management Meeting, Dallas, Texas, August 14.

Sternberg, R. J. (1985). *Beyond IQ*. New York: Cambridge University Press.

Wiggins, J. S. (1996). *The five-factor model of personality*. New York: Guilford.

Wilson, C. L., & Wilson, J. L. (1991). Teams and leaders: *A manual for the Clark Wilson Publishing Company training and development programs*. Silver Spring, MD: The Clark Wilson Group.

II

Models of Leadership and Multiple Intelligence

6

The Curious Role of Cognitive Resources in Leadership

Fred E. Fiedler
University of Washington

COGNITIVE RESOURCES AND LEADERSHIP

"*Multiple Intelligences and Leadership*" focuses on how different intellectual abilities affect leadership. However, this topic involves two distinctly different questions. First, what specific aspects of the leader's intellectual equipment are most relevant in the leadership process; and second, under what conditions do these intelligences contribute to the leadership process? This chapter deals with the latter question, specifically, what are the obstacles that prevent a leader's intellectual abilities and other cognitive resources from contributing to the effective performance of the task?

Common sense tells us that leadership requires such "cognitive resources" as intelligence, experience, and technical knowledge. This is the basis for administering admission tests and interviews by military academies and other organizations, and for requesting detailed information about the candidate's previous work history, intellectual abilities, and technical expertise. The basic assumption is that leaders will make effective use of their abilities and other attributes for which they are hired. However, we have known for many years (e.g., Stogdill,

1948; Ghiselli, 1963; Fiedler, 1970) that such "cognitive resources" as intellectual abilities, expertise, and experience by themselves do not predict leadership performance to any appreciable degree (e.g., Bass, 1990; Fiedler, 1970, Fiedler & Garcia, 1987, Ghiselli, 1963).

These findings have considerable practical as well as theoretical importance. The United States alone spends billions of dollars selecting and training leaders and managers. And in a substantial number of cases, experience and technical expertise are the main—and sometimes only—reasons why a particular manager is hired.

It would be foolish to suggest that the leader's intellectual functions do not affect leadership performance. The important question is, rather, under what specific conditions do they contribute, and under what conditions might they even be detrimental to leadership performance? In this chapter, we shall consider some of the conditions in the leadership situation that impede or block the effective utilization of the leader's intellectual resources.

The typical approach to testing how leader intelligence, experience, or technical competence predicts performance, has been to correlate the leader's scores (e.g., intelligence, experience) or other predictor data with appropriate performance measures. As mentioned before, these approaches have not been very successful. In fact, our studies show that correlations between performance and leader intelligence, experience, and technical expertise are essentially zero (Fiedler & Garcia, 1987).

One reason why measures of cognitive resources have generally failed to predict leadership performance is that the selection and training process is based on untenable implicit assumptions. First, it assumes that leaders who are bright or experienced will be able, or in a position, to use their abilities on behalf of the organization. In effect, we implicitly expect that a correlation between the leader's ability score and performance means that what's in the leader's head will translate into effective behaviors by subordinates.

Second, selection and training procedures assume that the leader effectiveness is independent of the immediate environment or the "leadership situation." This assumption is contradicted by more than three decades of research that tell us that the leader's performance depends on the leadership situation and not just the leader's abilities and attributes. Some leadership situations simply do not allow the leader to make effective use of his or her ideas, or they prevent the leader from exerting influence over the group that is to do the work.

Relevant Research

A study of U.S. Army dining halls conducted by Blades and Fiedler (1976), is a particularly good example of a situation in which the leader's behavior and group support were required to permit the leader's cognitive resources to contribute to group performance. Each dining hall crew consisted of a dining hall steward, then called the mess sergeant, and several cooks. We measured the mess

TABLE 6.1
Correlations between leader intelligence scores and performance in groups in which leaders were relatively directive or nondirective, and groups were either supportive or not supportive of their leader. (Source of data: Blades & Fiedler, 1976)

Correlations Between Intelligence and Performance		
Directive Behavior		
HIGH GROUP SUPPORT	**High**	**Low**
	.56* (13)	–.09 (13)
LOW GROUP SUPPORT	**High**	**Low**
	.21 (11)	–.05 (11)

sergeant's intelligence on a standard test, experience as time in service, and expertise gained through training in food service principles. In addition, we obtained ratings indicating the group members' acceptance of their leader. We also obtained a description of the leader's directive versus nondirective behavior. Performance was evaluated by the Post Food Service Officer and the unit's company commander.

The groups were divided into those with directive, moderately directive, and nondirective leaders, and we then correlated the leader's intelligence scores with ratings of the dining hall's performance. (For more detailed descriptions of the studies, also see Fiedler & Garcia, 1987, p. 161.)

Table 6.1 shows the contribution of leader intelligence to the performance of army dining hall crews whose mess stewards were either directive or nondirective and whose group members were supportive or not supportive. These data clearly tell us that the leader's intelligence contributed to group performance when the leader was willing and able to instruct group members what to do, and if group members are willing and able to "listen" to his instructions.

Training Simulation

A second study of simulated technical training shows similar results. Organizations differ in the degree to which they foster a democratic, participative climate; that is, in which leaders are expected to be nondirective and participative in their management. Alternatively, the climate (e.g., in the military and paramilitary services) may call for autocratic management and directive leadership.

Two related experiments (Murphy, Blyth, & Fiedler, 1992) examined the effect of these group climates and organizational cultures on the leader's use of task knowledge gained from training. The experiment used 60 three-person teams of college students. Their task was to rank the usefulness of various items of equipment (e.g., a mirror, a tarpaulin) for surviving a hypothetical plane crash in the desert during the summer. Half of the leaders received a short training lecture on survival in the desert. The team rankings were evaluated by comparing them with rankings by a team of Army desert survival experts.

The 60 teams worked with leaders who were either (a) trained and directive, (b) trained and participative, (c) not trained and directive, or (d) neither trained nor participative. As Fig. 6.1 shows, the only set of groups that benefited from the leader's training and technical knowledge were those in which the leader had been given not only relevant information but also told to be directive.

In a companion study, only the group members—but not the leader—received the brief training on how to survive an airplane crash. Again, one-half of the leaders were told to be directive, the other half were told to be participative. In this case, the team members contributed to performance only if the leader was participative. Thus, training and knowledge alone helped group performance only if the leader was participative and nondirective. This enabled group members to utilize the knowledge they had gained from training (Fig. 6.2).

The lesson from these two studies is obvious and clear: The leader who does not communicate what he or she wants the group to do is also unable to contribute the knowledge from training to the group process. Conversely, members' knowledge cannot contribute to group performance if the leader is directive and does all the talking. These studies, therefore, clearly fail to support the assumption that leaders who are selected for certain abilities or background will auto-

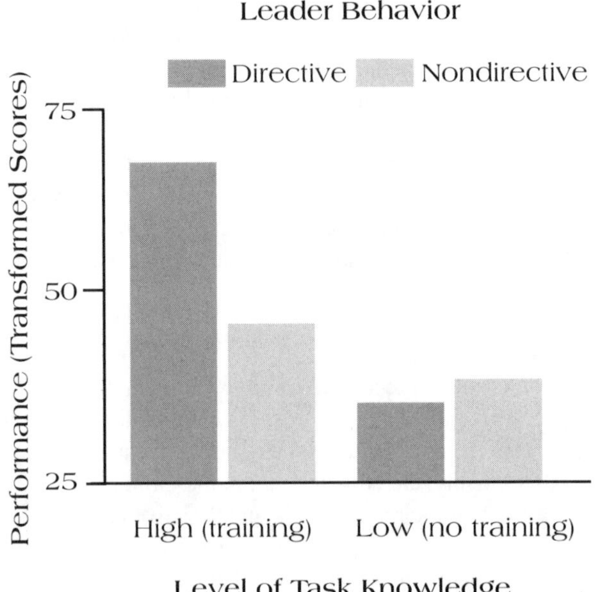

FIG. 6.1. Mean performance of leaders who had or had not been trained and who had been instructed to be directive or nondirective. *Source: Murphy, Blyth, & Fiedler (1992).*

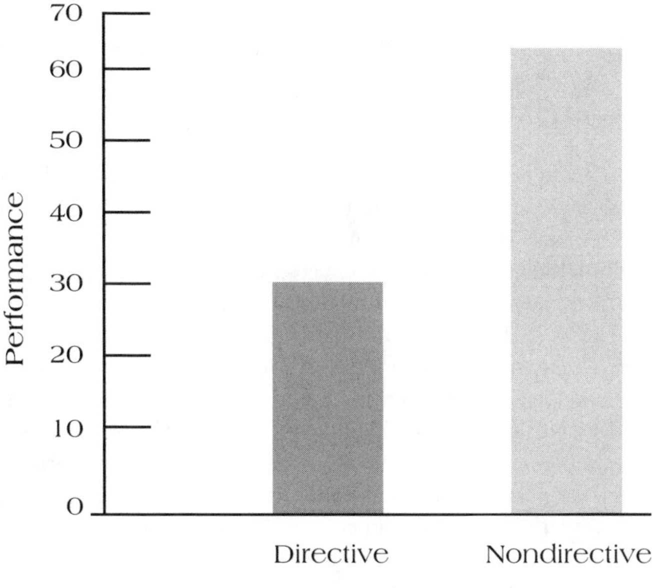

FIG. 6.2. Average performance of groups whose members had been given task-relevant training and whose leaders had been instructed to be directive or nondirective. *Source: Murphy, Blyth, & Fiedler (1992).*

matically be able to make effective use of them. The studies show that the leadership situation plays a major role in determining the extent to which the leader's abilities and knowledge contribute to the task.

Stress and the Leader's Cognitive Resources Utilization

Stress is another major block to the utilization of cognitive resources, and this is especially true of a stressful relationship with one's immediate superior or boss. Stress diverts the leader's intellectual focus from the task to the troubled interpersonal relationship.

In fact, most employees cite conflict or a stressful relationship with their bosses as their most troubling problem on the job. Even if subordinates do not think much of their boss, a poor performance evaluation affects their self-esteem and is highly ego threatening. And, of course, a poor evaluation by the immediate superior can have very serious consequences for an individual's career. The following studies illustrate the point that the stress in the leader's environment or in his or her interpersonal relations can block the leader's intellectual processes from influencing the task, and, in fact, detract from the individual's ability to function intellectually while enhancing his or her reliance on previously learned responses. The next study shows that stress has a different effect on the way in which two of the leader's intellectual attributes, namely, intelligence and experience, are affected by stress.

Infantry division leaders. A large study of an entire infantry division (Borden, 1980) illustrates this point particularly well. Data came from 314 company commanders, platoon leaders, and platoon sergeants of an infantry division. Borden obtained intelligence test scores, experience (time of army service), and ratings of stress the leaders had in their relations with their immediate superiors (see Fig. 6.3 and Fig. 6.4). Two to five of each leader's superiors evaluated leadership performance. (Incidentally, the amount of stress that the leaders had with their superior was unrelated to the superior's rating of the leader's performance.)

Figure 6.3 shows that the more intelligent leaders performed substantially better than less intelligent leaders when stress was low, but they performed substantially less well when stress was high. In other words, stress blocked or impeded the use of the leader's intelligence. In contrast, high stress enabled the more experienced leaders to perform substantially better than inexperienced leaders. In other words, stress energized experienced leaders but was detrimental to inexperienced leaders. Figure 6.4 shows that low stress impeded the effective use of experience.

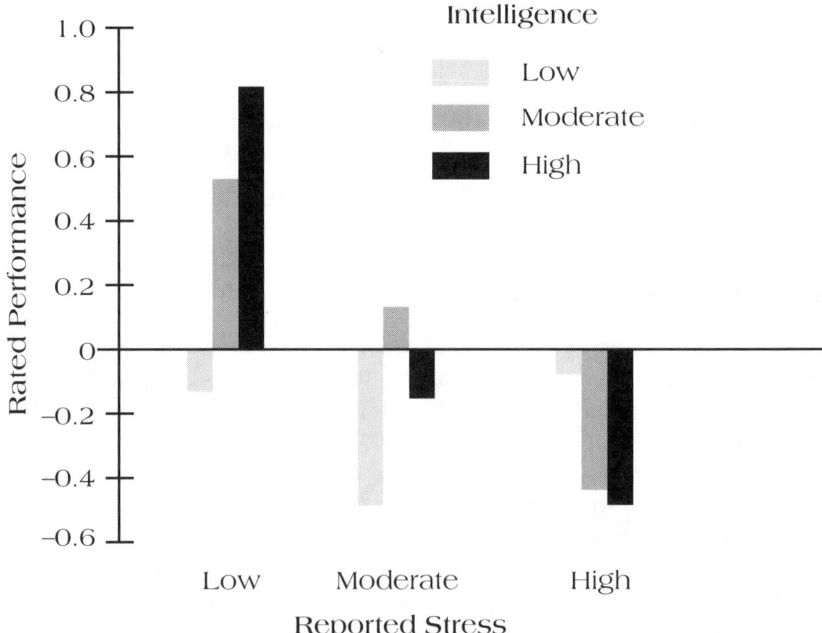

FIG. 6.3. The effect of boss stress on the contribution of intelligence to the performance of army troop leaders.

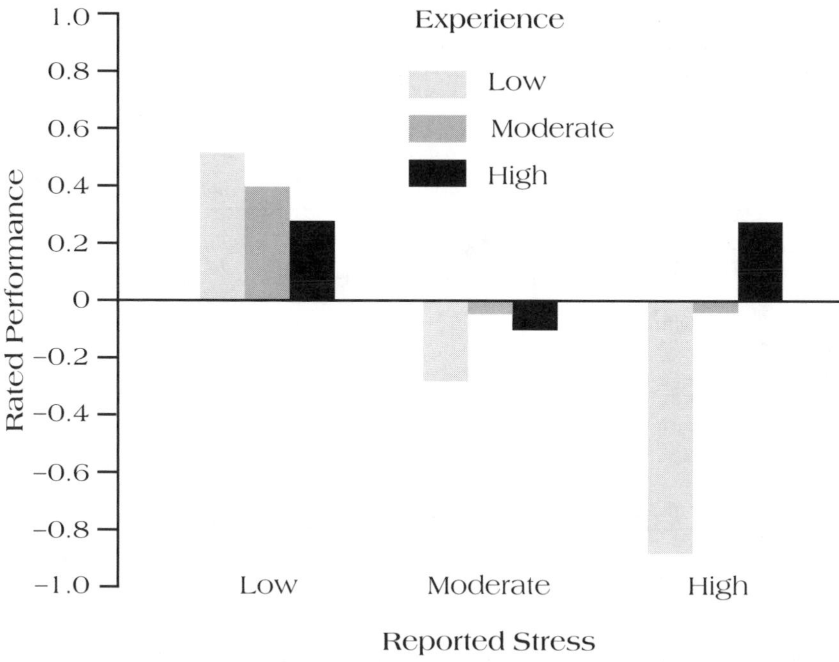

FIG. 6.4. The effect of boss stress on the contribution of experience to the performance of army troop leaders.

Very similar results have been found in a wide range of other studies. For example, in a study of high school basketball teams, where the percent of games won in league competition with comparable teams was the criterion (Fiedler, McGuire, & Richardson, 1989), we found that teams whose leaders had a stressful relationship with their coaches performed better if they were relatively experienced, but less well if they were relatively high in intelligence.

Fire department captains. The way in which the organization affects the utilization of experience is clearly apparent in such organizations as fire departments that operate under unusual levels of stress. Fire captains command the fire station, and they are in charge of training, maintenance, and administrative details. If they are the senior officers at the scene of a fire, they are in charge of all other companies as well as their own fire fighters. (Frost, 1981)

The performance of fire captains was rated on two distinct functions. One part of the job consists of administering the fire station (e.g., personnel training, and the maintenance of physical plant and equipment). The second major function is to direct fire-combat, which involves directing fire fighters at the scene of the fire and guarding the safety of firefighters and civilians. When a captain is the senior officer at the scene of the fire, his command extends to all other units combating the fire. Needless to say, fire combat is highly stressful.

TABLE 6.2
Correlations Between Intelligence and Experience with Performance of Fire Captains at the Scene of the Fire and in Administrative Assignments (Source: Frost 1981)

	Job Stress	
	Low	*High*
ADMINISTRATION	(25)	(20)
Intelligence	–.08	.03
Time in Service	–.41*	–.06
Time as Officer	–.58*	.10
	Low	*High*
FIRE COMBAT		
Intelligence	–.09	–.10
Experience	–.34	.41
Time as Officer	–.40	.68**

*$p < .05$; **$p < .01$

We divided the fire captains into those who reported low and high subjective stress with their bosses, thus permitting us to construct a four-point scale from low stress (low stress with boss and administrative functions, to high stress with boss and job stress at the scene of the fire).

As the results of this study show, the lower the job and interpersonal stress, the poorer the performance of experienced captains. The greater the stress, the better the performance of experienced fire captains (Table 6.2). Correlations between the captains' intelligence scores and their rated performance were low and nonsignificant. The effective use of experience increases with stress, regardless of whether the stress is interpersonal or job related. The common assumption that experience is, by itself, a highly valuable leader attribute, is here clearly refuted. High experience under low stress, as it was shown in the infantry and fire service studies, is detrimental to the leader's performance. The effective utilization of experience is thus in large part determined by the stressfulness of the leadership situation.

The Nature of the Task

It should not be surprising that certain intellectual abilities are more useful for dealing with intellectually demanding tasks than with routine tasks that present little or no intellectual challenge. This is shown in a study conducted by Fiedler, McGuire, and Richardson (1989). This study compared intellectually demanding and relatively undemanding tasks in a study of ROTC cadets in which we could also identify the aspect of leader intelligence most affected by stress. Thirty-four male ROTC cadets were assigned to respond to the Army In-basket exercise (Frederikson, Saunders, & Ward, 1957), a management simulation exercise that requires the individual to make decisions about various items which he or she presumably finds in his or her in-basket.

In this case, the cadets were told to assume that they were new second lieutenants who had just returned to their platoon from an assignment and were to leave again within half an hour on a second assignment away from their platoon. They had to make decisions about a variety of items (e.g., letters asking for leave, complaints about disciplinary infractions, directives to develop a training plan, etc.). Some of these decisions were rated as being substantive (e.g., making judgments, analyzing the problem) while others were instrumental (e.g., maintaining administrative control, clarity of written communication). The cadets' responses were then rated independently on the basis of the Army scoring manual for this exercise.

The cadets also took a short version of Horn's (1968) measures of crystallized and fluid intelligence, which identifies two major categories of thinking. Crystallized intelligence basically measures the individual's ability to learn from books, in school, and from the culture. This measure most closely resembles the standard intelligence test for predicting school performance. Fluid intelligence indicates the individual's ability to use concepts in novel ways in order to solve problems; it is a measure of resourcefulness and original thinking.

Half of the cadets performed this task under moderate boss stress, that is, the cadets were in uniform and a military officer monitored the exercise. The cadets were also told that they might have to justify their responses to the ROTC battalion commander. The other half of the cadets performed the task under low stress. They were in civilian clothes and they were monitored by a disinterested and sloppy looking undergraduate. A subsequent rating of stress supported the validity of the stress manipulation.

Two trained judges, following the Army In-basket's manual, categorized and scored the cadets' responses. That is, they judged whether the responses require judgment, decision making, administrative matters, personal sensitivity, etc. A different set of Army judges further rated the responses as to their appropriateness and probable effectiveness. These ratings were then correlated with the individual's crystallized and fluid intelligence.

The study found that stress had relatively little effect on crystallized intelligence. However stress led to negative correlations between fluid intelligence and such intellectually demanding functions as judgments and decision making, It also had little effect on the correlations between fluid intelligence and such routine administrative functions as communication and implementing orders.

None of the correlations between crystallized intelligence and the In-Basket dimensions were significant, or differed significantly from each other in the low and high stress conditions. This is shown in Table 6.3.

TABLE 6.3
Correlations Between Fluid Intelligence and In-Basket Dimensions Under Conditions of Low and High Perceived Stress (Source: Fiedler, McGuire, & Richardson 1991)

	Perceived Stress Condition		
In-Basket Dimension	*Low (N = 19)*	*High (N = 15)*	*Diff p*
Substantive Dimensions			
Problem Analysis	.54*	–.13	.06
Sound Judgment	.12	–.56*	.05
Planning & Organizing	.48*	–.33	.02
Decisiveness	.43	–.58*	.004
Showing Initiative	.35	–.07	NS
Instrumental Dimensions			
Delegation	.40*	–.33	.04
Administrative Control	–.20	–.37	NS
Sensitivity	.22	.28	NS
Written Communication	.23	.24	NS

*$p < .05$; NS = not significant

Interference Between Intelligence and Experience

One of the most interesting and unexpected findings in our research is the apparent conflict between intelligence and experience under high and low stress. That is, the leader's intellectual abilities correlate positively with performance under low stress but negatively under high stress. The leader's experience correlates negatively with performance under low stress but positively under high stress. In other words, under high stress, leaders use their experience but misuse their intelligence; under low stress, leaders use their intelligence but misuse their experience. It is, then, the stress in the immediate work environment or the leadership situation that determines whether an individual's intelligence and experience will contribute to leadership performance. Selecting leaders based on their experience or on their intellectual prowess alone will not ensure effective performance. And, as we saw from the Murphy, Blyth, and Fiedler (1992) study, the same holds for training.

Although we may not think of experience as an intellectual function, it is clearly related to perception, interpretation, and memory of events that happen to an individual. In fact, as was also shown in the study of infantry leaders, experience seems to substitute for typical intellectual problem solving under stress and in emergencies when analytical and problem-solving abilities fail to contribute to leadership performance.

Our research strongly suggests that stress has the effect of causing the individual's manner of behavior and thinking to regress to a less mature level (Goldenson, 1970; Carver & Scheier, 1992, pp. 236–238). Thus, in a study that required creative thinking, we found that the leaders with high fluid intelligence communicated less well than they did under low stress, and that they "babbled" more. That is, they spoke more but their statements had relatively little substantive content. Again, stress had no appreciable effect on the leader's verbal behavior (Gibson, Fiedler, & Barret, 1991).

Our findings also contradict the widely held belief that only bright people learn from experience while those who are not so bright make the same mistakes over and over. It behooves us to ask, "What really is 'experience?'" The dictionaries have long strings of definitions, but in this context, it is basically overlearned behavior based on having to deal with the same or similar problems over and over again. And how do we deal with them? Typically by automatic processing. As Herbert Simon (1992) pointed out, in the face of high uncertainty, we react on the basis of hunch and intuition derived from experience.

Consider the case of the fire captain at the scene of the disaster. He is responsible for fighting the fire, but at the same time, his major responsibility is for the safety of his fire fighters and of the individuals who may be trapped in a building. There is very little time to weigh alternatives, or to puzzle out various strategies since every minute may bring disaster. The experienced fire captain has dealt with situations of this type before and can act on hunch, intuition, and behavior previously acquired in the course of many years of service. We cannot simultaneously react by automatic processing on the basis of previously overlearned behavior and also deal with the problem in a logical, analytical way by carefully weighing alternative options and strategies.

This scenario also suggests why there might well be interference between intelligence and experience. Consider that bright people have learned to rely on their intellectual problem-solving abilities, and that they will, therefore, prefer to use them in preference to relying on their intuition and hunch. Likewise, old-timers rely on what they have learned from the past and tend to be suspicious of newfangled ideas, and impatient with "still another study" when they feel that they already know the answer. Think of the intellectual component and the experience component as two separate forces within the same person. Research shows that these two forces exert opposite pulls of action under conditions of low stress and high stress. A word of caution is in order, however. Our data are based on leaders at the low and middle levels of the organization. Whether the same effects occur at the highest levels of organizations still needs to be determined.

The inherent conflict between intelligence and experience is especially well shown in a re-analysis of a laboratory experiment conducted by Murphy (1992). The study dealt with two types of leadership experience: (a) the amount of time the individual reported as having spent in leadership positions in high school, college, as a paid manager, and as an emergent leader; and (b) "perceived leadership experience," that is, the estimated percentage of time in leadership roles as compared to others in the age group. In addition, half the leaders were given task experience by performing two similar tasks in succession to see how much they improved from the first to the second task. Leader intelligence was measured on Horn's (1968) scales of fluid and crystallized intelligence.

Sixty 3-person teams of college students performed group decision-making tasks similar to tasks developed by the U.S. National Aeronautics and Space Agency (NASA). These tasks required the groups to imagine that their plane had crashed in a desert (Lafferty & Pond, 1974). A parallel task was that they had crash-landed on a mountaintop in winter (Kast & Rosenzweig, 1976). Only 15 undamaged items remained. The group had to rank these items in order of their usefulness for survival. Performance was measured by comparing the group's ranking with the ranking by a panel of desert or mountain survival experts.

Interference of intelligence with experience is clearly seen when we divided the group of leaders into those in the high and low thirds on intelligence. We then determined the utilization of experience by correlating their previous experience as leaders with the group's performance. We also split the groups into those with leaders in the most experienced and least experienced thirds, and then correlated their intelligence scores with their performance (Table 6.4).

For highly intelligent leaders, experience did not predict performance, but for less intelligent leaders, the correlation between experience and performance was high and significant. Likewise, we correlated intelligence and performance for the most and least experienced leaders. There was no correlation between leader intelligence and performance for highly experienced leaders, but a significant correlation between intelligence and performance for moderate and low experienced leaders.

Can one be bright and experienced? The answer is, of course, "Yes." People can be experienced and bright or experienced and stupid. But the performance of a particular job requires the leader to give priority either to experience or to analytical or creative analysis in solving the particular problem.

TABLE 6.4

Correlations Between Intelligence and Performance of Leaders with Relatively High and Low Leadership Experience, and Correlations Between Experience and Performance of Leaders with Relatively High and Low Intelligence. (Source: Murphy, 1992)

Leader Intelligence	*High*	*Moderate*	*Low*
Correl. Exper and Perform	–.42 (19)	.07 (22)	.34 (19)
Leader Experience	*High*	*Moderate*	*Low*
Correl. Intell and Perform	–.06 (24)	.34 (13)	.45* (23)

$^{*}p < .05$

CONCLUSION

Probably the most important implications of our research are that we have to go well beyond the usual selection and training procedures that pick leaders on the basis of their particular attributes and abilities. Leadership performance depends on the leadership situation as well as the abilities and attributes leaders bring to their jobs. Leaders can use their cognitive resources only when the leadership situation—the leader's immediate work environment—permits this to happen.

Clearly, we cannot make leaders more intelligent, nor can we produce in the short run more experience or knowledge. Above all, we cannot hope to predict what an individual's leadership situation will look like months or years from now. Leadership situations and tasks change all the time. We can, however, attempt to train leaders and those who supervise them to modify the leadership situation so that leaders can use their cognitive resources to better advantage.

Thus, to mention a few methods, we can provide stress reduction training for knowledge workers to reduce stress with their bosses, we can assign experienced leaders to more stressful tasks and inexperienced leaders to less stressful tasks, and we can teach leaders how to face potentially stressful situations with greater equanimity. Above all, we need to devote more research effort to understanding the effect of the leadership situation in leadership performance.

REFERENCES

Bass, B. M. (1990). *Bass and Stogdill's Handbook of Leadership.* (3rd ed.). New York: Free Press.

Blades, J. W. & Fiedler, F. E. (1976). The influence of intelligence, task ability, and motivation on group performance. Tech Report 76–78, Seattle: Organizational Research Group, University of Washington.

Bond, G. E. (1995). Leadership behavior: How personality, stress, and gender affect leader behavior. Unpublished doctoral dissertation. University of Washington, Seattle.

Borden, D. F. (1980). *Leader-boss stress, personality, job satisfaction, and performance: Another look at some old constructs in the modern large bureaucracy.* Doctoral dissertation, University of Washington, Seattle.

Carver, C. S. & Scheier, M. F. (1992). *Perspectives in Personality.* Needham Heights, MA: Allyn & Bacon.

Fiedler, F. E. (1970). Leadership experience and leader performance—Another hypothesis shot to hell. *Organizational Behavior and Human Performance, 5*, 1–14.

Fiedler, F. E. (1995). Cognitive resources and leadership performance. *Applied Psychology—An International Review, 44(1)*, 5–28.

Fiedler, F. E. & Garcia, J. E. (1987). *New approaches to effective leadership: cognitive resources and organizational performance.* New York: Wiley

Fiedler, F. E., McGuire, M., & Richardson, M. E. (1989). The role of intelligence and experience in successful group performance. *Journal of Applied Sport Psychology, 1*(2), 132–149.

Frederikson, N., Saunders, D. R., & Ward, B. (1957). The in-basket test. *Psychological monographs: General and applied, 71*(9), No. 438.

Frost, D. E. (1981). *The effects of interpersonal stress on leadership effectiveness.* Unpublished doctoral dissertation. University of Washington, Seattle.

Ghiselli, E. F. (1963). Intelligence and Managerial Success. *Psychological Reports*, 23.

Gibson, F. W., Fiedler, F. E., & Barrett, K. (1993). Stress, babble, and the utilization of the leader's intellectual abilities. *Leadership Quarterly, 4(2),* 189–208.

Goldenson, R. M., (1970). *The Encyclopedia of Human Behavior: Psychology, Psychiatry, and Mental Health.* Garden City, NY: Doubleday.

Horn, J. L. (1968). Organization of abilities and the development of intelligence. *Psychological Review, 75*, 242–259.

Kast, M. & Rosenzweig, J. E. (1976). *Experiential exercises and cases in management.* NY: McGraw-Hill.

Lafferty, J. C. & Pond, A. W. (1974). The desert survival program. Plymouth, MI: Human Synergetics, Inc.

Murphy, S. E., Blyth, D., & Fiedler, F. E. (1992). Cognitive resources theory and the utilization of the leader's and group members' technical competence. *Leadership Quarterly, 3*(3), 237–355.

Murphy, S. E. (1992). *The contribution of leadership experience and self-efficacy to group performance under evaluation apprehension.* Doctoral dissertation, University of Washington, Seattle.

Potter, E. H., III & Fiedler, F. E. (1981). Utilization of staff member intelligence and experience under low and high stress. *Academy of Management Journal, 24*(2), 361–376.

Simon, H. (1992). What is an explanation of behavior? *Psychological Science, 3*, 150–161.

Stogdill, R. M. (1948). Personal factors associated with leadership: A survey of the literature. *Journal of Psychology, 25*, 35–71.

7

Cognitive, Social, and Emotional Intelligence of Transformational Leaders

Bernard M. Bass
Center for Leadership Studies
Binghamton University

TRANSFORMATIONAL LEADERSHIP

In 1985, I speculated on what personal traits would correlate with the tendency to be appraised as a transformational leader by one's subordinates (Bass, 1985). Fifteen years later, I will try to assemble some of the findings since then, both here and abroad. The driving question is to what extent cognitive, social, and emotional intelligences predispose leaders to be transformational. The preliminary answer furnished by correlational studies suggests that cognitive, social, and emotional intelligence all contribute to some degree.

All three intelligences, cognitive, social and emotional, contribute to emergent and successful leadership in general (Bass, 1990), and transformational leadership in particular (Bass, 1998). First, I will review theories and speculation about the extent to which transformational leaders are likely to be more cognitively, socially, and emotionally intelligent than the general population. Then I will present some of the empirical support from investigations of leaders from business, the community, and the military.

The Multiple Intelligences

Personality represents an integration of one's multiple intelligences. Allport (1937) listed 50 different definitions of personality. It is the sum total of all the qualities that make one person distinct from another (Super & Crites, 1962). The qualities are not independent of each other. They interact and form a pattern or gestalt whose whole may be greater than the sum total of the qualities. The qualities may include abilities, aptitudes, and physical attributes in the integrated brew. They are integrated as a consequence of their interactions. We treat them separately for purposes of discussion. Thus, physically attractive people get more time with a job placement interviewer so they have more opportunity to demonstrate their cognitive competencies. Emotionally competent persons are better able to make use of their intellectual and social competencies when danger threatens.

Among the most important intelligences are cognitive, social, and emotional intelligence. Our discussion will be limited to these three forms of multiple intelligence, although there are more such as tacit intelligence and mechanical intelligence. Additionally, there are many other attributes such as sense of humor, ethnocentricity, and health that form the total personality pattern. Again, although we treat the three intelligences separately, they overlap and influence each other. The cognitively capable manager is derailed in career by a lack of emotional intelligence. Another manager, with greater emotional intelligence but less cognitive intelligence, succeeds the derailed manager.

Cognitive intelligence includes the verbal, spatial, and numerical aptitude factors along with various aptitudes dealing with abstraction and complex problem solving, both fluid and concrete. Intellectual talents, skills, and achievements are also included.

Social intelligence embraces a variety of competencies dealing with effective interpersonal relations such as sociability, social boldness, friendliness, cooperativeness, thoughtfulness, and self-monitoring. It includes the extroversion, agreeableness, and openness dimensions of the Big Five Model of personality (Barrick & Mount, 1991).

Emotional intelligence is a new labeling by Salovey and Mayer (1990) and by Goleman (1995) of a complex of the social intelligence traits listed above and traits such as emotional maturity, moral maturity, conscientiousness, and emotional stability, as well as freedom from narcissism, neuroticism, depression, anxiety, and mood swings.

Transactional and Transformational Leadership

While *transactional* leadership emphasizes the exchange that takes place among leaders, colleagues, and followers in which the leader discusses with followers what is required and its consequences if they do or don't fulfill those requirements, *transformational* leaders achieve superior results by raising followers' consciousness about goals and values, by arousing needs higher on Maslow's hierarchy and motivating followers to go beyond their own individual interests for the good of the group, organization, or society (Burns, 1978). They employ one or more of the four components of transformational leadership.

Leadership is *charismatic* such that the followers seek to identify with the leader and emulate him or her. The leadership *inspires* the followers with challenge and persuasion, providing them with meaning and understanding. The leadership is *intellectually stimulating,* expanding the followers' use of their competencies. Finally, the leadership is *individually considerate* providing the followers with support, mentoring, coaching, and treating them with reference to their individual differences (Bass, 1985; Howell & Avolio, 1993; Bycio, Hackett, & Allen, 1995; Avolio, Bass, & Jung, 1999).

Each of these components can be measured with the Multifactor Leadership Questionnaire (MLQ) as follows:

Charismatic Leadership (or Idealized Influence). Transformational leaders are role models for their followers. The leaders are admired, respected, and trusted. Followers identify with the leaders and want to emulate them. The leaders are endowed by their followers as having extraordinary capabilities, persistence, and determination. The leaders are willing to take risks and are consistent rather than arbitrary. They can be counted on to do the right thing, demonstrating high standards of ethical and moral conduct. We should expect to find many strong correlations between Charismatic Leadership and the traits of cognitive, social, and emotional intelligence.

Inspirational Motivation. Transformational leaders motivate and inspire followers by providing meaning and challenge to their followers' work. Team spirit is aroused. Enthusiasm and optimism are displayed. The leader shares with followers a vision of an attractive future and articulates expectations on how to attain it. The multiple intelligences should contribute to being an inspirational leader.

Charismatic leadership and inspirational motivation combine into a single *Charismatic-inspirational* leadership factor (Avolio, Bass, & Jung, 1999).

Intellectual Stimulation. Transformational leaders stimulate their followers into being innovative and creative. The leader questions assumptions and reframes problems. Creativity is encouraged. Followers are galvanized into trying new approaches. Their ideas are not criticized because they differ from those of the leader or others. Both cognitive and social intelligence would appear to be particularly important to being intellectually stimulating.

Individualized Consideration. Transformational leaders pay special attention to each individual follower's needs for achievement and growth by acting as coach or mentor. Followers and colleagues are developed to successively higher levels of potential. Learning opportunities are created along with a supportive climate. Individual differences in needs and desires are recognized. Individually considerate leaders listen effectively. They delegate tasks as a means of developing followers. Social and emotional concerns for others should be prominent in predicting Individualized Consideration.

Along with the components of transformational leadership, the model of the Full Range of Leadership (FRL) includes the components of transactional leadership behavior and laissez-faire, or nonleadership, behavior. The components form a hierarchy from laissez-faire leadership at the bottom to transformational leadership at the top. Leaders are least active and effective at the bottom and most active and effective at the top. Numerous research studies have been completed in business and industry, government, the military, educational institutions, and nonprofit organizations, showing that transformational leaders, as measured by the MLQ survey instrument representative of the FRL variables (Avolio & Bass, 1997), were more effective and satisfying as leaders than were transactional leaders, although the best of leaders frequently were both transformational and transactional.

All the components of transformational leadership correlate positively with each other, which may justify a pooled transformational leadership score. Nonetheless, confirmatory factor analyses of 14 samples indicate that the best fitting model of transformational leadership contains three factors: Idealized Influence/Inspirational Motivation, Intellectual Stimulation, and Individualized Consideration (Avolio, Bass, & Jung, 1999). The separate factors provide differential utility for selection, training and policy.

Traits of cognitive, social, and emotional intelligence have been correlated with transformational leadership concurrently, retrospectively, and as forecasts of transformational leadership. In studies where participants have completed personality scales about themselves and leadership has been appraised by others, the MLQ frequently has been the instrument of choice to measure the leadership, but sometimes in a truncated form.

PERSONALITIES OF TRANSFORMATIONAL LEADERS

When it comes to predicting transformational leadership and its components from individual differences in personality traits, there is no shortage of hypotheses. Between 1900 and 1945, leadership commentaries and studies featured the listing of traits associated with leadership. Stogdill summarized 128 of these studies. He concluded that compared to nonleaders, leaders had more (intellectual) capacity and greater achievement, took more responsibility, participated more, and had higher status. But in addition to these individual strengths, the leaders' traits better matched the situational requirements.

Starting with Freud (1913/1946), psychoanalytic psychohistorians of leadership have focused attention on traits underlying cognitive, social, and emotional intelligence. Charismatics have been seen to have unresolved oedipal guilt and ambivalence, the desire for immortality, and a heightened sense of self. For Weber (1946) and the neocharismatic theorists who succeeded him, charismatics were endowed with extraordinary talents, willingness to take risks, sensitivity to the needs of their followers, articulation, and idealism (Conger & Kanungo, 1998). They were likely to be more emotionally expressive, self-confident, self-determined, eloquent, energetic, and insightful (Bass, 1990).

Chapter 10 of *Leadership and Performance Beyond Expectations* (Bass, 1985) provided a model of how personality contributed to transformational leadership. Transformational leaders were expected to be the offspring of strong mothers and absent fathers. They were expected to be ambitious, socially bold, idealistic, thoughtful, introspective, and energetic. They were expected to have strong egos and to experience little id-superego conflict. Transformational leaders may be authentic or pseudotransformational. This id-ego-superego pattern would involve less ego and more superego if the leaders were authentic transformational leaders, for they must have a strong moral sense (Burns, 1978; Bass & Steidlmeier, 1999). Without this moral sense, leaders might resemble authentic transformational leaders in their outward manifestations, but would be pseudotransformational. Authentic leaders are true to themselves and to others in how they think and behave. Pseudotransformational leaders, on the surface, may seem authentic but privately they deceive others and sometimes, themselves. While authentic transformational leaders can be trusted, pseudotransformational leaders ask to be trusted, but cannot be trusted. Authentic transformational leaders envision attainable futures for their followers; pseudotransformational leaders arouse the collective fantasies of their followers. Authentic transformational leaders develop their followers into leaders; pseudotransformational leaders develop submissive followers.

Cognitive intelligence is measured by traditional intelligence tests, competencies in technical skills, task completion, and problem solving. Indirectly, it is assessed by measures of task and problem-solving orientation, and tendencies to be iconoclastic and skeptical. It was expected to be linked to Intellectual Stimulation.

Social intelligence is the ability to relate effectively to others. Traits include friendliness, openness, supportiveness, relations orientation, empathy, sympathy, closeness and warmth, and nurturance. It was expected to contribute particularly to Individualized Consideration (Bass, 1985; Bass, 1990; Kirkpatrick & Locke, 1991).

For our purposes, *emotional intelligence*, includes several interrelated facets. There are abilities and feelings about principles that give rise to individual differences in traits such as: inner direction, moral sense, idealism, persistence, determination, vitality, hardiness, honesty, and integrity. How we relate to others gives rise to individual differences in traits such as: extroversion, ascendancy, dominance, esteem, credibility, and coping with conflict. How we deal with tasks, jobs, and assignments gives rise to individual differences in such traits as conscientiousness, originality, imagination, proactivity, risk-taking, optimism, self-efficacy, self-confidence, self-esteem, and decisiveness.

THE FINDINGS

Based on the earlier literature summarizing the linkages of personality traits to leadership (e.g., Stogdill, 1948; Bass, 1990), it was expected that traits representing all three intelligences would correlate with transformational leadership. We will now look at some of the empirical findings for managers, executives, and community leaders from a variety of sectors, and for military officers, cadets, and midshipmen.

Cognitive Intelligence and Transformational Leadership

Southwick (1998) contrasted scales from Owens' Biographical Questionnaire with MLQ ratings of 782 managers as rated by subordinates. With regard to cognitive intelligence, high school achievement correlated .13 to .16 with the Charisma and Inspirational Motivation scales. Hater and Bass (1988) found that for management committees' evaluations of midlevel executives for cognitive intelligence represented by good judgment correlated .33 with Charisma and .33 with Inspirational Motivation, and .23 with Intellectual Stimulation as assessed by the managers' subordinates. In several studies of midshipmen and cadets, intelligence tests such as the SAT failed to attain statistical significance in forecasting transformational leadership (Atwater & Yammarino, 1993; Avolio, Bass, et al. 1994). A search of a different literature dealing with decision making and strategic planning rather than personality might uncover further individual differences of consequence. A wider range of cognitive capabilities may be needed to obtain significant correlations with transformational leader behavior. For samples of executives likely to be higher in cognitive intelligence than the general population, more difficult cognitive tests are needed that discriminate between the average, the bright, and the brightest.

Social Intelligence and Transformational Leadership

As expected, traits of social intelligence tended to predict transformational leadership. Particularly strong associations were found with communication styles.

For social intelligence, Southwick found that *persuasiveness* as obtained from biodata, correlated .18 to .22 with MLQ Charisma and Inspirational Motivation, .14 with MLQ Intellectual Stimulation and MLQ Individualized Consideration. Social sensitivity correlated .14 to .18 with Charisma and Inspiration and .15 with Individualized Consideration. According to the Hater and Bass (1988) study at Federal Express, social intelligence expressed in *communications* and *persuasiveness*, correlated with subordinate-rated MLQ Charisma and Inspirational Motivation (.32 and .33) and Intellectual Stimulation (.29, .18). When Berson (1999) correlated the Klauss and Bass (1982) scales of communication style with MLQ ratings of their superiors by 968 Israeli employees and managers in a switchboard manufacturing firm, he found transformational leaders to be more careful listeners (.32 to .41), open (.55 to .64), informal (.30 to .32), careful transmitters (.45 to .48), and frank (.45 to .51).

Avolio and Bass (1994) correlated the Gordon Personal Profile (GPP) with MLQ profiles of 188 community leaders, half male and half female, based on followers' ratings. The leaders came from a variety of sectors in the community: education, government, health care, business, and social and protective services. Charisma was associated with social intelligence as seen in correlations of (.21) with GPP ascendance and .23 with GPP sociability. MLQ Inspirational Motivation correlated similarly with GPP ascendance (.23) and sociability (.25).

Emotional Intelligence and Transformational Leadership

The reader may quarrel with some of the traits we have included here in the clusters of emotional intelligence, but with a few exceptions their inclusion seemed to be self-evident. In a study of managers in a Canadian financial institution, Howell and Avolio (1993) demonstrated the linkage to transformational leadership of emotional intelligence. They found that the MLQ components and inner-directed locus of control, as measured by 13 items from Rotter's (1966) scale, were significantly related according to path coefficients of .33 with MLQ Individualized Consideration, .25 with Intellectual Stimulation and .18 with Charisma. In questionnaires and interviews with Digital Equipment executives, Gibbons (1986) obtained similar results for inner locus of control using Shostrom's (1974) Personality Orientation Inventory (POI). She correlated subordinates' MLQ ratings of 20 senior executives employed by Digital Equipment and their POI scale scores. Self-assessed inner direction of the executives correlated .37 with their subordinates' ratings of the executives' Charisma, .44 with Individualized Consideration, and .33 with Inspirational Motivation. Self-acceptance correlated .41 with Charisma, .46 with Individualized Consideration, and .43 with Inspirational Motivation. However, Avolio and Bass (1994) failed to find the same results for community leaders.

With further reference to emotional intelligence, according to Southwick (1998), for the 782 managers rated by their subordinates, MLQ Charisma and Inspirational Motivation correlated .11 to .18 respectively with being energetic (being a fast worker on the go), and between .11 and .14 with other biodata traits including strong work ethic, sense of responsibility, setting difficult self-goals, comfort in new situations, self-esteem, and self-confidence.

In the Hater and Bass investigation, emotional intelligence as evidenced in management committee appraisals of the FedEx managers' risk-taking propensities, correlated .45 with MLQ Charisma and Inspirational Motivation and .18 with Intellectual Stimulation. But with this sample, correlations of transformational leadership with the Myers-Briggs Type Indicator (MBTI) were somewhat mixed in meeting expectations. Thinking correlated –.25 with MLQ Charisma but insignificantly with MLQ Inspiration. Likewise, MBTI Feeling correlated .18 with MLQ Charisma but insignificantly with MLQ Inspiration. But MBTI Sensing correlated .20 with Inspiration and not with Charisma. Individualized Consideration correlated significantly: .19 with MBTI Feeling, .19 with MBTI Extroversion, and –.25 with Thinking.

Forty focal commissioned officers who were in charge of 40 cadet squadrons at the Air Force Academy were assessed by Ross and Offermann (1997) with truncated measures from the MLQ as rated by the cadets within the squadrons. A single MLQ transformational leadership scale correlated respectively as follows with inventoried personality traits of emotional intelligence as measured by the Gough and Heilbrun Adjective Check list (1983): self-confidence and personal adjustment, .63; pragmatism, .69; need for change, .39; nurturance, .67; feminine attributes, .54; lack of aggression, –.47, and criticalness, –.49.

Atwater and Yammarino (1993) studied the composite MLQ transformational leadership scores of 99 men and 8 women midshipmen at the U.S. Naval Academy who served as plebe summer squad leaders. They also completed the MBTI, the Epstein and Maier Constructive Thinking Inventory (CTI), and Cattell's (1950) 16PF Inventory, which provided indicators of multiple intelligence.

The MBTI Thinking/Feeling scales correlated –.29 and –.30 respectively with subordinates' and superiors' MLQ ratings of the focal squad leaders' transformational leadership. CTI Emotional Coping correlated –.25 with transformational leadership, according to subordinates' MLQ ratings. Superiors' MLQ ratings of the transformational leadership of the squad leaders correlated .22 with Behavioral Coping, –.20 with Superstitious Thinking, –.26 with negative thinking, and .22 with Naive Optimism. Subordinates' MLQ transformational ratings of their leaders correlated .20 with the 16PF intelligence scale score. Superiors' MLQ ratings correlated .22 with 16PF Conformity.

Avolio, Bass, Atwater, Lau, et al. (1994) analyzed results for 141 Virginia Military Academy cadets in their junior year, whose MLQ transformational leadership scores according to subordinates were forecast with a battery of tests and measures. Kobasa, Maddi, and Kahn (1982) scale of hardiness correlated .23, .15, and .37 with transformational leadership as did a measure of physical fitness, .21. The Defining Issues Test of Moral Reasoning (Rest, 1986) failed to correlate significantly with transformational leadership although it was expected to do so. This may be a consequence of our inability to discriminate between authentic and pseudotransformational leaders. It is only the authentic who are likely to have a strong moral sense (Bass & Steidlmeier, 1999).

In sum, the most extensive empirical evidence of correlations with transformational leadership rests with the traits of emotional intelligence, less so for social intelligence, and least with cognitive intelligence (assuming that we have properly surveyed the available relevant literature for the lattermost). There is a good deal of theory (Bass, 1960) and empirical evidence (Bass, 1990) that leaders, in general, are usually more cognitively intelligent and competent than those they lead—but not too much more so. However, this may apply to leaders whether or not they are transformational. As Cronin (1980) noted, U.S. presidents must be bright, but not too bright. Franklin Roosevelt and John F. Kennedy fit this description, but so did Calvin Coolidge and Herbert Hoover. At the time of this writing, the front-runners for the American presidency are Al Gore and George W. Bush—one is perceived as bright, the other as not so bright. Al Gore may be handicapped.

NEEDED RESEARCH

The strong impact of heredity on personality traits such as shyness has led to the expectation that leaders are both born as well as made. Tony Vernon and I almost succeeded in convincing the National Science Foundation to support a project to determine the variance due to heredity of MLQ ratings obtained from colleagues by comparing the agreement in leadership styles of identical twins with agreement in styles of fraternal twins. One problem seems to be that a minority of reviewers is convinced that heredity is important but there is no need to confirm or quantify the effects. Also, political correctness may be an issue with some of them. Nevertheless, McCarthy, Johnson, Vernon, et al. (1998), reported that as much as 50% of the variance comparing identical and fraternal twins in MLQ transformational scale self-ratings was accounted for by heritability. I expect that all three intelligences—cognitive, social, and emotional—are involved. Still needed is a confirmation of the effects of heredity based on 360-degree ratings of the focal leaders.

If heredity is as important to transformational leadership as it seems, some people will be less ready for positions of leadership than others. In the same way, some are more likely to profit from leadership education and training. Such was a finding when using 20 groups of seven women each who were first assessed for their leadership. Those of the seven who ranked 2nd and 6th were coached on improving their leadership performance. Only those ranked 2nd benefited from the coaching (Bass, McGehee, et al. 1953). More preparation time and energy will be required for some to reach the same level of performance as others. On the other hand, some people may be "natural leaders" requiring little training and experience to step into the leadership role.

Positive associations with transformational leadership are likely to be obtained with the Orientation Scales of the Campbell Leadership Index (CLI) involving checking adjectives to describe one's multiple intelligences. The adjectives include: competitive, forceful, adventuresome, risk-taking, enthusiastic, inspiring, impressive, resourceful, savvy, well-connected, insightful, forward-looking, creative, imaginative, convincing, fluent, active, and healthy. CLI scales that also might prove predictive include those assessing *consideration*, *empowering,* and *friendly* to predict Individualized Consideration. Being *credible* and *optimistic* on the CLI is likely to correlate with the transformational components of Charisma and Inspirational Motivation.

I would expect that MLQ Intellectual Stimulation would be higher with those higher in *task orientation* as measured by the Orientation Inventory (ORI) (Bass, 1967); Individualized Consideration would be higher for those higher in ORI *relations orientation*; and Charismatic-Inspirational Motivation would be higher for those higher in both *task* and *relations* orientations and for those lower in ORI *self-orientation*. However, self-orientation might be a good indicator of pseudo-transformational leadership.

Atwater and Yammarino (1993) showed that supervisors with more legitimate and reward power due to their positions were more likely to be transformational. Need for power as well as need for achievement (Winter, 1973) might generate more transformational leader behavior; need for affiliation might predict more individualized consideration.

Other uninvestigated measures of the multiple intelligences likely to predict transformational leadership include tests of integrity and honesty (Camara & Schneider, 1994), tests of the ability to play competing roles (Hart & Quinn, 1993), consistency of belief and action (Raelin, 1993), and working with paradox (Handy, 1994).

There are now a sufficient number of studies of traits related to transformational leadership to make possible one or more meta-analyses of the personality antecedents of transformational leadership. Situational variables need to be brought into play. Hardiness may be more important to VMI cadets than to comparable college students.

CONCLUSION

It is clear that the multiple intelligences, particularly social and emotional, contribute to the frequency with which individual leaders are seen as transformational. Consistent with what has been found for the emergence and success of leaders, in general, a sampling of correlational studies mainly using various forms of Multifactor Leadership Questionnaire ratings from followers to generate their leader's charismatic, inspirational, intellectually stimulating, and individually considerate scores, have yielded significant but modest correlations with measures of cognitive, social, and emotional intelligence. Results have been obtained for managers and executives, community and government leaders, and military officers, cadets, and midshipmen.

Cognitive Intelligence. Charismatic and inspirational managers were found to make better decisions and use better judgment. But traditional measures of intellectual achievement and cognitive intelligence, although usually associated with appointment to higher levels of leadership, do not seem to distinguish between transformational leaders and nontransformational leaders at the same organizational level (possibly due to restrictions in range). However, relevant achievements and requisite competencies may discriminate among them. To detect the cognitive differences among higher levels of executives who are able to transform their organizations and those who fail or do not try, will be an important endeavor and require an array of sophisticated instruments ranging from projectives to special in-basket tests. In the era of the Information Revolution, we need to test whether the proposition is still valid that leaders need to be more intelligent than those they lead, but not too much more intelligent.

Social Intelligence. The positive associations of *ascendancy* (social boldness) and *sociability* were expected to correlate with Charisma and Inspirational Motivation as well as Individualized Consideration. Individually considerate leaders were also expected to be more *extroverted* and *nurturing* (Bass, 1985). However, *sociability* appears to be much less important than *ascendancy*. In spite of that, transformational leaders are more careful listeners and transmitters, they communicate more openly, are more informal and frank. They are more persuasive, socially sensitive, and comfortable in new situations. Yet, to emerge and remain in a position of leadership, it is more important to take key initiatives than just be friendly and sociable.

Emotional Intelligence. Transformational leaders are more behavioral and less emotional in coping with stress and conflict. *Locus of control* is internal, particularly for those high in Intellectual Stimulation. *Self-confidence* and *self-acceptance* are high in charismatic leadership. Feelings are more important for the charismatic and the individually considerate. They are less aggressive and less critical. They are better adjusted and see more need for change. They have a strong sense of responsibility and set difficult goals for themselves. Their goals in life are clear.

The search for individual dispositions to behave as transformational leaders will go on. While different situations may moderate what is required, various traits of social and emotional intelligence along with more discriminating and sophisticated measures of cognitive intelligence will be of importance above and beyond situational considerations.

REFERENCES

Allport, G. W. (1937). *Personality.* New York: Holt.

Atwater, L. E., & Yammarino, F. J. (1993). Personal attributes as predictors of superiors' and subordinates' perceptions of military leadership. *Human Relations, 46,* 645–668.

Avolio, B. J., & Bass, B. M. (1994). *Evaluate the impact of transformational leadership training at individual, group, organizational, and community levels.* Final report to the W. K. Kellogg Foundation, Binghamton University, Binghamton, New York.

Avolio, B. J., & Bass, B. M. (1997). *The full range of leadership development: Manual,* Redwood City, CA: Mind Garden.

Avolio, B. J., Bass, B. M., Atwater, L. E., Lau, A. W., Dionne, S. Camembreco, J. & Whitmore, N. (1994). *Antecedent predictors of the "full range" of leadership and management styles.* (Contract MDA-903-91-0131). Binghamton, NY: Center for Leadership Studies.

Avolio, B. J., Bass, B. M., & Jung, D. I. (1999). Reexamining the components of transformational and transactional leadership using the Multifactor Leadership Questionnaire. *Journal of Occupational and Organizational Psychology.*

Avolio, B. J., & Gibbons, T. C. (1988). Developing transformational leaders: A lifespan approach. In J. A. Conger & R. N. Kanungo (eds.), *Charismatic leadership: The elusive factor in organizational effectiveness* (pp. 276–308). San Francisco, CA: Jossey-Bass.

Barrick, M. R., & Mount, M. K. (1991). The big five dimensions and job performance. *A meta-analysis. Personnel Psychology, 44,* 1–26.

Bass, B. M. (1960). *Leadership, psychology, and organizational behavior.* New York: Harper.

Bass, B. M. (1985). *Leadership and performance beyond expectations.* New York: Free Press.

Bass, B. M. (1990). *Bass and Stogdill's handbook of leadership: Theory, research, and applications* (3rd ed.). New York: Free Press.

Bass, B. M. (1967). Social behavior and the orientation inventory: A review. *Psychological Bulletin, 68,* 260–292.

Bass, B. M. (1998). *Transformational leadership: Industrial, military, and educational impact.* Mahwah, NJ: Lawrence Erlbaum Associates.

Bass, B. M., Avolio, B. J., & Atwater, L. (1996). The transformational and transactional leadership of men and women. *International Review of Applied Psychology, 45,* 5–34.

Bass, B. M., McGehee, C. R., Hawkins, W. C., Young, P. C., & Gebel, A. S. (1953). Personality variables related to leaderless group discussion behavior. *Journal of Abnormal and Social Psychology, 48,* 120–128.

Bass, B. M., & Steidlmeier, P. (1999). Ethics, character, and authentic transformational leadership behavior. *Leadership Quarterly, 10,* 181–217.

Bass, B. M., Wurster, C. R., Doll, P. A. & Clair, D. J., et al. (1953). Situational and personality factors in leadership among sorority women. *Psychological Monographs, 67,* 1–23.

Berson, Y. (1999). A comprehensive assessment of leadership using triangulation of qualitative and quantitative methods. Doctoral dissertation. State University of New York at Binghamton, Binghamton, NY.

Burns, J. M. (1978). *Leadership.* New York, NY: Harper & Row.

Bycio, P., Hackett, R. D., & Allen, J. S. (1995). Further assessment of Bass's (1985) conceptualization of transactional and transformational leadership. *Journal of Applied Psychology, 80,* 468–478.

Camara, W. J., & Schneider D. L. (1994). Integrity tests: Facts and unresolved issues. *American Psychologist, 49 (2),* 112–114.

Cattell, R. (1950). *Personality: A systematic, theoretical, and factual study.* New York: McGraw-Hill.

Conger, J. A., & Kanungo, R. A. (1988). *Charismatic leadership: The elusive factor in organization effectiveness.* San Francisco: Jossey-Bass.

Conger, J. A., & Kanungo, R. A. (1998). *Charismatic leadership in organizations.* Thousand Oaks, CA: Sage Publications.

Cronin, T. (1980). *The state of the presidency.* Boston: Little, Brown.

Dubinsky, A. J., Yammarino, F. J., & Jolson, M. A. (1995). An examination of linkage between personal characteristics and dimensions of transformational leadership. *Journal of Business and Psychology, 9,* 315–335.

Freud, S. (1913/1946). *Totem and taboo.* New York: Vintage Books.

Gibbons, T. C. (1986). *Revisiting: The question of born vs. made: Toward a theory of development of transformational leaders.* Doctoral dissertation, Fielding Institute, Santa Barbara, CA.

Goleman, D. (1995). *Emotional intelligence.* New York, Bantam.

Goleman, D. (1998). *Emotional intelligence at work.* New York: Bantam.

Gough, H. G., & Heilbrun, A. (1983). *The Adjective Checklist.* Palo Alto, CA: Consulting Psychologists Press.

Handy, C. (1994). *Age of paradox.* Cambridge, MA: Harvard Business School.

Hart, S. L., & Quinn, R. E. (1993). Roles executives play: CEOs, behavioral complexity, and firm performance, *Human Relations, 46,* 543–574.

Hater, J. J., & Bass, B. M. (1988). Superiors' evaluations and subordinates' perceptions of transformational and transactional leadership. *Journal of Applied Psychology, 73* (1), 695–702.

Howell, J. M., & Avolio, B. J. (1993). Transformational leadership, transactional leadership, locus of control, and support for innovation: Key predictors of consolidated business-unit performance. *Journal of Applied Psychology, 78,* 891–902.

Kirkpatrick, S. A., & Locke, E. A. (1991). Leadership: Do traits matter? *Academy of Management Executive,* 5(2), 48–60.

Klauss, R. & Bass, B. M. (1982). *Interpersonal communication in organizations.* New York: Academic Press.

Kobasa, S., (1979). Stressful life events, personality, and health: An inquiry into hardiness. *Journal of Personality and Social Psychology, 5,* 1–11.

Kobasa, S., Maddi, S., & Kahn, S. (1982). Hardiness and health: A prospective study. *Journal of Personality and Social Psychology, 43,* 168–177.

McCarthy, J. M., Johnson, S. A., Vernon, P. A., et al. (1988, April), Born to lead? A genetic investigation of leadership style. Symposium Paper, and *Society for International Organizational Psychology,* Dallas, TX.

Raelin, J. A. (1993). The Persean ethic: Consistency of belief and action in managerial practice. *Human Relations, 46,* 575–621.

Rest, J. (1986). *Moral development: Advances in research and theory.* New York: Praeger.

Ross, S. M., & Offermann, L. R. (1997). Transformational leaders: Measurement of personality attributes and work group performance. *Personality and Social Psychology Bulletin, 23,* 1078–1086.

Rotter, J. B. (1966). Generalized expectancies for internal versus external control of reinforcement. *Psychological Monographs (General and Applied) 80(1),* 1–28.

Salovey, P., & Mayer, J. D. (1990). Emotional intelligence. *Imagination, cognition, and personality, 9,* 185–211.

Shostrom, E. L. (1974). *POI Manual: An inventory for the measurement of self actualization.* San Diego, CA: Educational Industrial Testing.

Southwick, R. B. (1998). Antecedents of transformational, transactional, and laissez-faire leadership. Doctoral dissertation, University of Georgia, Athens, GA.

Stogdill, R. M. (1948). Personal factors associated with leadership: a survey of the literature. *Journal of Psychology, 25,* 35–71.

Super, D. E., & Crites, J. O. (1962*). Appraising vocational fitness by means of psychological tests.* New York: Harper & Brothers.

Weber, M. (1946). The sociology of charismatic authority. (Eds. & Tr.: H. H. Mills & C. W. Mills) *Essays in sociology.* New York: Oxford University Press.

Winter, D. G. (1973). *The power motive.* New York: Free Press.

8

The Motivational Dimensions of Leadership: Power, Achievement, and Affiliation[1]

David G. Winter
Department of Psychology, University of Michigan

THE MOTIVATIONAL ASPECTS OF LEADERSHIP

In this chapter I focus on the motivational aspects of leadership. Motives, both as conscious representations of desired states of affairs and as unconscious or implicit strivings, represent the "purposes" or end points—the goals toward which we use our many and varied intelligences to guide our behavior. As we have seen in the other chapters of this book, the domain of leadership involves many different kinds of "intelligence"—cognitive resources, social and sociopolitical intelligence, emotional intelligence, tacit knowledge and practical intelligence, and cultural intelligence. In the end, however, it is the leaders' motives that determine the leadership goals toward which these multiple intelligences will be mobilized and directed.

Motives, in other words, supply the "energy" and "direction," while cognitive resources and the various forms of leadership intelligence constitute the "mechanisms." Not every person with the sociopolitical skills to lead actually has the motivation to do so, and the corridors of corporate and political power are full of

[1]Comments may be addressed to the author at the following address: Department of Psychology, University of Michigan, 525 E. University Ave., Ann Arbor, MI 48109-1109; e-mail: dgwinter@umich.edu

people who *want* to lead but who lack the requisite cognitive and emotional intelligences to be a good leader.

MOTIVES AND LEADERSHIP

We begin with a question: Since leadership involves the exercise of power, isn't it obvious that all leaders are motivated by one major motive, namely the drive for power? Such a question confuses an *action* or outcome—in this case, power—with the leader's *purpose* or goal. Actually, people try to gratify many needs or motives through leadership. To be sure, some do seek power, but many highly successful leaders do not. For example, in the early years of the Roman Republic (fifth century B.C.E.), the farmer Cincinnatus was twice made dictator during an emergency; each time when the emergency was over, however, he gladly returned to his farm. Similarly, George Washington was drawn away from his beloved Virginia plantation home only by a sense of duty, to serve as the first United States president under the newly adopted Constitution. And Harry Truman found the renunciation of power at the end of his presidential years in the "White Prison" (his term) a welcome experience.[2]

Besides power, leaders may also be looking for assurance that they are loved, or trying to bolster their self-esteem through accomplishments and public acclaim. Leaders' motives, whatever they are, influence how they construe the leadership role. Motives sensitize perceptions of leadership opportunities and dangers; they affect the accessibility of different leadership styles and skills; and they determine sources of leadership satisfaction, stress, frustration, and vulnerability.

Three Motives

In this chapter, I discuss the implications for leadership of three major human motives: the drives for power, achievement, and affiliation. Empirically and theoretically, these three motives are independent, and so they can be represented by a three-dimensional space, as shown in Fig. 8.1: power as "up/down," achievement as "forward/backward," and affiliation as "near/far" (see Winter, 1996a, chap. 5; also Bales, 1970). The three motives are conceptually similar to Freud's (1940/1964, chap. 2) motivational concepts of mastery or aggression (a combination of power and achievement) and libido (affiliation). They are also conceptu-

[2]Miller (1974) records several anecdotes that reflect Truman's views about power. Once Truman told him that: "If a man can accept a situation in a place of power with the thought that it's only temporary, he comes out all right. But when he thinks he is the cause of the power, that can be his ruination" (p. 355). After the inauguration of his successor, Truman returned to his home in Independence, Missouri. The next day, a television reporter asked him what was the first thing he did when he walked into his house. Truman replied that he "carried the grips [suitcases] up to the attic" (p. 17). Neighbors in Independence said, "He hadn't changed a bit after being President . . . if you didn't know he'd been [president], he'd never tell you . . . He's not proud in *that* way" (p. 394).

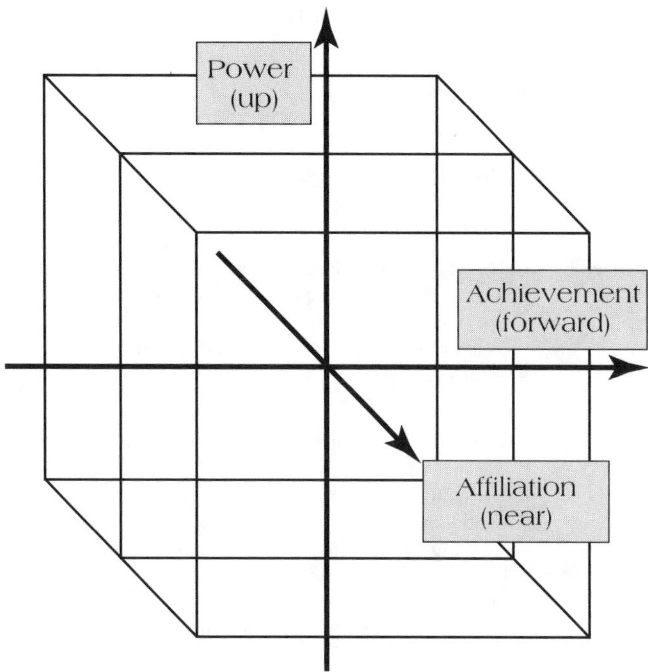

FIG. 8.1. Three-Dimensional Representation of Power, Achievement, and Affiliation Motives

ally and empirically related to Bakan's (1966) more modern dualism of agency and communion (see Helgeson, 1995; McAdams, Hoffman, Mansfield, & Day, 1996; Stewart & Malley, 1987).[3]

In the research tradition I draw upon, these motives are measured through content analysis of verbal material (Thematic Apperception Test stories, speeches, diaries, fiction, government communications; see Winter, 1991a), through experimentally derived methods developed by David McClelland and his colleagues (Smith, 1992; Winter, 1998b).[4] Brief outlines of these three scoring systems are presented in Table 8.1, and a summary of personality research findings about the behaviors and outcomes correlated with each motive is shown in Table 8.2 (see Winter, 1996a, chap. 5; also Smith, 1992).

[3]The achievement and power motives can be distinguished from each other in the words of an old proverb: "Build a better mousetrap and the world will beat a path to your door." Achievement-motivated people would want to build the better mousetrap, but wouldn't care about what the world thought. In contrast, power-motivated people would try to get the world coming to their door without building the better mousetrap.

[4]The indirect or "implicit" motive measures, employed by researchers in the McClelland tradition, do not correlate with direct questionnaire measures; further, the two methods predict different kinds of behavior (McClelland, Koestner, & Weinberger, 1989; Spangler, 1992; Weinberger & McClelland, 1990). The implicit motivational system will be the focus of this chapter.

TABLE 8.1
Scoring Systems for Achievement, Affiliation, and Power Motives

Motive	*Brief Scoring Definition*
Achievement	Concern about a standard of excellence: —Mentioning quality of performance —Success in competition —Unique, unprecedented accomplishment
Affiliation	Concern about establishing, maintaining, or restoring friendly relations among persons or groups: —Warm, positive, friendly feelings —Sadness about separation or disruption of a friendly relationship —Affiliative, companionate activities —Friendly, nurturant acts
Power	Concern about having impact, control, or influence on another person, group, or the world at large: —Strong, forceful actions that have impact on others —Controlling or regulating others —Trying to influence, persuade, convince, make a point, or argue —Unsolicited help or advice —Impressing others, prestige —Arousing strong emotions in another person

TABLE 8.2
Behavior Correlates of the Achievement, Affiliation, and Power Motives

	Achievement Motive	*Affiliation Motive*	*Power Motive*
Actions	—Moderate risks —Use information to modify performance —Entrepreneurial success —May be dishonest when necessary to reach goal	—Cooperative and friendly when "safe" —Defensive and even hostile under threat	Depending on level of responsibility, *either:* —Successful leadership —High subordinates' morale ——*or*—— —Profligate impulsivity
Negotiating style	Cooperative and "rational"	Cooperative when "safe"; defensive and hostile under threat	Exploitative Aggressive
Seeks help from	Technical experts	Friends and similar others	Political "experts"

The achievement motive is related to moderate risk-taking and using feedback to modify performance. Achievement-motivated people are rational negotiators, and seek information and help from technical experts. In contrast, affiliation-motivated people are cooperative and friendly, but only when they feel secure and safe; under threat, they can become prickly and defensive, even hostile. They seek help and advice from friends and others who appear to them as similar to themselves. Finally, power-motivated people engage in a variety of "impact" and prestige-seeking behaviors. If they are also high in responsibility, their power-seeking is prosocial and involves successful leadership; but if they are low in responsibility, their power-seeking reflects a pattern of "profligate impulsivity"—drinking, multiple drug use, exploitative sex, verbal and physical aggression, and other high risk behaviors.[5]

The research cited in this chapter comes from a variety of sources: systematic studies, at a distance, of United States presidents and other political world leaders, research on corporate leaders, and case studies of particular leaders. Leadership outcomes and characteristics were measured by a variety of methods: sociometric leadership success (i.e., voting), ratings of historians and other experts, promotion rates, and other objective criteria.

The Power Motive and Leadership

Several lines of research suggest that power motivation is associated with successful leadership, especially in political or bureaucratic settings. For example, McClelland and Burnham's (1976) study of corporate sales managers showed that managers scoring high in power motivation created higher morale and "team spirit" among their subordinates. The subordinates also rated the organizational climate as higher in clarity. In other words, power-motivated managers are able to establish clearly defined goals and tasks, and then arouse the motivation and enthusiasm of their subordinates to accomplish the tasks and reach the goals. Winter (1979) studied U.S. Navy officers in nontechnical positions, and found that power motivation was associated with higher ratings by superior officers. A longitudinal study of leaders in a large multinational corporation showed that managers with higher power motivation (assessed at entry) advanced to higher levels of management after 8 and 16 years (McClelland & Boyatzis, 1982; Winter, 1991b).

Studies of U.S. presidents, illustrated in Table 8.3, show that presidential power motivation (assessed through content analysis of the president's first inaugural address[6]) is associated with historians' ratings of "greatness" and "great decisions" (Winter, 1987; 1991a). House, Spangler, and Woycke (1991) also found presidential power motivation to be related to various measures of charismatic leadership. On the other hand, power-motivated presidents also tend to involve the United States in war (Winter, 1987; 1991a). Perhaps the connections between power motivation, war, and rated greatness suggest an evolutionary origin of the power motive in the cycle of capturing prey and avoiding being captured as prey

[5]Despite the presumptions of many psychologists and some widely cited early studies, there are no consistent sex differences in the average levels, structure of verbal content, or behavioral correlates of each of these three motives (see Stewart & Chester, 1982 in general; also Winter, 1988, in the case of the power motive).

[6]See Winter (1995) for a discussion of the many methodological issues in the scoring of political speeches for motive imagery, and Winter (1996, chap. 5) for a discussion of the reliability, validity, and other psychometric credentials of the motive measures.

TABLE 8.3
Motives and Leadership Outcomes Among U.S. Presidents: Rated Performance

	Correlation with Motive Score for:		
Variable[a]	*Power*	*Achievement*	*Affiliation*
Rated Greatness ($N = 29$)	.40*	.07	.09
Great Decisions ($N = 29$)	.51**	.09	.29
Charisma ($N = 31$)[b]	.23*	–.19*	–.09
War ($N = 31$)	.52**	–.03	.16

*$p < .05$
**$p < .01$
[a]Based on Winter (1987).
[b]Based on House, Spangler, and Woycke (1991); figures in this row are standardized regression coefficients.

(see Canetti, 1962, Ehrenreich, 1997). Alternatively, the power-war connection could be specific to the Western context of political leadership and images of power, while in Asian cultures (for example), power might assume different images and connotations (see Pye, 1985).

From all these studies, we may conclude that the power motive is related to successful leadership, especially when it is combined with some kind of internal control (measured by variables such as "activity inhibition" [McClelland & Burnham, 1976; see also McClelland, 1975] or "responsibility" [Winter, 1991b]).[7] Such variables appear to moderate expression of the power motive, channeling it in the direction of prosocial (versus antisocial) leadership. Thus activity inhibition or responsibility function in ways similar to Freud's concept of sublimation or Erikson's (1969, pp. 410–440) analysis of Gandhi's "rules" about the beneficial exercise of power, as well as modern concepts of emotional intelligence (Mayer, chap. 4, this volume), maturity, or wisdom. These findings also echo Max Weber's (1919/1948) description of the psychological prerequisites of "politics as a vocation":

> [The leader] works with the striving for power as an unavoidable means. Therefore, [a power motive] belongs indeed to his normal qualities. The sin against the lofty spirit of [politics], however, begins where this striving for power ceases to be objective and becomes purely personal self-intoxication. (p. 116)

[7]The categories of the responsibility measure include moral and legal standards, internal obligation, concern for consequences, concern for other people, and self-judgment (see Winter & Barenbaum, 1985).

The Achievement Motive and Leadership

McClelland's (1961) landmark studies of the "achieving society" show that achievement motivation predicts success in one kind of leadership: as an entrepreneur, especially in small "research and development" enterprises or other situations and climates that allow personal control and responsibility. However, achievement motivation is *not* particularly adaptive in most large, bureaucratic corporations (see Andrews, 1967), or in politics. This is one more illustration of Fiedler's argument (chap. 6, this volume) about the interaction of personality and situation in explaining leadership. As shown in Table 8.3 previously, achievement-motivated presidents are *not* conspicuously successful in terms of historians' ratings or displaying charisma. In fact, although they may start out with high ideals and lofty goals, the findings shown in Table 8.4 suggest that they often end up as "active negative" types (Barber, 1992): becalmed, frustrated, and frozen into a pattern of self-defeating rigidity (as compared with the "active-positive" style of power-motivated presidents[8]). Examples include Wilson, Lyndon B. Johnson, and Nixon.

TABLE 8.4.
Motives and Leadership Outcomes Among U.S. Presidents: Political Style

Ratings on style characteristic[a]	*Correlation with Motive Score for:* Power	Achievement	Affiliation
	Power	*Achievement*	*Affiliation*
Idealism (*N*=29)	.19	.51**	.19
Flexibility (*N*=29)	.26	–.22	.27
"Active positive" type[b] (*N*=11)	.87***	–.07	.37
"Active negative" type[b] (*N*=11)	–.32	.84***	.03

**$p < .01$
***$p < .001$
[a]Based on Maranell (1970); see also Winter (1987).
[b]See Barber (1992).

[8]Barber suggests that the Active-Negative character type involves excessive power concerns, but his analysis is based on the observation of outcomes, rather than the use of actual independent measures of motivational concerns. In my view, it is frustration that drives achievement-motivated presidents to behaviors that may seem like power, but actually reflect a possible latent authoritarian and autocratic style of achievement motivation that emerges under stress.

Achievement and Frustration in Political Leadership

Why should the achievement motive, which is so closely related to success in business, lead to such conspicuous failures in politics? What happens to unbridled achievement motivation in political life? Other findings presented in Table 8.4 suggest an explanation. Maranell's (1970) data, drawn from polls of American historians, suggests that achievement-motivated presidents are seen as idealistic but inflexible (Woodrow Wilson is a classic example). But why should they display rigidity instead of willingness to use feedback?

Let us analyze, as an example of such presidents, the case of Jimmy Carter. He scored quite high in achievement motivation. The title of his 1976 campaign autobiography, *Why Not the Best?* (Carter, 1975), is a prototypical achievement image. Yet his administration ended in a fog of frustration, "malaise,"[9] and defeat. What went wrong with Carter's presidency, and what did his achievement motivation have to do with it?

Carter's own rhetorical question can serve as a convenient point of departure for our discussion. "Why not the best?" Well, first, in politics different people have different ideas about what is "the best." This is especially true in a democracy, perhaps, but it is also true in an oligarchy. It is not enough to decide for one's self about what is best; there are always other people to persuade, cajole, and compromise. In the end, "the best" gives way to "the possible." To an achievement-motivated leader concerned to reach the "one best solution," such compromises may appear to be "selling out."

Modern politicians often describe politics as the "art of the possible," but the idea goes back a long way. Thus in 1861, as the United States Senate was trying to find some compromise that would avert an imminent civil war, Senator William H. Seward of New York expressed the necessity of reconciling aspirations and realities in politics (1861):

> In political affairs we cannot always do what seems to us absolutely best. Those with whom we must necessarily act, entertaining different views, have the power and the right of carrying them into practice. We must be content to lead when we can, and to follow when we cannot lead; and if we cannot at any time do for our country all the good that we would wish, we must be satisfied with doing for her all the good that we can. (p. 344)

Then "the best" often costs too much. As the historian Merk (1967) put it:

> On the floor of Congress a [program and plan], attractively packaged . . . is opened. Its items are individually inspected. The price tags on them are

[9]The phrase national "malaise" was not used by Carter, but was coined by presidential advisor Clark Clifford (1991) to characterize a speech Carter gave in the summer of 1979, after retreating to Camp David for several days to ponder a bewildering variety of national problems—notably the Teheran embassy hostages and the economic disaster of simultaneous inflation and unemployment.

> read with dismay, especially those still to be paid; mislabelings and confused labelings . . . are detected and denounced. Members . . . begin throwing epithets and charges at each other . . . The victory celebration ends; the fight over measures begins. (p. 371)

Finally, in politics "the best" usually has to be implemented by "less-than-the-best" officials—people whom the leader did not appoint, does not fully trust, and cannot remove from their positions.

Presidents whose power motivation was higher than their achievement motivation (for example, Franklin D. Roosevelt, Truman, Kennedy, Reagan) often find ways around these problems; indeed, they may not even be experienced as problems or obstacles, but rather as the very characteristics that make political life interesting. That is, power motivation enables or activates a whole series of specific "leadership intelligences" in political situations. For example, Roosevelt dealt with the problem of uncooperative subordinates by assigning the same task to several different people, which put him in the position of arbiter of everybody's performance. This meant that officials often competed to win his favor (see Burns, 1956). In other words, power-motivated political leaders also seem to take pleasure from the process of politics—maneuvering, "schmoozing," compromising, trading—as well as from the results.[10]

In contrast, presidents whose achievement motivation was higher than their power motivation (for example, Wilson, Hoover, Lyndon B. Johnson, Nixon, and Carter) seem to be worn down by the process of implementing the lofty goals with which they began their administrations. In the words of a recent political journalist (Wintour, 1999):

> [It is] a relatively simple process to think up and launch a new policy. But in government there are interest groups to fix, budgets to agree, white papers to publish, legislation to pass, pilot studies to implement, and then sometimes many years before the impact is felt on the ground. It is altogether a slower and more grinding business. (p. 21)

Faced with a strong inner demand to achieve in this "grinding business," achievement-motivated leaders may be tempted to go over the heads of their political and legislative colleagues and appeal directly "to the people" (as did Wilson, until a stroke crippled his body and his presidency), to cut moral and

---

[10]The potential maladaptiveness of pure achievement motivation, in a leadership context, can be illustrated by a speech of Edwin Land, the founder of the Polaroid Corporation. In many respects, Land was a prototypical achievement-motivated leader: energetic, restless, innovative, and an entrepreneur. Yet he preferred running a small enterprise, where he could maintain personal control, and in a 1942 speech to Polaroid employees, he described his complete lack of interest in politics and the real world of human relations: "If you dream of something worth doing and then simply go to work on it and don't think anything of personalities, or emotional conflicts, or of money, or of family distractions . . . it is a wonderful dream . . . " (quoted in McElheny, 1998, p. 1).

legal corners (as did Nixon, until he was forced to resign), or to micromanage (as did Carter, until he was defeated in his 1980 bid for reelection).

A MOTIVATIONAL ANALYSIS OF THE CLINTON PRESIDENCY

This discussion can be applied to an analysis and interpretation of the tortuous path of Bill Clinton's presidency. Both in the 1992 campaign and in his 1993 inaugural address, Clinton clearly scored higher in achievement motivation than power (Winter, 1995). Based on these scores, he most closely resembled Lyndon B. Johnson and Jimmy Carter.

Such a motive profile was clearly displayed in the fiasco of health care reform: a panel of "experts," meeting in secret, produced a 1,342-page document covering every feature of health care. Without paying any attention to politics and the arts of power—that is, the skills of recognizing possible obstacles, alliances, and powerful stakeholders in the status quo; of holding public interest; and of rallying public support through exhortation and compelling images—Clinton's health care team apparently expected to win a simple, single up-and-down vote.[11] Such a style is more characteristic of the "command and compliance" corporate world in which achievement motivation, when situated at the top of a hierarchy, has a relative untrammeled path toward the "single best way."

Even Clinton's "Slick Willie" image (referring to his tendency to change views and modify positions, reminiscent of another achievement-motivated president nicknamed "Tricky Dick"; see Winter & Carlson, 1988) can be seen as reflecting the tendency of achievement-motivated people to modify their performance on the basis of the results of previous actions. His retreats on health care, his withdrawals of contested appointments, and his acceptance of the Republican framework for welfare reform, as well as his more centrist agenda in 1995–1996 all reflect the avoidance of extreme risks and the use of feedback that are characteristics of achievement motivation.

During his first term, then, Clinton's motives predisposed him to the risks and vulnerabilities—the failures of "leadership intelligence"—that are characteristic of achievement motivation in a political context. Clinton's policies were often indecisive and ever-changing, leading to the erosion of domestic and foreign alliances. He got bogged down in the frustrating morass of politics. He may have taken illegal shortcuts, and he was certainly drawn toward micromanagement. The parallels with Nixon, Johnson, and Carter were compelling.

Suddenly, however, a "new Clinton" emerged after the Republican shutdown of the government in the winter of 1995–96. Clinton skillfully challenged and attacked the Republican-controlled Congress. His prospects for re-election, dis-

[11]See the accounts of the Clinton plan in Aaron (1996), Marmor (1998), and Moynihan (1996).

missed as hopeless, steadily rose during 1996 and culminated in a sweep of the Republican candidate. What happened?

In motivational terms, Clinton's power motive scores steadily rose during 1994–96, the last three years of his first term (Winter, 1998a), as illustrated in Fig. 8.2. For example, the ratio of power-to-achievement images increased from a value of 1.19 in his 1993 State of the Union message to a value of 2.03 in his 1996 message.

Many features of Clinton's second term are consistent with this change. Perhaps the most memorable signs were the bombings of suspected terrorist sites in the Sudan and Afghanistan, as well as the more aggressive stance toward Serbian ethnic cleansing in Kosovo that culminated in the 78-day NATO bombing campaign in 1999. In his relationship to the Republican-dominated Congress, Clinton also displayed improved political skills of maneuver, compromise, and persuasion. Even his well-publicized sexual relationship with Monica Lewinsky (which apparently began after the change toward power in Clinton's motive profile) can be understood as part of the "Don Juan" or exploitative sexual style that is often associated with male power motivation (see Winter, 1973, chap. 6).

Clinton's presidency, then, can be characterized as an initial two years in which his achievement motivation (with its associated intelligences and vulnerabilities) predominated, followed by six years in which his power motivation (with its associated intelligences and vulnerabilities) was ascendant.

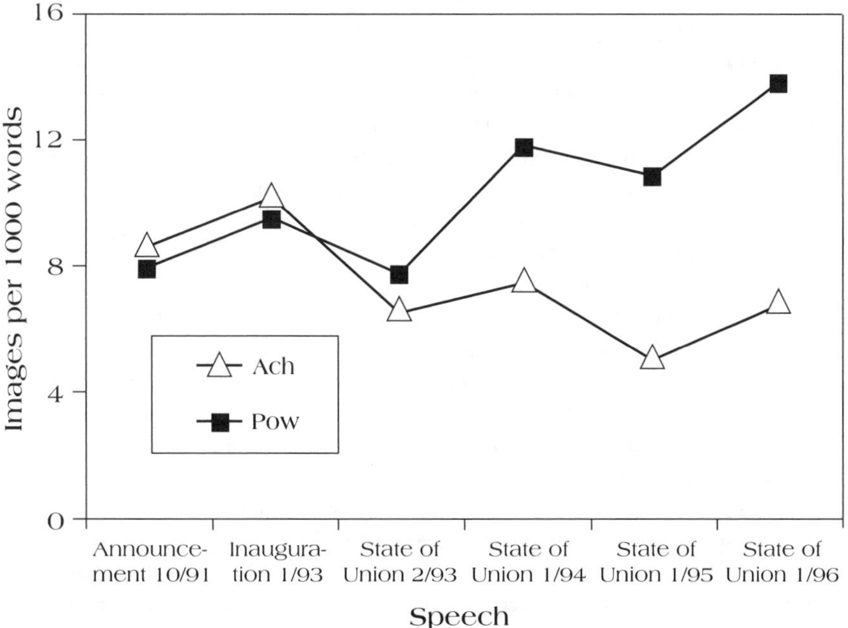

FIG. 8.2. Clinton's Achievement and Power Motives over Time

Power, Achievement, and Leadership in Bureaucracies

This discussion of the relative strengths and vulnerabilities of achievement and power motivation in different contexts suggests an important conclusion about the skills and intelligences needed for successful leadership in political contexts: Political bureaucracies may not be very hospitable to pure achievement needs. The achievement-motivated person may have a strong desire for success and excellence, but only under conditions of personal control can this be realized. To make an analogy from the game of chess: Achievement motivation involves skill at moving the pieces. Most leadership roles, however, require the skills of influence; that is, getting the pieces to move by themselves. To develop, energize, and engage these essential leadership intelligences, leaders need the capacity to enjoy exercising influence (i.e., having an effect on the behavior of others) for its own sake and not merely because it helps them reach a goal.

Power Motivation and the Multiple Intelligences of Leadership

What are the skills and intelligences engaged by the power motive? Many have already been suggested above: the ability to scan the political "landscape" for stakeholders, obstacles, and alliances; the ability to attract and hold public interest; and the ability to rally public support through exhortation and the articulation of compelling images.

The ways in which power motivation engages and energizes these forms of intelligence and tacit knowledge can be further illustrated by the analysis of changes in Clinton's motives and performance during his first term. (In the following discussion, these aspects of political tacit knowledge and sociopolitical intelligence appear as emphasized terms.) First, Clinton changed his sources of advice and assistance. Instead of relying on technical experts, as in the health care reform fiasco, he recruited political experts—people such as Dick Morris and David Gergen—experienced in developing political strategy and managing communication both to Congressional insiders and to the public at large.

As a result, the Clinton administration grew more successful at aggregating interests. For example, the welfare reform proposals passed by Congress and signed by Clinton in 1996 drew support from Republicans and moderate Democrats. While many liberal Democrats opposed the measure, they really had no alternative but to continue support of the president in the 1996 campaign. Of course the welfare proposals were inherently a compromise of many competing interests, cobbled together after extensive negotiations with key power brokers in the Congress. In contrast, the health care reform proposals had been developed essentially outside the political process, so that their fate was to aggregate oppositions, inviting attack from a broad range of constituencies ranging from Republicans who wanted little change, to Democrats who wanted a Canadian-style complete overhaul of the system.

Clinton's first response to the debacle of the 1994 Congressional elections, in which Democrats lost control of both houses of Congress, was the plaintive claim that, as the president, he was still "relevant." Shortly afterward, however, he mounted a more direct confrontation, even an attack. For example, a landmark April 7, 1995 speech contained the phrase "I will veto" seven times. And during his January 1996 annual message to Congress, he issued thirteen direct challenges ("I challenge you" or "I challenge the Congress") to Congress and fifteen other direct challenges to various other groups. (These words and phrases are a clear echo of Harry Truman's 1948 "give 'em hell" attack on the "do-nothing" Republican-dominated 80th Congress.)

Clinton also displayed a deft kind of political jujitsu, an art of interpretation, in which he turned the strength of Republican opposition back on itself. In 1995–96, for example, he was able to interpret the Republicans' opposition to his budget in such a way as to make them responsible, in the public view, for the shutdowns of government. Later, he was able to cast himself as the defender of highly popular programs such as Medicare and Social Security against irresponsible Republican tax cuts for the rich.

Success at political (re)interpretation requires several kinds of emotional intelligence. First, leaders have to control their own emotions. Early in his first term, Clinton was prone to outbursts of anger and hurt feelings when he sensed that the media and the public were unfair or ungrateful (see Wenner & Greider, 1993). By 1995–96, however, these emotions were either better managed or at least better concealed. At the same time, Clinton and his advisors shared an improved ability to sense the nuances of popular emotion, so that their policies (welfare reform, "protection" of Social Security and Medicare, "family values" through maternal leave, HMO regulation as a marginal change to health care) could be presented in ways that had emotional resonance with the public mood.

While Clinton's relative increase in power motivation engaged these and other forms of leadership intelligence, they may also have heightened certain vulnerabilities and risks ("anti-intelligences," as it were). Thus the successful exercise of power often makes leaders prone to an exalted view of themselves, and a dehumanized view—often wrapped in metaphors of sexuality—of others (Kipnis, 1976; Winter, 1996b; 1999b). While it is difficult to know the exact details of any public figure's sex life, Clinton's sexual involvement with Monica Lewinsky, beginning during the 1995–96 government shutdown, as well as his brazen attempts to conceal that involvement, may illustrate how motives can engage their characteristic vulnerabilities and "negative intelligences," as well as positive ones.[12]

[12]The interpretation of Clinton's relationship with Lewinsky in power terms is certainly the opposite of Hillary Rodham Clinton's (public) explanation that his extramarital sexual behavior is triggered by a sense of weakness, based on abuse he suffered as a child and his attempts to please two conflicting women. This raises the question of whether power motivation originates as a compensation for early experiences of weakness, or as a result of direct reinforcement of childhood power behaviors (see Winter, 1999a).

TABLE 8.5
Motives and Leadership Outcomes Among U.S. Presidents: Reporters' Ratings

White House reporters' ratings of[a]	*Correlation with Motive Score for:*		
	Power	*Achievement*	*Affiliation*
Combative skill	.76+	.25	.59
Humor	.91*	.23	.19
Candor	.06	.13	–.22

Note: $N = 6$.
+$p < .10$
*$p < .05$
[a]Based on Shearer (1982).

Two additional kinds of leadership intelligence associated with power motivation are suggested by ratings assembled by a veteran television correspondent, Robert Pierpoint (Shearer, 1982). Pierpoint and several of his White House correspondent colleagues rated U.S. presidents from Eisenhower through Reagan on several characteristics. Although the sample is small, it does consist of men who occupied the most powerful and important leadership position in the world during an era of grave international crises and danger. As shown in Table 8.5, presidential power motive scores were significantly associated with the correspondents' ratings of combative skill and humor. We might think that these two skills conflict with each other: How can the same leader be both "combative" and have a sense of "humor"? That very combination, I suggest, may be the essence of one important political "leadership intelligence"—the ability to be engaged and fight, and the detachment to be able to laugh.[13]

Exercising leadership often involves a good deal of dissatisfaction and frustration, especially when the followers become dependent or demanding. Thus, for example, during the many years that the followers of Moses wandered in the desert, some grew tired and began to imagine that their lives had been better in Egypt. In despair, Moses cried out to God: "Am I their mother? Have I brought them into the world, and am I called upon to carry them in my bosom, like a nurse with her babies . . . ?" (Numbers 11:12). As another example, in *Henry V*, Shakespeare's king eloquently soliloquizes about the burdens of leadership, while awaiting the next day's crucial battle of Agincourt:

[13]As an illustration of the relationship between presidential power motivation and humor, imagine those presidents whose power motivation was higher than their achievement motivation (Roosevelt, Truman, Kennedy, Reagan). We usually recall them as smiling or laughing (even at their own expense). Now imagine presidents with achievement higher than power (Wilson, Hoover, Lyndon Johnson, Nixon, and Carter). In our "imagined pictures," each of these presidents is likely to have a grim countenance.

We must bear all.
. . . What infinite heart's-ease
Must kings neglect, that private men enjoy!

Referring to the perquisites of power such as titles, a throne, and pomp, Henry laments that:

Not all these, laid in bed majestical,
Can sleep so soundly as the wretched slave. . . .
(Act IV, Scene 1)

In such situations of follower demands and dependency, power motivation—the capacity to take pleasure from having impact on the behavior of others—can help to sustain the leader's personal morale and focus.

THE AFFILIATION MOTIVE AND LEADERSHIP

Laboratory and field studies (McClelland, 1975; McClelland & Boyatzis, 1982) have shown that affiliation motivation is unrelated (or even negatively related) to successful leadership. Among U.S. presidents, as shown previously in Table 8.3, the affiliation motive shows nonsignificant (albeit positive) correlations with the three measures of presidential leadership.

Presidential affiliation motivation does have two important correlates, as illustrated in Table 8.6. First, affiliation-motivated presidents are peacemakers, in the sense of supporting agreements with other major powers for the limitation or abolition of major weapons systems (e.g., the 1922 Washington Naval Conference agreements on battleship ratios, the SALT agreements, or the renunciation

TABLE 8.6
Motives and Leadership Outcomes Among U.S. Presidents: Peace and Scandals

	Correlation with Motive Score for:		
Variable[a]	*Power*	*Achievement*	*Affiliation*
Arms limitation treaty ($N = 14$)	–.05	.13	.40
Scandal ($N = 29$)	.01	.15	.40*

*$p < .05$
[a]Based on Winter (1987).

of chemical and biological warfare). This is consistent with the cooperative orientation of affiliation-motivated people in everyday life—so long as they are comfortable with their "counterplayers."[14]

As shown in Table 8.6, affiliation-motivated presidents are also vulnerable to scandals. That is, they (or top-level figures in their administration) engage in political practices that are judged to be illegal or inconsistent with established constitutional principles. This may be the result of affiliation-motivated leaders being more readily influenced by others who are perceived to be similar and friendly (Winter, 1996a, chap. 5). Alternatively, it may simply be that all presidential administrations have scandals and affiliation-motivated presidents are simply less adept at concealing them.

In any case, affiliation motivation seems to work against pure Weberian precepts of bureaucracy with respect to such matters as the personal ownership of the tools of office, the separation of "public" and "personal" spheres of action, and the objective application of universalistic principles. On the other hand, the prominence of affiliation as a human motive, and the prevalence of "scandals" as a feature of politics suggest that political bureaucracies may require some affiliative "grease" in order to work effectively.[15] As the writer Tom Wolfe expressed it in *Bonfire of the Vanities* (1988), a novel about justice, politics, and money in late twentieth-century New York City:

> Everything . . . operates on favors. Everybody does favors for everybody else . . . If you make a mistake, you can be in a whole lotta trouble, and you're gonna need a whole lotta help in a hurry . . . But if you've been making your regular deposits in the Favor Bank, then you're in a position to make contracts. That's what they call big favors, contracts. (pp. 400–401)

Affiliative grease, then, may constitute yet another kind of leadership intelligence. Yet at the same time it poses a dilemma for the leader. While every bureaucratic system may require some minimal level of personal relations (or particularism) in order to function properly, such particularism can, by overriding more universalistic bureaucratic standards, corrode morale and thereby destroy support on the part of those followers who feel excluded from the leader's favored inner circle of personal relations. Thus exercising a motivational capacity for "personal relations" requires great caution on the part of the leader, lest it arouse a sense of unfairness in the minds of some followers.

---

[14]Thus George Bush's very high affiliation motive did not prevent him from reacting to the Iraqi invasion of Kuwait with fury and an assertion that "this shall not stand." Probably Bush's rage was fueled by a sense of having been "double-crossed" after his previous friendly overtures, which continued as late as the famous conversation of U.S. Ambassador April Glaspie with Saddam Hussein that took place only a few days before the invasion of Kuwait (see Winter, Hermann, Weintraub, & Walker, 1991).

[15]Similarly, soldiers at war are said to fight not because of abstract principles, nor because of orders in the chain of command, but rather because of ties to their immediate companions or "buddies" (Kellett, 1990, p. 225).

TWO MAJOR MOTIVATIONAL AXES OF LEADERSHIP

While the three motives for power, achievement, and affiliation are empirically uncorrelated and so constitute a three-dimensional space, as shown previously in Fig. 8.1, for purposes of understanding leadership, we may find a two-dimensional representation more useful, as shown in Fig. 8.3.

The affiliation motive, in this figure represented as the vertical axis, represents the extent to which ties of friendship or close similarity and personal relations make a difference in, setting goals, evaluating others, and making decisions. As suggested, the dilemma of personalization versus universalism confronts every leader. By drawing closer to some followers and peers, moreover, the leader necessarily draws away from others. Thus the motive for friendship, unless carefully managed, has the paradoxical potential for increasing suspicion and paranoia and actually decreasing "friendship" at the collective or mass level.

The balance between power and achievement, shown in Fig. 8.2 as the horizontal axis, represents the relative tendency of leaders toward either (1) restlessness and even rigidity as their "great ideals" become enmeshed in the mire of the political process (the left-hand pole, of achievement higher than power) or (2) exploitation and oppression of others (the right-hand pole, of power greater than achievement). Thus an "absolute" power motive, unmitigated by ideals of achievement, responsibility, or affiliation, "corrupts absolutely."

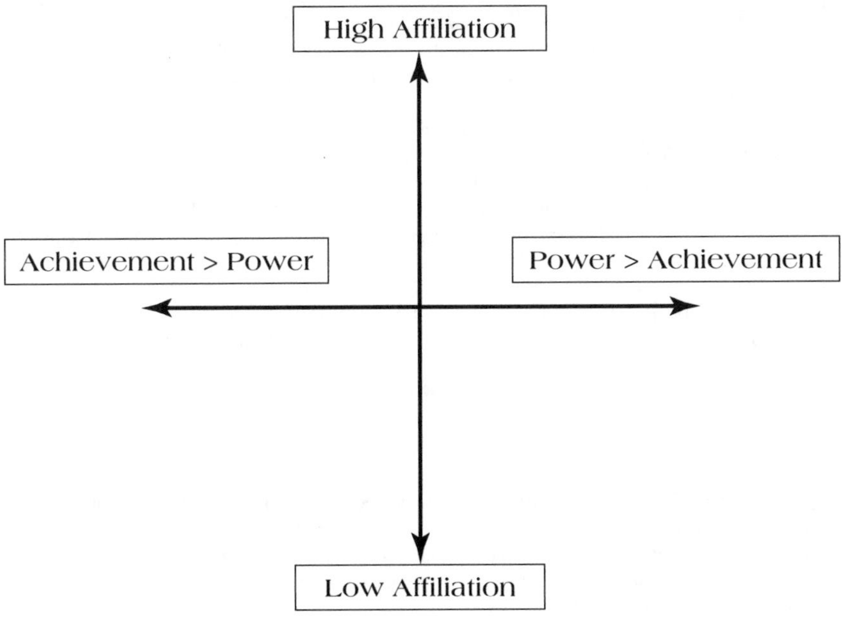

FIG. 8.3. Motivational Axes of Leadership

CONCLUSION

What has our analysis of the role of motivation contributed to an understanding of the intelligences of leadership? Leaders' motives influence their perceptions and construals of the leadership situation, and affect their own satisfactions and vulnerabilities in the leadership process itself. Each of the dimensions of motivation discussed in this chapter is complex, in the sense that it engages both advantages and liabilities, and energizes skills and styles that have the potential for both good and bad leadership outcomes. A motivational prescription for effective leadership would therefore involve some degree of balance: balance between achievement and power concerns, balance or tempering of power with responsibility or similar forms of control, and balance among the benefits and liabilities of affiliative concerns.

The motives of leadership are a little like *fire*: they can cook our food and keep us warm, but they must always be controlled, trimmed back, and guarded—lest they burn and destroy our homes, our institutions, and ourselves.

REFERENCES

Aaron, H. J. (Ed.). (1996). *The problem that won't go away: Reforming U.S. health care financing.* Washington, DC: Brookings Institution.

Andrews, J. D. W. (1967). The achievement motive in two types of organizations. *Journal of Personality and Social Psychology, 6,* 163–168.

Bakan, D. (1966). *The duality of human existence.* Chicago: Rand McNally.

Bales, R. F. (1970). *Personality and interpersonal behavior.* New York: Holt, Rinehart, and Winston.

Barber, J. D. (1992). *The presidential character: Predicting performance in the White House* (4th ed.). Englewood Cliffs, NJ: Prentice Hall.

Burns, J. M. (1956). *Roosevelt: The lion and the fox.* New York: Harcourt Brace.

Canetti, E. (1962). *Crowds and power.* New York: Viking.

Carter, J. (1975). *Why not the best?* Nashville, TN: Broadman Press.

Clifford, C. (1991). *Counsel to the president: A memoir.* New York: Random House.

Ehrenreich, B. (1997). *Blood rites: Origins and history of the passions of war.* New York: Metropolitan Books.

Erikson, E. H. (1969). *Gandhi's truth.* New York: Norton.

Freud, S. (1964). *An outline of psycho-analysis.* In J. Strachey (Ed.), *The standard edition of the complete psychological works of Sigmund Freud* (Vol. 23, pp. 144–207). London: Hogarth Press. (Original work published 1940)

Helgeson, V. S. (1995). Relation of agency and communion to well-being: Evidence and potential explanations. *Psychological Bulletin, 116,* 412–428.

House, R. J., Spangler, W. D., & Woycke, J. (1991). Personality and charisma in the U.S. presidency: A psychological theory of leader effectiveness. *Administrative Science Quarterly, 36,* 364–396.

Kellett, A. (1990). The soldier in battle: Motivational and behavioral aspects of the combat experience. In B. Glad (Ed.), *Psychological dimensions of war* (pp. 215–235). Newbury Park, CA: Sage.

Kipnis, D. (1976). *The powerholders.* Chicago: University of Chicago Press.

Maranell, G. (1970). The evaluation of presidents: An extension of the Schlesinger poll. *Journal of American History, 57,* 104–113.

Marmor, T. R. (1998). *Steering health care systems: Observations on managerial fashions in the United States and in the Netherlands.* 's-Hertogenbosch, Netherlands: SWOOG.

McAdams, D. P., Hoffman, B. J., Mansfield, E. D., & Day, R. (1996). Agency and communion in significant autobiographical scenes. *Journal of Personality, 64,* 339–377.

McElheny, V. K. (1998). *Insisting on the impossible: The life of Edwin Land.* Reading, MA: Perseus Books.

McClelland, D. C. (1961). *The achieving society.* Princeton, NJ: Van Nostrand.

McClelland, D. C. (1975). *Power: The inner experience.* New York: Irvington.

McClelland, D. C., & Boyatzis, R. E. (1982). The leadership motive pattern and long-term success in management. *Journal of Applied Psychology, 67,* 737–743.

McClelland, D. C., & Burnham, D. H. (1976, March-April). Power is the great motivator. *Harvard Business Review,* pp. 100–110, 159–166.

McClelland, D. C., Koestner, R., & Weinberger, J. (1989). How do self-attributed and implicit motives differ? *Psychological Review, 96,* 690–702.

Merk, F. (1967). *The Oregon question: Essays in Anglo-American diplomacy and politics.* Cambridge, MA: Harvard University Press.

Miller, M. (1974). *Plain speaking: An oral biography of Harry S. Truman.* New York: Berkley Publishing Corporation.

Moynihan, D. P. (1996). *Miles to go: A personal history of social policy.* Cambridge, MA: Harvard University Press.

Pye, L. W. (1985). *Asian power and politics: The cultural dimensions of authority.* Cambridge, MA: Harvard University Press.

Seward, W. H. (1861, January 12). Transcript of remarks in Senate debate. *Congressional Globe* (36C2, p. 344). Washington, DC: Congressional Globe Office.

Shearer, L. (1982, January 17). Intelligence report: Pierpoint's presidential report card. *Parade: The Sunday Newspaper Magazine,* p. 8.

Smith, C. P. (Ed.). (1992). *Motivation and personality: Handbook of thematic content analysis.* New York: Cambridge University Press.

Spangler, W. D. (1992). Validity of questionnaire and TAT measures of need for achievement: Two meta-analyses. *Psychological Bulletin, 112,* 140–154.

Stewart, A. J., & Chester, N. L. (1982). Sex differences in human social motives: Achievement, affiliation, and power. In A. J. Stewart (Ed.), *Motivation and society,* pp. 172–218. San Francisco: Jossey-Bass.

Stewart, A. J., & Malley, J. E. (1987). Role combination in women: Mitigating agency and communion. In F. Crosby (Ed.), *Spouse, parent, worker: On gender and multiple roles* (pp. 44–62). New Haven, CT: Yale University Press.

Weber, M. (1948). Politics as a vocation. In H. Gerth & C. W. Mills (Eds.), *From Max Weber: Essays in sociology.* London: Routledge & Kegan Paul. (Original work published 1919)

Weinberger, J., & McClelland, D. C. (1990). Cognitive versus traditional motivational models: Irreconcilable or complementary? In E. T. Higgins & R. M. Sorrentino (Eds.), *Handbook of motivation and cognition* (Vol. 2, pp. 562–597). New York: Guilford Press.

Wenner, J. S., & Greider, W. (1993, December 9). President Clinton: The *Rolling Stone* interview. *Rolling Stone,* pp. 40–45, 80–81.

Winter, D. G. (1973). *The power motive.* New York: Free Press.

Winter, D. G. (1979). *An introduction to LMET [Leadership and management education and training] theory and research.* Boston: McBer & Company.

Winter, D. G. (1987). Leader appeal, leader performance, and the motive profiles of leaders and followers: A study of American presidents and elections. *Journal of Personality and Social Psychology, 52,* 196–202.

Winter, D. G. (1988). The power motive in women—and men. *Journal of Personality and Social Psychology, 54,* 510–519.

Winter, D. G. (1991a). Measuring personality at a distance: Development of an integrated system for scoring motives in running text. In A. J. Stewart, J. M. Healy, Jr., & D. Ozer (Eds.), *Perspectives in personality: Approaches to understanding lives* (pp. 59–89). London: Jessica Kingsley Publishers.

Winter, D. G. (1991b). A motivational model of leadership: Predicting long-term management success from TAT measures of power motivation and responsibility. *Leadership Quarterly, 2,* 67–80.

Winter, D. G. (1995). Presidential psychology and governing styles: A comparative psychological analysis of the 1992 presidential candidates. In S. A. Renshon (Ed.), *The Clinton presidency: Campaigning, governing, and the psychology of leadership* (pp. 113–134). Boulder, CO: Westview.

Winter, D. G. (1996a). *Personality: Analysis and interpretation of lives.* New York: McGraw-Hill.

Winter, D. G. (1996b, June). *What does power "do" for you and to you, and what can we do to power?* Invited address at the annual meeting of the Society for the Psychological Study of Social Issues, Ann Arbor, Michigan.

Winter, D. G. (1998a). A motivational analysis of the Clinton first term and the 1996 presidential campaign. *Leadership Quarterly, 9,* 253–262.

Winter, D. G. (1998b). "Toward a science of personality psychology": David McClelland's development of empirically derived TAT measures. *History of Psychology, 1,* 130–153.

Winter, D. G. (1999a, August). *Origins of power motivation in males: Data from a longitudinal study.* Paper presented at the annual meeting of the American Psychological Association, Boston.

Winter, D. G. (1999b, July). *Power, sex, and violence: A psychological reconstruction of the twentieth century and an intellectual agenda for political psychology.* Presidential address at the annual meeting of the International Society of Political Psychology, Amsterdam.

Winter, D. G., & Barenbaum, N. B. (1985). Responsibility and the power motive in women and men. *Journal of Personality, 53,* 335–355.

Winter, D. G., & Carlson, L. (1988). Using motive scores in the psychobiographical study of an individual: The case of Richard Nixon. *Journal of Personality, 56,* 75–103.

Winter, D. G., Hermann, M. G., Weintraub, W., & Walker, S. G. (1991). The personalities of Bush and Gorbachev measured at a distance: Follow-up on predictions. *Political Psychology, 12,* 457–464.

Wintour, P. (1999, January 17). Things have only got worse. *The Observer,* p. 21.

Wolfe, T. (1988). *Bonfire of the vanities.* New York: Bantam Books.

9

Efficacy and Effectiveness: Integrating Models of Leadership and Intelligence

Martin M. Chemers
University of California at Santa Cruz

THE ROLE OF INTELLIGENCE IN LEADERSHIP EFFECTIVENESS

Except for one very notable exception, contemporary leadership researchers and theorists have largely ignored the role of intelligence in leadership effectiveness. Among leadership theories of the last thirty or forty years, only Cognitive Resources Theory (Fiedler & Garcia, 1987) regards intelligence as an important variable. This was not always true. Early approaches to the study of leadership were strongly influenced by the apparent success of intelligence tests in the prediction of important outcomes, e.g., performance during military training. Stogdill's (1948) review of leadership traits, which showed that traits alone were not sufficient to predict either leadership emergence or effectiveness, also acknowledged that intelligence was one of the traits with the strongest association with leadership. (About 35% of the studies involving measures of intelligence and leadership revealed a significant relationship between the two variables.)

In this chapter, I will develop the premise that not only is intelligence a useful variable for understanding the processes that underlie effective leadership, but even more, that contemporary intelligence theories can serve as useful models for similar approaches in leadership research. Indeed, there are intriguing parallels in the research histories of the two constructs. Leadership ability, like intellectual ability, was first regarded as a trait that people either had or didn't have, and little attention was paid to situational or environmental factors that might mitigate the utility of particular capabilities.

Later models began to emphasize an interaction between the characteristics of the individual and the nature of the environment with this interaction being the somewhat mechanical fit between stable traits and a relatively static environment. In leadership, this approach might manifest as a hypothesis that one type of leadership behavior (e.g., giving directions versus being emotionally supportive) would be more effective in some situations than in others (e.g., in situations of high versus low clarity and structure).

Finally, contemporary approaches (Sternberg, 1988; Cantor & Kihlstrom, 1987; Chemers, 1997) are moving in the direction of the conceptualization of a more fluid interaction between person and environment with an acknowledgement of the individual's actions in construction and shaping of the environment rather than just reacting to it. Thus, rather than a fixed and unchanging capacity, intelligence (or leadership) becomes a set of skills and knowledge that change and develop in interaction with an environment that can, in turn, be shaped and modified to facilitate a good (i.e., effective) fit.

A FUNCTIONAL MODEL OF LEADERSHIP EFFECTIVENESS

Before turning to the application of contemporary intelligence models to leadership theory, it is useful to develop a model of leadership effectiveness that integrates what is currently known about what makes some leaders more effective than others. I will define leadership as "a process of social influence in which one person is able to enlist the aid and support of others in the accomplishment of a common task" (Chemers, 1997, page 1). The important points of this definition are that leadership is social, involves influence, and is centered on a task. The definition is quite simple, but the reality of leadership is very complex.

Part of that complexity is rooted in the nature of organizational functioning. To be effective, an organization must attend to two critical demands. First, it must develop a system of rules, norms, and standards that provide the internal order, reliability, and predictability necessary to address recurrent and routine events. Organizations must assign jobs, titles, and offices, meet payrolls, pay suppliers, file governmental reports, etc. However, because organizations also exist within a dynamic environment, they must develop the systems and strategies that foster the sensitivity and flexibility that make it possible to respond to novel challenges. Organizational prosperity (even survival) depends on the appropriate balance between these two somewhat incompatible functions—stability and change.

Organizational effectiveness depends on leadership effectiveness. Leaders must help groups and individuals accomplish the tasks on which the organization's internal stability and external adaptability depend. To do this, leaders must enlist the aid and support of followers, guide and encourage the efforts of those followers, and direct the collective efforts of the team toward task accomplishment. Leadership effectiveness depends on the leader behaving in a manner that (1) elicits the trust and loyalty of followers (image management); (2) motivates followers toward enthusiastic effort (relationship development); and (3) applies the efforts, knowledge, and material resources of the group to mission accomplishment (resource deployment). Although the leadership literature is large, extensive, and somewhat fragmentary, it is the case that considerable agreement exists on the factors that determine these three key elements.

Image Management

It is important to recognize that the decision to act as a follower (i.e., to give up some of one's autonomy and independence of action) represents a social cost that must be balanced by some benefit. The benefit that makes the exchange equitable and attractive occurs when the leader appears able to increase the likelihood that the follower will be able to satisfy personal needs and achieve personal goals.

Hollander's (1958; 1964; Hollander & Julian, 1970) "idiosyncrasy credit" model of status accrual in groups directly addressed this exchange. Hollander showed, both through laboratory and field studies, that when a leader is seen as competent in task-related domains and committed to the group's core values, followers are willing to give the leader greater latitude of action and authority. The task-related competency provides the basis for the leader moving the group toward goal accomplishment, and the loyalty to group values fosters the assurance that the goal pursued by the leader will be one that serves the collective interests of the group. How are such judgments normally made by followers?

Although many researchers have written about leadership attributions, the most integrated and comprehensive treatment of the subject is in the writings of Robert Lord and his associates (Lord, 1985; Lord, Foti, & De Vader, 1984). Lord and Maher's (1991) information processing model posits that leadership is assessed through both recognition and inferential processes. Recognition-based processes are dependent on the implicit theories that each person holds about the traits and characteristics that comprise leadership. The implicit models of "good" leadership result in prototypes (Rosch, 1978; Cantor & Mischel, 1979), sets of characteristics that we consciously or unconsciously associate with the leadership role. When an individual seems (through appearance or behavior) to possess a sufficient number of these characteristics, observers make a generalized attribution (i.e., reach a conclusion) that the individual has leadership capacity. Once a decision is made that an individual is "leaderly," subsequent attention, interpretation, and memory are likely to be consistent with and reinforce the initial judgment.

Inferential attributional processes occur when we ascribe the causes for a group's success to the leader's actions or abilities. The tendency to assign causality as internal to the actor (in this case, the leader) is so pervasive that social psychologists have dubbed it the "fundamental attribution error" (Jones & Nisbett, 1971). Leaders who are associated with successful outcomes are seen as effective, based on the assumption that the leader caused the outcome. Meindl (1990) argues that tendency to credit leaders for anything—good or bad—that happens within an organization is so strong in our culture that it constitutes a "romance of leadership."

Several studies have been done on the particular characteristics that make up the leadership prototype (Lord, Foti, & De Vader, 1984). Although there are some differences between the prototypes for different classes of leaders (i.e., business, military, sports, etc.), there are common elements across these categories. In a simple study reported by Kouzes and Posner (1987), 1,500 managers and workers were asked to describe the characteristics of an outstanding leader they had known. Honesty and competence led the list, with over 80% of the respondents mentioning honesty, reaffirming Hollander's (1964) early results along the same lines.

A consistent theme in the literature on perceptions and attributions of leadership is that such judgments are fraught with biases. Assumptions, implicit theories, and romantic notions may induce observers to see what they are expecting to see and to remember what is consistent with their expectations. Nonetheless, creating the impression of competence and trustworthiness is an essential element of effective leadership, and little influence is possible until a leadership image is established.

Relationship Development

The establishment of a leader's legitimacy through competence and trustworthiness provides the basis for a relationship between leader and follower. The features of a successful leader–follower relationship are threefold. First, the leader must provide the follower with a supervisory context that is motivating and allows the follower to perform effectively. Second, the ability to provide such positive guidance and support depends on accurate judgments of the followers, needs, goals, and capabilities. Finally, the relationship must be equitable and fair.

Research on intrinsic motivation (Deci & Ryan, 1985; Hackman & Oldham, 1976) reveals that tasks are motivating to the extent that they provide one with autonomy, feedback, and an opportunity to engage one's skills and abilities toward meaningful goals. Feedback about performance makes possible a positive self-evaluation for a job well done. Autonomy (i.e., control over one's work) enhances the personal significance of positive feedback. The opportunity to use a variety of skills is interesting, and the entire endeavor is made more meaningful if the goal of the task is important. These characteristics of intrinsic motivation provide the bases for effective supervision.

A leader must provide the follower with direction and guidance that is sufficient to allow the subordinate to perform well and reap the benefits of positive feedback. However, the level of supervisory directiveness is a critical and subtle element. Too little direction might make the task overly ambiguous and difficult, reducing the likelihood of positive feedback. On the other hand, too much direction robs the follower of the autonomy necessary to make the feedback personally meaningful.

Path-goal theory (House, 1971; House and Dessler, 1974) prescribes that two general classes of behavior available to the leader are structuring (i.e., providing direction and task-related feedback) and consideration (i.e., providing emotional support). According to the theory, leader-structuring behavior will have the most positive effects on subordinate morale and performance when the ambiguity or difficulty of the subordinate's task makes direction valuable for goal attainment. Conversely, when the task is well understood by the subordinate, structuring behavior will be seen as overly close monitoring, pushing for performance, and robbing the subordinate of autonomy. Consideration and morale-boosting leader behavior should have their most positive effects when the subordinate's task is aversive by being boring or unpleasant. If the subordinate's task, however, is interesting and engaging, leader consideration will be regarded as unnecessary and distracting. The leader must be familiar with both the demands of the task and the capabilities of the follower to judge how much structuring and consideration would be useful. However, it is more complex than that.

The research findings on path-goal theory are quite mixed. One reason for the lack of consistent findings may be revealed in a study by Griffin (1981). In addition to measuring the nature of the subordinates' tasks, Griffin also measured a subordinate's personality characteristics—"growth need strength," Hackman and Oldham's (1976) measure of an individual's desire for growth and challenge in the workplace. Griffin found that growth need strength (GNS) moderated the predicted relationship between leader behavior and follower motivation and performance. High GNS subordinates, who were energized by difficult and unstructured tasks, responded negatively to leader structuring regardless of task condition, but responded quite positively to leader consideration when the task was highly structured and boring. Low GNS subordinates showed the opposite pattern. Boring tasks did not create as strong a positive reaction to supportive, considerate behavior by the leader, and structuring was well appreciated even when tasks were already fairly structured. Griffin's findings indicate that leaders must be sensitive not only to task features and follower skill levels, but also to followers' personality, needs, and expectations. Accurate judgment becomes a critical part of effective leadership.

The leader–follower relationship is a dynamic one. Subordinates are assigned tasks that they perform well or poorly. Follow-up actions are taken by the leader, and new tasks are assigned. Subordinates are rewarded or chastised; sent for training or given enhanced responsibilities; promoted or not. Thus, another important feature of leadership judgments centers on how the leader interprets this flow of actions and performance. Research by Mitchell and his associates (Green & Mitchell, 1979; Mitchell, Larson, & Green, 1977; Mitchell & Wood, 1980) indicates that attributions about followers by leaders obey many of the principles of classic attribution theory (Jones & Davis, 1965; Kelley, 1967). That is, leaders integrate information about how well the subordinate has performed on other tasks, and at other times, and how well other workers perform at similar tasks. Consistent and distinctive performance outcomes (i.e., success or failure that is consistent over time, but different from other workers) are likely to lead to strong attributions about the subordinate's ability, which lead to actions consistent with those judgments.

However, attributional processes in the leadership relationship have some additional features not usually addressed in social psychological studies of person perception. These additional processes are related to the fact that the leader and follower are engaged in a relationship with reciprocal causality and connected outcomes. By this I mean that follower performance may be caused by the leader. Poor leadership is a potential explanation for poor follower performance. Furthermore, poor performance by a follower has important implications for the leader's success and evaluation by superiors.

This mutual dependence makes the subordinate's behavior and performance and subsequent explanations surrounding that performance very important to the leader. This increases the tendency for judgments by the leader to be ego-defensive, self-protective, and occasionally extreme. Because the leader is taking action with respect to the subordinate based on these judgments, biased processes can have serious negative outcomes. Followers who are blamed for failures outside their control are likely to become resentful and problematic employees. The leader–follower relationship can become a descending spiral. This possibility leads to a discussion of the third element of relationship development—equity and fairness.

At base, the leader–follower relationship is a transaction in which the follower provides effort and loyalty to the group and leader in exchange for help in attaining personal goals. Graen (1976; Graen & Cashman, 1975; Graen, Cashman, Ginsburgh, & Schiemann, 1978; Graen & Scandura, 1987) has presented a model of leader–follower exchange that acknowledges the qualitative range of such transactions. Because a leader needs the help of followers to accomplish the leader's and the group's goals, the leader and follower will undergo a perhaps unspoken but important negotiation of the nature of their relationship. The leader may regard a subordinate as a valued partner who is given interesting tasks, made privy to inside information, provided training and development opportunities, and rewarded well, or may be regarded as a "hired hand" who is afforded far less attractive options. Research indicates better leader–follower exchanges are associated with better job-related communication (Graen & Schiemann, 1978) and greater satisfaction (Graen & Ginsburgh, 1977).

Resource Deployment

The successful negotiation of image management and relationship development provides the leader with a legitimate basis for authority that can be used to develop a team of motivated subordinates ready to direct their knowledge, skills, and energy toward mission accomplishment. The actual effectiveness of the team is determined by how successfully the intellectual, motivational, and material resources of the team are utilized to achieve the goal. Like a military commander who must deploy troops, weapons, and materials based on an informed estimate of the enemy's strengths and strategies, an effective leader must deploy the team's resources based on an informed judgment of the critical demands created by the task and mission environment.

Resource deployment is achieved on two levels. First, each member of the group must make the most effective use of his or her personal resources, i.e., intelligence, knowledge, skills, etc. Second, the individual efforts of team members must be coordinated and applied to the task environment in a manner that makes the most efficient use of those resources. Both self-deployment and team deployment are strongly influenced by the match between situational variables and team and personal characteristics.

Self-deployment addresses the ability to make the best use of personal resources. The basic premise of the Contingency Model of leadership effectiveness (Fiedler, 1967; Fiedler & Chemers, 1974; 1984) is that leaders function most effectively when their personal orientation or motivational pattern (i.e., toward task versus interpersonal accomplishment) is appropriate to (i.e., "matched" with) the situation. Extensive research (see meta-analyses by Peters, Hartke, & Pohlmann, 1983; Strube & Garcia, 1981) indicates that task-motivated leaders are most effective when the leadership situation (i.e., task, authority, and relationship with subordinates) provides the leader with a stable and predictable leadership environment. Relationship-motivated leaders perform most effectively—i.e., lead groups with high performance and satisfied subordinates—when situational contingencies create an environment of some complexity, ambiguity, and unpredictability.

Applying the Contingency Model to job stress, Chemers, Hays, Rhodewalt, and Wysocki (1985) found that "in-match" leaders reported lower levels of job stress and stress-related illness than did "out-of-match" leaders. Chemers, Ayman, Sorod, and Akimoto (1991) reported that in-match leaders evidenced more positive moods, greater confidence, and greater satisfaction than out-of-match leaders in both laboratory and field studies.

Fiedler and Garcia (1987) extended the logic of the Contingency Model to explain the effective deployment of leaders' cognitive resources (i.e., intelligence and experience) to effective group performance. Studies with the Cognitive Resources Model have indicated that the most effective use of intelligence and experience depends on two factors—the level of stress the leader is experiencing, and the willingness of the leader to provide clear direction to subordinates. Leaders under stress are less able to use their intelligence to solve problems, ostensibly because of the interference of anxiety on thought process, but are able to make good use of highly learned information provided by previous experience in similar situations. We see here the effect of positive and negative emotional states on the ability to make use of personal resources.

Fiedler and Leister (1977) have also shown that unless the leader is active in directing the activities of subordinates, intelligence and experience do not have much impact on the group's success. Fiedler (1993) suggests that match between leadership style and situation is related to the leader's level of directiveness. This notion is consistent with Eagly and Johnson's (1990) conclusions based on a meta-analysis of gender effects in leadership. They found that when a leadership situation was judged to be "congenial" (i.e., a situation in which a leader would be most comfortable) leaders were found to be more directive and judged to be more effective by observers.

Staw and Barsade (1992) who observed M.B.A. students in an assessment center simulation, found leaders with more positive affect to be more effective in the in-basket decision-making task, using more information and making more complex decisions, and were also more likely to be judged as an emergent leader in a leaderless discussion group. Individuals with positive affect are also more likely to take risks (Isen, Nygren, & Ashby, 1988), solve problems creatively (Isen, Daubman, & Nanicki, 1987), and make better decisions (Carnevale & Isen, 1986)—all of which are characteristics that are related to effective leadership.

It appears, then, that confidence plays an important role in the ability of individuals to make the most effective use of personal resources. One contributor to confidence is the degree of fit between the leader's personality, leadership style, gender, or other personal characteristics with features of the task, group, or organizational environment. I will develop this idea a bit more fully in a later section.

Team deployment refers to the effective coordination and application of the individual and collective resources of the team to the accomplishment of the group or organization's mission. The contingency theories (e.g., Fiedler, 1967; Vroom & Yetton, 1973) provide the most relevant explanatory premises for understanding team deployment.

All of the leadership functions discussed in earlier sections are dependent on subjective perceptions. The extent to which the leader looks likes a leader (i.e., matches the leadership prototype) or the degree to which the leader's structuring and considerate behavior are seen by the subordinate as appropriate and motivating are influenced primarily by perceptions and judgments that are endogenous to the leader–follower relationship.

However, the strategies and actions that are used to affect the coordination of team resources for task accomplishment have their interface with the more concrete constraints of the external environment. Generally speaking, situations of high predictability make the use of directive, highly structured strategies more likely to yield positive results, while more complex and unpredictable circumstances benefit from the information sharing and creative problem solving made possible by more participative and flexible strategies. For example, Vroom and Yetton (1973) maintain that the wrong decision-making strategy (e.g., the use of autocratic [low follower input], decision making when the leader lacks relevant information and structure) is likely to lead to less efficient use of resources and lower effectiveness. A voluminous literature on the Contingency Model (Fiedler, 1978; Strube & Garcia, 1981) supports the notion that team effectiveness is dependent on the proper match between leadership style and situational factors.

Effective coordination of team resources requires the use of communication and decision-making structures that are compatible with the environment. Successful leaders must make accurate judgments about the nature of the environment and implement strategies that fit.

Transformational Leadership

Leadership researchers have always been interested in that class of exceptionally effective leaders that political historian James McGregor Burns (1978) referred to as "transformational" leaders—i.e., leaders who transcend the "transactional," quid pro quo bases of leadership authority to transform their followers into dedicated agents of collective achievement (Bass, 1985; 1998; Conger, 1989; Conger & Kanungo, 1987; House, 1977; House & Shamir, 1993). Like Weber's (1947) "charismatic" leaders, this class of exceptional leaders is seen as qualitatively different from their more mundane counterparts. I don't find this to be a defensible or useful distinction. Rather, I would argue that so-called transformational leaders are those who exhibit the highest levels of the three elements of image management, relationship development, and resource deployment.

The transformational theories all stress the important role of impression management in eliciting the high levels of follower commitment that define charismatic or transformational leadership. House's (1977) analysis of historical figures with charismatic effects on followers emphasizes the use of image management, such as bold gestures and risk-taking, to establish an image of commitment and trust-evoking dedication to the mission. Conger and Kanungo (1987) place great importance on the leader's technical expertise and "depth of knowledge" for achieving desired objectives. Bass (1985) uses the term "idealized influence" to refer to the leader's image as supremely competent, and "inspirational motivation" to underscore the necessity of stating the group's goal in terms that inspire trust and dedication to the leader and to the mission. House (1977) and House and Shamir (1993) stress that transformational leaders evince extremely high levels of confidence in themselves and their followers. This confidence leads to followers' self-perceptions of competence and subsequently to high expectations and high goals.

Relationship development with its components of judgment and guidance is an important feature of the transformational theories. Bass (1985) argues that transformational leaders employ "individualized consideration" (i.e., a highly personalized understanding of and reaction to follower needs and abilities) to create "intellectual stimulation" (i.e., providing guidance that stretches subordinates to think independently and creatively). This is very similar to the basic elements of relationship development, which are the sensitive understanding of follower needs and abilities in order to provide coaching, and guidance that stretch the follower's capacities and promote growth of knowledge and skills.

Finally, the notion that leaders must coordinate group activities through judgment and process for effective resource deployment is most clearly expressed by Conger and Kanungo (1987), who maintain that an important component of outstanding leadership is the ability to accurately assess the strategic factors affecting the attainment of the leader's vision.

Effective leadership can be conceived of as a continuum from very poor to very excellent. The successful fulfillment of the three elements of image management, relationship development, and resource deployment provides the basis for movement towards the positive pole of that dimension.

THE ROLE OF INTELLIGENCE IN LEADERSHIP EFFECTIVENESS

Leadership research has never been strongly focused on specific skills or knowledge bases that leaders might possess. Since Stogdill's (1948) critical examination of leadership traits, only minimal interest had been shown in intelligence—either as a trait or skill—until Fiedler and Garcia's (1987) presentation of Cognitive Resources Theory. However, in recent years, the conceptualization of intelligence has moved from a trait to a process. These modern approaches to intelligence hold great promise for illuminating the bases of successful leadership. I will address three of the most prominent of the modern conceptualizations of intelligence and examine how they might contribute to the functional, integrative view of leadership presented previously. The three intelligence models are Sternberg's (1988) Triarchic Theory of Intelligence, Cantor and Kihlstrom's (1987) Social Intelligence Theory, and Salovey and Mayer's (1990; Mayer & Salovey, 1993) Theory of Emotional Intelligence.

Contemporary Models of Intelligence

What sets apart the newer conceptualizations of intelligence from the older "intelligence as stable trait" approaches is the view of intelligence as a process of adaptation. Cognitive skills and knowledge interact with environmental demands in a mutual shaping and development that enhances the adaptive fit of the individual to the environment. Robert Sternberg's Triarchic Theory of Intelligence (1988), which led the way in this approach, regards the individual as possessing internal resources in the form of cognitive abilities, such as specific knowledge and learning strategies that are applied to the solution of problems in the life environment. The relative utility of these internal resources are defined by the degree to which they are appropriate to the environmental demands. By interacting with the environment, the individual develops and refines the resources necessary to be effective, and in the process selects, shapes, and adapts elements of the environment for better fit with existing and developing internal resources. A central process in effective adaptation is the turning the novel and unfamiliar into the predictable and routine, which can then be managed for attaining desired goals. The intelligent person, then, is one who can muster current knowledge and ability to relate to the problem environment in a flexible way that allows for the acquisition of new skills and knowledge that help the individual to develop the solutions necessary for goal attainment.

Cantor and Kihlstrom's (1987) Theory of Social Intelligence proceeds from a similar position of intelligence as "problem solving in a context." The socially intelligent person is one who possesses a sophisticated "perceptual readiness" to interpret social life accurately and respond to social situations effectively, i.e., managing interpersonal interactions to attain personal goals. Like Sternberg's "metacomponents," individuals possess internal resources or expertise in the social domain, consisting of concepts, interpretive rules, scripts, etc. These internal resources are applied to "life-task contexts" that afford the opportunity for the individual to accomplish his or her central life tasks. Intelligence becomes the ability to act wisely in human relations and involves the selection and shaping of contexts to provide the best fit with knowledge and abilities. The intelligent person understands the cultural expectations and normative processes governing social interaction and can recognize when and how social rules are applied.

Salovey and Mayer (1990; Mayer & Salovey, 1993) have directed attention to the extent to which emotional as well as cognitive knowledge is an important component of effective mastery of the personal environment. They discuss four types of emotional intelligence: (1) the accurate perception of one's own and others' emotions, (2) the use of emotions to facilitate thinking (i.e., the ability to create task-congruent emotions that help one focus on task demands), (3) emotional knowledge and understanding, including empathy and judgment, and (4) regulation of one's emotions to promote personal growth (i.e., self-control, coping with stressful situations). Emotional intelligence contributes to an individual's ability to control oneself and to understand and influence others.

Intelligences as Contributors to Leadership Effectiveness

A reexamination of the key elements of effective leadership affords an opportunity to recognize the role of the various types and aspects of intelligence.

Image management involved the establishment of the credibility and legitimacy of authority by matching subordinate prototype-based expectations for leadership. The strongest components of the leadership prototype across all types of leaders are competence and honesty. A potential leader's ability to match observer expectations depends on two factors; the understanding of what the content of the prototype is, and the capability for presenting the expected behaviors and attitudes. Social intelligence is clearly the basis for the first requirement, and emotional intelligence is a significant contributor to the latter.

Social intelligence includes the knowledge of prototypical characteristics and situational scripts. The socially intelligent person is adept at reading the characteristics of the situation for cues and clues that define the nature of the interpersonal context and the appropriate behaviors for the context. The effective leader knows when a situation requires a formal authority and presentation or a more informal and intimate interactional style. A CEO who attends the corporation's shareholders meeting dressed in jeans and a sweatshirt and gives the annual report while leaning against a table would be as out of place and unconvincing as one who attends the company picnic in a three-piece suit. Social knowledge is a requisite for appearing as a credible leadership figure.

It is also the case that leadership prototypes involve more than appropriate clothing. The projection of competence includes proper attitude, emotions, and demeanor. "Cool under pressure," "calm and self-assured," and "possessing a fire in the belly" have all become common phrases used to describe valued leaders in our culture. Social intelligence contributes to the ability to discern when one should be calm or fiery, but emotional intelligence plays a critical role in the would-be leader's ability to regulate self-control and emotional state to meet situational demands.

If the foregoing descriptions of the uses of intelligence in image management give the impression of a manipulation or insincerity, it would be misleading. Understanding where others "are coming from" and being able to harness and control one's emotions in order to meet the challenges of demanding situations need not imply any insincerity. In the long run, it is the person who is really "calm under pressure" but can "rise to the challenge" that will be recognized and afforded the status to lead.

Relationship development has, as its most central feature, the ability to accurately judge the needs and expectations of followers so that coaching and guidance can be given in a manner that encourages motivation and promotes growth. Again, both social and emotional intelligence are the bases for that ability. Coaching, with its sometimes oppositional components of correction and encouragement, is one of the most subtle and potentially volatile of social interactions. An understanding of the norms surrounding such interactions and a knowledge of the impact of feedback and of how to phrase both praise and criticism is essential for acting effectively in the coaching situation. This ability to understand others and act in ways that are in tune with the feelings of followers is what we mean by the term "consideration."

However, transformational leadership theory (Bass, 1985) makes clear that outstanding leadership goes beyond a generalized knowledge of what considerate behavior is to achieve an "individualized consideration" that is sensitive to the unique personality and situation of a particular follower. We have also discussed the impediments to sensitive understanding of subordinates that are inherent in the leader's own vulnerability to criticism and need to defend self-esteem. It is at this deeper level of understanding that emotional intelligence becomes critical. The leader needs first to control his or her own emotional reactions to the coaching situation, both in terms of anxiety about delivering feedback, as well as in terms of threats to one's own sense of competence. Second, the ability to read and understand the emotions of others, i.e., empathy, forms the basis for truly individualized consideration.

Resource deployment is the facet of leadership that mobilizes and applies the group's collective resources to accomplish the task or mission. At this level, intelligence theories may provide both strikingly apt metaphors as well as useful models for understanding effective leadership. Sternberg's (1988) triarchic model presents intelligence as the employment (or read "deployment") of the individual's internal resources to attain desired goals. To do this, the individual engages the environment in order to both bring to bear existing knowledge and to sample environmental demands to determine what new knowledge or skills must be developed. This interface with the environment is shaped to fit the individual's capabilities just as capabilities are expanded and developed to fit the environment. The hallmark of this process is the turning of the novel and unpredictable aspects of the environment into the well understood and routinely manageable—thus freeing the individual's capabilities to access new novel problems.

If we make a few substitutions in words, we have a very good description of effective leadership. For a group to attain its goals and accomplish its mission, it must bring to bear the individual capabilities, knowledge, skills, and energy of its members to address the demands of the task environment. It begins by selecting and shaping the problem to fit existing knowledge, as well as by activating the learning processes of each individual member. Just as with individual intelligence, the group's immediate goal is to process information and make decisions that turn novel and unpredictable environmental features into routine events that can be reliably and predictably managed to effect solutions.

Although aspects of this metaphor are obvious, some less obvious ideas are brought into relief. The notion of the group as a learning organism reorganizing and expanding knowledge and skills to meet challenges may be more or less explicit in some approaches to organization (Senge, 1990), but those ideas have not been as clearly integrated into leadership theory. Likewise, the idea that effective problem solving is the conversion of novelty into order is not a new concept, but it is relatively new to contemporary leadership theory.

Social and emotional intelligences may also affect the resource deployment process. Clearly, emotional intelligence, i.e., the regulation of one's own emotion and others' emotions, is central to self-deployment—the effective release of personal resources. By managing anxiety, maintaining a positive attitude, and successfully coping with stress, leaders and followers are more able to make use of the resources of knowledge and skill that they possess. In addition, as House and Shamir (1993) point out, the arousal of motives that are appropriate to task performance (e.g., achievement motivation for difficult tasks or "aggression" for competitive situations) enhance ability. Emotional intelligence provides a basis for understanding how a leader's behavior might arouse appropriate moods or motivations in oneself or in one's followers.

Summary

Thus far, I have made the case that effective leadership involves (a) establishing credibility with followers by behaving in ways that reflect competence and trustworthiness; (b) encouraging high levels of motivated and self-regulated task-relevant behavior among subordinates through effective coaching guided by sensitive understanding of follower capabilities and needs; and (c) using the knowledge, skills, and motivated effort of self and followers to accomplish the organizational mission by understanding the nature of the group's task environment and matching group problem solving and decision-making strategies to environmental demands. General, social, and emotional intelligence are central contributors to a leader's ability to accomplish each of these functions. However, I believe that we can understand the effects of intelligence in a broader sense. Intelligence may provide the basis for a leader to approach a situation with a feeling of confidence knowing that he or she possesses the skills and knowledge to deal with situational demands or the resources to adapt personal resources and situational parameters to achieve an effective match.

In the discussion of outstanding or transformational levels of leadership effectiveness, confidence was described as playing a key role. Highly confident leaders are able to project an image of competence, have lower levels of personal anxiety and defensiveness allowing for more effective interpersonal communication and judgment, and possess a calmer demeanor, which facilitates complex and effective decision making. Where, then, are the roots of leadership confidence?

In an earlier section in this chapter describing the self-deployment of leadership, I summarized research that indicated that leaders with a good match between leadership orientation and situational characteristics tended to perform more effectively (Fiedler & Chemers, 1974), express greater job satisfaction (Chemers & Ayman, 1985), report less job stress and stress-related illness (Chemers, et al. 1985), and most interestingly, describe themselves as upbeat, confident, and in control of the leadership situation compared to leaders who are "out-of-match" (Chemers, Ayman, Sorod, & Akimoto, 1991). The positive mood and confidence associated with match are similar to other affect-related constructs discussed in the social psychological literature, e.g., hopefulness (Snyder, et al. 1991), mood, and self-efficacy (Bandura, 1982; 1997). The next section focuses on the role of positive dispositional affect and leadership efficacy on leadership performance.

LEADERSHIP EFFICACY AND LEADERSHIP PERFORMANCE

Personal Dispositions and Leadership Capabilities

Except for some work on self-esteem (Korman, 1968), the empirical literature on leadership has not reflected a great deal of interest in constructs related to positive affect or self-perception. Comprehensive reviews of leadership trait research (Bass, 1990; Yukl, 1994) reveal just a few studies of confidence, with mixed results. And in most of the studies of leadership confidence (e.g., Kipnis & Lane, 1962), constructs of self-esteem, self-confidence, and self-efficacy were not clearly differentiated from one another.

More qualitative approaches to leadership have touched on these issues. For example, after a loosely structured interview study of 90 outstanding leaders in the public and private sectors, Bennis and Nanus (1985) concluded that all of these individuals shared high levels of self-confidence about their own capabilities and optimism about the outcomes of their actions. Corporate CEOs, political leaders, professional sports coaches, symphony conductors, and others shared the beliefs that a) they were capable of doing what had to be done (self-efficacy), and b) if they did what they should do, the environment would respond positively (optimism). In a similar vein, Boyatzis (1982) conducted critical incident interviews with 253 managers preselected on the basis of high effectiveness ratings. Content analyses of the interviews revealed that effective managers demonstrated a strong belief in their own capabilities (self-efficacy) and an internal locus of control.

In purely theoretical analyses, House and Shamir (House, 1977; House & Shamir, 1993; Shamir, House, & Arthur, 1992) have included self-confidence and high expectations for self and followers among the list of traits that have distinguished charismatic leaders throughout history. In other words, traits like confidence and optimism crop up when analysts think about very effective leaders, but these constructs are less prevalent in the empirical work that addresses the more mundane aspects of organizational leadership.

In some empirical studies, positive affect has been found to be associated with better relations between soldiers and their superiors (Solomon, Mikulincer, & Hobfall, 1986). High levels of self-esteem have been related to a greater sense of personal locus of control (Deci & Ryan, 1985), and a greater willingness to assume positions of leadership (Linimon, Barron, & Falbo, 1984). Self-efficacy has been related to work motivation (Gist & Mitchell, 1992) and to better leadership performance under stress (Murphy, 1992).

An extensive literature on self-efficacy (Bandura, 1982; 1997) reveals that perceptions of efficacy can enhance or impair motivation and performance in a variety of ways, e.g., by influencing the kinds of activities in which people choose to engage (Bandura, 1982), the level of the goals they set (Locke, Frederick, Lee, & Bobko, 1984), and their effort and persistence at achieving those goals (Bandura & Cervone, 1983). Self-efficacy judgments are important because they influence not only what skills people perceive themselves to have, but also what they believe they can do with the skills they possess. Self-efficacy beliefs can affect attentional and thinking processes, eliciting either confidence with positive concomitants or debilitating self-doubt (Bandura & Wood, 1989) with a resultant tendency to withdraw or give up (Carver, Peterson, Follansbee, & Scheier, 1983). Bandura and Jourdan (1991) found that M.B.A. students given efficacy-enhancing feedback showed improved performance in a management simulation, decision-making task.

Although these various personal dispositions do not describe a single, unidimensional construct, they do share a focus on the positive effects of confidence in one's ability and positive expectancies about the outcomes of one's actions. In summary, feelings of enhanced self-efficacy should be related to high levels of motivation, which could affect levels of aspiration, goal setting, perseverance in the face of difficulty, and enthusiasm, causing a leader to work harder and longer to achieve group goals. Such feelings might also be contagious to followers, affecting their confidence and related perceptions.

Leadership Efficacy and Effectiveness

Bandura (1982; 1997) has maintained that self-efficacy is quite domain-specific. Therefore, only leadership efficacy, not generalized self-esteem or positive affect, should lead specifically to leadership effectiveness. In a series of recent studies, my colleagues and I (Chemers, Watson, & May, 2000; Watson, Chemers, and Preiser, 1996; Murphy (this volume), have found strong support for the predictive utility of leadership self-efficacy in group and organizational performance.

Chemers, Watson, and May (2000) measured the leadership self-efficacy of approximately 100 cadets enrolled in the Reserve Officer Training Corps (ROTC) at five colleges and universities in southern California and Arizona. Third-year cadets (i.e., juniors) responded to a measure of self-esteem, the Revised Janis-Field Scale (Brockner, 1988); to a measure which asked for their self-evaluation of a number of leadership skills (e.g., decision making, delegation, oral communication) and general leadership capabilities (e.g., "I know how to get a group to work well together"); and to a measure of generalized optimism, the Life Orientations Test (LOT; Scheier & Carver, 1985). The cadets were rated on leadership potential by their military science class instructors (career military officers). Results indicated that leadership efficacy and optimism, but not general self-esteem, were strongly related to the leadership potential ratings.

Follow-up data on these same cadets were collected during their attendance at a U.S. Army six-week summer leadership training camp. Companies of approximately 40 cadets lived in common barracks and rotated through leadership duties. Cadets also underwent extensive training in leadership, as well as in nonleadership skills (e.g., marksmanship, navigation), and participated in highly realistic and demanding leadership simulation exercises. Leadership ratings were obtained from cadet peers, superior officers (regular army), and from simulation observers (Pentagon-trained evaluators). In all analyses, leadership efficacy (but not self-esteem or optimism) was strongly related to leadership ratings by all parties, but not to nonleadership measures. The authors conclude that the leadership efficacy measure provided evidence of strong concurrent (instructor ratings), predictive (summer camp ratings and score), and discriminant (nonleadership measures) validity.

Watson, Chemers, and Preiser (1996) examined the effects of leadership efficacy on collective efficacy and team performance among men's and women's college basketball teams. Small college basketball team members responded to measures of leadership efficacy, individual basketball efficacy, and team collective efficacy prior to the beginning of the basketball season and also identified the player regarded as the team leader. Results indicated that the leadership efficacy of the identified leader (usually the team captain) was strongly predictive of the team's collective efficacy, which, in turn, was strongly predictive of the team's win-loss record during the season. Leaders with high leadership efficacy led more confident and more successful teams. Efficacy was, in fact, a better predictor of performance than more frequently used "objective" measures of talent, such as previous year's win-loss record, number of returning lettered players, or players out for the team.

Murphy (this volume) reported the results of three studies employing leadership efficacy as a predictor. These studies revealed that the relationship of leadership efficacy to leader, group, and organizational performance becomes stronger when the leader's situation is more stressful or demanding. The paper included a laboratory study in which groups were randomly assigned to high or low stress conditions on a creative task, and leadership efficacy was found to be more strongly related to performance under high stress conditions. A second study done on managers in a state governmental bureaucracy indicated that leadership efficacy was related to performance ratings by superiors for women managers, but not for their male counterparts. A third study of unit managers of outlets of a fast food chain found leadership efficacy to be significantly related to restaurant performance (company ratings) for women and minority group managers, but not for white male managers. The authors interpret the results of these studies to show that leadership efficacy is a resource that allows people to deploy their knowledge and skills, and that as the leadership situation becomes more difficult and demanding, the more useful and impactful leadership efficacy becomes.

CONCLUSION

This chapter has presented an integrated theory of leadership that regards effective leadership as grounded in three critical functions. Image management is essential to the development of credibility of the leader and the acceptance of influence by followers and is dependent on follower perceptions of the leader as competent and trustworthy. Relationship development is the basis for the development of a motivated and competent group of followers and is dependent on a leader's ability to recognize follower capabilities and needs, and to provide intrinsically motivating coaching and direction. Finally, resource deployment encompasses a leader's ability to get the most out of individual and collective effort by the appropriate matching of strategy to environment.

An additional thesis of this chapter is that all of these leadership capabilities are dramatically enhanced by a leader's sense of personal efficacy in the leadership role, and in fact, outstanding levels of leadership are not possible without high levels of confidence. Empirical evidence from three major studies support the value of leadership efficacy as a predictor of leadership, group, and organizational performance as measured in a variety of ways.

The chapter also presents an intriguing hypothesis to guide future research—i.e., that situational self-efficacy (leadership efficacy in this case) is rooted in intelligence, which provides the actor with a sense of personal agency. In particular, social and emotional intelligence may be very highly related to a leader's success at image management and relationship development, and general intelligence to a leader's ability to read and respond to task environments. An exciting direction for future research would be to probe the effects of social and emotional intelligence on leadership efficacy and leadership performance.

REFERENCES

Bandura, A. (1982). Self-efficacy mechanism in human agency. *American Psychologist, 37*, 122–147.

Bandura, A. (1997). *Self-efficacy: The exercise of the self.* New York: W. H. Freeman & Company.

Bandura, A. & Cervone, D. (1983). Self-evaluative and self-efficacy mechanisms governing the motivational effects of goal systems. *Journal of Personality and Social Psychology, 45*, 1017–1028.

Bandura, A. & Jourdan, F. J. (1991). Self-regulatory mechanisms governing the impact of social comparison on complex decision making. *Journal of Personality and Social Psychology, 60*, 941–951.

Bandura, A. & Wood, R. (1989). Effect of perceived controllability and performance standards on self-regulation of complex decision making. *Journal of Personality and Social Psychology, 56*, 805–814.

Bass, B. M. (1985). *Leadership and performance beyond expectations.* New York: Free Press.

Bass, B. M. (1990). *Bass & Stogdill's handbook of leadership: Theory, research, and managerial applications.* (3rd ed.). New York: Free Press.

Bass, B. M. (1998). *Transformational leadership: Industry, military, and educational impact.* Mahwah, NJ: Lawrence Erlbaum Associates.

Bennis, W. G., & Nanus, B. (1985). *Leaders: The strategies for taking charge.* New York: Harper & Row.

Boyatzis, R. E. (1982). *The competent manager.* New York: John Wiley.

Brockner, J. (1988). *Self-esteem at work: Research, theory, and practice*. Lexington, MA: D. C. Heath and Company.

Burns, J. M. (1978). *Leadership*. New York: Harper & Row.

Cantor, N. & Kihlstrom, J. F. (1987). *Personality and social intelligence*. Englewood Cliffs, NJ: Prentice Hall, Inc.

Cantor, N. & Mischel, W. (1979). Prototypes in person perception. In L. Berkowitz (Ed.), *Advances in experimental social psychology*, (Vol. 12). New York: Academic Press.

Carnevale, P. J. D. & Isen, A. M. (1986). The influence of positive affect and visual access on the discovery of integrative solutions in bilateral negotiation. *Organizational Behavior and Human Decision Processes, 37*, 1–13.

Carver, C. S., Peterson, L. M., Follansbee, D. J., & Scheier, M. F. (1983). Effects of self-directed attention on performance and persistence among persons high and low in test anxiety. *Cognitive Therapy and Research, 7*, 333–354.

Chemers, M. M. (1997). *An integrative theory of leadership*. Mahwah, NJ: Lawrence Erlbaum Associates.

Chemers, M. M. & Ayman, R. (1985). Leadership orientation as a moderator of the relationship between performance and satisfaction of Mexican managers. *Personality and Social Psychology Bulletin, 11*, 359–367.

Chemers, M. M., Ayman, R., Sorod, B., & Akimoto, S. (1991). Self-monitoring as a moderator of leader-follower relationships. Presented at the International Congress of Psychology, Brussels.

Chemers, M. M., Hays, R., Rhodewalt, F., & Wysocki, J. (1985). A person-environment analysis of job stress: A contingency model explanation. *Journal of Personality and Social Psychology, 49*, 628–635.

Chemers, M. M., Watson, C. B., & May, S. (2000). Dispositional affect and leadership effectiveness: A comparison of self-esteem, optimism, and efficacy, *Personality and Social Psychology Bulletin, 26*, 267–277.

Conger, J. A. (1989). The dark side of the charismatic leader. In J. A. Conger (Ed.), *The charismatic leader*. San Francisco: Jossey-Bass.

Conger, J. A. & Kanungo, R. A. (1987). Towards a behavioral theory of charismatic leadership in organizational settings. *Academy of Management Review, 12*, 637–647.

Deci, E. L. & Ryan, R. M. (1985). *Intrinsic motivation and self-determination in human behavior*. New York: Plenum Press.

Eagly, A. H. & Johnson, B. T. (1990). Gender and leadership style: A meta-analysis. *Psychological Bulletin, 108*, 233–256.

Fiedler, F. E. (1967). *A theory of leadership effectiveness*. New York: McGraw-Hill.

Fiedler, F. E. (1978). The contingency model and the dynamics of the leadership process. In L. Berkowitz (Ed.), *Advances in experimental social psychology*, Vol. 11. New York: Academic Press.

Fiedler, F. E. (1993). The leadership situation and the black box in contingency theories. In M. M. Chemers & R. Ayman (Eds.), *Leadership theory and research: Perspectives and directions*. San Diego: Academic Press.

Fiedler, F. E. & Chemers, M. M. (1974). *Leadership and effective management*. Glenview, IL: Scott, Foresman & Company.

Fiedler, F. E. & Chemers, M. M. (1984). *Improving leadership effectiveness: The Leader Match concept* (2nd ed.). New York: Wiley.

Fiedler, F. E. & Garcia, J. E. (1987). *New approaches to effective leadership: Cognitive resources and organizational performance*. New York: Wiley.

Fiedler, F. E. & Leister, A. F. (1977). Leader intelligence and task performance: A test of the multiple screen model. *Organizational Behavior and Human Performance, 20*, 1–14.

Gist, M. E. & Mitchell, T. R. (1992). Self-efficacy: A theoretical analysis of its determinants and malleability. *Academy of Management Review, 17*, 183–211.

Graen, G. (1976). Role-making processes within complex organizations. In M. D. Dunnette (Ed.), *Handbook of industrial and organizational psychology*. Chicago, IL: Rand McNally.

Graen, G. & Cashman, J. (1975). A role-making model of leadership in formal organizations: A developmental approach. In J. G. Hunt and L. L. Larson (Eds.), *Leadership frontiers*. Kent, OH: Kent State University Press.

Graen, G., Cashman, J. F., Ginsburgh, S., & Schiemann, W. (1978). Effects of linking-pin quality on the quality of working life of lower participants: A longitudinal investigation of the managerial understructure. *Administrative Science Quarterly, 22*, 491–504.

Graen, G. & Ginsburgh, S. (1977). Job resignation as a function of role orientation and leader acceptance: A longitudinal investigation of organizational assimilation. *Organizational Behavior and Human Performance, 19*, 1–17.

Graen, G. & Scandura, T. A. (1987). Toward a psychology of dyadic organizing. *Research in Organizational Behavior, 9*, 175–208.

Graen, G. & Schiemann, W. (1978). Leader-member agreement: a vertical dyad linkage approach. *Journal of Applied Psychology, 63(2)*, 206–212.

Green, S. G. & Mitchell, T. R. (1979). Attributional processes of leaders in leader-member interactions. *Organizational Behavior and Human Performance, 23*, 429–458.

Griffin, R. N. (1981). Relationships among individual, task design, and leader behavior variables. *Academy of Management Journal, 23*, 665–683.

Hackman, J. R. & Oldham, G. R. (1976). Motivation through the design of work: Test of a theory. *Organizational Behavior and Human Performance, 16*, 250–279.

Hollander, E. P. (1958). Conformity, status, and idiosyncrasy credit. *Psychological Review, 65*, 117–127.

Hollander, E. P. (1964). *Leaders, groups, and influence*. New York: Oxford Press.

Hollander, E. P. & Julian, J. W. (1970). Studies in leader legitimacy, influence, and innovation. In L. Berkowitz (Ed.), *Advances in experimental social psychology*, Vol. 5. New York: Academic Press.

House, R. J. (1971). A path-goal theory of leadership. *Administrative Science Quarterly, 16*, 321–338.

House, R. J. (1977). A 1976 theory of charismatic leadership. In J. G. Hunt & L. L. Larson (Eds.), *Leadership: The cutting edge*. Carbondale, IL: Southern Illinois University Press.

House, R. J. & Dessler, G. (1974). The path-goal theory of leadership: Some post-hoc and a priori tests. In J. G. Hunt & L. L. Larson (Eds.), *Contingency approaches to leadership*. Carbondale, IL: Southern Illinois University Press.

House, R. J. & Shamir, B. (1993). In M. M. Chemers & R. Ayman (Eds.), *Leadership theory and research: Perspectives and directions*. San Diego: Academic Press.

Isen, A. M., Daubman, K. A., & Nanicki, G. P. (1987). Positive affect facilitates creative problem solving. *Journal of Personality and Social Psychology, 51*, 1122–1131.

Isen, A. M., Nygren, J. E., & Ashby, G. F. (1988). The influence of positive affect on the subjective utility of gains and losses: It's not worth the risk. *Journal of Personality and Social Psychology, 55*, 710–717.

Jones, E. E. & Davis, K. E. (1965). From acts to dispositions: The attribution process in person perception. In L. Berkowitz (Ed.), *Advances in experimental social psychology*, Vol. 2. New York: Academic Press.

Jones, E. E. & Nisbett, R. E. (1971). *The actor and the observer: Divergent perceptions of the causes of behavior*. Morristown, NJ: General Learning Press.

Kelley, H. H. (1967). Attribution theory in social psychology. In D. Levine (Ed.), *Nebraska symposium on motivation*. Lincoln: University of Nebraska Press.

Kipnis, D. & Lane, W. P. (1962). Self-confidence and leadership. *Journal of Applied Psychology, 46*, 291–295.

Korman, A. K. (1968). The prediction of managerial performance: A review. *Personnel Psychology, 21*, 295–322.

Kouzes, J. M. & Posner, B. Z. (1987). *The leadership challenge: How to get extraordinary things done in organizations*. San Francisco: Jossey-Bass.

Linimon, D., Barron, W. L., & Falbo, T. (1984). Gender differences in perceptions of leadership. *Sex Roles, 11*, 1075–1089.

Locke, E. A., Frederick, E., Lee, C., & Bobko, P. (1984). Effect of self-efficacy, goals, and task strategies on task performance. *Journal of Applied Psychology, 69*, 241–251.

Lord, R. G. (1985). An information-processing approach to social perceptions, leadership, and behavioral measurement in organizations. In B. M. Staw & L. L. Cummings (Eds.), *Research in organizational behavior*, Vol. 7. Greenwich, CT: JAI Press.

Lord, R. G., Foti, R. J., & De Vader, C. (1984). A test of leadership categorization theory: Internal structure, information processing, and leadership perceptions. *Organizational Behavior and Human Performance, 34*, 343–378.

Lord, R. G. & Maher, K. J. (1991). *Leadership and information processing: Linking perceptions and performance*. Boston: Unwin Hyman.

Mayer, J. D. & Salovey, P. (1993). The intelligence of emotional intelligence. *Intelligence, 17*, 433–442.

Meindl, J. R. (1990). On leadership: An alternative to the conventional wisdom. In B. A. Staw (Ed.), *Research in organizational behavior* (Vol. 12, pp. 159–203). New York: JAI Press.

Mitchell, T. R., Larson, J. R., & Green, S. G. (1977). Leader behavior situational moderators in group performance: An attributional analysis. *Organizational Behavior and Human Performance, 18*, 254–268.

Mitchell, T. R. & Wood, R. E. (1980). Supervisor's responses to subordinate poor performance: A test of an attribution model. *Organizational Behavior and Human Performance, 25*, 123–138.

Murphy, S. E. (1992). The contribution of leadership experience and self-efficacy to group performance under evaluation apprehension. Unpublished doctoral dissertation, University of Washington, Seattle.

Peters, L. H., Hartke, D. D., & Pohlmann, J. T. (1983). Fiedler's contingency theory of leadership: An application of the meta-analysis procedure of Schmidt and Hunter. *Psychological Bulletin, 97*, 274–285.

Riggio, R. E., Murphy, S. E., & Pirozzolo, F. J. (2001). *Multiple intelligences and leadership*. Mahwah, NJ: Lawrence Erlbaum Associates.

Rosch, E. (1978). Principles of categorization. In E. Rosch & B. B. Lloyd (Eds.), *Cognition and categorization*. Hillsdale, NJ: Lawrence Erlbaum Associates.

Salovey, P. & Mayer, J. D. (1990). Emotional intelligence. *Imagination, Cognition, and Personality, 9*, 185–211.

Scheier, M. F. & Carver, C. S. (1985). Optimism, coping, and health: Assessment and implications of generalized outcome expectancies. *Health Psychology, 4*, 219–247.

Senge, P. M. (1990). *The fifth discipline: The art and practice of the learning organization*. New York: Doubleday.

Shamir, B., House, R. J., & Arthur, M. B. (1992). The motivational effects of charismatic leadership: A self-concept-based theory. *Organizational Science, 4*, 577–594.

Snyder, C. R., Harris, C., Anderson, J. R., Holleran, S. A., Irving, L. M., Sigmon, S. T., Yoshinobu, L., Gibb, J., Langelle, C., & Harney, P. (1991). The will and the ways: Development and validation of an individual-differences measure of hope. *Journal of Personality and Social Psychology, 60*, 570–585.

Solomon, Z., Mikulincer, M., & Hobfall, S. E. (1986). Effects of social support and battle intensity on loneliness and breakdown during combat. *Journal of Personality and Social Psychology, 51*, 1269–1276.

Staw, B. M. & Barsade, S. G. (1992). Affect and managerial performance: A test of the sadder-but-wiser vs. happier-and-smarter hypothesis. *Administrative Science Quarterly, 38*, 304–331.

Sternberg, R. J. (1988). *The triarchic mind: A new theory of human intelligence*. New York: Viking.

Stogdill, R. M. (1948). Personal factors associated with leadership: A survey of the literature. *Journal of Psychology, 25*, 35–71.

Strube, M. J. & Garcia, J. E. (1981). A meta-analytical investigation of Fiedler's Contingency Model of leadership effectiveness. *Psychological Bulletin, 90*, 307–321.

Vroom, V. H. & Yetton, P. W. (1973). *Leadership and decision-making.* Pittsburgh: University of Pittsburgh Press.

Watson, C. B., Chemers, M. M., & Preiser, N. (1996, June). *Collective efficacy: A multi-level analysis.* Presented at the annual meetings of the American Psychological Society, San Francisco, CA.

Weber, M. (1947). *The theory of social and economic organization.* (A. M. Henderson & T. Parsons, Transls.; T. Parsons, Ed.). New York: Free Press. (Originally published in 1924.)

Yukl, G. (1994). *Leadership in organizations* (3rd. Ed.). Englewood Cliffs, NJ: Prentice Hall.

III

Applications of Multiple Intelligences to Leader Effectiveness

10

Leader Self-Regulation: The Role of Self-Efficacy and Multiple Intelligences

Susan E. Murphy
Claremont McKenna College

LEADERSHIP AND SELF-REGULATION

While there exist many different conceptualizations of leadership, and almost as many different measures of effectiveness, little research has focused on the underlying processes a person must engage in to enact the social role of leadership. Current leadership theories represent three main emphases. The first emphasis asks, What do leaders do? That is, how do they behave in order to influence followers' performance? These include transformational (Bass, 1985; Avolio & Bass, 1988) and charismatic theories (Conger & Kanungo, 1988; House, 1977) of leadership. This category may also include how leader personality characteristics might influence the tendency to behave in a particular way. The second category of leadership theories represents a more reciprocal or dyadic view of leadership and covers leadership from the leader and follower perspectives. For example, Leader Member Exchange (LMX; Dansereau, Graen, & Haga, 1975; Graen, 1976; Graen & Scandura, 1987) suggests that it is the reciprocal nature of the relationship that develops over time between a leader and follower that affects performance. A final category of theories asks the question, How does the situation determine the appropriateness of leader behavior or style? These theories include Fiedler's Contingency Model (Fiedler, 1967); and Hersey and Blanchard's (1982) Situational Leadership Theory.

A handful of existing leadership theories, however, have begun to investigate and incorporate the process of leadership. For example, within transformational leadership theory, Bass (1985) discusses how the leader's behavior affects particular follower motivational states, which then eventually lead to increased performance. Also, within LMX theory, recent research focuses on how the quality of leader member exchange develops over time (Liden, Wayne, & Stilwell, 1993). Another line of research, however, focuses on the processes that explain how leaders effectively utilize the complement of skills and abilities as applied to the task of leadership (Fiedler & Garcia, 1987). Examining leadership performance from this perspective becomes important in understanding how today's leaders face difficult challenges on the job. While we can think of many examples of leaders who appear to face these challenges with amazing ease, we can also bring to mind those leaders who are paralyzed by similar situations. Differences in performance for these sets of leaders could be the result of different levels of abilities and training; however, there are many other leaders with virtually identical skill sets who react differently to situational challenges. In order to select and train leaders for future challenges, it is important to understand how leaders enact the role of leadership, or engage in self-regulation. Very few existing theories of leadership fully incorporate ideas of leader self-regulation.

This chapter presents a self-regulative view of leadership that describes how a leader utilizes his or her own abilities in the domain of leadership. This view incorporates the leader's own beliefs regarding these skills to enact the role of leadership. The chapter reviews past research contributions in leader self-regulation, and provides a model from a program of research on the role of social cognitive elements from leaders' own self-perceptions. The model also outlines a number of situational impediments that may influence success in the leadership role, including those faced by nontraditional leaders. And finally, this chapter introduces the potential role of social and emotional intelligence in self-regulation.

SOCIAL COGNITION AND SELF-REGULATION

The social cognitive movement in social psychology has produced a number of insights into a person's ability to participate in various situations as a social actor. Social cognition focuses on how people perceive others and themselves in social situations (Fiske & Taylor, 1991). Social cognition examines many topics including the influence of biases, stereotypes, categories, and schemas within the perceptual process and how people make causal explanations or attributions for their own or others' behaviors (Heider, 1958; Jones & Davis, 1965; Kelley, 1967). The field of social cognition also offers explanations for individual motivation from a self-regulatory perspective (Carver & Scheier, 1981).

Early social cognitive theories in leadership and management focused mainly on the followers' perceptual processes. In one line of research, for example, Lord and his colleagues (Lord & Maher, 1993; Hall & Lord, 1998) examine the affective and cognitive processing strategies used in the social perception of leaders. Their early work in this area showed that leadership behavior was inferred from performance outcomes (Lord & Maher, 1993). They also found that people hold particular leader prototypes that include specific leadership attributes. And finally they find that the leader perception has an affective component (Lewter & Lord, 1993), which according to Hall and Lord (1998), is thought to occur very quickly and sets the context for future cognitive processing. Another strong contribution examining followers' perceptions explores the notion of the romance of leadership. Within this theory, leadership is viewed as an attributional error because of the tendency for followers to give leaders excessive credit for affecting organizational outcomes (Meindl, 1990, 1993; Meindl, Ehrlich, & Dukerich, 1985). In other words, when we as social perceivers look around for an explanation for the success or failure of an organization, we tend to overestimate the leader's influence on the firm's performance.

One area of social cognition that has been relatively ignored in leadership research is how leaders think about themselves; that is, their mental representation of themselves within their role as leader and how they engage in behaviors to enact that role. Traditionally, in social cognition there are two broad areas of study with respect to the self (Fiske & Taylor, 1991). The first refers to the structure: how the self is represented in memory. This includes personality attributes, social roles, past experiences, and future goals. This specific structure of the self is often called a person's self-schema—in other words, the "cognitive-affective structure that represents a person's experience in a given domain" (Fiske & Taylor, 1991, pg. 182). For leaders, the structure of the self with respect to the domain includes both their schema regarding their general view of what leaders should look like (a prototype), and an assessment of their specific leadership abilities against this prototype.

The second main focus of study of the self in social cognition refers to the function of the self. This refers to how the self works to enact behavior, revise behavior, and alter the environment, or what is broadly called self-regulation (Markus & Wurf, 1987). Self-regulation includes goal setting, cognitive strategies of planning or rehearsing, and monitoring of goal attainment. Bandura's (1986) work in the process of self-regulation is one of the most comprehensive. Self-regulation begins with a level of self-awareness in which individuals observe their thoughts and behaviors. Next, they make judgments of their capabilities within a domain, or estimates of self-efficacy. Finally they engage in the thoughts, affect, motivation, and action. Self-efficacy is defined by Bandura (1986) as "judgments of capabilities to organize and execute courses of action required to attain designated types of performances" (p. 391). High self-efficacy has been shown to lead to increased performance in a wide range of situations (Bandura, 1997). Differences in levels of self-efficacy also explain individual reactions to discrepancies between personal standards and attainments. For those individuals low in self-efficacy, failure is seen as discouraging, while for those individuals high in self-efficacy, failure to attain a personal standard is motivating (Bandura & Cervone, 1983).

These conceptualizations of self-structure and function lead to the final enactment of behavior. Fig. 10.1 summarizes the relationships outlined for self-regulation within the leadership domain. It is adapted from Markus, Cross, and Wurf (1990). It begins with the structure of the self with respect to the domain of leadership. The structure requires that a leader holds a prototype of the role of leader and secondly, must hold a self-schema with respect to his or her abilities in that role. Those who either choose or find themselves in a leadership role must understand role requirements and make an assessment of their current complement of skills to fulfill that role. From where do these schemas regarding the prototypes of leaders come? While past research investigates the prototypes others hold of leadership (Lord & Maher, 1993), no research discusses the leader's own prototypes of effective leaders. When do these form? In working with young people to develop their leadership skills, students as young as age 12 hold definite ideas of how leaders behave and can explain why they hold certain people as examples of good leaders. Research by Avolio and Gibbons (1988) report that identity for leadership, in fact, occurs at an early age.

With respect to the function in the leadership domain, the leader must make further assessments of his or her capabilities to fulfill the leadership role under various conditions or situations. Self-efficacy for leadership (Murphy, 1992) and ego resiliency (Zaccaro, 1995; Zaccaro, et al. 1991) affect a leader's appraisal of capabilities to overcome potential stressors in a situation. As the leader moves to organize behavior and plan actions, issues of self-management become important (Manz & Sims, 1986). Within a self-regulative view of leadership, situational challenges can occur at two points in the process. First, potential stressors may interfere with the leader's ability to deploy the abilities contained in the leader's self-concept. For example, one can imagine many instances in which leaders have the necessary skills, but facing overwhelming demands, they may find that they cannot apply these skills in a given situation. Second, potential situational challenges may interfere with the leader's behavior resulting in ineffective performance. Within this linkage in the model, the situational challenges mostly reside in perceptions held by others of the leader's behavior, but eventually these perceptions interfere with the leader's ability to be effective. One way to think about this type of interference is to put it in terms of the concept of expectancy theories of motivation (Vroom, 1964). It is akin to the linkage between effort to performance, or the expectancy that certain behaviors will result in intended performance. The role of these situational challenges at each point in the self-regulation process will be explored in detail later in this chapter.

The next section of this chapter contains a review of leadership research that incorporates elements of this self-regulatory process summarized in Fig. 10.1.

FIG. 10.1 Self-Regulation within the leadership domain. *Adapted from Markus, Cross, & Wurf (1990) shown in Fiske & Taylor (1991).*

These theories are similar in that all recognize that a leader must engage in specific strategies to enact the leadership role; however, they vary in the degree to which they incorporate the many processes involved in self-regulation.

LEADERSHIP SELF-REGULATION: THE STRUCTURE AND FUNCTION OF THE SELF

Bass (1990) acknowledged that "how people think, feel, and act about themselves affects their tendencies to lead" (p.150). He speculated that a leader's self-concept contributes to effective performance when leaders strive for goals, or in Maslow's (1954) terms, work toward self-actualization. Furthermore, Bass proposes that these successful leaders have a higher level of self-understanding than less successful leaders and this self-understanding leads to an openness for receiving feedback. Many popular books on leadership, as well as management training programs, agree that overall self-awareness is an important leadership quality that is the first step for developing leadership capabilities (Hughes, Ginnett, & Curphy, 1998). In a recent *Fortune* magazine article (June, 1999), one of the major mistakes made by many top CEOs was that they were in denial about many aspects of their own actions, as well as those of their firms.

A series of studies on self-regulation within managerial decision making highlight some of the underlying issues that may affect a leader's ability to enact the role of leader and overcome challenges associated with that role. Wood and Bandura (1989) showed that managers who were led to believe that their ability on a managerial decision-making task was an innate ability had lower self-efficacy and lower performance over time than those who were led to believe that this ability was an acquirable skill. A similar pattern of results was found when another group of managers was told that the organizations in which they were managing were either controllable or difficult to control (Bandura & Wood, 1989). Self-efficacy and performance were lower when the organization was said to be difficult to control. And finally in another study, managers were given accurate performance feedback, but also received one of four types of feedback about their performance in relationship to other managers performing the same task (Bandura & Jourden, 1991). Of particular importance were two of the four conditions: a "progressive mastery condition" in which the managers were shown to be performing worse in the beginning but closing the performance gap later, and a "progressive decline condition" in which they were shown to be performing slightly better than others in the beginning but then falling behind. Self-efficacy and performance decreased over time for those managers in the progressive decline condition as compared to those in the progressive mastery condition. Within a model of leader self-regulation, thought patterns such as beliefs about ability and controllability of outside events could affect a leader's capability in the role. These studies provide an important basis for understanding factors that can undermine self-efficacy and possibly subsequent performance.

With respect to current leadership theories, two—transformational (Bass, 1985) and charismatic (Conger, 1989; Conger & Kanungo, 1988)—include elements of leader self-regulation. In a review of these theories, Hughes, Ginnett, and Curphy (1998) highlight leader qualities that differentiate charismatic leaders from noncharismatic leaders. Self-confidence is said to be required in displaying vision formation, rhetorical skills, image and trust building, and personalized leadership, as well as leaders' management of the impressions they make on others. Recently, Gardner and Avolio (1998) expanded charismatic leadership theory by including specific components of leader self-regulation. Using a "dramaturgical" perspective, Gardner and Avolio assert that "charismatic leaders' self-systems and situational assessments guide their efforts to manage follower's impressions of them, their vision, and their organization" (p. 32). Within the model, the leader's identification process explains how leaders work to construct their identity as leaders; more specifically their identity as charismatic leaders. Gardner and Avolio highlight the importance of the leader's self-system, which includes leader identity—including self-schema, high self-esteem, and high self-monitoring. This model provides important insights into the components of leader identity that are important for affecting organizational performance. However, it focuses somewhat exclusively on the leader's impression management activities. Leary (1989) makes a distinction between the types of leader behaviors that are necessary for managing the impressions of others and those necessary to function as a leader. Therefore, leader self-systems that apply more broadly to aspects of leader behavior, other than impression management, should be considered in examining leadership effectiveness.

Research by Sosik and Dworakivsky (1998) uncovered additional aspects of self-regulation that are important for charismatic leaders. They examined the effects of leader self-consciousness, self-monitoring, and purpose in life on subordinate ratings of charismatic leadership. They proposed that the leader's self-concept should work to motivate leaders to behave in ways that are consistent with their self-perception. They found that leaders who scored high on private self-consciousness, self-monitoring, and purpose in life were seen as more charismatic than leaders scoring low on these dimensions. These findings add some insight into some motivational elements of the leader's self-regulatory behaviors.

Chemers' (1997; see also this volume, Chap. 9) integrative view of leadership includes another component of leader self-regulation that has important implications for leadership performance. The "resource utilization function" requires that a leader engage in "self-deployment" activities. More specifically, this is defined as the "use of the physical and intellectual resources garnered from personality, training, experience, or other origins." (p. 159). These resources contribute to leadership performance when "successfully deployed." Within the self-regulative model of leadership presented earlier in Fig.10.1, self-deployment is the process that occurs as the leader uses his or her skills and abilities in the process of planning to engage in activities.

Finally, specific strategies of self-regulation are included in the theory of "self-leadership" (Manz, 1986) in which leaders use strategies of self-set goals, behavioral self-observations, positive cognitions, and positive and negative rewards to become more effective (Manz & Sims, 1980; Manz, 1986; 1990.) Self-leadership goes beyond the strategies of self-management, which mostly concentrate on methods to meet standards that are set by others, to also include self-regulatory methods to set one's own standards (see Neck, 1998, for discussion). In addition, Neck and Manz (1996) introduce the concept of "thought self-leadership" to further refine the notions associated with the use of inner cognitive strategies. These self-leadership strategies provide a compelling basis for understanding how leaders face and master challenges.

Together these leadership theories provide a useful basis for beginning to understand the process of leader self-regulation. In addition, each contributes uniquely to that process. However, these theories also leave unresolved issues and unexplained processes. For example, specific skills and abilities, such as different forms of intelligences may work to enhance the ease with which the leader can put to use his or her skills and abilities. Also ignored within these models are the situational factors that may interfere or enhance the leader's ability to succeed in the leadership role. Next, we turn to one additional leadership theory that provides an understanding of some of the situational constraints that affect a leader's ability to enact the leadership role and introduce additional leader abilities that may be important for effective self-regulation.

COGNITIVE RESOURCES THEORY WITHIN THE CONTEXT OF SELF-REGULATION

Overview of Cognitive Resources Theory

A compelling line of research by Fiedler and his colleagues demonstrates that situational factors can strengthen or weaken the relationship between a leader's resources and subsequent performance. Cognitive Resources Theory (Fiedler & Garcia, 1987; also see Fiedler, Chap. 6, this volume) proposes that in some conditions a leader's cognitive resources are quite predictive of performance, while in other situations, it is the leader's level of experience, or time in the job, that affects performance. Fiedler outlines a number of situations that help the leader effectively utilize his or her resources. These include the use of directive leader behavior, a supportive work group, and the absence, or surprisingly, presence of stress. Specifically, a number of studies by Fiedler and his colleagues (Fiedler & Garcia, 1987) have found that under stressful conditions, intelligence has a low, even negative, relationship with performance. Conversely, leadership experience, often measured as time in position, is positively related to performance under stress. Fiedler highlights the role of stress in cognitive resources theory. In studies with his colleagues, the sources of stress included stress with the boss (Bons, 1974), stress with subordinates (Blades & Fiedler, 1973), and stressful tasks such as firefighting (Frost, 1983).

Fiedler (1995) offers one explanation for the findings within Cognitive Resources Theory that is based on Zajonc's (1965) social facilitation theory. Experience is akin to the ability that is gained from performing a task over and over. Therefore, stress, or arousal, causes the dominant response (learned through repeated experience) to influence and improve performance. On newer, more novel tasks, arousal interferes with the use of intelligence, and experience is useless. In separate critiques of CRT, Zaccaro (1995) and Sternberg (1995) both explain the relationship between intelligence and experience in terms of the nature of specific task requirements. Zaccaro (1995) suggests that leadership experience facilitates the solving of well-defined problems because "experience results in the acquisition of extensive knowledge stores that are applicable to such problem domains" (p. 33). He further argues that "[I]n high stress situations leaders are likely to adopt a satisfying strategy, in which the goal is to determine as quickly as possible a solution that works, not necessarily the best possible or optimal solution" (p. 33). However, according to Zaccaro, stress will not facilitate performance for ill-defined problems because these types of problems require the generation of novel solutions. Leaders with higher intelligence, therefore, will perform better on ill-defined problems than those with lower intelligence, regardless of stress levels.

Sternberg also explains Fiedler's findings with respect to the task type choosing to distinguish between novel and automatic decision tasks. He argues that crystallized intelligence, or what is learned from day-to-day life experience (Horn, 1968), is akin to what leaders learn from years of experience and should predict performance on automatic decision tasks. Fluid intelligence should predict performance on novel tasks and especially under low stress circumstances. During high levels of stress, a leader cannot use fluid intelligence because resources are diverted to dealing with stress, and therefore, "automised" strategies learned from experience will work best in stressful conditions.

The Role of Self-Efficacy Within Cognitive Resources Theory

The mechanisms that allow leaders to apply their cognitive resources to given situations are important self-regulatory processes that are ignored in Cognitive Resources Theory. Specifically, self-efficacy for leadership should play a central role in the process of leader self-regulation. Within Cognitive Resources Theory, increased experience may work to enhance a leader's belief in his or her ability to cope with a stressful situation. In other words, an outcome of increased leadership experience may be a correspondent increase in self-efficacy for the task of leadership. Bandura (1997) reports that within the organization context, "It requires a strong sense of efficacy to deploy one's cognitive resources optimally and to remain task-oriented in the face of the many organizational complexities . . ." (p. 452). Individuals with high self-efficacy exhibit little stress reaction, while subjects with low self-efficacy experience a high level of stress and autonomic arousal (Bandura, Cioffi, Taylor, & Brouillard, 1988). Increased self-efficacy for leadership, therefore, should increase a leader's ability to succeed under stressful circumstances.

Although self-efficacy for leadership has not been incorporated into existing theories of leadership, related constructs of self-confidence and generalized self-efficacy have been examined. Within transformational theories of leadership, for example, charisma is said to be displayed through self-confidence (Bass, 1985). A recent study by Smith and Foti (1998) found that leaders with particular patterns of personality, which included generalized self-efficacy, most often emerged as leaders. While the use of specific self-efficacy estimates for leadership competencies is narrower than the concept of generalized self-efficacy, it is more broad-based than other self-efficacy measures tied to a particular task. Early studies of self-efficacy estimates were investigated in the contexts of specific abilities such as creative problem solving (Locke, Frederick, Lee, & Bobko, 1984) and physical exertion (Bandura & Cervone, 1983). In all of these studies, self-efficacy estimates of ability had virtually a one-to-one relationship with the outcome of interest, and individuals estimated their self-efficacy by indicating whether or not they could perform a specific task at a specified level. Later studies of self-efficacy, however, have used relatively complex tasks. Self-efficacy has been found to be related to weight control (Glynn & Ruderman, 1986), academic performance (Lent, Brown, & Larkin, 1984; Wood & Locke, 1987), sales performance (Barling & Beattie, 1983), and as mentioned previously, managerial decision making (Wood & Bandura, 1989). Therefore, a measure of a person's estimates of their ability to carry out the leadership role captures the complexity of leadership, but it is more specific than a person's general level of self-confidence, or even generalized self-efficacy.

Murphy (1992) developed a measure of self-efficacy for leadership in order to examine the relationship of self-efficacy and experience within Cognitive Resources Theory. This measure was used in a laboratory study of leadership effectiveness in which half of the groups were placed under conditions of evaluation apprehension. It was found that leaders high in leadership self-efficacy reported less stress than those low in leadership self-efficacy, and they did not experience performance decline under stress conditions as did those leaders low in self-efficacy. The results of a laboratory study by Watson and Chemers (1995), using this same measure of leadership self-efficacy, showed that in the face of negative feedback from their work groups, leaders high in self-efficacy persevered and continued working on the task, even when they were told that their group members wanted to dismiss them. Two additional field studies showed that high levels of self-efficacy were related to rated leadership performance (Murphy, Chemers, Kohles, & Macaulay, 2000). However, self-efficacy did not mediate the relationship between a leader's years of experience and performance as might be suggested by Cognitive Resources Theory. In a later laboratory study, Hoyt, Watson, and Murphy (1997) found that leaders high in self-efficacy reported less anxiety and had better-performing groups than leaders low in self-efficacy. Moreover, the leader's level of self-efficacy contributed independently over and above the group member's own self-efficacy for group performance.

Zaccaro (1995) offers a further explanation of Cognitive Resources Theory within his own model of leader effectiveness (see Chap. 3, this volume) that provides one possible explanation for the role of self-efficacy in leader self-regulation. The two requirements of effective leadership within Zaccaro's theory are ego resiliency and social intelligence (Zaccaro, et al. 1991). Ego resiliency refers to a disposition reflecting "resourceful adaptation to changing circumstances and environmental contingencies and flexible invocation of a repertoire" (Mumford, Baughman, Threlfall, Uhlman, & Costanza, 1993, p. 250). The second component is social intelligence, which includes social perceptiveness and behavioral flexibility. Social perceptiveness provides an ability to perceive the requirements of organizational situations and respond appropriately to these requirements (Zaccaro, et al. 1991). According to Zaccaro (1995), "successful leaders are less likely to be caught in situations of high interpersonal stress and, when confronted by interpersonal stressors, less likely to be thwarted by them" (p. 34). Why is this the case? Both ego resiliency and social intelligence provide "emotional mechanisms to either cope with stressors or by providing the capacity to develop coping strategies that ameliorate or eliminate interpersonal stressors" (p. 34). Experience by definition should enhance ego resiliency, social intelligence, or other personal qualities that promote stress management.

Leadership self-efficacy, therefore, appears to be an important component in understanding leadership self-regulation. Self-efficacy as a measure of a person's belief in the ability to execute a course of action and overcome obstacles should also be what leaders learn through years of experience. Self-efficacy helps the leader reevaluate stressors in situations. High self-efficacy leaders in our studies perceived less stress than those low in self-efficacy when stress was manipulated in laboratory studies, or they reported fewer stress symptoms and workplace stressors in field studies (Hoyt, Watson, & Murphy, 1997; Murphy, 1992; Murphy, Halverson, & Riggio, 1999; Murphy, Chemers, Kohles, & Macaulay, 2000).

THE ROLE OF EMOTIONAL AND SOCIAL INTELLIGENCE IN SELF-REGULATION

Cognitive Resources Theory incorporates a limited set of leader cognitive resources; choosing to focus on leader experience, and traditional measures of intelligence. Two additional forms of intelligence, social and emotional, are important leader resources that have implications for leader self-regulation. These intelligences may work in two ways. The first, and most obvious manner, is as a general ability that has a direct and positive effect on leadership functioning. The second way emotional and social intelligence may contribute to effective leadership is more indirect through their interaction with situational challenges. Leaders high in social and emotional intelligence may be better able to engage in self-regulatory processes. In this capacity, these forms of intelligence may operate in the same manner in which experience contributes to performance as Fiedler (1995), Zaccaro (1995), and Sternberg (1995) describe.

The concept of emotional intelligence recently has received much attention in the popular press (Goleman, 1995). Emotional intelligence is defined as a person's ability to manage their emotions successfully and also to understand the emotions of others (Salovey & Mayer, 1990). The specific components include the ability to recognize your own emotions or your feelings as they happen; the ability to handle these emotions; the ability to engage in self-control to motivate oneself; the ability to recognize the emotions of others, and the ability to handle relationships. In addition, emotional intelligence has been cited as an important component in successful leadership (Goleman, 1998). But these types of skills—such as regulating emotions and reading others' emotional messages—have long been recognized as important components of effective leadership. For example McCall, Lombardo, and Morrison (1988) outline many of these same factors in their studies of what leaders learn from experience.

Previous research on the concept of social intelligence paved the way for much of the current thinking on emotional intelligence. Social intelligence gives people the readiness for the events of social life according to Cantor and Kihlstrom (1987). Social intelligence includes both declarative (concepts and memories of events) and procedural expertise (rules that operate on concepts and memories) for working on social tasks (Cantor & Kihlstrom, 1987). Social intelligence has a distinct definition that is different from emotional intelligence, but the constructs are not necessarily independent from one another. For example, part of understanding the subtleties of social situations and acting appropriately, therefore demonstrating social intelligence, requires emotional intelligence. Emotional intelligence should increase sensitivity to cues in a social environment and help control a person's responses to that situation. Social and emotional intelligence are also more broad-based than the concept of self-monitoring (Synder, 1974). The construct of self-monitoring, defined as the ability to monitor and control expressive behaviors, is more limited in that it only explains a portion of social and emotional intelligence components.

Both emotional and social intelligence have important implications for the social role of leadership (Zaccaro, see Chap. 3, this volume; Zaccaro, et al. 1991). Within the context of charismatic leadership theory, for example, these types of intelligence relate directly to a leader's ability to influence others. More successful leaders have the ability to communicate persuasively, either through the creative use of words that paint a compelling vision of the future for the organization or work group, or by the certainty with which the leader introduces the mission and the strategic plans to accomplish that mission (Conger, 1991). The second potential for influence comes from a leader's ability to tune into the needs of the followers. Those people who feel that they are truly understood may be more likely to listen to the leader's ideas and implement his or her plans. Both influence processes for leadership suggest the need for high levels of social and emotional intelligence. For example, sharing positive emotions in the form of enthusiasm, or monitoring negative emotions in order to maintain positive motivation for a work team, are both very important skills.

Our own research has looked at how forms of social and emotional intelligence contribute to leadership performance. The first exploratory studies attempted to identify patterns of contribution for the different dimensions of emotional intelligence. In one study of college seniors, a survey revealed that students highly involved in leadership activities had significantly different constellations of emotional intelligence dimensions than those less involved in leadership activities (Murphy, Johnson, & Johnson, 1996). Also SAT scores were not related to any of the dimensions of emotional intelligence, yet those with higher grade point averages reported engaging in more delay of gratification than did those with lower GPAs. In the second study, we used the statistical technique of cluster analysis to find how five components of emotional intelligence, as defined by Goleman (1995), combined into distinctive groupings that were related to measures of career success for a group of college alumni. The cluster analysis technique statistically separates dimensions that provide significant differences in distinctive groupings. There were three significantly different clusters across the five dimensions of emotional intelligence. One group consisted of alumni who scored high on all five dimensions. Another group was one in which the alumni scored high on knowing their own emotions and those of others, but were relatively low in other dimensions. Finally, members of the third group scored high in delaying gratification and moderately in self-control, but very low in knowing their own emotions and knowing those of others. Interestingly, those in the first group who had high scores on all dimensions had statistically significantly lower college GPAs than did the other two clusters, and they were more likely to be involved in high school leadership activities. In addition, the study showed overall that alumni who were high in managing their own emotions and delaying gratification reported higher levels of career satisfaction than those who scored lower on these dimensions (Murphy, Weiner, & Gopez, 1998). Both of these studies point to the importance of looking at how different dimensions of emotional intelligence either contribute uniquely or combine to produce positive outcomes.

In a recent study, Murphy, Halverson, and Riggio (1999) used the Social Skills Inventory (SSI), a self-report questionnaire that asks individuals to provide a self-rating of their own abilities to express and control their own emotions, and read others' emotions (Riggio, 1989). The questionnaire also measures the person's ability to express and control oneself in social situations, as well as sensitivity to appropriate behavior in social settings. Therefore, the measure includes an assessment of abilities and of self-regulatory strategies within both the social and emotional domains. For this laboratory study, leaders worked in groups of three (n = 70) on a personnel placement task that required the groups to make placement decisions fitting 30 resumes into 13 jobs. Half of the leaders were assigned to conditions of stress in which they were told that their performance as leaders, as recorded by videotapes, was to be forwarded to the career services office and scored for leadership potential. The remaining leaders were told only that their performance was being videotaped. The leaders in the stress condition were also told that they were to prepare a briefing to explain the strategies that their groups used. We obtained measures of leaders' self-efficacy, as well as recorded heart rate throughout the experiment. We hypothesized that self-efficacy would be negatively related to heart rate. We also hypothesized that leaders with higher emotional and social skills would have better group performance and group satisfaction across stress and no stress conditions. And finally, we predicted that stress would moderate the relationship between social skills and performance, such that a leader's social skills would be more strongly related to performance under stressful conditions. In other words, these types of social and emotional skills would act similarly to experience within Cognitive Resources Theory.

The results showed that self-efficacy was not related to heart rate in the low stress condition at task completion, but was related as hypothesized for the high stress condition. Further analysis using repeated measures ANOVA for the three heart rate measures showed that leadership self-efficacy predicted heart rate only in the stress condition. Both dimensions of the SSI were positively related to leadership self-efficacy ($r = .25$, $p < .05$ emotional skills, and $r = .38$, $p < .01$ for social skills). We were also interested in whether social and emotional intelligence became even more important under stressful situations. We found that a leader's level of emotional sensitivity to their own emotions and to those of others predicted group member satisfaction with leader performance across both conditions ($r = .26$, $p < .05$) and even more so for leaders in the stress condition ($r = .44$, $p < .01$). Emotional skills had a stronger correlation under stress than did social skills. With regard to task performance under stress, however, leaders high in social and emotional skills had poorly performing groups compared to leaders low in these skills ($r = -.52$, $p < .01$). In other words, leaders who cared little about their group members had better group performance as measured by quantity. It makes sense that more emotionally and socially skilled leaders will have more satisfied subordinates, but these same leaders may not necessarily have better performing groups for all types of tasks.

In summary, self-regulatory mechanisms shed additional light on the relationships of leader cognitive resources and situational challenges within Cognitive Resources Theory. A number of questions regarding underlying mechanisms, however, remain. For example, how do highly efficacious leaders convey their confidence in order to increase the group's performance? Emotional expressiveness may be a useful skill. Does self-efficacy mediate the relationship between abilities and successful performance? Also, while the role of stressors in Cognitive Resources Theory has been outlined extensively, there are additional sources of stressors not currently included in the model, that have further implications for explaining difficulties in enacting the role of leadership.

Threats to Successful Enactment of the Role of Leadership

The added pressure that women and minorities find in nontraditional roles or occupations within organizations may produce a number of stress reactions that affect their ability to lead in certain circumstances. Even though women and minorities have made tremendous inroads toward work equality as evidenced by their increasing numbers in many middle management jobs, women and minorities are still underrepresented in the upper echelons of America's top corporations (Morrison & Von Glinow, 1990). In addition, there are many professions that still remain dominated by White males. Women and minorities, therefore, continue to face situations in which their membership in underrepresented groups produces many challenges.

Biases and negative stereotypes can affect these nontraditional leaders in two ways. First, stereotypes that others hold can interfere with accurate appraisals of performance and subsequent selection or promotion decisions. In a meta-analysis of gender and leader performance evaluation, Eagly, Makhijani, and Klonsky, (1992) found that women who acted in more masculine ways were rated more negatively than women who did not act in stereotypically masculine ways. However, these researchers did not find significant overall differences in performance evaluations of men and women leaders.

Women and minorities who are the first of their kind to fill organizational positions may find that they must work hard to overcome coworker stereotypes based on gender or ethnicity. Lord and Maher (1991) suggest that stereotypes of women, for example, that are incompatible with stereotypes/prototypes of effective managers, affect expectations of performance of female leaders. Furthermore, Ayman (1993) suggests that role-appropriate behavior for either females or minority leaders may be in conflict with behaviors that are role-appropriate for managers. These stereotypes, therefore, can greatly affect perceptions of women and minorities.

A second manner in which biases and negative stereotypes can affect nontraditional leaders is that they can produce numerous psychological thoughts or self-doubts about one's capabilities that may interfere with successful performance. Bandura (1997) cites studies showing "that even highly talented individuals make poor use of their capabilities under circumstances that undermine their beliefs in themselves" (pg. 37, from Bandura & Jourden, 1991). Claude Steele and his colleagues discuss the vulnerability that comes from the thoughts surrounding the possibility of fulfilling a negative stereotype, or what they have called "stereotype threat," and the implications for that person's performance (Steele & Aronson, 1995, Steele, 1997; 1999). In a number of studies, participants are placed in evaluative situations and through various means reminded of their membership in a stigmatized group. The results showed that when Black students were led to believe that the test would be diagnostic of their ability, they brought to mind the stereotypes others hold of them and they performed less well than when they were told the test was not diagnostic of ability (Steele & Aronson, 1995). This same type of threat was activated when White males were exposed to the stereotype that Asians perform better at math (Aronson, et al. 1998). For stereotype threat to occur, a person must identify with the domain in question. For example, research showed that women who were highly identified with respect to math ability were affected by stereotype threat and had decrements in performance, while those not so identified had no decrements in performance (Steele, 1999). Nontraditional leaders, especially those for whom leadership is important (highly identified), may suffer performance decrements when they are reminded of their membership in stigmatized groups, and therefore have stereotypes activated that others might hold regarding their potential leadership performance.

Organizational characteristics such as structures and policies may foster additional biases or stereotypes for women or minority leaders. For instance, policies such as affirmative action, and perhaps some ineffective diversity training efforts, can increase self-doubt for women and minorities if they are led to believe that they are unfair recipients of preferential treatment. In a series of studies by Heilman and her colleagues, it was found that implying that an individual receives a managerial position based on preferential treatment rather than merit affects both others' ratings of that candidate (Heilman, Block, & Lucas, 1992; Heilman, Block, & Stathatos, 1997), and the candidates' own ratings of their capabilities if the candidate is a female (Heilman, Simon, & Repper, 1987; Heilman, Battle, Keller, & Lee, 1998). Organizational demography, or the extent to which the organization is homogenous or heterogeneous along demographic lines (Pfeffer, 1983; Tsui, Egan, & O'Reilly, 1992), may also affect the level of self-doubt experienced by these new leaders. This self-doubt can be the result of actual biases, or self-inflicted because of perceived token status. Finally, power differentials in organizations also have implications for successful enactment of the leadership role. According to Ragins (1995), power differentials in organizations stem from cultural, structural, and behavioral factors. Cultural factors include the organizational factors that determine what behaviors will be rewarded in the organization. Certain styles, of leadership for example, will be encouraged and rewarded. In addition, according to Ragins, power holders in the organization will maintain the status quo of the organizational culture. Structural factors within organizations dictate power bases, and historically women and minorities are often in less powerful positions within the organization. These positions can be based on rank or function. Finally, behavioral factors suggest that even if women and minorities engage in the same influence behaviors, these behaviors will be perceived differently than if White males exhibit the same behaviors. All of these factors, affirmative action policies, organizational demography, and power differentials in organizations, produce added challenges for women and minorities when enacting the role of leader.

In two studies examining both self-efficacy and optimism levels of leaders new to their positions, we found that these self-concepts were helpful in understanding performance (Murphy, Chemers, Kohles, & Macaulay, 2000). A study of state employees revealed that while self-efficacy and optimism were positively related to both male and female managers' rated performance, moderated regression analyses revealed that these abilities were even more important for female managers. In other words, the nature of the relationship was stronger for female managers compared to male managers. A study of fast food restaurant managers produced a similar set of results. In this study, we obtained multiple measures of restaurant performance. We found an overall small relationship between leadership self-efficacy or leader optimism and measures of quality performance. However, this relationship was moderated by the leader's objective status in the organization. Leaders with low levels of job-related experience, and leaders who were either female or male minority status, had better-performing restaurants with respect to quality of food and service when they possessed high levels of self-efficacy and optimism.

In summary, these additional sources of stressors have important implications within a self-regulative view of leadership. First, certain stressors will interfere with the utilization of specific skills and abilities. In other words, a leader with sufficient intelligence, experience, and social skills may have difficulty translating these into behaviors because of self-doubt or lowered self-efficacy. Secondly, stressors in a situation may impede the effectiveness of exhibited behaviors to contribute to performance. As mentioned previously, the second form of interference is similar to the thinking we see in expectancy theories of motivation in the path from effort to performance (or expectancy) (Vroom, 1964). Imagine a leader who has behaved in a situationally appropriate manner, yet because of coworkers' negative stereotypes about the leader's group membership, or the leader's low power base, those behaviors are ineffective in producing high performance. Furthermore, if these behaviors are initially ineffective, the leader will eventually change his or her behavior to attempt to find something that works.

UNRESOLVED ISSUES AND IMPLICATIONS OF A SELF-REGULATIVE APPROACH TO LEADERSHIP

The self-regulative approach provides a rich area for future research to understand effective leader performance. Moreover, this approach affords an understanding of how situational factors enhance or distract an individual from enacting the leadership role. The area of social cognition, however, still contains a number of additional insights that may help explain successful and less than successful leadership performance, but are beyond the scope of this chapter. For example, there is a large literature explaining motivational components of self-assessment (see Fiske & Taylor, 1991 for review). These components include accurate self-assessment (Trope, 1983), self-enhancement (e.g., Greenwald, Bellezza, & Banaji, 1988; Taylor & Brown, 1988), self-evaluation with respect to other's behavior (Tesser, 1988), and self-confirmation or verification (Swann & Read, 1981) to name a few. Some of these motivational aspects have been explored within the area of impression management in organizations (e.g. Arkin & Sheppard, 1989), and have further implications of how the self will be presented to others. Issues of self-handicapping (see Arkin & Baumgardner, 1985, for different forms of handicapping behavior), or self-affirmation (Steele, 1988), and self-inflation determine the types of activities a leader will use to manage others' impressions. In addition, Carver and Scheier (1981; 1998) have a cybernetic model of self-regulation that incorporates some of these motivational processes, but provides more detail regarding underlying processes than the model presented in this chapter. All of these areas provide an extremely fertile ground for additional research to understand leader behavior. While the approach described in this chapter almost exclusively emphasizes leadership from the leader perspective at the exclusion of followers, future research could also include the reciprocal nature of leadership by examining follower reactions to leader self-regulation.

Incorporating social and emotional intelligence within a self-regulative view of leadership is an important contribution, but does not represent a throwback to standard trait theory approaches to leadership. These constructs fall within a new approach to understanding the role of traits along the lines of the ideas of Zaccaro, Foti, and Kenny (1991). Their research shows that certain traits, such as self-monitoring, actually contribute to performance to a greater degree than once thought. A high level of self-monitoring may give leaders behavioral flexibility that leads to better performance. Social and emotional intelligence may work in the same way. Leaders with high levels of these skills are perceptive of situational requirements and then have the skills to change their behavior to act in ways that are appropriate to the situation (Zaccaro, et al. 1991). Cognitive resources theory also helps us understand how situational factors will determine when social and emotional intelligence will contribute to task performance. For example, stress may interfere with the effective use of a leader's social intelligence on novel tasks, but not with the use of emotional intelligence. Social intelligence requires resources to determine features of the situation and decide how to behave appropriately. However, emotional intelligence may act more like experience and will help deal with stress and respond effectively. Further research is needed to understand exactly how these new forms of intelligence help leader performance.

There are a number of advantages that are the outgrowth of a social cognitive view of leadership from the perspective of leader self-regulation. A major implication of this perspective lies in enhancing leadership development strategies. In order for leaders to effectively enact the role of leader, appropriate prototypes for leadership, as well as self-schema, must be developed. In addition, training and experiences must work to increase self-efficacy for the role of leadership. This would include overcoming issues of self-doubt, faulty attributions, and self-inflicted stereotypes for all leaders. According to Bandura (1997) behavior change occurs in a number of ways—including enactive mastery, persuasion, and vicarious learning. A number of researchers have used Bandura's ideas (e.g., Gist & Mitchell, 1992) and those of self-management to improve individual job-related behavior. Direct application of self-management strategies in organizational functioning has been examined in the context of self-management strategies for reducing absenteeism (Frayne & Latham, 1987; Latham & Frayne, 1989); and also within the context of improving self-efficacy and the subsequent use of training on the job (Gist, Stevens, Bavetta, 1991). These techniques can be incorporated into existing leadership development programs.

CONCLUSION

In conclusion, expanding leadership research by understanding how people think and feel about themselves (self-efficacy), and how they use their skills and self-regulation strategies (emotional and social intelligence), is a unique area for understanding ways to choose and develop successful leaders.

REFERENCES

Arkin, R. M., & Baumgardner, A. H. (1985). Self-handicapping. In J. H. Harvey & G. Weary (Eds.), *Attribution: Basic issues and applications* (pp. 169–202). New York: Academic Press.

Arkin, R. M., & Sheppard, J. A. (1989). Self-presentation styles in organizations. In R. Giacalone & P. Rosenfeld, (Eds.), *Impression management in the organization*, pp. 125–139, Hillsdale, NJ: Lawrence Erlbaum Associates.

Aronson, J., Lustina, M. J., Good, C., Keough, K., Steele, C., & Brown, J. (1999). When white men can't do math: Necessary and sufficient factors in stereotype threat. *Journal of Experimental Social Psychology, 35,* 29–46.

Aronson, J., Quinn, D. M., & Spencer, S. J. (1998). Stereotype threat and the academic underperformance of minorities and women. In J. Swim and C. Stangor (Eds.*), Prejudice: The target's perspective*. Academic Press.

Avolio, B. J. & Bass, B. M. (1988). Transformational leadership, charisma, and beyond. In J. G. Hunt, B. R. Balliga, H. P. Dachler, & C. A. Schriesheim, *Emerging leadership vistas.* Lexington, MA: D. C. Heath.

Avolio, B. J., & Gibbons, T. C. (1988). Developing transformational leaders: A life span approach. In J. Conger & R. Kanungo (Eds.), *Charismatic leadership: The elusive factor in organizational effectiveness*, pp. 276–308, New York: Wiley.

Ayman, R. (1993). Leadership Perception: The role of gender and culture. In M. Chemers & R. Ayman, (Eds.), *Leadership theory and research: Perspectives and directions*, pp. 137–166, San Diego, CA: Academic Press.

Bandura, A. (1986). *Social foundations of thought and action*. Englewood Cliffs, NJ: Prentice Hall.

Bandura, A. (1988). Reflection on nonability determinants of competence. In R. J. Sternberg & J. Kolligian, Jr (Eds.), *Competence considered: Perceptions of competence and incompetence across the lifespan*, pp. 315–362. New Haven, CT: Yale University Press.

Bandura, A. B. (1997). *Self-efficacy: The exercise of control.* New York: W.H. Freeman.

Bandura, A., & Cervone, D. (1983). Self-evaluative and self-efficacy mechanisms governing the motivational effects of goal systems. *Journal of Personality and Social Psychology*, 45, 1017–1028.

Bandura, A., Cioffi, D., Taylor, C. B., & Brouillard, M. E. (1988). Perceived self-efficacy in coping with cognitive stressors and opioid activation. *Journal of Personality and Social Psychology, 55*, 479–488.

Bandura, A. & Jourden, F. J. (1991). Self-regulatory mechanisms governing the impact of social comparison on complex decision making. *Journal of Personality and Social Psychology, 8*, 99–108.

Bandura, A., & Wood, R. (1989). Effects of perceived controllability and performance standards on self-regulation of complex decision making. *Journal of Personality and Social Psychology, 56*, 805–814.

Barling, J. & Beattie, R. (1983). Self-efficacy beliefs and sales performance. *Journal of Organizational Behavior Management, 5*, 41–51.

Bass, B. M. (1990). *Bass & Stogdill's handbook of leadership*. New York: Free Press.

Bass, B. M. (1985). *Leadership and performance beyond expectations*. New York: Free Press.

Blades, J. W. & Fiedler, F. E. (1973). *The influence of intelligence, task ability, and motivation on group performance*. (Organizational Research Tech. Rep. 76–78). Seattle: University of Washington.

Bons, P. M. (1974). *The effects of changes in leadership environment on the behavior of task- and relationship-motivated leaders*. Unpublished doctoral dissertation, University of Washington, Seattle.

Cantor, N. & Kihlstrom, J. F. (1987). *Personality and social intelligence*. Englewood Cliffs, NJ: Prentice Hall.

Carver, C. S., & Scheier, M. F. (1981). *Attention and self-regulation: A control theory approach to human behavior*. New York: Springer-Verlag.

Carver, C. S., & Scheier, M. F. (1998). *On the self-regulation of behavior*. Cambridge: Cambridge University Press.

Chemers, M. M. (1997). *An integrative theory of leadership*. Mahwah, NJ: Lawrence Erlbaum Associates.

Chemers, M. M. & Murphy, S. E. (1995). Leadership and diversity in groups and organizations. In M. M. Chemers, S. Oskamp, and M. A. Costanzo, (Eds.), *Diversity in organizations,* Thousand Oaks, CA: Sage.

Conger, J. A. (1989). *The charismatic leader*. San Francisco: Jossey-Bass Publishers.

Conger, J. A. (1991). Inspiring others: The language of leadership. *Academy of Management Executive, 5(1)*, 31–45.

Conger, J. A. & Kanungo, R. N. (1988). *Charismatic leadership: The elusive factor in organizational effectiveness*. San Francisco: Jossey Bass Publishers.

Dansereau, F., Jr., Graen, G., & Haga, W. J. (1975). A vertical dyad linkage approach to leadership within formal organizations: A longitudinal investigation of the role-making process. *Organizational Behavior and Human Performance, 13*, 46–78.

DeMatteo, J. S., Dobbins, G. H., Myers, S. D., Facteau, C. L. (1996). Evaluations of leadership in preferential and merit-based leader selection situations. *Leadership Quarterly, 7(1)*, 41–62.

Eagly, A. H., Makhijani, M.G., & Klonsky, B. G., (1992). Gender and the evaluation of leaders: A meta-analysis. *Psychological Bulletin, 111*, 3–22.

Fiedler, F. E. (1967). *A theory of leadership effectiveness*. New York: McGraw-Hill.

Fiedler, F. E. (1995). Cognitive resources and leadership performance. *Applied Psychology: An International Review, 44*, 5–28.

Fiedler, F. E. (1994). *Leadership experience and leadership performance*. Seattle, WA: United States Army Research Institute for the Behavioral and Social Sciences.

Fiedler, F. E., & Garcia, J. E. (1987). *New Approaches to Effective Leadership: Cognitive Resources and Organizational Performance*. New York: Wiley.

Fiske, S. T. & Taylor, S. E. (1991). *Social cognition*. New York: McGraw Hill.

Fortune Magazine, June 21, 1999. P. Sellers, pp. 80–82.

Frayne, C. A. & Latham, G. P. (1987). Application of social learning theory to employee self-management of attendance. *Journal of Applied Psychology, 72(3)*, 387–92.

Frost, D. E. (1983a). *The effects of interpersonal stress on leadership effectiveness*. Unpublished doctoral dissertation, University of Washington, Seattle.

Frost, D. E. (1983b). Role perceptions and behavior of the immediate supervisor; Moderating effects on the prediction of leadership effectiveness, *Organizational Behavior & Human Decision Processes, 31,* 123–142.

Gardner, W. & Avolio, B. J. (1998). The charismatic relationships: A dramaturgical perspective. *Academy of Management Review, 23*(1), 32–58.

Gist, M. E., & Mitchell, T. R. (1992). Self-efficacy: A theoretical analysis of its determinants and malleability. *Academy of Management Review, 17*, 183–211.

Gist, M. E., Stevens, C. K., & Bavetta, A. G. (1991). Effects of self-efficacy and post-training intervention on the acquisition and maintenance of complex interpersonal skills. *Personnel Psychology, 44(4)*, 837–861.

Glynn, S. M., & Ruderman, A. J. (1986). The development and validation of an eating self-efficacy scale. *Cognitive Therapy and Research, 10*, 403–420.

Goleman, D. (1995). *Emotional intelligence*. New York: Bantam Books.

Goleman, D. (1998). *Working with emotional intelligence*. New York: Bantam Books.

Graen, G. (1976). Role-making processes in complex organizations. In M. D. Dunnette (Ed.), *Handbook of industrial and organizational psychology* (1201–1245). Chicago: Rand McNally.

Graen, G., & Scandura, T. (1987). Toward a psychology of dyadic organizing. In B. Staw & L. L. Cumming (Eds.), *Research in organizational behavior* (Vol. 9, pp. 175–208). Greenwich, CT: JAI Press.

Greenwald, A. G., Bellezza, F. S., & Banaji, M. R. (1988). Is self-esteem a central ingredient of the self-concept? *Personality and Social Psychology Bulletin, 14,* 34–45.

Hall, R. J. & Lord, R. G. (1998). Multilevel informal-processing explanations of followers' leadership perceptions. In F. Dansereau & F. Yammarino, (Eds.), *Leadership: Multiple-level approaches*. (Monographs in organizational behavior and industrial relations, vol. 24, part B, pp. 159–183, S. Bacharach (Ed).) Stamford, CT: JAI Press.

Heider, F. (1958). *The psychology of interpersonal relations*. New York: Wiley.

Heilman, M. E., Battle, W. S., Keller, C. E., & Lee, R. A. (1998). Type of affirmative action policy: A determinant of reactions to sex-based preferential selection? *Journal of Applied Psychology, 83(2),* 190–205.

Heilman, M. E., Block, C. J., & Lucas, J. A. (1992). Presumed incompetent? Stigmatization and affirmative action efforts. *Journal of Applied Psychology, 77,* 536–544.

Heilman, M. E., Block, C. J., & Stathatos, P. (1997). The affirmative action stigma of incompetence: Effects of performance information. *Academy of Management Journal, 40*, 603–625.

Heilman, M. E., Simon, M. C., & Repper, D. P. (1987). Intentionally favored, unintentionally harmed? The impact of sex-based preferential selection on self-perceptions and self-evaluations. *Journal of Applied Psychology, 72*, 62–68.

Hersey, P. & Blanchard, K. H. (1982). *Management of organization behavior: Utilizing human resources* (4th ed.). Englewood Cliffs, NJ: Prentice Hall.

Horn, J. L. (1968). Organization of abilities and the development of experience. *Psychological Review, 75*, 242–259.

House, R. (1977). A 1976 theory of charismatic leadership. In J. G. Hunt & L. L. Larson (Eds.), *Leadership: The cutting edge*. Carbondale: Southern Illinois University Press.

Hoyt, C. L., Watson, C. B., Murphy, S. E. (1997). *Group leadership: The stress buffering effects of confidence and optimism.* Paper presented at the Western Psychological Association, Seattle Washington, April.

Hughes, R. L., Ginnett, R. C., & Curphy, G. J. (1998). *Leadership: Enhancing the lessons of experience, 3rd Ed.* Chicago: Irwin.

Jones, E. E. & Davis, K. E. (1965). From acts to dispositions: The attribution process in person perception. In L. Berkowitz (Ed.), *Advances in experimental social psychology* (Vol. 2, pp.220–266). New York: Academic Press.

Kelley, H. H. (1967). Attribution theory in social psychology. In D. Levine (Ed.), *Nebraska Symposium on Motivation* (Vol. 15, pp.192–240). Lincoln: University of Nebraska Press.

Latham, G. P. & Frayne, C. A. (1989). Self-management training for increasing job attendance: A follow-up and a replication. *Journal of Applied Psychology, 74(3)*, 411–416.

Leary, M. R. (1989). Self-presentational processes in leadership emergence and effectiveness. In R. Giacalone & P. Rosenfeld, (Eds.), *Impression management in the organization*, Hillsdale, NJ: Lawrence Erlbaum Associates.

Lent, R. W., Brown, S. D., & Larkin, K. C. (1984). Self-efficacy in the prediction of academic performance and perceived career options. *Journal of Counseling Psychology, 33,* 265–269.

Lewter, J. & Lord, R. G. (1993). *Affect, self-schemas, and transformational leadership*. Unpublished manuscript.

Liden, C., Wayne, S. J., & Stilwell D. (1993). A longitudinal study on the early development of leader-member exchanges. *Journal of Applied Psychology, 78(4),* 662–674.

Locke, E. A., Frederick, E., Lee, C., & Bobko, P. (1984). The effect of self-efficacy, goals, and task strategies on task performance. *Journal of Applied Psychology, 69*, 241–251.

Lord, R. G. & Maher, K. J. (1991). Cognitive theory in industrial and organizational psychology. In M. D. Dunnette & L. M. Hough (Eds.), *Handbook of industrial and organizational psychology* (Vol.2, pp.1–62), 2nd ed. Palo Alto, CA: Consulting Psychologists Press.

Lord, R. G. & Maher, K. J. (1993). *Leadership and information processing: Linking perceptions and performance*. Boston, MA: Rutledge.

Manz, C. C. (1986). Self-leadership: Toward an expanded theory of self-influence process in organizations. *Academy of Management Review, 11*, 585–600.

Manz, C. C. (1990). Beyond self-managing work teams: Toward self-leading teams in the workplace. In R. Woodman & W. Pasmore (Eds.), *Research in organizational change and development* (Vol. 4, pp. 273–299). Greenwich, CT: JAI Press.

Manz, C. C., & Sims, H. P., Jr. (1980). Self-management as a substitute for leadership: A social learning perspective. *Academy of Management Review, 5,* 361–367.

Manz, C. C., & Sims, H. P., Jr. (1986). Leading self-managed groups: A conceptual analysis of a paradox. *Economic and Industrial Democracy, 7*, 141–165.

Markus, H. & Wurf, E. (1987). The dynamic self-concept: A social psychological perspective. *American Review of Psychology, 38,* 299–337.

Markus, H., Cross, S., & Wurf, E. (1990). The role of the self-system in competence. In R. J. Sternberg & J. Kolligian, Jr. (Eds.), *Competence considered* (pp. 205–225). New Haven, CT: Yale University Press.

Maslow, A. (1954). *Motivation and personality*. New York: Harper.

Mayer, J. D., Salovey, P., & Caruso, D. R. (1996). *Multifactor Emotional Intelligence Scale*.

McCall, M. W., Lombardo, M. M., & Morrison, A. M. (1988). *The lessons of experience*. Lexington, Massachusetts: Lexington Books.

Meindl, J. R. (1990). On leadership: An alternative to the conventional wisdom. In B. M. Staw & L. L. Cummings (Eds.), *Research in organizational behavior* (Vol. 12, pp. 159–203). Greenwich, CT: JAI Press.

Meindl, J. R. (1993). Reinventing leadership: A radical, social psychological approach. In J. K. Murnighan (Ed.), *Social psychology in organizations*. Englewood Cliffs, NJ: Prentice Hall.

Meindl, J. R., Ehrlich, S. B., & Dukerich, J. M. (1985). The romance of leadership. *Administrative Science Quarterly, 30*, 78–102.

Morrison, A. M. & Von Glinow, M. A. (1990). Women and minorities in management. *American Psychologist, 45,* 20–208.

Mumford, M. , Baughman, W., Threlfall, K. V., Uhlman, C. E., & Costanza, D. P. (1993). Personality, adaptability, and performance: Performance on well-defined and ill-defined problem-solving tasks. *Human Performance, 6,* 241–285.

Murphy, S. E., (1992). *The contribution of leadership experience and self-efficacy to group performance under evaluation apprehension*. Unpublished doctoral dissertation, University of Washington.

Murphy, S. E., Halverson, S. & Riggio, R. *Effects of leader self-regulation on group performance under stress*. Paper presented at the Western Psychological Association, April 1999, Irvine, CA.

Murphy, S. E., Weiner, S., & Gopez, A. (1998). *Factors contributing to perceived career success: The role of emotional intelligence and other self-referent attitudes*. Paper presented at the Western Psychological Association, April 1998, Albuquerque, NM.

Murphy, S. E., Johnson, C. S., & Johnson, M. B., (1996). *A study of high school experiences and college outcomes: The role of confidence, optimism, and power motive in leadership roles*. (Working paper).

Murphy, S. E., Chemers, M. M, Kohles, J., & Macaulay, J. L. (2000). The contribution of leadership self-efficacy to performance under stress: An extension of cognitive resource theory. Paper under review.

Neck, C. P. (1998). The rest of the self-leadership story. In F. Dansereau & Yammarino, *Leadership: The multiple-level approaches*. Stanford, CT: JAI Press.

Neck, C. P., & Manz, C. C. (1996). Thought self-leadership: The impact of mental strategies training on employee cognition, behavior, and affect. *Journal of Organizational Behavior*, 17(5), 445–467.

Pfeffer, J. (1983). Organizational demography. In L. L. Cummings & B. M. Staw (Eds.), *Research in organizational behavior* (Vol. 5, pp. 299–357). Greenwich, CT: JAI Press.

Ragins, B. R. (1995). Diversity, power, and mentorship in organizations: A cultural, structural, and behavioral perspective. In M. Chemers, S. Oskamp, & M. Costanzo, *Diversity in organizations: New perspectives for a changing workplace*, (pp. 91–132). Thousand Oaks, CA: Sage.

Riggio, R. E. (1989). *Manual for the social skills inventory*. Palo Alto, CA: Consulting Psychologists Press.

Salovey, P. & Mayer, J. D. (1990). Emotional intelligence. *Imagination, cognition, and Personality, 9(3)*, 185–211.

Sarason, I., Potter, E., & Sarason, B. (1986). Recording and recall of personal events: Effects on cognition and behavior. *Journal of Personality and Social Psychology, 51*, 357–356.

Scheier, M. F., & Carver, C. S. (1985). Optimism, coping, and health: Assessment and implications of generalized outcome expectancies. *Health Psychology, 4*, 219–247.

Smith, J. A. & Foti, R. J. (1998). A pattern approach to the study of leader emergence. *Leadership Quarterly, 9(2)*, 147–160.

Sosik, J. J., & Dworakivsky, A. C. (1998). Self-concept based aspects of the charismatic leader: More than meets the eye. *Leadership Quarterly, 9(4)*, 503–526.

Steele, C. M. (1988). The psychology of self-affirmation: Sustaining the integrity of the self. In L. Berkowitz (Ed.), *Advances in experimental psychology*, (Vol.21, pp. 261–302). New York: Academic Press.

Steele, C. M. (1997). A threat in the air: How stereotypes shape the intellectual identity and performance. *American Psychologist, 52*, 613–629.

Steele, C. M. (1999). Thin ice: "Stereotype threat" and black college students. *Atlantic Monthly, 284(2)*, 44–54.

Steele, C. & Aronson, J. (1995). Stereotype threat and the intellectual test performance of African Americans. *Journal of Personality and Social Psychology, 69*, 797–811.

Sternberg, R. (1995). A triarchic view of "cognitive resources and leadership performance." *Applied Psychology: An International Review, 44,* 29–32.

Swann, W. B., & Read, S. J., (1981). Self-verification processes: How we sustain our self-conceptions. *Journal of Experimental Social Psychology, 17*, 351–370.

Synder, M. (1974). The self-monitoring of expressive behavior. *Journal of Personality and Social Psychology, 30,* 526–537.

Taylor, S. E., & Brown, J. D. (1988). Illusion and well-being: A social psychological perspective on mental health. *Psychological Bulletin, 103*, 193–210.

Tesser, A. (1988). Toward a self-evaluation maintenance model of social behavior. In L. Berkowitz (Ed.), *Advances in experimental social psychology* (Vol. 11, pp. 289–338). New York: Academic Press.

Trope, Y. (1983). Self-assessment in achievement behavior. In J. M. Suls and A. Greenwald, (Eds.), *Psychological perspectives on the self* (Vol. 2, pp. 93–122). Hillsdale, NJ: Lawrence Erlbaum Associates.

Tsui, A. S., Egan, T. D., & O'Reilly, C. A., III. (1992). Being different: Relational demography and organizational attachment. *Administrative Science Quarterly, 37*, 549–579.

Vroom, V. H. (1964). *Work and motivation*. New York: McGraw-Hill.

Watson, C. B., & Chemers, M. M. (1995). *The resilience of confident and optimistic leaders*. Paper presented at APA in New York, August 1995.

Weiner, B. (1979). A theory of motivation for some classroom experiences. *Journal of Educational Psychology, 71*, 3–25.

Wood, R. E. & Bandura, A. (1989). Impact of conceptions of ability on self-regulatory mechanisms and complex decision making. *Journal of Personality and Social Psychology*, 56, 407–415.

Wood, R. E. & Locke, E. A. (1987). The relation of self-efficacy and grade goals to academic performance. *Educational and Psychological Measurement, 47*, 1013–1024.

Zaccaro, S. J. (1995). Leader resources and the nature of organizational problems. *Applied Psychology: An International Review, 44*, 32–36.

Zaccaro, S. J., Foti, R. J., & Kenny, D. A. (1991). Self-monitoring and trait-based variance in leadership: An investigation of leader flexibility across multiple group situations. *Journal of Applied Psychology, 76*, 308–315.

Zaccaro, S. J., Gilbert, J. A., Thor, K. K., & Mumford, M. D. (1991). Leadership and social intelligence: Linking social perceptiveness to behavioral flexibility. *Leadership Quarterly, 2*, 317–347.

Zajonc, R. B. (1965). Social facilitation. *Science, 149*, 269–274.

11

Culturally Intelligent Leadership for a Diverse World

Lynn R. Offermann and Ly U. Phan
George Washington University

Less than a mile from our university is a branch of a major organization that currently employs 815 people in the Washington, DC area. At present, their workers speak at least 36 languages, representing a wide variety of cultures. Managers supervise a staff where about 65% are foreign-born. No, we are not talking about one of those well-known international organizations housed in DC—their staff would be even more diverse—we are talking about the Washington Hilton, a large hotel dependent on the collaborative efforts of men and women from around the world to serve and satisfy their equally diverse customers. For the Hilton, and many other organizations throughout the U.S., cultural diversity is not merely a concept for the future, it is today's reality.

What is also a reality is the fact that those in positions of leadership have, by and large, not been trained to deal with this kind of cultural diversity. Nor have we, as scholars of leadership, devoted much time to carefully rethinking our traditional theories and models to accommodate this far more diverse followership (Offermann, 1998). Yet research taking an organizational demography perspective has shown clear effects of employee demographic attributes on organizational outcomes. For example, racial/ethnic dissimilarity compared to others in the group has been found to predict low commitment and intention to stay in the organization, as well as greater absenteeism (Tsui, Egan, & O'Reilly, 1992). Such dissimilarity has also been associated with less favorable attitudes toward the group and the perception of poorer promotion opportunities (Riordan & Shore, 1997).

In terms of leadership, demographic differences between leaders and the led have been shown to make a difference in terms of both effectiveness and satisfaction. In their study of supervisor-subordinate demographic similarity, Tsui and O'Reilly (1989) found that increasing disparity between superior-subordinate demographic characteristics was associated with lower superior ratings of subordinate effectiveness, less attraction toward subordinates, and the experience of greater role ambiguity by subordinates. Work by Chong and Thomas (1997) with ethnic groups in New Zealand also found higher levels of follower satisfaction when leaders and followers were ethnically similar. This suggests that leaders may need to make greater efforts to overcome tendencies to work more effectively with demographically similar staff if the talents of a diverse workforce are to be fully realized. We are suggesting that the ability to engage in the mental processes and adaptive behaviors needed to function effectively as a leader in collective environments in which there is a diverse followership is culturally intelligent leadership.

WHY CULTURAL INTELLIGENCE?

In recent years, the concept of intelligence has broadened immensely. Indeed, the primary emphasis of this book is on the many ways in which people can express superior capabilities that reflect high "intelligence." We argue that one of them is the ability to function effectively in a diverse context where the assumptions, values, and traditions of one's upbringing are not uniformly shared with those with whom one needs to work. If culture is considered the collective mental programming that distinguishes members of one human group from another (Hofstede, 1980), then cultural intelligence is the ability to successfully function in environments where individuals have experienced different programming. This is decidedly a type of "intelligence in context," where the "right answers" are dependent on the situation and people involved. In many situations, there may be no single appropriate response, and successful responses made by one person may not be successful when tried by another. Hence, effective responding will likely require as much understanding of self as of other.

Cultural intelligence as so defined is new research terrain. We are not dealing with global comparisons of leadership behavior, an area that has been and continues to be researched (see House, Wright, & Aditya, 1997). Though familiarity with this literature on leadership patterns in different cultures is instructive for those aspiring to culturally intelligent leadership, it does not deal with the capability of altering one's behavior to fit the situation, or determining when it is in one's best interest to do so. As some U.S. women managers have found out, trying to lead "like a man" often backfired, as some behaviors acceptable in men were seen as inappropriate for women (Morrison, White, & Van Velsor, 1992). Followers are not easily fooled. Rather, there must be an attempt to find that portion of one's own style that maintains effectiveness across a variety of situations. Our focus here will be on broadly pluralistic situations, where the simpler (but by no means simple) identification and learning of a single additional culture's traditions is impractical.

We view cultural intelligence as a life skill in today's pluralistic societies that is particularly relevant to those who seek to lead. Though cultural intelligence is adaptive and desirable for all who function in multicultural environments, leaders and followers alike, the responsibility for maximizing the value of a diverse workforce disproportionately falls on those who seek to lead. Leaders are, and will be, increasingly called upon to be the champions of diversity, the models of skillful cross-cultural behavior, and the mediators of cross-cultural conflict. More and more, successful leadership will become synonymous with culturally intelligent leadership.

In this chapter, we briefly discuss cultural differences in intelligence, taking a contextualistic position that cultural variability in the adaptiveness of specific behaviors affects concepts of intelligence cross-culturally, and arguing that individual leaders may be more prone to define intelligence according to their own cultural traditions to the detriment of capable but differing staff. We then focus on differences in cultural values and expectations as they relate to leadership and expectations of leadership, and highlight literature on the successful management of cultural diversity within work organizations. Finally, implications for leadership will be discussed, including equity issues, the role of organizations in developing shared norms and practices, and options for developing more culturally intelligent leadership.

Cultural Variations in "Intelligence"

Cross-cultural researchers often differentiate between those concepts that are common across cultures, called etics, and those concepts that are more specific to particular cultures, called emics. The concept of intelligence clearly has both etic and emic aspects. For example, solving novel problems is one etic aspect of intelligence, though how one goes about doing this may be emic (Brislin, 1993). Within any culture, "intelligence" will be defined as the possession of key, valued skills and behaviors in the eyes of members of that culture. We now understand that because cultures may differ in the salience attached to particular skills and the ideal combination of cognitive processes, it is reasonable to expect that people from different cultural backgrounds would vary in the way in which they solve problems and in the patterns of skills they acquire (Segall, Dasen, Berry, & Poortinga, 1990). Different socialization practices will emphasize the development of modes of knowing that have relevance and value in a particular cultural context. Children practice thinking in the context of goal-directed activities, and these activities and their goals are expressions of culture (Gauvain, 1998). Thus, cultural differences in cognition are increasingly acknowledged, though interpreted through the lens of cultural relativism. Although components of intelligence may be universal across cultures, their manifestations are not (i.e., Segall, et al. 1990; Sternberg, 1988). Simply put, what it means to be smart depends on where you are.

Trouble begins when we mistake our own cultural emic view of intelligence for a universal etic. As noted by Hall (1981), "Western man uses only a small fraction of his mental abilities; there are many different and legitimate ways of thinking; we in the West value one of these ways above others—the one we call "logic," a linear system that has been with us since Socrates" (p. 9). Thus, traditional Western intelligence tests may measure well the values of Western society such as academic achievement, quick responses, and analytical thinking processes, but provide poor measurement of the forms of knowing that are adaptive and valued in other types of societies (Miller, 1997). For example, many African views of intelligence encompass not only the more "technological" aspects of intelligence concerning aptitude and know-how, but a "social" component as well (Mundy-Castle, 1974). In these societies, school-based knowledge would not be considered part of intelligence unless it could be put to use in service of one's social groups, namely, family and community (i.e., Dasen, et al. 1985; Mundy-Castle, 1974). It is only recently that concepts of social intelligence are beginning to be reflected in Western thinking about intelligence as well (see Murphy, Chap. 10, this volume), as more current models of intelligence broaden to encompass more than merely analytic forms of intelligence (e.g., Gardner, 1983; Sternberg, 1985).

Given these differences, it is possible to be considered highly intelligent in one culture and intellectually lacking in another, based on the same skills or behaviors exhibited. For example, one common emic aspect of intelligence in many parts of the world deals with processing speed, a feature built into many Western intelligence tests. Yet speed is not universally valued. For example, the Baganda people of Uganda associate intelligence with careful, slow, and deliberate thought (Wober, 1974). They value the careful consideration of many alternative solutions, with slow internal examination before sharing thoughts with others. Imagine one of the Baganda in a U.S.-style corporate brainstorming session!

Cultural intelligence, then, encompasses many of the skill sets now referred to as different forms of intelligence. For example, emotional intelligence, defined as the ability to perceive and understand emotions as well as to regulate them (Mayer & Salovey, 1997), is clearly important in cultural intelligence. The greater self-awareness and empathy associated with emotional intelligence (Goleman, 1995) would be expected to promote better cross-cultural interaction. Likewise, social knowledge and expertise, components of social intelligence (Cantor & Kihlstrom, 1987) would also be important. We see cultural intelligence as a meta-intelligence, encompassing a variety of forms of intelligence (including the traditional analytic skills) and enacting them outside of the frame of reference in which they were developed. Most of us have developed intelligences within a particular cultural frame, and the most successful among us presumably function better in that context. Yet these intelligences may be culture-dependent (e.g., Willmann, Feldt, & Amelang, 1997). Cultural intelligence is what allows us to transcend our cultural programming and function effectively in cross-cultural situations, either within or between nations. It is the capability of leaving behind those intelligent behaviors learned in one context when what is intelligent in another context differs.

In order for a leader to function effectively across cultural boundaries, that is, to embody what we have called cultural intelligence, a leader needs to accept that individual followers will come to the workplace with different patterns of intelligent behavior that may or may not be seen as intelligent in the present setting. Leaders need to be able to identify the behaviors that are truly required by the work involved or that are so valued as to be undisputedly mandated by the organization. Is on-the-spot responding really critical, or would a predistributed agenda with questions allow those with more reflective thinking patterns to participate more fully? Our experience suggests that leaders may unduly limit the domain of acceptable job behavior to that with which they are culturally familiar, and attempt to force others into that mold, experiencing predictable difficulties in the process. Yet the true prospect for leading a diverse workforce is to capitalize on the varied skills and capabilities brought by diverse staff rather than attempt to homogenize them.

We suggest that culturally intelligent leadership with diverse followers requires a three-prong approach: 1) understanding the impact of one's own culture and background in terms of the values (and hence, often biases) one brings to the workplace, as well as the expectations held for self and other in a leader-follower relationship; 2) understanding the other(s), and their comparable values, biases, and expectations; and 3) being able to diagnose and adaptively match appropriate leadership behaviors and expectations to specific cross-cultural situations. We will turn first to the two elements of cultural understanding—of self and others—and then to the issue of adaptation.

CULTURAL VALUES AND LEADERSHIP

Leader behavior may take many forms, but will nonetheless be consistent with cultural norms (Erez & Earley, 1993). Culture is the primary shaper of everyone's behavior (Segall, Lonner, & Berry, 1998), and leaders are no exception. Of the available categorizations of cultural values, the most noted has been the work of Hofstede (1980, 1991). Based on his pioneering study of about 88,000 IBM employees in over 60 countries, Hofstede proposed four dimensions of organizationally relevant cultural value differences: Power Distance, Uncertainty Avoidance, Individualism-Collectivism, and Masculinity-Femininity. His work suggests the relevance of these cultural values to understanding leadership behavior worldwide.

Perhaps the most heavily investigated of the four dimensions is Individualism-Collectivism, a value that differentiates between cultures in which individual identity, goals, and personal choice are revered and those in which a strong collective identity exists linking individuals to cohesive in-groups over a lifetime (Triandis, McCusker, & Hui, 1990). In individualistic cultures, organizational practices may allow for and expect greater individual initiative, while in collectivistic cultures, there may be a greater emphasis on teams. The promotion of leadership as an ideal is an inherently individualistic notion, as opposed to advocating the value of group membership. Likewise, the concept of power distance is clearly relevant to the study of leadership in that it deals directly with expectations of and relationships to authority. Power distance is defined as the extent to which there is an acceptance of unequal distribution of power within a culture. In low power distance cultures, leader-subordinate relations are theoretically close and less formal in nature; in high power distance cultures these relationships are expected to be more distant, hierarchically ordered, and reserved. High power distance scores indicate a preference for autocratic and paternalistic management, while low power distance should be more compatible with managerial consultation and approachability.

Uncertainty avoidance is the extent to which members of a culture prefer certainty and predictability and find ambiguity stressful. Members of high uncertainty avoidance cultures prefer rules and stable jobs with long-term employers; members of low uncertainty cultures may be more willing to take risks, change employers, and tolerate organizational ambiguity and change. High uncertainty avoidance cultures have been called "tight" in that there are clear norms and expectations that people behave exactly as specified by those norms; "loose" cultures allow more latitude in behavior (Triandis, 1994). Given the strong theoretical relationship of perceptions of uncertainty and ambiguity with aspects of decision making and policy formation (i.e., Jackson & Dutton, 1988), relationships between uncertainty avoidance and leadership behavior in organizations is likely. Leaders from high uncertainty avoidance cultures should be more likely to find ways to exert and keep control (certainty) in their work units. In addition, the masculinity-femininity dimension distinguishes between cultures in which assertiveness, challenge, and ambition are highly valued (so-called masculine cultures) and cultures in which greater emphasis is placed on cooperation and good working relationships (so-called feminine cultures). These differences have implications for what goals leaders may reasonably pursue and the behaviors that they may expect from followers. A summary of these four cultural values and their potential impact on leadership and followership appears in Table 11.1.

Subsequent multinational studies by a group of 24 researchers calling themselves the Chinese Culture Connection (1987), as well as work by Schwartz (1992) and Trompenaars (1994), have acted as a validity check on Hofstede's dimensions, producing substantial overlap with Hofstede's work (Helmreich & Merritt, 1998). The Chinese study was designed with an intentionally non-Western bias as a balance to Hofstede's work, and identified another unique dimension not

TABLE 11.1
Cultural Implications for Organization Leadership

INDIVIDUALISM/COLLECTIVISM:

Individualism	**Collectivism**
Leadership is idealized	Membership is the ideal
Emphasis on individual initiative and achievement	Emphasis on belonging to groups
Fulfill obligations to self (self-actualization)	Fulfill obligations to in-group
Value standards apply to all: "Universalism"	Value standards differ for in and out-group members: "particularism"
Staff members are expected to defend their own interests	Staff expect the leader and organization to defend loyal members
Freedom and challenge in jobs important	Training and use of skills in jobs important
Individual initiative encouraged	Individual initiative frowned upon
Everyone has a right to their own private life and opinions	Private life is integrated with in-groups; opinions are predetermined

POWER DISTANCE:

Large Power Distance	**Small Power Distance**
Everyone has rightful place in social order	Inequality in society should be minimized
Leaders are entitled to special privileges	All should have equal rights
Power is based on family/friends/charisma/force	Power is based on position and expertise
Respect for advanced age	No respect for advanced age per se
Greater centralization; leaders make decisions	Less centralization; decision making spread out
Inaccessibility of leaders accepted	Leaders should be accessible
Subordinates expect to be told what to do by leaders	Subordinates expect to be consulted by leaders

UNCERTAINTY AVOIDANCE:

Strong Uncertainty Avoidance	**Weak Uncertainty Avoidance**
Concern with security in life	More willing to take risks
Clear social norms, written rules	Few clear norms or written rules
Intolerance of deviance; different is dangerous	Tolerant of deviance; difference is curious
Belief in experts and their knowledge	Belief in generalists and common sense
Leaders more involved in details	Leaders more involved in strategy
Subordinates expect leaders to have answers	Leader can legitimately say "I'll find out"
Subordinate initiative should be controlled	Delegation to subordinates can be complete

(Continued)

TABLE 11.1
(Continued)

MASCULINITY/FEMININITY:

Feminine	**Masculine**
Roles for men and women overlap	Separate roles for men and women
Quality of life and environment important	Performance and growth important
Interdependence idealized	Independence idealized
Small and slow are beautiful	Big and fast are beautiful
Equality and solidarity are emphasized	Equity and competition emphasized
Work is less central in people's lives	Work is more central in people's lives
Lower job stress; shorter hours preferred	Higher job stress; more salary preferred over shorter hours

found by Hofstede, a dimension they called Confucian Dynamism. This factor reflects a long-term orientation incorporating perseverance and thrift adopted by many Confucian cultures in Asia, and was integrated by Hofstede as a fifth dimension into his recent thinking as well (Hofstede, 1991). Together, these various researchers have identified multiple cultural values that appear broadly applicable and relevant to the study of leadership in cross-cultural environments.

Understanding the Self

These cultural values theoretically affect both the leader and the led. However, it is more often the case that discussions of leadership focus on the need for understanding others without a comparable consideration of understanding oneself. Yet, as Hall (1981) states, "Culture hides much more than it reveals, and, strangely, it hides itself most effectively from its own participants. The real job is not to understand foreign cultures, but to understand one's own." Though the impact of a leader's own culture may not be apparent to him or her, followers can see it. For example, Offermann and Hellmann (1997) present evidence that cultural values held by managers can relate to what subordinates see as their manager's leadership style. In this study, both power distance and uncertainty avoidance were associated with leadership ratings. As predicted, power distance was significantly and negatively associated with leader communication, delegation, approachability, and team building. This is consistent with the view that high power distance is associated with a greater tendency for the leader to autocratically retain power him or herself, rather than empower others through sharing information, delegation, and team building. Uncertainty avoidance was significantly associated with the leadership behaviors displaying control, and significantly negatively associated with delegation and approachability. Leaders taught to value certainty may be more likely to act on this value by exerting more control over staff and sharing less power with them.

It is interesting to note that the findings that cultural values predicted leadership behavior previously described were discovered with a sample of internationally well-traveled managers. These managers had not been isolated from exposure to other views, and indeed the nature of their work guaranteed substantial exposure. Yet cultural differences in the leadership behaviors they were perceived as exhibiting closely followed predictions based on elements of cultural background. Theorists of cultural influences have long maintained that the impact of early cultural socialization is felt throughout one's lifetime despite exposure to other cultures. For example, work by Shackelton and Ali (1990) showed that Pakistanis in Great Britain scored closer on power distance and uncertainty avoidance to Pakistan than their current home, despite a lifetime spent in Britain. Thus, experience and travel alone appear insufficient in eliminating basic culturally endorsed values.

Care must always be taken in interpreting such cross-cultural data. In any culture, individuals will show patterns of within-country variation around the central tendency representing the values of the society in general. Thus, conclusions should be viewed at the group level. It should not be construed that any particular leader or manager will behave in a particular way, but rather that when a group of managers from countries with a certain value orientation are averaged, that average may differ in predictable ways from averages based on groups of individuals from cultures with other value orientations. Further, any single cultural value may be less informative than the pattern produced by examining multiple values simultaneously and in interaction. However, together these values yield important information about the orientation and potential predilection of many leaders.

Unfortunately, many leaders, like people in general, are unaware of the cultural lenses they use to view the world, or how their own acculturation affects the way in which they view others. The ethnocentric tendency to use one's own group as the standard of correctness against which all others are judged sets the stage for in-group bias (Triandis, 1994; Gudykunst & Bond, 1997). Bias is not, however, inevitable. As noted by Gudykunst and Bond (1997), it is possible for people to value their own heritage without denigrating that of others.

In the U.S., many people dislike the notion of being "programmed" by culture and prefer to deny the impact of the collective on individual thought and behavior, sometimes even denying that there is a U.S. "culture." Consistent with the U.S. ranking as one of the most highly individualistic nations in the world, many Americans do not like being grouped into any cultural category, preferring to see their behavior as freely and individually chosen. Yet non-Americans see clear patterns of U.S. cultural values just as we see those of others, primarily through differences with our own. In Hofstede's (1980) terms, the U.S. is individualistic, low in power distance, low in uncertainty avoidance, and masculine in orientation. This translates into a culture that values individual happiness, equality, practicality, is comfortable with change, achievement-oriented, and data-driven (Hoppe, 1998). Of course, not all Americans share these values any more than citizens of other nations share theirs. It is, however, a cultural heritage that underlies much of current U.S. management philosophy, including an emphasis on individual responsibility, individual rewards, action-orientation, valuing tasks over relationships, a measurement-driven approach, and a focus on short-term gains and "quick wins," just to name a few. It is also a cultural heritage that needs to be acknowledged and understood before trying to understand others.

Understanding Others

The same cultural dimensions affecting leader behavior affect followers as well, and they, too, often go through life unaware of how their views have been shaped by culture. Understanding at a practical level the implications of cultural values on everyday work behavior is a wise investment in cross-cultural sensitivity. However, while leaders can, and we believe should, learn about core dimensions of cultural values, they must also take care not to categorize or stereotype individual persons based on group membership. We as individuals are not our cultural categories. Leaders must remember that within-culture variation can be as great or greater as that between cultures.

As observers of staff behavior, leaders, like any of us, presumably make certain attributions for the causes of the behaviors observed. Psychological research on attribution theory suggests that people commonly make attributional errors, the most basic of which is the tendency to overestimate the contribution of personal, dispositional factors in observed outcomes as opposed to situational factors (i.e., Nisbett & Ross, 1980). Though well-documented with Euro-American samples, people from other cultural groups may attribute the sources of behavior elsewhere. For example, there is evidence that Asians may focus more on social roles, obligations, and situational constraints (Markus, Kitayama, & Heiman, 1996). Regardless of the direction of bias, if leaders make erroneous attributions for the performance of diverse followers, their behavior may also be inappropriate. Recent U.S. work by Offermann, Schroyer, and Green (1998) found that leader attributions about the causes of subordinate performance can affect the way in which a leader subsequently interacts with them, with leaders more behaviorally active in working with groups who they believed performed poorly due to effort (an unstable cause) rather than ability (a stable cause). Based on this work, if a leader misattributes unsatisfactory performance of culturally different staff to lack of ability (rather than, say, lack of clarity about what they were supposed to do or knowledge of how to do it to the leader's satisfaction), it would be predicted that the leader may give up on them and miss the opportunity to coach people who could perform well. The leader then may harbor low expectations of those who are different, denying them needed support, which in turn becomes a self-fulfilling prophecy (Eden, 1990). Understanding others builds on self-knowledge, including knowledge of one's own attributional biases, so that leaders can more appropriately diagnose difficulties and select more effective responses.

Culturally intelligent leadership also means a commitment to understanding the strengths and weaknesses of the various approaches represented by multicultural staff, and combining them creatively for maximum organizational performance. For example, Hofstede (1991) suggests the potential for synergy between innovating (low uncertainty avoidance) cultures that are more tolerant of new or deviant ideas and implementing cultures (stronger uncertainty avoidance) that may have superior skills with detail in making innovative ideas become reality. He notes that consistent with their levels of tolerance for uncertainty, the U.K. has produced more Nobel Prize winners than Japan, but Japan has put more new products on the world market. At the individual level, culture may be one of a number of factors affecting capabilities on the job, and allowing each person to contribute their best, combined with others with different strengths, offers the best prospects for maximum achievement.

This view represents the antithesis of assimilation and homogenization: the metaphor of the U.S. melting pot has justifiably given way to a mosaic, maintaining the identity and contribution of different pieces in the context of a larger organizational creation. Research on diversity in groups has found great potential for enhanced creativity and performance in diverse groups, as different perspectives are combined (Triandis, Kurowski, & Gelfand, 1994). Unfortunately, this potential may not be realized if effective communication and cooperation cannot simultaneously be preserved. Evidence suggests that multicultural groups in practice can be either highly effective or ineffective depending on whether diversity is successfully managed (Adler, 1990). If destructive conflict is allowed to fester, performance will be hurt; if divergent perspectives are used to generate and develop new ideas in a mutually supportive and learning-oriented environment, performance can be enhanced. Often, it falls on the group's leader to be able to bring out the best from diverse perspectives in a way that maintains positive interpersonal relations.

Based on cultural differences in values, follower expectations of their leaders may also differ significantly. Hence, endorsement of any particular leadership strategy as universally "best" or most desired by followers is unlikely. Although extensive multinational studies are currently underway to further examine leadership in global perspective and assess commonalities (House, Wright, & Aditya, 1997), even where commonalities are found, leadership expectations and preferences are still likely to be affected by cultural values in important ways. For example, leader consideration (a commonly found leadership dimension in many studies) may be widely favored by staff, yet expectations for what consideration entails may be very different based on culture. Smith, Misumi, Tayeb, Peterson, and Bond (1989) supported the universal relevance of leader consideration, but also indicated that a leader who discusses a follower's personal problems with others in their absence was viewed as considerate in Japan but as violating the follower's privacy in the U.S. Likewise, Schmidt and Yeh (1992) identified common leader influence strategies across Australian, English,

Japanese, and Taiwanese managers, but noted that both their relative importance and tactical definition differed by nationality.

Other leadership behaviors are very likely to differ significantly in degree of cross-cultural endorsement. For example, while in some countries delegation may be seen as positive behavior for a leader, high use of delegation may be viewed by individuals from other countries (particularly those high in power distance) as weak leadership. Followers from different backgrounds may come with very different expectations of their leaders, and behave in accordance with those expectations. Therefore, the culturally intelligent leader must be prepared and able to adapt their ways of interacting with diverse staff to accommodate cultural differences and to help their multicultural staff to better adapt to the demands of their organizations.

CULTURALLY ADAPTIVE LEADERSHIP

Understanding oneself and others in terms of cultural conditioning is the foundation of successful leader adaptation. And it is leader adaptation that is at the heart of culturally intelligent leadership. Many organizational models and approaches have historically advocated some tailoring of style to situation, with the core aspects of the situation attended to defined differently by different models. Traditional needs models of work motivation suggest core individual differences in what people want from work, and what they find most satisfying, preferences that may well be affected by culture. The path-goal model of leadership (House, 1996) and the expectancy models of work motivation on which it is based advocate that leaders help staff to feel efficacious in their work, assigning them tasks which are within their competence, and removing barriers that would inhibit their successful performance. In this view, it is the role of the leader to provide that which the task itself does not, to clarify if needed, to provide necessary resources, or otherwise support the staff member in his or her progress towards goal accomplishment. Given that staff members have different needs and backgrounds, different leadership behaviors would be required with different staff members.

More recently, models of transformational leadership (i.e., Bass, 1997) have emphasized the importance of individualized consideration—a tailoring of leader consideration behavior to the developmental needs of different staff. While all of these models suggest the importance of modifying leadership to situational needs, we suggest that one of the key bases for tailoring is cultural differences. Unfortunately, many "tailored" theories progress to categorize followers into groups based on some commonality (i.e., in-group vs. out-group, level of maturity), and the temptation to try to categorize staff by culture is strong as well. We worry that some diversity programs in the U.S. have gone awry in teaching leaders new categorical "boxes" into which they can place unsuspecting staff based on culture of origin. Though these attempts may be well meaning, they may be ineffective, or worse yet, offensive. For example, despite cultural traditions, not all Japanese dislike being singled out for praise, and some Americans do. Errors can be costly in terms of good will and employee motivation.

In addition, our world is developing into one in which a hybridization of culture is more common, and where "different and contrasting cultures can be part of a repertoire of collective voices playing their part in a multivoiced self" (Hermans & Kempen, 1998, p. 1118). To artificially categorize a complex human being on the basis of membership in a single group—even on the basis of a strong force like culture—is to limit understanding of what makes that person give or withhold his or her talents to a project or organization. Every person belongs to multiple groups. Ferdman (1995) has proposed the concept of cultural identity, that is, one's personal image of the cultural features of one's group(s), together with one's own feelings about those features and how they may be reflected in oneself. Given this complexity, true adaptation—true cultural intelligence—means a willingness to forgo the boxes, and to treat people as unique combinations of values, preferences, and needs. Understanding each individual in all his or her complexity holds the best promise of developing meaningful and positive leader–follower relations.

This is no easy task. Culturally intelligent leadership is not for the so-called "cognitive miser." Although the literature suggests that people are capable of individuating thought in processing information, shortcutting category-based stereotyping is commonly believed to require cognitive effort or motivation (Fiske & Neuberg, 1990). Marshaling the effort required depends on the clear understanding of why it is "intelligent" for the leader to do so.

WHY MANAGE DIVERSITY?

Cox and Blake (1991) reviewed the major benefits of diversity management, which include reducing cost due to decreased turnover rate among members of minority groups and broadening creativity from people with various perspectives. The benefits of diversity appear at many levels. Research has shown that top management teams in multinational corporations also benefit from cultural heterogeneity, and can achieve better performance without a loss of cohesion (Elron, 1997). Evidence suggests that companies that implement good diversity management programs are more likely to attract and retain employees as well as create a good reputation in the market. In contrast, poor diversity management can substantially hold back the organization. For example, Williams and Bauer (1994) found that individuals examining alleged organizational recruiting materials that either did or did not feature a managing diversity program evaluated the organization with the diversity program as significantly more attractive to them. This suggests that providing support for a diverse workforce may be a potent recruiting tool. As the workforce continues to diversify, maintaining a positive environment for diverse staff may differentiate those organizations able to attract and keep the best talent from those who cannot.

In contrast, failure to manage diversity effectively may lead to increases in stress for both leaders and followers. Indeed, Andre (1995) coined the term diversity stress to capture the negative feelings that can occur when personal resources are inadequate to understand and respond effectively in multicultural situations. For diverse staff, perceived discrimination has been found to be a significant organizational stressor, affecting levels of organizational commitment and job satisfaction (Sanchez & Brock, 1996). Dissatisfaction and stress can then lead talent to look elsewhere for employment.

Successful diversity management also appears to be good for organizational profit. Wright, Ferris, Hiller, and Kroll (1995) present evidence that investors bid up the stock price of organizations that were recognized by the U.S. Department of Labor for their high quality affirmative action programs. In addition, these authors also found that announcements of discrimination settlements were associated with significant negative changes in stock prices. Taken together, these studies strongly suggest that superior diversity management provides competitive benefits to an organization in a variety of ways. These benefits, in addition to the obvious reality that the U.S. workforce continues to diversify and hence failure to manage diversity becomes increasingly critical, should provide strong incentives for organizations to find new and better ways to optimize the potential of their diverse talent pools. For leaders, the benefits of success and the risks of failure should create potent motivation to see it in the best interests of both themselves and their organizations to develop the skills of culturally intelligent leadership.

SUCCESSFUL LEADERSHIP WITH DIVERSE FOLLOWERSHIP

One way to begin to answer the question of how culturally intelligent leadership behavior can be developed is to examine the "best practices" used by organizations to help those in leadership positions work with diverse staff. Unfortunately, many U.S. organizations still put more emphasis on acquiring a diverse staff than they do on assisting leaders in working with these diverse followers once on board. Yet it is the leadership of diversity that most promises net business rewards as well as the sought-after retention of diverse staff.

Managing diversity in U.S. organizations is slowly moving from an orientation toward mere regulatory compliance to a view that the effective management of diversity is a mandatory requirement for financially competitive organizations. However, the inevitability and complexity of diversity still pose great challenges to organizational leaders, not only because diversity is multifaceted, but also because of the many environmental and organizational factors involved. Jamieson and O'Mara (1991) note the narrow U.S. perspective where more often than not, managing diversity initiatives only focus on differences in gender and ethnic groups. Indeed, many organizations claiming to aim at managing diversity effectively still devote the majority of their resources and energy to affirmative action programs, and measure success in terms of whether recruiters achieve quantitative requirements or goals. This focus is itself a reflection of the American value on objective quantification—if we have the right numbers, all must be well. We argue that actively recruiting a representative workforce or implementing affirmative action is only the first step in managing diversity. While it is certainly important to bring diversity into organizations, working successfully with the resulting diverse workforce requires further actions. Table 11.2 summarizes the theoretical and practical distinctions between affirmative action and diversity management approaches.

Diversity management is the organization's answer to the question of what does an organization do to maximize such diverse resources and to minimize potential problems that spring from cultural differences once a representative workforce has been achieved. Jamieson and O'Mara (1991) note that conventional approaches to managing diversity often isolated those who were viewed as "different" and usually

TABLE 11.2
Distinctions Between Affirmative Action and Diversity Management

Affirmative Action	*Diversity Management*
• Women, people of color, veterans, persons with disabilities	• All employees, customers, vendors, constituents, etc.
• Defined analysis steps (workforce analysis, availability, goal setting, etc.)	• Undefined
• Mandated for government contractors	• Voluntary
• Compliance reviewed by government	• Progress reviewed internally by management/stockholders
• Inclusion, upward mobility, terms and conditions of employment	• Inclusion, productivity, upward mobility, goal governance, competition, etc.

What's the Real Difference?

Affirmative Action	*Diversity Management*
• No linkage to business	• Linkage to business is everywhere
• If you do business with the government, you must do Affirmative Action	• If you do business in the global market, you must effectively manage diversity to become effective
• Builds a workforce including women and people of color	• Management strategies and actions that effectively recognize, accept, and utilize all employees. It creates and maintains an environment where employees can contribute creative ideas.

Source: Conference Board, 1997

assigned responsibility for diversity management solely to human resource departments. This approach is highly undesirable in that failure to retain diverse staff may be blamed on ineffective selection rather than poor management, producing a vain search for better recruitment methods (Thomas, 1990). Yet the prevention and management of diversity problems more reasonably falls to leaders throughout the organization, at all levels.

In general, facing the challenge of managing diversity often leads to the use of either an avoidance strategy (i.e., "do nothing"), a reactive strategy (i.e., respond to inquiry), or a proactive strategy (i.e., initiate interaction) (Mamman, 1996). Resistance to changing the organization's culture is a major obstacle for many diversity initiatives. According to Arredondo (1996), expressions of this resistance are revealed in defensive mechanisms such as denying the need for action and hoping problems will just go away, blaming those who complain, or projecting responsibility to higher levels of management. As Norton and Fox (1997) indicate, managing diversity requires elements of change at all levels of the organization and effective organizational change must maximize utilization of diversity. Practically, this means that the traditional organizational focus on conformity through assimilation needs to be replaced by a true understanding of integration and mutual adaptation (Offermann & Gowing, 1990).

BEST PRACTICES IN DIVERSITY MANAGEMENT: LESSONS LEARNED

Many organizations have initiated programs that are attempting to achieve significant cultural change in embracing and using diversity as an organizational strength. Table 11.3 briefly summarizes some types of initiatives, focusing mainly on those that help managers to work with a culturally diverse workforce. They are not guaranteed to be successful in all places, as success comes as much through commitment and careful implementation as form or design. Organizations vary widely in the scope and intensity of programs offered, requirements for participation, and opportunities for cross-cultural exchange. However, extracting from the experiences of many organizations, there are some commonalities that offer suggestions to leaders for developing competencies in managing in culturally different environments. Some illustrations follow, though this is by no means an exhaustive list.

- *View managing diversity as a business imperative.* Organizational culture is very important for an effective diversity program. Managing diversity must be a business priority of the organization to convey the message that actions are being taken in the best interests of the profitability and competitiveness of the organization. Leaders must be evaluated on their success in building and maintaining a diverse workforce (Conference Board, 1997;

TABLE 11.3
Common Diversity Management Initiatives

Goal	*Options*	*Purpose*
Organizational Support for Diversity	Caucus Groups	Communication links with upper management; Environments for personal and professional development Maintain/support relationship between majority and minority staff
	Recruitment	Maintaining a representative workforce
	Mentoring programs	Help staff learn unwritten rules Provide support and career guidance
	Targeted Training for Women/Minorities	Provide forum for dealing with additional issues faced by group members (i.e., harassment, stereotyping, prejudice) as well as basic training
Changing Attitudes	Cultural Sensitivity Programs	Increase knowledge of cultures, issues in working in a multicultural environment
	"Core Groups"	Informal network of discussion groups Identify unspoken stereotypes, break barriers
	Celebrating Differences Events	Awareness of contributions of other cultures
Leadership Training and Development	Diversity Management Programs	Teach managers how to work with a diverse workforce Develop interpersonal skills Understand the business case for diversity
	Coaching	One-on-one support for leader change

Sessa, 1992). Doing so emphasizes the intelligence of efforts to develop appropriate skills in working with multicultural staff.

- *Learn from other organizations, but import with care.* There is no one single recipe for managing diversity: each organization is unique in terms of demands, resources, and applicant pools (Jackson, 1992). Hence, strategies for managing diversity will need to be localized in consideration of each particular organization's needs and employees. What works in one organization with a different staff profile in terms of culture may not work in your organization. The earlier admonishment to know yourself and your own culture first can be extrapolated here to knowing your own organization and creatively addressing local needs.

- *Leaders must champion the implementation of diversity initiatives.* Top organizational leaders play an important role in diversity initiatives through their guidance and continuous support. Leaders can influence implementation of new policies, facilitate information flow at all levels of the organization, and provide financial support (Sessa, 1992). Leaders at lower levels likewise can see the vision through into practice, hopefully serving as models for other staff.

- *Set high expectations for all staff.* In their work examining the experiences of minorities in selective U.S. universities, Bowen, Bok, and Burkhart (1999) present evidence that a student with an 1100 admission board score in a school where others are in the 1300s does better on almost every count than the student with an 1100 score admitted to a school with an 1100 average. Their conclusion is simple: So-called "less-qualified" students rise to the challenge because that is what is expected of them. This conclusion is supported by years of organizational research on goal setting that likewise suggests that challenging goals promote superior performance (Locke & Latham, 1994). Organizations that do not expect as much from culturally dissimilar staff are likely to get less, hence perpetuating a self-fulfilling prophecy (i.e., Eden, 1990).

- *Provide training as an ongoing education process.* Subsequent to recruitment of a representative workforce, well-designed training is necessary to promote and to maintain this workforce. For example, Cox and Blake (1991) advocate the importance of training in managing and valuing diversity in order to increase awareness of diversity-related issues such as cultural biases and cross-cultural sensitivity, and in building essential skills for intercultural interactions. Aim at behavior change in support of chosen organizational values rather than attempt to change personal beliefs, and find ways to encourage cooperation despite differences.

- *Listen and watch—patiently*. Americans are not known to be patient people. Many in leadership positions in particular are highly action-oriented and expect prompt—even immediate—responses from staff. Meetings are to begin on time, and if someone doesn't make a point quickly enough, someone else is likely to finish the sentence for him or her. Other cultures are more reflective and are put off by the American focus on speed and time. High power distance and respect for position may make some persons reluctant to share their thoughts with their organizational leaders. Understanding others requires taking the time to actively listen and to carefully watch for potential cultural factors that may be interfering with a staff member's ability to function successfully. Listening to employees was a key theme for success articulated in a recent meeting of 400 executives dealing with workplace diversity issues (Conference Board, 1997), and recent work with international organizations suggests patience as an important quality for global leaders (Thorn & Prosper, 1999).

- *Mentor and share the informal rules*. People working in a foreign culture need assistance to help them learn new culture norms and expectations. For example, a Haitian woman attending Princeton credited a professor with helping her to adapt to her new environment. In her culture, she was taught not to openly disagree with her elders, and hence would not say anything when she disagreed with her professor. Through his prompting, both in class and throughout college, he encouraged her to say what she thought. With his help, she came to realize that "at Princeton, you have to talk. Otherwise people won't know that you understand the issue at hand or that you have your own opinion" (Bowen, Bok, & Burkhart, 1999, p. 147). Mentoring is a key way that culturally intelligent leaders can develop and nurture their staff toward effective performance.

- *Emphasize the importance of trust*. Dialogue among members of a diverse workforce must be a process of learning rather than a product of conflict settlements. As people with different values, beliefs, and traditions come together in dialogues, they rely on each other to help them struggle through their biases and assumptions. Because this is sensitive and can be threatening at times, the extent to which people are comfortable with sharing and learning depends greatly on their perception of psychological safety in the group (Walker & Hanson, 1992).

- *Watch out for backlash*. AT&T sent about 100,000 employees through programs to promote a multicultural workforce, only to find out that some of their White male employees felt left out and attacked. They ultimately designed a course to discuss issues of White men in diverse environments, only to be challenged by others who felt that diversity programs should stick to concerns of women and minorities (Swisher, 1995). Xerox had a similar experience with White men feeling left out, and learned that successful initiatives must make it clear that diversity is everyone, including White men (Sessa, 1992). Diversity programs need to be carefully evaluated, with those that exacerbate cultural tensions discarded in favor of those increasing tolerance and curiosity about other views (Nemetz & Christensen, 1996).

IMPLEMENTING CULTURALLY INTELLIGENT LEADERSHIP

Measurement issues. For those more culturally inclined towards measurement, new concepts call for new measures. In the case of cultural intelligence, work is needed to flesh out the concept and develop appropriate measures to identify it. Work on the measurement of social and tacit intelligences may provide models for this development, with the creation of scenario-based situational judgment tests to evaluate behavior-in-situation. Work on intercultural competence, too often insulated from the social sciences and focused exclusively on an elusive search for generic traits (Dinges & Baldwin, 1996), can nonetheless be an important resource in developing a more interdisciplinary approach that might have greater relevance to issues of leadership and followership.

Fairness issues. One of the practical difficulties with implementing a more individualized leadership style concerns potential fairness issues. Though it may mean different things in different places, one of the more universal (etic) ethical premises is that of fairness (Kidder, 1994), and leaders are typically charged with ensuring fairness in their units. However, operational definitions of fairness may be more emic. In the U.S., there is often a basic confusion between fairness and equality that dampens leader willingness to individualize treatment of staff. Some leaders believe that fairness must mean exactly equal treatment, without consideration to individual needs or capabilities, that is, all in a given position should have the same training, the same conditions, and the same freedoms. Clearly, such "equality" will limit the ability of leaders to give each staff member what he or she needs to be successful. In one local situation where Moslem staff requested to work through lunch and leave earlier during the daytime-fasting month of Ramadan rather than face the smells of the staff cafeteria, it was a manager's peers who objected to her accommodating the wishes of these religiously observant staff, not other staff (Grimsley, 1999). These managers apparently feared setting a precedent of accommodation that would then be difficult to break. Individualizing may require not only the intelligence to discern culturally appropriate adaptations, but also the courage to stand by one's judgments and defend them to one's own peers and management.

Individual factors. Cultural differences may also affect how willing a person is to work effectively in diverse company. It has been suggested that one of the legacies of high uncertainty avoidance is the belief that "what is different, is dangerous" (Hofstede, 1991, p. 109). Persons holding this value are likely to be more uncomfortable working in multicultural environments, as they may find the unpredictability of coworkers' behaviors to be anxiety-producing. In addition, the strong belief in the importance of rules—and their uniform application—may make leaders favoring uncertainty avoidance unable or unwilling to individualize treatment of staff with differing needs. They may need additional support in making the transition to a culturally diverse world.

Future research is needed to examine further the personality characteristics of individuals who are successful in functioning in diverse environments. One relevant example may be Snyder's (1979) concept of self-monitoring: the ability to diagnose situations and produce different behaviors depending on what would be most desirable in a given context. According to his research, high self-monitors are "chameleons" who can change adaptively in response to environmental needs. Self-monitoring has already been extended into the leadership literature, with evidence showing that high self-monitors are more likely to emerge as leaders than low self-monitors (Day, Schleicher, & Unckless, 1996) and may have better promotion rates (Kilduff & Day, 1994). Interestingly, a recent study by Warech, et al. (1998) found that managers with high self-monitoring ability were rated as more interpersonally effective by supervisors and assessment center assessors, though not by subordinates. Further examination of self-monitoring in cross-cultural leadership contexts including subordinate perceptions would certainly be appropriate.

Phillips and Ziller (1997) suggest another promising option. Drawing on the classic work of Allport (1954), who referred to the "habitual openmindedness" (p. 24) of tolerant people who resist categorizing others, they propose the concept of nonprejudice. Nonprejudice, to them, implies a universal orientation where perceivers accentuate similarities rather than differences between the self and others. Their work suggests that people high in universal orientation may be more accepting and less discriminating between members of majority and minority groups, and that individuating thought may be less effortful for them. Research extending this concept with organizational leaders and followers would be most instructive.

Organizational culture. Every organization can be thought of as having its own form of culture, which in turn may impact the advocated leadership styles and behaviors exhibited by its managers. Either through selective reward or promotion, organizational leaders may be encouraged to lead in certain ways and not others. Culturally intelligent leadership at senior levels within organizations needs to focus on what the organization is trying to accomplish and the role of diversity in accomplishing that mission. As the U.S. workplace continues to diversify, we believe that more organizations will come to understand that diversity is a business imperative, where continuing organizational success rides on the ability to nurture and develop culturally diverse staff. Success is certainly possible; many multinational and international organizations have thrived despite significant value differences among their culturally diverse employees. They have done it not by denying differences in values or perspectives, but rather by coalescing around shared organizational expectations and practices.

People do not need to think, feel, and act in similar ways in order to come to agreement on practical issues and work cooperatively (Hofstede, 1991). Culturally intelligent leaders have important roles in developing and communicating shared norms and practices in their diverse organizational communities. In their creative responses to the demands of diversity, leaders can help their organizations forge a collective perspective on "how we do things around here" that is an amalgam of different approaches, known by all, and which diverse people can endorse as their own even if it differs in significant respects from some of their culturally formed values. To the extent that different perspectives are integrated into organizational practices, we may expect greater comfort with them from a greater proportion of staff, as opposed to a more autocratic development approach emphasizing the traditions of a single national culture.

Leadership development. Consistent with our heritages, we believe that culturally intelligent leadership can be developed. The notion that leadership can be developed or learned at all is not be universally shared, and certainly the preferred means and purpose of such development may vary cross-culturally. It is absurd to think that development techniques created in one country will necessarily prove universally relevant and effective. Theoretical frameworks and assessment techniques must be carefully examined to determine cultural appropriateness. For example, the 360-degree feedback processes now widely popular in the U.S. are not universally embraced, and often experience problems when used cross-culturally (Leslie, Gryskiewicz, & Dalton, 1998). In the U.S., leadership development tends to emphasize practical experience and the development of the individual; in other parts of the world an emphasis on theoretical aspects, power dynamics, and development of shared collective leadership might be more appropriate (Hoppe, 1998). There are many ways in which one can learn the skills of culturally intelligent leadership.

Fortunately, there are many intercultural training and education opportunities available for leaders hoping to develop greater facility in this area (see Landis & Bhagat, 1996), and evidence suggests that even short-term training is usually beneficial (Triandis, 1994). Development goals often focus on three areas: changing people's thinking (increasing knowledge of cultural differences and issues), affective reactions (how to manage challenges and enjoy diversity rather than merely tolerate it), and changing actual behaviors (Brislin & Horvath, 1997). What is required from the student is a willingness to learn and a willingness to make mistakes and correct them. As Dalton (1998) notes, "An attitude of deep-seated courtesy and respect often buys forgiveness of behavior based on cultural misunderstanding" (p. 386). For U.S. leaders, the cultural heritage of greater risk tolerance and comfort with ambiguity may be a positive force for success in such intercultural training.

In their work on learning ability in international executives, Spreitzer, McCall, and Mahoney (1997) identified 14 behaviors and competencies that they suggest are indicative of those who are able to be effective in international experiences. Although their focus is on global executives, many of these behaviors are likely to be related to success in domestic experiences with international staff as well. In particular, skills like seeking opportunities to learn, being insightful and open to criticism, flexibility, seeking and using feedback, sensitivity to cultural differences, and being able to bring out the best in people are characteristics that bode well for any leader in diverse environments, at home or abroad.

Learning the competencies of cultural intelligence may take time and practice. The learner needs to be willing to acknowledge deficits and be willing to make mistakes in perfecting new approaches. There is evidence that concerns about performance, particularly early in skill acquisition, can override learning objectives (e.g., Kanfer & Ackerman, 1989). Successful leader-learners need to manage such performance concerns if they wish to move from initial states of unconscious incompetence in cultural matters, to conscious incompetence (awareness of learning needs), to become consciously competent in leading their culturally diverse staff. Over time, the skills of cultural intelligence may become more habitual, and the conscious competence of the learner may be replaced with the unconscious competence of the skilled leader (Wheeler, 1994).

CONCLUSION

Most current leadership theories have been created by and for persons from low power distance, low uncertainty avoidance, and highly individualistic cultures (particularly the U.S.). The generalizability of U.S.-based leadership approaches to other types of cultures must be determined, with the hope of developing a more globally relevant understanding of leadership behavior. Future emphasis in leadership theory must be given to greater meaningfulness from a global perspective (Peng, Peterson, & Shyi, 1991). As organizations become more global, it is critical that leadership theory and practice be increasingly reexamined through the lens of culture. In this chapter, we have tried to underscore the need for leadership theory to embrace a concept of cultural intelligence as a vital requirement for effective leadership in pluralistic societies.

What's a leader to do? It is clear that leaders in our global society will increasingly need to extend their skills in developing mature leader–follower relationships with culturally diverse followers (Graen & Wakabayashi, 1994). We have made a number of suggestions here, focusing on self-understanding, understanding others, and adapting one's own leadership behaviors to the needs of culturally diverse followers. This is the essence of culturally intelligent leadership. Changing laws and expectations is the easier part of moving toward diversity in organizations; the hard part is changing the myriad everyday behaviors and assumptions that often unintentionally exclude, demean, and limit the prospects of a culturally diverse workforce. Despite their more typically limited emphasis on gender and race, there are lessons to be learned from the experiences of U.S. organizations in their attempts at managing diversity. These lessons can help organizations develop practices compatible with today's diverse workforce, train both leaders and followers in cultural awareness and sensitivity, and help their staff to become more interculturally competent.

The most important step is to begin. As William Edwards, general manager of the Washington Hilton has learned, "If you don't have empathy and aren't able to communicate in diversity, or are uncomfortable around a multicultural workforce, or if you are not confident enough to give an opportunity to someone who has a heavy accent or is different, you'll be a miserable failure as a manager" (Grimsley, 1999, p. 12). The more successful alternative is what we call cultural intelligent leadership.

REFERENCES

Adler, N. J. (1990). *International dimensions of organizational behavior.* (2nd ed.). Boston, MA: Kent.

Allport, G. (1954). *The nature of prejudice.* Cambridge, MA: Addison-Wesley.

Andre, R. (1995). Diversity stress as morality stress. *Journal of Business Ethics, 14,* 489–496.

Arredondo, P. (1996). *Successful diversity management initiatives: A blueprint for planning and implementation.* Thousand Oaks, CA: Sage.

Bass, B. M. (1997). Does the transactional-transformational paradigm transcend organizational and national boundaries? *American Psychologist, 52,* 130–139.

Bowen, W. G., Bok, D., & Burkhart, G. (1999, January-February) A report on diversity: Lessons for business from higher education. *Harvard Business Review*, 139–149.

Brislin, R. (1993). *Understanding culture's influence on behavior.* Fort Worth: Harcourt Brace Jovanovich.

Brislin, R., & Horvath, A. (1997). Cross-cultural training and multicultural evaluation. In J. W. Berry, M. H. Segall, & C. Kafitgibasi (Eds.), *Handbook of cross-cultural psychology*, (Vol. 3, pp. 327–369). Boston, MA: Allyn & Bacon.

Cantor, N., & Kihlstrom, J. F. (1987). *Personality and social intelligence.* Englewood Cliffs, NJ: Prentice Hall.

Chinese Culture Connection (1987). Chinese values and the search for culture-free dimensions of culture. *Journal of Cross-cultural Psychology, 18*, 143–164.

Chong, L. M. A., & Thomas, D. C. (1997). Leadership perceptions in cross-cultural context. *Leadership Quarterly, 8,* 275–293.

Conference Board (1997). *Managing diversity for sustained competitiveness: A conference report.* Report No. 1195-97-CH. New York, NY: The Conference Board.

Cox, T. H. & Blake, S. (1991). Managing cultural diversity: Implications for organizational competitiveness. *Academy of Management Executive, 5*, 45–56.

Dalton, M. (1998). Developing leaders for global roles. In C. D. McCauley, R. S. Moxley, & E. Van Velsor (Eds.). *Handbook of Leadership Development*, (pp. 379–402). San Francisco: Jossey-Bass.

Dasen, P. R., Dembele, B., Ettien, K., Kabran, K., Kamagate, D., Koffi, D. A., & N'Guessan, A. (1985). N'glouele, l'intelligence chez les Baoule. {N'glouele, intelligence among the Baoule}. *Archives de Psychologie, 53,* 293–324.

Day, D. V., Schleicher, D. J., & Unckless, A. L. (1996, San Diego). Self-monitoring and work-related outcomes: A meta-analysis. Paper presented at the meeting of the Society for Industrial and Organizational Psychology.

Dinges, N. G., & Baldwin, K. D. (1996). Intercultural competence: A research perspective. In D. Landis & R. S. Bhagat (Eds). *Handbook of intercultural training*, 2nd ed. (pp. 106–123). Thousand Oaks, CA: Sage.

Eden, D. (1990) *Pygmalion in management: Productivity as a self-fulfilling prophecy*. Lexington, MA: D.C. Heath.

Elron, E. (1997). Top management teams within multinational corporations: Effects of cultural heterogeneity. *Leadership Quarterly, 8*, 393–412.

Erez, M., & Earley, P. C. (1993). *Culture, self-identity, and work*. New York: Oxford University Press.

Ferdman, B. M. (1995). Cultural identity and diversity in organizations: Bridging the gap between group differences and individual uniqueness. In M. M. Chemers & S. Oskamp (Eds). *Diversity in organizations: New perspectives for a changing work place*, (pp. 37–61). Thousand Oaks: Sage.

Fiske, S. T., & Neuberg, S. L. (1990). A continuum of impression formation, from category-based to individuating processes: Influences of information and motivation on attention and interpretation. In M. P. Zanna (Ed.), *Advances in experimental social psychology* (vol. 23, pp 1–74). New York: Academic Press.

Gardner, H. (1983). *Frames of mind: The theory of multiple intelligences*. New York: Basic Books.

Gauvain, M. (1998). Cognitive development in social and cultural context. *Current directions in psychological science, 7,* 188–192.

Goleman, D. (1995). *Emotional intelligence*. New York: Bantam Books.

Graen, G., & Wakabayashi, M. (1994). Cross-cultural leadership making: Bridging American and Japanese diversity for team advantage. In H. C. Triandis, M. D. Dunnette, & L. M. Hough (Eds.), *Handbook of industrial and organizational psychology*, (2nd ed.), Vol. 4, (pp. 415–446). Palo Alto, CA: Consulting Psychologists Press.

Grimsley, K. D. (1999). The world comes to the American workplace. *Washington Post,* March 20, p. A1..A12.

Gudykunst, W. B., & Bond, M. H. (1997). Intergroup relations across cultures. In J. W. Berry, M. H. Segall, & C. Kagitgibasi (Eds.). *Handbook of cross-cultural psychology* (Vol. 3, pp. 119–161). Boston, MA: Allyn & Bacon.

Hall, E. T. (1981). *Beyond culture*. New York: Doubleday.

Helmreich, R. L. & Merritt, A. C. (1998). *Culture at work in aviation and medicine: National, organizational, and professional influences*. Brookfold, VT: Ashgate.

Hermans, H. J. M., & Kempen, H .J. G. (1998). Moving cultures: The perilous problems of cultural dichotomies in a globalizing society. *American Psychologist, 53,* 1111–1120.

Hofstede, G. (1980). *Culture's consequences*. Newbury Park, CA: Sage.

Hofstede, G. (1991). *Cultures and organizations: Software of the mind*. London: McGraw-Hill.

Hoppe, M. (1998). Cross-cultural issues in leadership development. In C. D. McCauley, R. S. Moxley, & E. Van Velsor (Eds.). *Handbook of Leadership Development*.(pp. 336–378). San Francisco: Jossey-Bass.

House, R. (1996). Path-goal theory of leadership: Lessons, legacy, and a reformulated theory. *Leadership Quarterly*, 7, 323–352.

House, R. J., Wright, N. S., & Aditya R. N. (1997). Cross-cultural research on organizational leadership: A critical analysis and a proposed theory. In P. C. Earley & M. Erez (Eds.), *New perspectives on international Industrial/Organizational Psychology* (pp. 535–625). San Francisco: New Lexington Press.

Jackson, S. E. (1992). *Diversity in the workplace: Human resources initiatives*. New York: Guilford Press.

Jackson, S. E., & Dutton, J. E. (1988). Discerning threats and opportunities. *Administrative Science Quarterly, 33*, 370–387.

Jamieson, D. & O'Mara, J. (1991). *Managing workforce 2000: Gaining the diversity advantage*. San Francisco, CA: Jossey-Bass.

Kanfer, R., & Ackerman, P. L. (1989). Motivation and cognitive abilities: An integrative/aptitude-treatment interaction approach to skill acquisition. *Journal of Applied Psychology, 74,* 657–690.

Kidder, R. M. (1994). *How good people make tough choices*. New York, NY: William Morrow & Co.

Kilduff, M., & Day, D. V. (1994). Do chameleons get ahead? The effects of self-monitoring on managerial careers. *Academy of Management Journal, 37,* 1047–1060.

Landis, D., & Bhagat, R. S. (Eds.). (1996). *Handbook of intercultural training*. Thousand Oaks, CA: Sage.

Leslie, J. B., Gryskiewicz, N. D., & Dalton, M.A. (1998). Understanding cultural influences on the 360-degree feedback process. In W. W. Tornow & M. London (Eds.) *Maximizing the value of 360-degree feedback: A process for successful individual and organizational development.* (pp. 196–216). San Francisco: Jossey-Bass.

Locke, E. A., & Latham, G. (1994). Goal setting theory. In H. P. O'Neill & M. Drillings (Eds.), *Motivation: Theory and research* (pp. 13–29). Hillsdale, NJ: Lawrence Erlbaum Associates.

Mamman, A. (1996). A diverse employee in a changing workplace. *Organization Studies, 17(3)*, 449, 477.

Markus, H. R., Kitayama, S., & Heiman, R. (1996). Culture and "basic" psychological principles. In E. T. Higgins & A. W. Kruglanski (Eds). *Social psychology: Handbook of basic principles.* (pp. 857–913). NY: Guilford Press.

Mayer, J. D., & Salovey, P. (1997). What is emotional intelligence? In P. Salovey & D. J. Sluyter (Eds.), *Emotional development and emotional intelligence: Educational implications.* New York: Basic Books.

Miller, J. G. (1997). A cultural-psychology perspective on intelligence. In R. Sternberg & E. Grigorenko (Eds.). *Intelligence, heredity, and environment,* (pp. 269–302), Cambridge University Press.

Morrison, A. M., White, R. P., & Van Velsor, E. (1992). *Breaking the glass ceiling: Can women reach the top of America's largest corporations?* Reading, MA: Addison-Wesley.

Mundy-Castle, A. C. (1974). Social and technological intelligence in Western and non-Western cultures. *Universitas (University of Ghana, Legon), 4,* 46–52. (Also in S. Pilowsky (Ed.), (1975) *Cultures in collision.* Adelaide: Australian Nat. Association for Mental Health.)

Nemetz, P. L., & Christensen, S. L. (1996). The challenge of cultural diversity: Harnessing a diversity of views to understand multiculturalism. *Academy of Management Review, 21,* 434–462.

Nisbett, R. E. & Ross, L. (1980). *Human inference: Strategies and shortcomings in social judgment.* Englewood Cliffs, NJ: Prentice Hall.

Norton, J. R. & Fox, R. E. (1997). *The change equation: Capitalizing on diversity for effective organizational change.* Washington, DC: American Psychological Association.

Offermann, L. R. (1998). Leading and empowering diverse followers. In G. Hickman (Ed.), *Leading organizations: Perspectives for a new era* (pp. 397–404). Thousand Oaks: Sage.

Offermann, L. R., & Gowing, M. K. (1990). Organizations of the future: Changes and challenges. *American Psychologist, 45,* 95–108.

Offermann, L. R., & Hellmann, P. S. (1997). Culture's consequences for leadership behavior: National values in action. *Journal of Cross-cultural Psychology, 28,* 342–351.

Offermann, L. R., Schroyer, C. J., & Green, S. K. (1998). Leader attributions for subordinate performance: Consequences for subsequent leader interactive behaviors and ratings. *Journal of Applied Social Psychology, 28,* 1125–1139.

Peng, T. K., Peterson, M. F., & Shyi, Y. (1991). Quantitative methods in cross-national management research: Trends and equivalence issues. *Journal of Organizational Behavior, 12*, 87–107.

Phillips, S. T., & Ziller, R. C. (1997). Toward a theory and measure of the nature of nonprejudice. *Journal of Personality and Social Psychology, 72,* 420–434.

Riordan, C. M. & Shore, L. M. (1997). Demographic diversity and employee attitudes: An empirical examination of relational demography within work units. *Journal of Applied Psychology, 76,* 873–877.

Roberson, L. & Gutierrez, N. C. (1992). Beyond good faith: Commitment to recruiting. In S. E. Jackson (ed.), *Diversity in the workplace: Human resources initiatives* (pp. 65–88). New York, NY: Guilford.

Sanchez, J. I., & Brock, P. (1996). Outcomes of perceived discrimination among Hispanic employees: Is diversity management a luxury or a necessity? *Academy of Management Journal, 39*, 704–718.

Schmidt, S. M., & Yeh, R. (1992). The structure of leader influence: A cross-national comparison. *Journal of cross-cultural psychology, 23,* 251–264.

Schwartz, S. H. (1992). Universals in the content and structure of values: Theoretical advances and empirical tests in 20 countries. In M. Zanna (Ed), *Advances in Experimental Social Psychology* (Vol. 25). Orlando, FL: Academic Press.

Segall, M. H., Dasen, P. R., Berry, J. W., & Poortinga, Y. H. (1990). *Human behavior in global perspective*. New York: Pergammon.

Segall, M. H., Lonner, W. J., & Berry, J. W. (1998). Cross-cultural psychology as a scholarly discipline: On the flowering of culture in behavior research. *American Psychologist, 53*(10) 1101–1110.

Sessa, V. (1992). Managing diversity at the Xerox corporation: Balanced workforce goals and caucus groups. In S. E. Jackson (ed.), *Diversity in the workplace: Human resources initiatives* (pp. 37–64). New York, NY: Guilford.

Shackleton, V. J., & Ali, A. H. (1990). Work-related values of managers: A test of the Hofstede model. *Journal of cross-cultural psychology, 21*, 109–118.

Smith, P. B., Misumi, J., Tayeb, M., Peterson, M. F., & Bond, M. (1989). On the generality of leadership style measures across cultures. *Journal of occupational psychology, 62*, 97–109.

Snyder, M. (1979). Self-monitoring processes. In L. Berkowitz (Ed.), *Advances in experimental social psychology,* vol.12. (pp. 85–128). New York: Academic Press.

Spreitzer, G. M., McCall, M. W., Jr., & Mahoney, J. D. (1997). Early identification of international executive potential. *Journal of Applied Psychology, 82*, 6–29.

Sternberg, R. (1988) A triarchic view of intelligence in cross-cultural perspective. In S. H. Irvine & J. W. Berry (Eds.), *Human abilities in cultural context* (pp. 60–85) New York: Cambridge University Press.

Sternberg, R. J. (1985). *Beyond IQ: A triarchic theory of human intelligence.* New York, NY: Cambridge University Press.

Swisher, K. (1995). Diversity's learning curve: Multicultural training's challenges include undoing its own mistakes. *Washington Post,* February 5, p.H1..H4.

Thomas, R. R., Jr. (1990, March-April). From affirmative action to affirming diversity. *Harvard Business Review,* 170–117.

Thorn, I. M., & Prosper, G. (1999, November). *Leadership in international organizations: Lessons learned through the International Monetary Fund.* Selected proceedings of the 1998 annual meeting of the Leaders/Scholars Association, Los Angeles.

Triandis, H. (1994). *Culture and social behavior*. New York, NY: McGraw-Hill.

Triandis, H. C., Kurowski, L. L., & Gelfand, M. J. (1994). Workplace diversity. In H. C. Triandis, M. D. Dunnettte, & L. M. Hough (Eds.), *Handbook of industrial and organizational psychology*, 2nd ed., vol 4 (pp. 769–827). Palo Alto, CA: Consulting Psychologists Press.

Triandis, H. C., McCusker, C., & Hui, C. H. (1990). Multimethod probes of individualism and collectivism. *Journal of Personality and Social Psychology, 59*, 1006–1020.

Trompenaars, F. (1994). *Riding the waves of culture: Understanding diversity in global business.* New York, NY: Union.

Tsui, A. S., Egan, T. D., & O'Reilly, C. A. III (1992). Being different: Relational demography and organizational attachment. *Administrative Science Quarterly, 37*, 549–579.

Tsui, A. S. & O'Reilly, C. A. III. (1989). Beyond simple demographic effects: The importance of relational demography in superior-subordinate dyads. *Academy of Management Journal, 32*, 402–423.

Walker, B. A. & Hanson, W. C. (1992). Valuing differences at Digital Equipment Corporation. In S. E. Jackson (Ed.), *Diversity in the workplace: Human resources initiatives* (pp.119–137). New York, NY: Guilford.

Warech, M. A., Smither, J. W., Reilly, R. R., Millsap, R. E., & Reilly, S. P. (1998). Self-monitoring and 360-degree ratings. *Leadership Quarterly, 9,* 449–473.

Wheeler, M. (1994). *Diversity training: A research report.* (Report No. 1083-94-RR). New York: Conference Board.

Williams, M. L. & Bauer, T. N. (1994). The effect of a managing diversity policy on organizational attractiveness. *Group and Organizational Management, 19,* 295–308.

Willmann, E., Feldt, K., & Amelang, M. (1997). Prototypical behaviour patterns of social intelligence: An intercultural comparison between Chinese and German subjects. *International Journal of Psychology, 32,* 329–346.

Wober, M. (1974). Toward understanding of the Kiganda concept of intelligence. In J. Berry & P. Dasen (Eds.), *Culture and Cognition.* London: Methuen.

Wright, P., Ferris, S. P., Hiller, J. S., & Kroll, M. (1995). Competitiveness through management of diversity: Effects on stock price valuation. *Academy of Management Journal, 38,* 272–287.

12

Interpersonal Acumen and Leadership Across Cultures: Pointers from the GLOBE Study

Ram N. Aditya
Louisiana Tech University

Robert J. House
University of Pennsylvania

It was quite a challenge, but I sensed the union leaders were getting strong and wanted to dramatize the issue. So did I . . .

I acted very tough. Their leader thought I was bluffing . . . They were thinking I would have to give in . . .

I didn't give them a clue as to what I had in mind, but I held my bargaining ground up to the last minute . . .

When the strikers realized they had been outwitted, the humiliation was theirs. I had slipped out the back way and managed to get to the party at the hotel before it was over. They gave me a round of applause when I walked into the room, and the Prime Minister said Sony's attitude in confronting the extremists should be appreciated by others. The union gave up the strike . . .

Akio Morita in *Made in Japan*
(1986, pp. 156–158)

This chapter represents the confluence of two hitherto independent programs of research. One is an investigation into a component of social intelligence, conducted by the first author in collaboration with Ralph Rosnow at Temple University in Philadelphia. Based on Rosnow, Skleder, Jaeger, and Rind's (1994) work on what they termed interpersonal acumen, or the ability to read others' behavior, Aditya (1997) created and tested a measure for use with executives. The other research program is a cross-cultural study of leadership and national culture, initiated by the second author in 1993, with which the first author became associated in 1996. In this chapter, we draw on results from these two streams of research to explore the implications of culture for the association between interpersonal acumen and leadership effectiveness. Every leader of renown has engaged in a battle of wits, often many. At the heart of this game of the brain is the ability to decipher the underlying motives of other people's actions. The precise extent of the role played by interpersonal acumen in leadership may be a function of follower perceptions in a given culture—perceptions that vary widely across societies, according to findings from the GLOBE investigation.

INDIVIDUAL ABILITY IN LEADERSHIP

The topic of leadership has attracted political and academic writers from diverse disciplines from well before the twentieth century, with Machiavelli's well-known tome among the early treatises on the subject. In organizational contexts, the prediction of effective leadership is an evergreen issue for management scholars and practitioners alike. The chronological evolution of leadership theory through several perspectives has been traced by House and Aditya (1997). Particularly attractive to practitioners is the trait perspective (Aditya, House, & Kerr, 2000). A number of scholars have followed the priorities of practitioners and delved into personality traits and ability (e.g., House, Howard, & Walker, 1991; Meyer & Pressel, 1954), rather than situational factors, in the prediction of managerial success.[1] The reason for this emphasis on personal characteristics is not hard to see: The use of individual differences to predict leadership effectiveness promises to make the future less uncertain for organizations. Whereas situational contingencies arise from a continually changing mix of different environmental, social, organizational, and personal factors, measures of individual differences are relatively stable. Prediction of effective leadership through individual characteristics, if at all possible, would allow firms to identify future leaders who would be successful regardless of situational constraints. Although the results in this area have been promising at best, some evidence exists for individual differences as predictors of success in the management and leadership literature (e.g., Bass, 1990; Harrell, 1969, 1970; Harrell & Harrell, 1973; House & Aditya, 1997; House & Singh, 1987; Mann, 1959; McClelland & Boyatzis, 1982).

Until recently, general intelligence was held in high esteem as a potential predictor of managerial success in organizations. IQ is attractive as a predictor of leadership for at least two reasons. First, one can intuitively see a connection between intelligence and effective leadership. Second, the use of an index of general intelligence to predict managerial effectiveness should, in theory, minimize

[1]Some scholars draw a distinction between management and leadership, discussed elsewhere (e.g., House and Aditya, 1997; p. 444). However, for purposes of the present discussion, leadership is broadly defined to include managerial success and effectiveness at the higher levels of the organization.

errors common to other measures such as interview assessments of social skills and self-report measures of personal characteristics. Presumably, a measure of core ability would be less susceptible to biases (such as from socially desirable responding) than are personality inventories or observations from interviews.

The role of intelligence in leadership occurs prominently in two streams of research. Simonton (1994) elaborated on the relative levels of intelligence in leaders and followers that make for effective and productive leader-follower relationships. Fiedler (1994; see also Fiedler, Chap. 6, this volume; Fiedler, Potter, Zais, & Knowlton, 1979) expounded on the moderating role of stress in the impact of leader intelligence versus experience on performance. These authors referred to the traditional measures of IQ in their theorizing, although their findings (discussed later in this chapter) may be equally applicable to the emerging concept of social intelligence.

Notwithstanding the roles discussed previously, the direct influence of general intelligence on managerial success and leadership effectiveness has been notoriously ambiguous. Reviewing the results from 19 studies (of which only seven involved executive, as opposed to supervisor, samples), Korman (1968) found only four studies that indicated moderate correlations between tests of cognitive ability and executive mobility or criterion ratings. Korman, however, acknowledged the complexity of leadership behaviors, thus calling into question the validity of the measures of managerial potential used in these studies.

On the other hand, the adequacy of traditional measures of cognitive ability for use in predicting leadership potential has also come under scrutiny. In particular, social abilities relating to social adaptation and problem solving are widely acknowledged as important domains not addressed in traditional IQ tests (Snyderman & Rothman, 1987). Seen in this light, the modest correlation between IQ and managerial or leadership potential is not surprising. Leadership is inherently a social construct, as there can be no concept of a leader without the attendant one of a follower group. Mintzberg (1975) found that corporate CEOs spent a large portion of their time in interpersonal and informational roles involving social relationships. Such findings highlight the importance of social abilities to effective performance in leadership positions at higher echelons of human organization.

The acknowledgment of core abilities relatively independent of those assessed by conventional IQ tests has resulted in a more pluralistic view of intelligence (e.g., Ceci, 1990; Gardner, 1983, 1993; Mayer & Salovey, 1993; Sternberg, 1988) during the last two decades. Recognizing that the subtests of standardized IQ batteries do not explain much of performance in the real world, several scholars, management writers, and practitioners have applied themselves to the task of identifying abilities that can better explain performance. Elsewhere, the notions of emotional intelligence (Caruso, Mayer, & Salovey, Chap. 4, this volume) and practical intelligence (Sternberg, Chap. 2, this volume) have been elucidated. These concepts represent diverse perspectives on the social skills that are intuitively acknowledged as being crucial to dealing effectively with other people.

The next section begins with an outline of a typology of behavior (Tunis & Rosnow, 1983) and the construct of interpersonal acumen (Rosnow et al., 1994; Rosnow, Skleder, & Rind, 1995), a recent development in the study of social intelligence. This is followed by a discussion of the role of interpersonal acumen in managerial success (Aditya, 1997). The following section contains a brief description of the GLOBE project, a study of leadership involving approximately 170 investigators in 62 countries, initiated by Robert House in 1993. Relevant findings from the GLOBE study are discussed within the context of interpersonal acumen. The chapter concludes with a discussion of the theoretical implications of interpersonal acumen for the study and practice of leadership and proposed directions for future research.

INTERPERSONAL ACUMEN

Intention-Action Discrepancies in Social Behavior

Interpersonal acumen (henceforth IA) refers to the ability to decipher underlying intentions in other people's behavior. The measurement of IA is based on a typology of behavior, developed by Rosnow and his associates, that views all behavior in terms of the valence of overt actions and underlying emotive dispositions of the actors toward the target of the action (Tunis & Rosnow, 1983). Every action can be represented as overtly positive, neutral, or negative in valence. Similarly, the underlying motive of the actor toward the target can be represented as positive, neutral, or negative. Behavior can then be represented as a combination of overt action and underlying intention. With the valences of action along one axis and those of intention along the other, every act can be located in one of nine cells of a 3×3 matrix (Fig. 12.1). A colleague who drops in with a genuine word of praise for handling a difficult project at work would provide an example of behavior in cell A—a positive action is matched by a positive underlying intention. On the other hand, human interaction (indeed, several instances of behavior among other animal species as well) frequently involves a discrepancy between the valence of action and valence of intention. Those of us who have worked in executive or supervisory capacity know the familiar routine in which an employee appears to find fault with our work—not because of any negative intent toward us personally, but as a justification for something he or she did. Such behavior would belong to cell D in the matrix. While the scholarly literature on management and organizational behavior has focused primarily on situations in the three cells along the principal diagonal (cells A, E, and I), representing straightforward acts, Aditya and Rosnow (1999) have documented the existence of various intention-action discrepancies (abbreviated IAD) in organizations, through interviews with people in supervisory and managerial positions.

	Actor's Emotive Disposition Toward Target		
Appearance of Action	*Positive*	*Neutral*	*Negative*
Positive	A	D	G
Neutral	B	E	H
Negative	C	F	I

FIG. 12.1 Typology of Actions and Intentions (from Rosnow et al., 1994).

From the matrix typology, it can be seen that all behaviors, with the exception of those falling along the principal diagonal, involve a discrepancy between action and the underlying emotive disposition of the actor toward the target of the act. IADs can be classified as synthetic benevolence, synthetic malevolence, or synthetic indifference depending upon whether the observed act is positive, negative, or neutral. For instance, an act that appears positive (benevolence) but has a neutral or negative intention is labeled synthetic, because the intention does not match the observed act. Similarly, an act that appears to be neutral but has a positive or negative motive would be referred to as synthetic indifference. Finally, an act that appears to be negative but has a positive or neutral intent is termed synthetic malevolence. For ease of discussion, it is useful to introduce the concepts of positive and negative displacement. We would label intention that is negative with respect to the observed action as being negatively displaced, and intention that is positive (relative to the action) as being positively displaced.

Stages in Interpersonal Acumen

In the context of social intelligence, the matrix model of behavior and the existence of IADs lend themselves to a formal conceptualization of the ability to "read" other people's behavior. What is interesting about the model is not that IADs exist in organizations—in fact, such discrepancies may be expected in interpersonal interaction in general—but that these situations fall into distinct stages of difficulty with regard to the deciphering of true intentions underlying an overt action. The theoretical underpinnings of the stages in the model derive from Gardner's (1983) theory of multiple intelligences, specifically interpersonal intelligence. Projecting Gardner's rationale for the development of interpersonal intelligence onto the cells of the matrix model, Rosnow et al. (1994) theorized that behavior in cells A and I should be the easiest to decipher, connoting the first stage in the development of the ability to interpret social behavior. The reader will notice that these two cells represent simple, straightforward behavior in which a positive action is matched by a positive intention and a negative action by a negative intention. An example would be a genuine word of praise from a friend. Cell E, representing a neutral action matched by a neutral intention, also implies straightforward behavior. For instance, seated at a restaurant, we might be perturbed to see a colleague walk past our table without a greeting; in reality, the colleague may not have noticed us at all. Such situations are not as easy to interpret correctly, and therefore constitute Stage 2 in the ordinal sequence. Presumably, it is easier to attribute a negative or positive intention to a noncommittal act than to detect true neutrality in the act. Stage 3 involves behavior that is the direct opposite of intentions with regard to valence, represented by cells C and G. In other words, acts with negative motives that appear positive, and negative appearing acts with positive motives, constitute Stage 3. A colleague appears to be helpful while actually leveraging himself or herself into a better position to be promoted; or a well-meaning boss stalls our attempts to get a lucrative-sounding posting to a different branch, knowing that the position is not as good as it looks on paper. The theoretical framework predicts that these acts would be somewhat more difficult to interpret than the situations in Stage 2 or 1.

In Stage 4 come the situations in cells B and H. These are acts that appear to be neutral while being positively or negatively motivated. The con artist who projects a disinterested countenance while waiting to pick a pocket provides an example of this category of behavior. The reader can appreciate this strategy of the con artist, as opposed to engaging in positive acts—a stranger seeming overly friendly may be more open to suspicion than a stranger who appears disinterested. In organizational contexts, failure to voice support for an argument in a meeting, while appearing to be a neutral act, may be motivated by either positive or negative disposition toward the target.

The final stage comprises behaviors in cells D and F: positive or negative appearing acts that have neutral intent. As mature adults we nevertheless make frequent errors in judgment in such situations. The cashier at the counter who smiles and says, "Have a nice day!" provides an example of behavior in cell D. Unless the target of the act happens to know the cashier personally, there is no reason to attribute a positive intent to the gesture—the cashier is simply doing his or her job, and the customer is just one among the many in a day. The telephone salesperson who hangs up abruptly when a potential customer declines an offer cannot possibly have a negative emotive disposition toward the customer—the salesperson does not even know the customer. The salesperson is simply trying to meet a quota of calls for the day. However, the act appears rude, and provides an illustration of cell F.

Distinguishing IA from Related Constructs

Interpersonal acumen should be distinguished from other conceptually proximal constructs proposed in the literature on social intelligence. IA refers to a specific interpretive ability, although it is highly contextualized in nature. In contrast to some notions of intelligence that seek extensive coverage of all predictive factors with regard to performance, IA is a core ability well-defined in conceptual scope and empirical measurement. The operational foundations of IA are drawn from

Gardner's (1993, p. 239) exposition of interpersonal intelligence as "*the ability to notice and make distinctions among other individuals* and, in particular, among their moods, temperaments, motivations, and intentions. . . . " (Italics in original). At the most basic level, according to Gardner, interpersonal intelligence is reflected in the capacity of the young child to distinguish among people and their various moods. At its highest level, "interpersonal knowledge permits a skilled adult to read the intentions and desires—even when these have been hidden—of many other individuals and, potentially, to act upon this knowledge—for example, by influencing a group of disparate individuals to behave along desired lines" (p. 239). Interpersonal acumen reflects the ability to read underlying intentions and motivations in others' behavior. The measurement of IA, described elsewhere in the chapter, involves judgments about an actor's emotive disposition, or underlying motivation, toward the target. In making this judgment, the judge has to consider the temperament of the actor (an enduring component of the individual's personality) as well as the mood of the actor (a relatively transient component that lies at the intersection of situational context, personality, and relationship between actor and target). Further, although the term "judgment" connotes a cognitive process, understanding and interpretation of emotions play a significant role in this judgment.

A concept that sounds at first similar to IA is social insight (Chapin, 1942). However, Chapin's (1942) social insight test attempts to measure an individual's ability to make judgments on social problems and suggest solutions, while IA involves an interpretation of actors' motives from the observed behavior in social or interpersonal interaction. IA might therefore be seen as a core ability that can facilitate insight into social problems.

A concept that comes much closer to IA is empathy (Davis, 1983; Ickes, 1993). Empathy has been viewed both as a cognition-oriented (e.g., Deutsch & Madle, 1975; Dymond, 1949; Kerr & Speroff, 1954) and as an affect-oriented (e.g., Stotland, 1969) ability. Davis (1980) synthesized the various theoretical perspectives on empathy in a 28-item measure called the Interpersonal Reactivity Index (IRI). The multidimensional nature of empathy was recognized by Davis (1980, 1983), in the four subscales that represent subdomains of the IRI: the Perspective-Taking, Fantasy, Empathic Concern, and Personal Distress subscales. The Perspective-Taking scale measures the tendency to adopt others' points of view; the Fantasy scale measures the extent to which an individual gets into the role and affective states of fictitious characters; the Empathic Concern scale addresses the tendency to feel warmth, compassion, and concern for others; the Personal Distress scale evaluates the extent to which an individual is affected adversely by events with strong emotional content. Of these, Fantasy and Personal Distress do not lend themselves, theoretically, to a connection with IA. Perspective-Taking and Empathic Concern, to the extent that they represent a proclivity to think about other people and their feelings, may facilitate the development of IA. However, an ability to read other people's behavior does not presume a tendency to take the perspective of others, or to be concerned about them.

In the initial studies on interpersonal acumen, Rosnow et al. (1994) found a small correlation of .20 between their measure of IA and scores on the Empathic Concern scale, and even smaller correlations with the Perspective-Taking scale (r = .11), the Fantasy scale (r = –.011) and the Personal Distress scale (r = .058), consistent with expectations.

Ickes and his colleagues (e.g., Ickes, 1993; Hancock & Ickes, 1996; Stinson & Ickes, 1992) measure the accuracy with which an individual is able to read what is going on in another individual's mind at a given point in interpersonal interaction. Ickes calls his construct "empathic accuracy." The operational methodology makes empathic accuracy the most evolved measure of empathy. Ickes' measure includes all aspects of a conversation, involving a broad range of feelings and cognitions. However, empathic accuracy deals with the reading of another individual's thoughts at that point in time. Thus, from an empathic accuracy perspective, a parent scolding his or her child is probably thinking at that moment of providing an unpleasant experience that the child will not forget in a hurry. The underlying intention, from the IA perspective, is positive (under normal circumstances): The parent is trying to ensure that the child grows up to be a competent member of society. Thus, empathic accuracy may actually lead to errors on the IA task. Moreover, research suggests that the social relation between the target of the behavior (judge) and the actor (the individual whose intentions are being evaluated) does not influence empathic accuracy (Hancock & Ickes, 1996), while we would expect such a relationship to influence the judge's conclusion with regard to the valence of underlying intentions in the actor's behavior. In sum, there is no theoretical reason to believe that IA and empathic accuracy go together.

IA also differs from certain other forms of intelligence explicated in other chapters (e.g., Sternberg, Chap. 2, this volume; Zaccaro, Chap. 3, this volume). One such is social perceptiveness (Zaccaro, Gilbert, Thor, & Mumford, 1991), which involves the recognition of needs, problems, and goals of individuals, organizations, and groups as a whole. Social perceptiveness is characterized by Zaccaro et al. (1991, p. 326) as being "fundamentally linked to the breadth and depth of encoded declarative [social] knowledge structures." Their concept of behavioral flexibility, on the other hand, deals with the behavioral aspects of social intelligence, and is therefore seen as being linked to procedural social knowledge. Practical intelligence, or "common sense" (Sternberg, 1997; Sternberg & Wagner, 1986) makes use of what Sternberg calls tacit knowledge, a form of action-oriented procedural knowledge that is "acquired without direct help from others, that allows individuals to achieve goals they personally value" (Sternberg, 1997, p. 483). By comparison, IA is narrower in scope, with a relatively crystallized domain. It reflects the ability to deal with a particular facet of human interaction—the ability to read motives. IA engages both tacit knowledge and social perceptiveness. The rules and symbols in social interaction are not always explicitly taught, but are necessary for the accurate interpretation of behavior. Knowledge of personalities and other facts pertaining to a context are also needed in making accurate judgments about other peoples' intentions and motivations. The primary motivation in the conceptualization of IA is theoretical isolation of a core ability rather than the prediction of managerial performance or leader effectiveness that drives the concepts of practical intelligence, social perceptiveness, and behavioral flexibility.

The Measurement of Interpersonal Acumen

The notion of ordinal stages implies that the development of IA in individuals can be tracked by tapping into these stages. By creating scenarios keyed to the nine cells of the behavior typology, Rosnow et al. (1994) were able to study the scale structure of IA. Rosnow and associates used scripts and drawings depicting the behavior of children in various situations. Participants in the study were shown the drawings in sequence as the script was read out to them, and then asked to evaluate the intention of the actor as positive, negative, or neutral. The investigators examined, and found evidence for, the ordinal properties of the scale in a series of studies with undergraduate student samples. Put simply, subjects found it less or more difficult to correctly identify motives depending on the stage in which the situation belonged in the theoretical framework. The findings served to substantiate Gardner's (1983) rationale for a developmental trajectory for interpersonal intelligence.

While Gardner's seminal theory provided the explanation for the development of interpersonal intelligence, it did not address the issue of distinct stages in the ability to read other people's behavior beyond the developmental years. Also, there was the question of inherent qualitative differences in the life situations to which an individual is exposed. A child of ten may be expected to have encountered scenarios in all the nine cells of the typology, and may have mastered them all with regard to the interpretation of underlying emotive dispositions of actors. As the child grows to become an adult, however, there is a corresponding change in the individual's social environment, and in the nature of situations the person must face. Would this individual, who has mastered all stages of IA as a child of ten with regard to juvenile situations, exhibit mastery in interpreting scenarios in the adult environment? Intuitively, we would answer in the negative, sensing that adult scenarios constitute a qualitatively different domain involving a higher level of cognitive processing. However, the instances of adult interaction could also be mapped on to the basic typology of behavior described by Rosnow et al. (1994). The question then was whether we would find the same five stages of difficulty within the new context. Heuristically, the sequence of stages represented by the different cells of the behavior matrix could be applied to the new set of situations, except that the adult scenarios would be at a higher global level of difficulty than the juvenile situations portrayed in Rosnow et al.'s (1994) instrument. In short, a system of nested hierarchies was to be expected, with the five stages of IA being replicated within a larger hierarchy of social contexts.

To test these and other hypotheses, Aditya (1997) created a set of scenarios depicting adult interaction in the workplace. The scenarios had three components.

The first component, presented as the "situation," described a specific behavior of an individual (a superior, peer, or subordinate) in one or two sentences. A second component had a single statement about the relationship between the target and the actor (that is, whether the relationship was basically good or bad). The third part of the scenario contained historical information that could be relevant to the judging of underlying motives in the given situation. These three pieces of information were presented on the computer screen as three "boxes" labeled "situation," "relationship," and "history." The participant-judges (who were also the target of the behavior in the given situation) could click open one box at a time and read the information it contained. This arrangement was designed to mimic judgments in real life, where we rarely have information about a situation in written form when making judgments about others' behavior. In this instrument, participants judged the underlying motive in the actor's behavior toward the participant (the imagined target) by choosing one of three plausible motives keyed through pilot studies to be positive, neutral, or negative in valence. The basic situations portraying the behavior of the actor had also been similarly keyed through prior testing, and the phrasing refined through several iterative studies, detailed in Aditya (1997).

Three indices of IA were developed from this measure. First, the number of correct responses constituted the raw score (R score). Second, the correct responses weighted by the theorized level of difficulty constituted the weighted raw score (WR score). Finally, a stage score (S score) was obtained by counting the number of stages in which participants got more than a specified number of items "correct." Thus, if a respondent got the required number of items correct in Stages 1, 3, and 4, then the S score would be 3. Clearly, the WR score had the largest range of potential scores, and the S score was the most appropriate for testing the sequentiality hypothesis.

Scalogram analyses (Goodenough, 1944) established the ordinal properties of this scale with an executive sample as well as with a student sample. The notion of nested hierarchies was explored by comparing the percentages of correct responding in the two samples, and across the two measures, the executive measure (Aditya, 1997) and the juvenile measure (Rosnow et al. 1994). If indeed there were a nested hierarchical structure in the interpersonal acumen task, and if the contextual differences were large enough, we should expect to find a floor effect of the executive measure with the undergraduate sample. By implication, a) undergraduate students should score lower than executives would on all stages of the executive measure, and b) the student sample should score lower on the executive measure than on the juvenile measure. The empirical findings were as expected. The percentage of correct responding in the undergraduate sample was lower for every stage than that for the executive sample, and lower in the executive measure than in the juvenile measure.

The hierarchical structure of the adult measure of IA has been replicated subsequently with the executive measure on another undergraduate sample (Aditya, Darkangelo, & Morris, 1999). The cross-cultural validity of the sequentiality hypothesis has also been supported in a study with Korean subjects using the juvenile measure (Kim, 1997).

Interpersonal Acumen as a Core Competence

That IA addresses a core cognitive competency is supported by several empirical results. The initial studies by Rosnow, et al. (1994) with undergraduate samples used SAT-M and SAT-V scores respectively as measures of mathematical and verbal ability, and grade point average (GPA) as an indicator of general academic ability. Their results suggested that IA was relatively independent of these measures: IA correlated –.05 with SAT-V, –.09 with SAT-M, and .08 with GPA. In a study using the executive measure of IA and the WAIS-R (short version) for IQ on an undergraduate sample, Aditya (1997) found somewhat higher correlations, ranging from .22 to .35, with the three IA indices. However, these results compare favorably with intercorrelations between various component ability tests in the IQ battery, which have been found to range from .20 to .80 (Jensen & Weng, 1994). It appears, even from a *g*-centric perspective, that the small-to-moderate correlations between IA and IQ are well within the expected range.

Traditional tests of cognitive ability have been found to relate inversely with time spent on the task, with correlations ranging from –.30 to –.40 (Phillips & Rabbitt, 1995). A similar relationship was found by Aditya (1997) between time taken to inspect the scenarios (including supplemental information) and IA, in the executive sample. Correlations ranged from –.22 to –.27 with the three IA indices. Using this executive measure with a student sample, however, yielded positive correlations (r = .24 to .31). These results, puzzling at first, are actually consistent with the notion of nested hierarchies. While executives were familiar with the context (i.e., scenarios drawn from workplace situations) of the executive IA task, the undergraduate students were not—they had had little or no exposure to such situations. As a result, the student participants would have had to spend more time trying to understand and figure out the scenarios and motive choices.

Rosnow et al. (1994) have also investigated the association of IA with four measures of individual characteristics: the Interpersonal Reactivity Index (Davis, 1980, 1983), Interpersonal Trust Scale (Rotter, 1967), Self-Monitoring Scale (Snyder, 1974), and Need for Cognition Scale (Cacioppo & Petty, 1982). Davis' (1983) 28-item Interpersonal Reactivity Index is designed to measure self-reported empathy along four dimensions, addressing both cognitive and emotional aspects. The four dimensions are addressed, as described earlier, by subscales for Perspective-Taking, Fantasy, Empathic Concern, and Personal Distress. The 25-item Interpersonal Trust Scale (Rotter, 1967) is designed to measure the tendency to trust other people. Snyder's (1974) 25-item Self-Monitoring Scale is designed to measure the extent to which individuals engage in self-introspection and self-control in social situations. Following Briggs, Cheek, and Buss' (1980) demonstration of the multidimensionality of the construct, the Self-Monitoring scale has been broken down into three components—the Extraversion subscale, the Other-Directedness subscale, and the Acting subscale. The Extraversion subscale addresses the proclivity to be the center of attention in social gatherings, to entertain people, and to be outspoken in general. The Other-Directedness subscale focuses on the tendency to adjust one's behavior to suit others. The Acting subscale is designed to measure one's liking for activities that involve acting, speaking, and in general, entertaining. Finally, Cacioppo and Petty's (1982) 18-item Need for Cognition Scale is constructed as a measure of one's engagement and enjoyment of "thinking." Rosnow et al. (1994) found that IA scores were not strongly correlated with any of these scales or subscales (r ranging from –.06 to .11), with the exception of the Empathic Concern subscale (r = .20) reported earlier.

A personality characteristic not explored in the early studies was Machiavellianism (Christie & Geis, 1970). Machiavellian principles often involve pretense and deceit, among other strategies, to gain power and control in social structures. Effective use of these strategies presumes the ability to read other people's motives, although the presence of this ability does not imply that an individual should be Machiavellian in character. Using the executive measure of IA, Aditya (1997) examined its relationship with Machiavellianism, anticipating no more than a moderate relationship. Consistent with this expectation, small correlations (r = –.03 to .10) were observed in the student sample, and moderate correlations (r = .34 to .35) were found in the executive sample.

INTERPERSONAL ACUMEN AND LEADERSHIP

Empirical and Conceptual Links

In organizational behavior, the existence of IADs in interpersonal interaction, documented by Aditya and Rosnow (1999), speaks for the relevance of IA in the workplace. Aditya (1997) observed moderate correlations[2] of .27 to .31 between IA scores and indices of executive success such as number of promotions in career and management level. Since promotions, especially at the higher levels of organizations, are usually indicators of leadership potential, the obtained correlations are reflective of the association between IA and leadership potential.

The link between IA and leader effectiveness, however, is yet to be investigated. A theoretical exploration is initiated by revisiting the concept of nested hierarchies. The notion of nested hierarchies in IA represents a reconciliation of two seemingly conflicting perspectives on intelligence. On the one hand, there is

[2]Statistically significant at the .05 level. Correlations of one of the IA indices (stage score) with number of promotions and with management level were in the region of .17, not statistically significant. However, restriction of range in stage scores and in the number of management levels may account for the lower correlation in this case.

the idea, first stated by Piaget and Inhelder (1947), that intellectual development takes place in stages that are cumulative and irreversible, so that mastery of a given stage presumes the successful completion of earlier stages. On the other hand, there is also the view of intelligence as being contextualized and distributed (Gardner, 1993). The contextualist view of intelligence, in simple terms, refers to the fact that the definition of an intelligent act is embedded in the cultural setting of the act. Even a seemingly simple sorting task (e.g., Sternberg, 1988, p.19) can be loaded with cultural meaning that we frequently fail to recognize until we go outside of our own culture. Further, intelligence is distributed to the extent that it derives meaning from a host of environmental influences, such as the availability of tools, artifacts, and other resources that we take for granted in our everyday lives. For instance, the dexterity with which a teenager can troubleshoot a problem on her friend's computer is an index of intelligence among her peers, but that cognitive ability is born of a process to which the functional parameters of a computer chip are inextricably tied. These two components of the modern definition of intelligence imply that within a certain core ability, there could be multiple domains of development that are not necessarily cumulative or irreversible. In the context of interpersonal acumen, for instance, we may think of different domains of observation and of behavior that may represent parallel, rather than serial, stages of cognitive development. Thus an individual may be adept at reading visual cues in people's gestures and facial expressions, but quite inept at reading between the lines in written communication. These domains of development are not sequential or irreversible. It may just be that the individual grew up in a society or a social setting where there is little written communication. This has implications for organizational leaders who are suddenly moved to new environments and cultures on the basis of their effective leadership in a previous culture—whether organizational, societal, or, for that matter, industrial or occupational.

Leadership is not only about dealing with other people, but about being perceived by others as a leader (Lord & Maher, 1991; p.11). This view of leadership implies that an individual cannot be a leader unless that individual is perceived by a group of other individuals as a leader. People have their own perceptions of what constitutes a leader. These perceptions make up a mental model, or a leader prototype, in the mind of an individual. Leader prototypes serve to trigger recognition of a leader when a target person fits the image contained in the prototype. To the extent that prototypes are shared in a society, an individual aspiring to be an effective leader must conform to the prototype that exists in that culture.

A leader must also be able to understand correctly the behavior of other people—not only the followers, but also other individuals who provide meaning to the leader's position by virtue of their association with the leader's function. In the political arena, this means that a leader should know and understand his or her people's motivations and expectations, their profile of a prototypical leader. It also means the leader should understand the motivations of other political leaders, be they rivals within the same constituency or leaders of other constituencies. Within the organizational setting, the implicit leadership perspective requires that a leader understand the emotive dispositions of subordinates as well as of superiors and of leaders of other organizations with which the leader's organization interacts.

In both contexts, the requirements of a leader imply an ability to read behavior accurately in the context of the set of social norms within which the leader and the group operate. The level of interpersonal acumen required of a leader may depend on the leader prototypes operative in that setting and the social norms of the society. Research on the Leader Motive Profile (McClelland, 1975) and Charismatic Leadership (House, 1977; House, Spangler, & Woycke, 1991) based on studies conducted in the U.S. suggests that some attributes, such as displaying integrity, assertiveness, and prosocial dominance, may be correlated with effective leadership (House & Aditya, 1997; p. 416). Whether these prototypical attributes would be universally applicable is debatable, however. Results from the GLOBE study, described in the next section, indicate some rather startling differences among cultures on what is expected of an outstanding leader.

Simonton (1994) had found that leadership was most effective when the IQ of leaders was greater than the average intelligence of the followers. It is conceivable that this result may be observed in the case of IA as well. In other words, leadership will be most effective when the leader is more adept at deciphering the intentions underlying followers' acts than the followers are in deciphering the motives behind the leader's actions. Part of this effect would have to do with issues of power and influence. A leader who is utterly predictable may be less captivating and less influential than a leader who is not. If followers can predict a leader's behavior in every situation, then the leader becomes redundant, and leadership superfluous. Of course, infamous leaders in the annals of history have used unpredictability to great personal advantage and to the detriment of their subjects, but many good leaders have been described as presenting something of an enigma, giving them an almost immortal quality in the perception of their followers.

Interpersonal Acumen, Social Experience, and Stress

Elsewhere, Fiedler (Chap. 6, this volume; for more details see Fiedler, 1995; Fiedler & Garcia, 1987) has expounded the role of stress in moderating the relationship between intelligence and performance, and that between experience and performance. Specifically, Fiedler and his associates found that, under conditions of low stress, leader intelligence predicted performance better than did leader experience, but that under conditions of high stress, the reverse was true—that is, leader experience correlated better with performance than did leader intelligence. These results may have a neurological basis and may be observed not only in leadership effectiveness, but also in performance outside the realm of leadership.

The results have far-reaching implications for performance in all walks of life. Further, the theory may be extended to posit similar relationships between IA and socially involved task performance, as in leadership. It is reasonable to expect that perceptions of behavior, involving social judgment, may be distorted by stress so that in stressful situations IA will correlate less well with performance than will social experience. The contextualized nature of intelligence, as well as the results from the GLOBE study described in the following section, further enhances the probability that social experience will play a visible role in performance under conditions of stress.

IA and Leadership in Cross-Cultural Perspective

An interesting aspect of interpersonal acumen is that while it is invested heavily in social mores and cultural beliefs, its operationalization is based on a universal model. This feature makes it especially amenable to examination across cultural settings. IA becomes relevant in any culture that includes IADs in interpersonal behavior; by implication, IA is universally relevant to leadership. The question of interest in the cross-cultural context is the extent to which IADs play a role in the implicit leadership theories operative in different cultures. We might expect that the higher the involvement of IADs in the culturally endorsed expectations of leaders, the higher would be the relationship of IA to leader effectiveness. Some interesting pointers are available from the GLOBE research program, described next.

CULTURAL CONTINGENCIES IN LEADERSHIP

The GLOBE Study: An Overview

The Global Leadership and Organizational Behavior Effectiveness (GLOBE) research program was initiated by the second author in 1993 as a cross-cultural investigation of leadership and national culture. The primary objectives of the project were to determine: a) universal and culture-specific leader behaviors and organizational practices that contribute to effective leadership; b) the influence of societal and organizational culture on effective and universally accepted leader behaviors; and, c) the effect of violations of cultural norms relating to leader behaviors and organizational practices. To date, the project has brought together about 170 investigators from 62 countries in a unique cooperative research effort.[3] In the course of the past five years, data have been collected from approximately 17,000

[3]A complete listing of the co-investigators and the countries represented in the GLOBE research program is available in House et al. (1999).

individuals in 825 organizations in three industries. What follows here is a brief overview of the project, available in greater detail in House et al. (1999).

It is noteworthy that GLOBE is an investigation primarily of organizational leadership, and not leadership in general. At the first conference of GLOBE in 1994 at the University of Calgary, Canada, co-investigators from 38 countries concurred on a definition of leadership as "the ability of an individual to influence, motivate, and enable others to contribute toward the effectiveness and success of organizations of which they are members" (House et al., 1999).

Four phases were planned in Project GLOBE. The first stage of the project involved the construction and validation of measures addressing various dimensions of national culture and leadership based on extant theory. From an original pool of 753 items, 54 scales were developed for the culture and leadership dimensions based on data obtained from 36 countries. The culture scales were developed on the basis of existing theoretical dimensions. The leadership scales were derived empirically from two pilot studies conducted during the first phase. The scale properties were replicated with data obtained from an additional group of sixteen nations. The validation procedures and the scales developed are detailed by Hanges & Dickson (in press). A detailed report of the first phase is available in House et al. (1999).

Phase 2 of the project involved data collection to test several substantive hypotheses about the cultural influences on leader attributes, using the scales developed in the first phase. Two questionnaires, code-named Alpha and Beta, were constructed because the total number of questions in all the scales together was considered too lengthy to be administered to each participant. Each questionnaire contained five sections. Sections 1 and 3 addressed organizational practices and organizational values in Alpha, and societal practices and societal values in Beta. The other three sections in both questionnaires were the same—two sections (2 and 4) containing leader attribute items and the final section (5) containing demographics and some additional items added by individual co-investigators. Besides the collection of primary data through these individual questionnaires, a number of other methodologies have been employed in Phase 2. The Country Co-Investigators (abbreviated CCIs) completed another inventory, called the Participant Observation Questionnaire (POQ) and the Unobtrusive Measures Questionnaire (UMQ), which addressed many of the dimensions of national culture in a parallel effort at triangulation. Additionally, other qualitative and secondary research methodologies were employed. Interviews, content analyses of media reports, and focus groups were used to collect qualitative information to supplement, juxtapose with, or to otherwise help explain the results from the questionnaire data. Detailed guidelines were provided to the CCIs in order to ensure uniformity in data collection and in the format for reporting the findings. The qualitative information is being compiled in a set of anthologies soon to be published.

Phases 3 and 4 are yet to be conducted. Phase 3 envisages a longitudinal, within-culture investigation of the effects of leadership and organizational practices on organizational effectiveness. Also planned in Phase 3 is the investigation of the impact of specific leader behaviors and styles on subordinate attitudes, subordinate performance, and leader effectiveness. Phase 4 will involve field and laboratory experiments to confirm the findings from the previous phases.

Some Results From the GLOBE Program

A primary objective of the program was to identify leader attributes that are universally endorsed and those that are culturally contingent. Six distinct dimensions of culturally endorsed implicit leadership were identified. These are: 1) charismatic/value-based leader behaviors, 2) team orientation, 3) participative leadership, 4) self-protective behaviors, 5) humane orientation, and 6) autonomous leadership. Of these, the first two were observed to be universally endorsed across cultures as contributing to outstanding leadership. The third dimension, participative leadership, was nearly universal in endorsement as a facilitator. The fourth dimension—self-protective behaviors—was universally endorsed by all cultures as inhibiting leadership effectiveness. The last two, humane orientation and autonomous leadership, were culturally contingent. That is, behaviors comprising these two dimensions were reported as either impeding or facilitating leadership effectiveness, depending on the cultural setting. Details of the first and higher-order factors derived, and the criteria and procedures used in testing the hypotheses regarding cultural contingency, are set out in House et al. (1999).

The findings from the GLOBE program are detailed in a series of publications (House, Hanges, Javidan, Dorfman, et al., in press; House, Hanges, & Ruiz-Quintanilla, 1997; House, Hanges, Ruiz-Quintanilla, Dorfman, Javidan, Dickson, Gupta, & GLOBE Coordinating Team, 1999). Broadly, the findings from Phase 2 indicate that countries differ in the extent to which they endorse particular leader behaviors. In the context of social intelligence, the findings imply differences among cultures in the profiles of leader prototypes, or in follower expectations of leaders. The leadership items in the GLOBE study were designed to tap perceived traits of outstanding leaders in each culture. Respondents were asked to indicate the extent to which each trait or behavior was perceived as impeding or facilitating outstanding leadership. They rated specific attributes on a scale ranging from 1 ("This behavior or characteristic greatly inhibits a person from being an outstanding leader") to 7 ("This behavior or characteristic contributes greatly to a person being an outstanding leader"). The items, presented in Sections 2 and 4 of the Alpha and Beta forms, originally were meant to address 17 leadership scales, later expanded to 21 scales. The scale labels are listed in Table 12.1, along with the number of items in each scale, after elimination of some items based on psychometric analyses. In their final versions, all of the scales exhibit sound psychometric properties (Hanges & Dickson, in press).

Of particular interest to us in the current discussion are the responses to certain items in the GLOBE questionnaire that address leader behaviors involving

TABLE 12.1
Leadership Scales in the GLOBE Study

#	*Scale Label*	*# of items*
1.	Administratively Competent (formerly called Procedural)	4
2.	Autocratic	6
3.	Autonomous (formerly called Individualistic)	4
4.	Charismatic I: Visionary	9
5.	Charismatic II: Inspirational	8
6.	Charismatic III: Self Sacrificial	3
7.	Conflict Inducer	3
8.	Decisive	4
9.	Diplomatic	5
10.	Face-saver	3
11.	Humane Orientation	2
12.	Integrity	4
13.	Malevolent	9
14.	Modesty (formerly called Equanimity)	4
15.	Non-participative	4
16.	Performance Oriented	3
17.	Procedural (formerly called Bureaucratic)	5
18.	Self-centered	4
19.	Status Consciousness	2
20.	Team I: Collaborative Team Orientation (formerly called Collective)	6
21.	Team II: Team Integrator	7

IADs. Interestingly, several of such items do not appear in any of the 21 leadership scales. This is because the scales were empirically derived based on psychometric properties and factor analysis. Items that did not load on any theorized factor were excluded from the scales. What is left out can be as important as what is kept, and so it is in this case. Most of the items that went into the scales do not relate directly to the present discussion, and most of the pertinent items do not fit in with any of the scales. Also, these excluded items do not go together, or they would have formed another factor to be appropriately labeled.

An exhaustive report on all relevant items for all countries included would not only be tedious but superfluous to the purpose of this chapter. The intent here is to demonstrate cultural variations in certain leader attributes involving IADs. Therefore, we have selected four items from the questionnaire that display remarkable variability in attributes seen as describing outstanding leaders in different cultures. The nature of these questions has implications not only for the leader's ability to read other people's behavior, but also for followers' expectations of effective leaders. The four items describe various characteristics or behaviors and require the participant to rate the extent to which these characteristics inhibit or contribute to outstanding leadership in their cultures. The scale ranges from 1 (greatly inhibits outstanding leadership) to 7 (greatly contributes to outstanding leadership). One of the four items (Evasiveness) is part of a leadership scale (Face Saving). The other three items do not fit in with any of the scales. The results from the four items and their implication for implicit leadership and interpersonal acumen are discussed next. For each of the four items, three countries have been selected for discussion: the countries at the two extremes of the rating scale, and the United States as a point of reference.

Guileful behaviors. The first item under consideration is labeled "Cunning," and describes an individual as being sly, deceitful, and full of guile. Deceit, by definition, implies a discrepancy between overt action and underlying emotive disposition. This IAD usually takes the form of synthetic benevolence or synthetic indifference with negative displacement. Although other forms are also possible, it can be readily appreciated that deceitful or sly behavior is rarely necessary unless the actor's intention toward the target is negative. This item does not fit in with any of the leadership scales, and predictably so. Of course, that does not make the behavior disappear from human interaction, and responses to this item are informative. On the seven-point scale (1 = greatly inhibits outstanding leadership, 7 = greatly contributes to outstanding leadership), 314 responses from Switzerland yield a mean rating of 1.26, with a standard deviation of .62, as shown in Table 12.2. In sharp contrast, Colombia with 288 respondents has a mean rating of 6.37, with a standard deviation of .94. Thus in Switzerland, sly, deceitful, and guileful behaviors are seen as a characteristic that would serve to inhibit effective leadership; in Colombia, precisely the opposite is the case. By way of comparison, the U.S. sample of 395 responses yields a mean rating of 1.74, with a standard deviation of 1.12.[4]

In analyzing these and the following ratings, the actual difference between the means, and the standard deviations associated with the two means, arguably provide the most useful information about the differences in the two societies with regard to the particular perceived leadership attribute. A more formal statistic (such as from a t-test) might give a highly inflated picture of the difference, because of the small p-values associated with large sample sizes. For instance, the difference between the mean ratings of Colombia and Switzerland in terms of a t-test is highly significant ($t(600) = 79.3$, $p = 3.5E - 32$), but this significance is based on the sample size of respondents, not the leaders rated. It ignores the possibility that the ratings of these several respondents may be based on the characteristics of a relatively small number of leaders most salient in the participants' minds while completing the questionnaire. To the extent that some characteristics of a leader are prominent, ratings of that leader on the relevant attribute would tend to form a leptokurtic distribution. The relevant degrees of freedom in this case would be determined by the actual number of leaders in the minds of the

[4]The mean and standard deviation for the U.S. were earlier shown erroneously as 5.19 and 1.37 respectively at an earlier presentation of these results. These values could not be readily explained at the time, although they did not change the point of the discussion. A subsequent check uncovered the regrettable error, however inadvertent, in the extraction of figures from GLOBE results.

TABLE 12.2
Country Means on Selected Leadership Items

Detail	*Lowest mean rating*	*Reference mean rating*	*Highest mean rating*
Item 1 (4–3): Cunning—sly, deceitful, full of guile			
Country	Switzerland	U.S.	Colombia
Mean	1.26	1.74	6.37
Std. Dev.	.62	1.12	.94
N (respondents)	314	395	288
Item 2 (4–16): Indirect communication—does not go straight to the point, uses metaphors and examples to communicate			
Country	Colombia	U.S.	Taiwan
Mean	2.16	2.76	4.86
Std. Dev.	1.24	1.24	1.35
N (respondents)	287	396	234
Item 3 (2–2): Evasive—refrains from making negative comments to maintain good relationships or to save face			
Country	Finland	U.S.	Georgia
Mean	1.52	3.28	5.67
Std. Dev.	.93	1.88	1.47
N (respondents)	429	397	254
Item 4 (4–21): Sensitive—aware of slight changes in others' moods, restricts discussion to prevent embarrassment			
Country	Russia	U.S.	Ecuador
Mean	1.95	5.11	6.35
Std. Dev.	.99	1.24	.86
N (respondents)	302	396	49

Note: Figures in parentheses next to item numbers in the table identify the item in the original questionnaire.

respondents when they answered the questionnaire. Since this number will never be known, we have no precise way of estimating the p-value for the difference between the means. The best we can do is to compare the means directly with one another and with the ends of the scale.

Whatever the case, the ratings from Colombia do make sense from a practical viewpoint, if we keep recent history in perspective. In the U.S., on the other hand, even though many recent and present day political leaders are seen as sly and deceitful, there is presumably a tendency to deny to oneself that such characteristics could have contributed to the leader's popularity or fame.

Indirect communication. A second item addresses indirect communication: a leader who "does not go straight to the point, uses metaphors and examples to communicate." Indirect communication does not necessarily imply an IAD, but does suggest the ability to read between the lines. Thus, for a leader to be effective while using indirect communication, it is all the more important that the followers understand the language. Further, an individual using indirect communication may expect different overt responses than when using direct communication. Therefore, such an individual must be good at decoding such responses in order to be effective. This item also does not fit in with any of the leadership scales, but implies some interesting distinctions between countries. The mean rating from 287 respondents from Colombia is 2.16 (s.d. = 1.24), indicating that indirect communication is somewhat inhibiting to outstanding leadership. At the other extreme, 234 respondents from Taiwan indicate that such a form of communication is mildly characteristic of effective leaders (mean = 4.86, s.d. = 1.35). Clearly, the perceived characteristic of the Colombian leader is very different from that of the Taiwanese leader on this attribute. The U.S. sample (N = 396) yields a mean of 2.76 (s.d. = 1.24), as might be expected.

Evasive behaviors. A third item deals with the somewhat related issue of evasive behavior in interpersonal relationships. The item describes the leader as one who "refrains from making negative comments to maintain good relationships or to save face." Unlike the first two items discussed, this item is part of the "Face Saving" scale. Typically, face-saving behaviors involve a positive or neutral representation of a negative evaluation. In a culture where direct unpleasantness in interaction is avoided, the ability to pick up hidden cues in communication is presumed. On this item, 429 respondents from Finland yield an average response of 1.52 (indicating that such behaviors were highly inhibiting to outstanding leadership in their culture) with a standard deviation of .93. In contrast, the sample from Georgia (N = 254) yields a mean rating of 5.67, with a standard deviation of 1.47. It is interesting to note that Japan, much touted in the management and cross-cultural literature for "face-saving" behavior, actually yields a mean rating of only 3.56 (s.d. = 1.77). This suggests that such behaviors do not have much impact on leadership effectiveness, and may in fact have a negative impact on leadership in Japan. The U.S. sample (N = 397), with a mean of 3.28 (s.d. = 1.88), is consistent with what one might expect: Effective leaders in the U.S. would not shy away from making negative comments. The variability in responses, however, was just as high as Japan's on this attribute. The similarity between the U.S. and Japan on this attribute is interestingly different from what the management literature would suggest. In the U.S. as well as in Japan (and in most places around the world), embarrassment is unwelcome. However, the overall mean of ratings across countries is below the neutral rating of 4, suggesting that face-saving and accommodating behaviors may actually detract from effective leadership.

Sensitivity. Finally, the fourth item selected for this discussion examines sensitivity, and characterizes a leader as one who is "aware of slight changes in others' moods, restricts discussion to prevent embarrassment." This item comes closest to a behavioral definition of interpersonal intelligence. The first part of the statement addresses the ability to read other's motives and dispositions, while the second part of the statement gets at the ability to act on that judgment, albeit in a very limited sense. Almost uniformly across countries, this attribute was rated as contributing to outstanding leadership, with only Russia, Spain, and Portugal yielding means on the negative side of the rating scale. The lowest rating was from Russia, with a mean of 1.95 (s.d. = .99) from 302 executive respondents. At the other extreme was Ecuador, with a mean of 6.35 (s.d. = .86) from 49 respondents. A leader in Ecuador, clearly, would need to be very sensitive to the moods and inner motivations of followers to be effective. The U.S. (N = 396) yielded a mean rating of 5.11 (s.d. = 1.24) representing the bulk of responses from nations around the globe.

The foregoing results reflect the wide disparity in perceived characteristics of effective leaders in diverse cultures, with particular reference to a) those behaviors that involve discrepancy between action and underlying motive, and b) the capacity of the leader to detect such discrepancies in the behavior of others. The notion of IA becomes especially important for a leader in some cultures, if only because reading others' motives is central to political maneuvering. The more subtle the forms of expression in a given culture, the higher the level of IA required for social interaction, and presumably the stronger the relationship between IA and effective leadership. The mean ratings on indirect communication reflect the norms operative in societies that have developed subtle forms of expression. The use of metaphors and examples also implies a need for the ability to read between the lines, as it were.

CONCLUDING NOTES

The construct of interpersonal acumen addresses a fundamental aspect of social intelligence, namely, the ability to decipher underlying motives in other people's behavior. The first part of the chapter described the construct, distinguished it from similar concepts set out in the literature, and presented evidence from other studies supporting the notion of IA as a core cognitive competency. The measurement of IA is based on a typology of behavior that has cross-cultural validity, making it particularly amenable to examination across societal boundaries. The developmental rationale for the sequential structure in the measurement of IA was subsumed in a broader framework of nested hierarchies, facilitating the measurement of IA in adults and in specific contexts. The notion of nested hierarchies led to the discussion of IA with respect to leadership, and the contextual view of intelligence was invoked to specify the implication of IA for leadership in cross-cultural perspective. This led to an overview of the GLOBE research program and selected results that highlight differential levels of IADs in implicit leadership theories operative in different societies.

Where Do We Go From Here?

Interpersonal acumen (Rosnow et al., 1994) is a new concept that shows much promise as a useful predictor of performance in socially oriented tasks in all walks of life. An interesting aspect of this construct is that, although it addresses a cognitive capacity, it is based on an aspect of human interaction that is primarily emotional. The valence of underlying intentions (which we prefer to call emotive dispositions when inclined to be more precise) refers to feelings that result from knowing the intent behind an act. A good part of leadership, in current theorizing (e.g., House, Delbecq, & Taris, 1997; House & Shamir, 1993), has to do with subjective states of arousal in followers. The emotive content of leadership presupposes a cognitive ability to monitor and control it, so that IA assumes a central role in the successful discharge of leadership functions.

There is another side to the cognitive capacity of IA, however, that may be somewhat more predictive of effective leadership. An accurate judgment of an actor's motives does not influence outcomes in social interaction except through its translation into a reaction by the person making the judgment (the target of the actor's behavior). The way the target depicts the motives of the actor in outward behavior may be termed as *social portrayal* of the motive judgment. A target may judge the motive of an actor as negative, but may prefer to portray it as a neutral or even a positive motive in social interaction for a variety of reasons. The shift in valence between a personal judgment and social portrayal of a motive has been termed as *behavioral displacement* (Aditya, 1997). In the final analysis, a combination of IA, social portrayal, and behavioral displacement may be more predictive of leadership effectiveness or managerial success than any one aspect taken in isolation. The task ahead is to achieve this operational facility without sacrificing the reliability associated with measurement of core competencies. IA is by definition more socially embedded than any other traditional measure of cognitive ability.

In a state of stable equilibrium in the environment, the case for IA in leadership is not immediately clear. As long as things are running smoothly, the leader's role is subdued. However, part of the leader's role is to bring about change, and that road is not smooth at all. Incidents such as the one narrated by Akio Morita in the epigraph that began this chapter do not occur every day—but when they do occur, they constitute the ultimate test of a leader. Every leader, organizational or political, has fought a battle. And in the end, it always boils down to who outread the opponent.

It would be an error, however, to assume that the role of IA in leadership begins and ends with battles. IA plays a subtle but critical role in the maintenance of stability in leader-follower relationships to effect change in the smoothest possible manner. Followers' expectations and prototypes of leaders may often include the differences in intelligence between leaders and followers observed by Simonton (1994). What holds for traditional IQ can be extended to IA. An untested but logically sound expectation is that a leader should be able to not only outread an opponent, but should be able to outread his or her followers as well.

ACKNOWLEDGMENTS

The authors are grateful to Ralph Rosnow for reviewing earlier drafts of the manuscript. His invaluable suggestions have greatly improved this chapter. The authors are also thankful to graduate research assistants Chad Law, Arul Rajendran, and Robin Broyles for their dedicated clerical and library assistance.

REFERENCES

Aditya, R. N. (1997). *Toward the better understanding of managerial success: An exploration of interpersonal acumen.* Unpublished doctoral dissertation, Temple University, Philadelphia.

Aditya, R. N., & Rosnow, R. L. (1999). *To be or seem to be: Synthetic benevolence, malevolence, and indifference in the workplace.* (Manuscript in preparation), Louisiana Tech University, Ruston, LA.

Aditya, R. N., Darkangelo, D., & Morris, M. L. (1999). *The structure of interpersonal acumen in adult interaction.* Paper presented at the 11th Annual Conference of the American Psychological Society, June 3–6, Denver, CO.

Aditya, R. N., House, R. J., & Kerr, S. (2000). Theory and practice of leadership: Into the new millennium. In C. L. Cooper & E. A. Locke (Eds.), *Industrial and organizational psychology: Linking theory with practice.* Blackwell Publishers.

Bass, B. M. (1990). *Bass and Stogdill's Handbook of leadership: Theory, research, and managerial applications.* (3rd ed.). New York: Free Press.

Briggs, S. R., Cheek, J. M., & Buss, A. H. (1980). An analysis of the self-monitoring scale. *Journal of Personality and Social Psychology, 38*, 679–686.

Cacioppo, J. T., & Petty, R. E. (1982). The need for cognition. *Journal of Personality and Social Psychology, 42,* 116–131.

Ceci, S. J. (1990). *On intelligence . . . more or less: A bio-ecological theory of intellectual development.* Englewood Cliffs, NJ: Prentice Hall.

Chapin, F. S. (1942). Preliminary standardization of a social insight scale. *American Sociological Review, 7,* 214–225.

Christie, R., & Geis, F. L. (1970). *Studies in Machiavellianism.* New York: Academic Press.

Davis, M. H. (1980). A multidimensional approach to individual differences in empathy. *JSAS Catalog of Selected Documents in Psychology, 10*, 85.

Davis, M. H. (1983). Measuring individual differences in empathy: Evidence for a multidimensional approach. *Journal of Personality and Social Psychology, 44,* 113–126.

Deutsch, F., & Madle, R. (1975). Empathy: Historic and current conceptualizations, measurement, and a cognitive theoretical perspective. *Human Development, 18*, 267–287.

Dymond, R. F. (1949). A scale for the measurement of empathic ability. *Journal of Consulting Psychology, 43*, 522–527.

Fiedler, F. E. (1994). *Leadership experience and leadership performance.* United States Army Research Institute for the Behavioral and Social Sciences.

Fiedler, F. E. (1995). Cognitive resources and leadership performance. *Applied Psychology: An International Review, 44,* 5–28.

Fiedler, F. E., & Garcia, J. E. (1987). *New approaches to effective leadership: Cognitive resources and organizational performance.* New York: Wiley.

Fiedler, F. E., Potter, E. H., III, Zais, M. M., & Knowlton, W., Jr. (1979). Organizational stress and the use and misuse of managerial intelligence and experience. *Journal of Applied Psychology, 64*(6), 635–674.

Gardner, H. (1983). *Frames of mind: The theory of multiple intelligences.* New York: Basic Books.

Gardner, H. (1993). Intelligence and intelligences: Universal principles and individual differences. *Archives de Psychologie, 61*, 169–172.

Goodenough, W. H. A. (1944). A technique for scale analysis. *Educational and Psychological Measurement, 4*, 179–190.

Hancock, M., & Ickes, W. (1996). Empathic accuracy: When does the perceiver-target relationship make a difference? *Journal of Social and Personal relationships, 13*(2), 179–199.

Hanges, P. J., & Dickson, M. W. (in press). Scale development and validation. In R. J. House, P. J. Hanges, M. Javidan, P. W. Dorfman, & GLOBE Associates, Cultures, Leadership, and Organizations: GLOBE—A 62 Nation Study, Thousand Oaks, CA: Sage.

Harrell, T. W. (1969). The personality of high earning MBA's in big business. *Personnel Psychology, 22*, 457–463.

Harrell, T. W. (1970). The personality of high earning MBA's in small business. *Personnel Psychology, 23*, 369–375.

Harrell, T. W., & Harrell, M. S. (1973). The personality of MBA's who reach general management early. *Personnel Psychology, 26*, 127–134.

House, R. J. (1977). A 1976 theory of charismatic leadership. In J. G. Hunt and L. L. Larson (Eds.), *Leadership: The cutting edge*. (pp.189–207). Carbondale, IL: Southern Illinois University Press.

House, R. J. & Aditya, R. N. (1997). The social scientific study of leadership: Quo vadis? *Journal of Management, 23*, 409–473.

House, R. J., Delbecq, A. L., & Taris, T. (1997). *Value-based leadership: A theory and an empirical test*. Working paper, Reginald H. Jones Center for Strategic Management, Wharton School of Management.

House, R. J., Hanges, P. J., Javidan M., & Dorfman, P. W., & GLOBE associates (in press.) Cultures, leadership, and organizations: GLOBE—A 62 nation study. Thousand Oak, CA: Sage.

House, R. J., Hanges, P., & Ruiz-Quintanilla, A. (1997). GLOBE: The Global Leadership and Organization Behavior Effectiveness research program. *Polish Psychological Bulletin, 28*(3), 215–254.

House, R. J., Hanges, P. J., Ruiz-Quintanilla, S. A., Dorfman, P. W., Javidan, M., Dickson, M. W., Gupta, V., and GLOBE Coordinating Team (1999). Cultural influences on leadership and organizations: Project GLOBE. In W. H. Mobley (Ed.). *Advances in global leadership*. Stamford, CN: JAI Press.

House, R. J., Howard, A., & Walker, G. (1991). *The prediction of managerial success: A test of the personal-situation debate.* Working paper no. WP 91–17. Reginald H. Jones Center for Management Policy, Strategy and Organization, University of Pennsylvania.

House, R. J., & Shamir, B. (1993). Towards the integration of transformational, charismatic, and visionary theories. In M. M. Chemers & R. Ayman (Eds.). *Leadership theory and research: Perspectives and directions*. San Diego, CA: Academic Press.

House, R. J., & Singh, J. V. (1987). Organizational behavior: Some new directions for I/O psychology. *Annual Review of Psychology, 38*, 669–718.

House, R.J., Spangler, D., & Woycke, J. (1991). Personality and charisma in the U.S. presidency: A psychological theory of leadership effectiveness. *Administrative Science Quarterly, 36*, 364–396.

Ickes, W. (1993). Empathic accuracy. *Journal of Personality, 61*(4), 587–610.

Jensen, A. R., & Weng, L. (1994). What is a good g? *Intelligence, 18*, 231–258.

Kerr, W. A., & Speroff, B. G. (1954). Validation and evaluation of the empathy test. *Journal of General Psychology, 50*, 369–376.

Kim, G. H. (1997). *Interpersonal acumen: A test of the sequentiality hypothesis on a Korean sample.* Unpublished honors thesis, Temple University, Philadelphia.

Korman, A. K. (1968). The prediction of managerial performance: A review. *Personnel Psychology, 21*, 295–322.

Lord, R. G. & Maher, K. J. (1991). *Leadership and information processing: Linking perception and performance.* Boston: Unwin Hyman.

Mann, R. D. (1959). A review of the relationships between personality and performance in small groups. *Psychological Bulletin, 56*, 241–270.

Mayer, J. D., & Salovey, P. (1993). The intelligence of emotional intelligence. *Intelligence, 17*, 433–442.

McClelland, D. C. (1975). *Power: The inner experience*. New York: Irvington.

McClelland, D. C., & Boyatzis, R. E. (1982). The leadership motive pattern and long-term success in management. *Journal of Applied Psychology, 67*, 737–743.

Meyer, D., & Pressel, L. (1954). Personality test scores in the management hierarchy. *Journal of Applied Psychology, 38*, 73–80.

Mintzberg, H. (1975). The manager's job: Folklore and fact. *Harvard Business Review, 53*(4), 49–61.

Morita, A. (with E. M. Reingold & M. Shimomura). (1986). *Made in Japan: Akio Morita and SONY.* New York: NAL Penguin.

Phillips, L. H., & Rabbitt, P. M. A. (1995). Impulsivity and Speed-Accuracy Strategies in Intelligence Test Performance. *Intelligence, 21*, 13–29.

Piaget, J., & Inhelder, B. (1947). Diagnosis of mental operations and theory of the intelligence. *American Journal of Mental Deficiency, 51*, 401–406.

Rosnow, R. L., Skleder, A. A., Jaeger, M. E., & Rind, B. (1994). Intelligence and the epistemics of interpersonal acumen: testing some implications of H. Gardner's theory. *Intelligence, 19*, 93–116.

Rosnow, R. L., Skleder, A. A., & Rind, B. (1995). Reading other people: A hidden cognitive structure? *The General Psychologist, 31*(1), 1–10.

Rotter, J. B. (1967). A new scale for the measurement of interpersonal trust. *Journal of Personality, 35*, 651–665.

Simonton, D. K. (1994). *Greatness: Who makes history and why*. New York: Guilford.

Snyder, M. (1974). Self-monitoring of expressive behavior. *Journal of Personality and Social Psychology, 30*, 526–537.

Snyderman, M. & Rothman, S. (1987). Survey of expert opinion on intelligence and aptitude testing. *American Psychologist, 42*, 137–144.

Sternberg, R. J. (1988). *The triarchic mind*. New York: Viking.

Sternberg, R. J. (1997). Managerial intelligence: Why IQ isn't enough. *Journal of Management, 23*(3), 475–493.

Sternberg, R. J., & Wagner, R. K. (Eds.). (1986). *Practical intelligence: Nature and origins of competence in the everyday world*. New York: Cambridge University Press.

Stinson, L. & Ickes, W. (1992). Empathic accuracy in the interactions of male friends versus male strangers. *Journal of Personality and Social Psychology, 62*(5), 787–797.

Stotland, E. (1969). Exploratory studies in empathy. In L. Berkowitz (Ed.), *Advances in experimental social psychology* (Vol. 4). New York: Academic Press.

Tunis S. L., & Rosnow, R. L. (1983). Heuristic model of synthetic behavior: Rationale, validation, and implications. *Journal of Mind and Behavior, 4*, 165–178.

Zaccaro, S. J., Gilbert, J. A., Thor, K. K., & Mumford, M. D. (1991). Leadership and social intelligence: Linking social perceptiveness and behavioral flexibility to leader effectiveness. *Leadership Quarterly, 2*(4), 317–342.

Commentary

Multiple Intelligences and Leadership: Implications for Leadership Research and Training

Ronald E. Riggio
Kravis Leadership Institute

Francis J. Pirozzolo
Kravis Leadership Institute and New York Yankees

IN CONCLUSION

This volume has explored some of the most recent developments in the investigation of leadership with a special emphasis on the role of multiple intelligences. The notion that there are multiple forms of intelligence, in addition to the well-known and generally accepted notion of IQ/academic intelligence, has intuitive appeal to practicing managers and leaders (and to just about everyone else). Almost from birth, and certainly throughout years of formal schooling, most people have either been formally tested and know their IQ scores, or they get a pretty good sense of their level of intelligence from grade point averages, from achievement and aptitude tests, or from feedback from teachers, parents, and peers. People also likely believe that aside from formal education, there is not a lot they can do to improve their IQ scores. Therefore, the idea that there are other forms of intelligence—practical intelligence, or what people refer to as "street smarts," or an "emotional intelligence"—suggests that an individual is not limited simply because he or she has a below average or average IQ. And, for those persons blessed with high IQs it is important to know that there are other areas of competence that may be required to be successful. This intuitive appeal has fueled great interest in these "other" forms of intelligence, with perhaps emotional intelligence getting the most attention, thanks largely to popular, best-selling books by Daniel Goleman (1995, 1998). Indeed, entire leadership development programs have been formed around improving emotional intelligence, and terms such as emotional intelligence and social intelligence have become quite commonplace, particularly in work settings. It is our contention, however, that the rush toward developing full-blown programs to dramatically improve one's emotional or social intelligence may be a bit premature.

Research has only just begun to explore these other dimensions of intelligence, and these forms of intelligence are fantastically complex. Moreover, unlike academic intelligence, which is highly verbal in nature, emotional intelligence is primarily nonverbal, while other domains of intelligence, such as social intelligence, practical intelligence, or the concepts of sociopolitical intelligence and cultural intelligence, introduced in this volume by Hogan and Hogan, and Offermann and Phan, respectively, are difficult to conceptualize verbally. As a result, there is great difficulty in operationalizing and measuring these types of intelligence. Additionally, although there have been several models proposed that seek to capture these multiple dimensions of intelligence, such as Gardner's Multiple Intelligences Theory (MIT; 1983, 1995, 1999), Sternberg's Triarchic Theory (1985), and earlier models such as Guilford's (1967), this research is relatively new and sparse in comparison to research on academic intelligence. In short, research on non-IQ domains of intelligence is still relatively new, and methods to measure these constructs are still in their very early stages. Despite these limitations, we firmly believe that these multiple intelligences constructs have important and potentially "earth-shaking" implications for leadership research and theory, and that they will open up new frontiers in leadership training and development.

To a large extent, this volume was the result of an explosion of interest in non-IQ domains of intelligence by leadership practitioners. We sought to bring together renowned leadership scholars and researchers in the area of multiple intelligences to address the question of what is currently known about multiple intelligences constructs and how these impact effective leadership. In other words, despite the hype, what do we really know? We think there are several clear findings.

First, there is general agreement that these different types of intelligence can be very important for effective leadership. Each of the leadership theorists from Fiedler to Bass to Chemers and Winter, incorporates multiple intelligences into their respective leadership theories. For instance, Fiedler in his Cognitive Resources Theory emphasizes that both intelligence (IQ) and experience are important to effective leadership, and he acknowledges that different forms of intelligence are part of the leader's "cognitive resources." Moreover, non-IQ forms of intelligence, such as social and emotional intelligence, may contribute to what Fiedler characterizes as a leader's "experience," a point expanded on by Susan Murphy in a later chapter. Fiedler, however, emphasizes the moderating role of the situation, particularly situational stress, in determining how cognitive resources and leadership experience interact to produce effective or ineffective leadership. From Fiedler's perspective, an important application of multiple intelligences would be to explore the role that emotional and social intelligence might play in helping the leader become more resistant to stress to avoid overtaxing the leader's cognitive processing.

Bass easily incorporates multiple intelligences into his conceptualization of transformational leadership. Operationalizing social and emotional intelligence in terms of associated personality traits (a topic that we will consider later), Bass presents evidence that suggests that both emotional and social intelligence, and to a lesser extent, cognitive intelligence, contribute to transformational leadership. This has obvious and important implications for leadership training, assuming that enhancing multiple intelligences increases a leader's tendency to be transformational.

David Winter's work in leadership emphasizes the importance of key leadership motives, particularly power and achievement. While these motives drive leadership, Winter suggests that multiple intelligences may represent some of the skills needed by effective leaders. He would perhaps view the Hogans' notion of sociopolitical leadership, or Offermann and Phan's cultural intelligence, as more important in this regard. As Winter notes, motives supply the "energy" while multiple intelligences "constitute the mechanisms" of effective leadership (p. 119). Because multiple intelligences are somewhat independent of motives, and because of the relative fidelity of motives, Winter's perspective may be more pertinent to the selection of leaders than to their training or development. In other words, although many individuals may be motivated by power or achievement to lead, relatively few may have the intelligence resources to be truly effective leaders.

In his recent "integrative theory of leadership," Martin Chemers (1997), asserts that there are three key elements of effective leadership: image management, relationship development, and resource deployment. In his chapter, Chemers explores the obvious connection between multiple intelligences and these three leadership elements. Similar to Winter, Chemers believes that the relationship between multiple intelligences and leadership may not be a direct one. According to Chemers, it is leadership efficacy—a sense of confidence and mastery in leadership situations—that connects multiple intelligences and successful leadership.

Although these noted leadership theorists agree that multiple intelligences play a part in leadership effectiveness, there is disagreement about that role. None assert that there is a direct role. Each theorist believes that there are mediators and/or moderators of the multiple intelligences-leadership relationship. For Fiedler and Chemers, the situation clearly moderates the role. For Bass, multiple intelligences contribute to transformational leadership, but transformational leadership is the "prerequisite" for successful leadership. For Winter and Chemers, multiple intelligences and leadership are mediated by motives and self-efficacy, respectively. In short, these leadership theorists are telling us that the relationship between multiple intelligences and leadership is a complex one—one that we are only just beginning to understand. Importantly, however, the notion of multiple intelligences has struck a responsive chord with these scholars, as each is able to integrate this notion into the leadership theories and concepts that each has studied in depth.

Second, there is as yet no generally agreed-upon or integrating framework for identifying multiple intelligences. Although there are at least two well-known frameworks for multiple intelligences (Sternberg's Triarchic Theory of Intelligence (1988), and Howard Gardner's Multiple Intelligences Theory (1983, 1999)), neither seems to adequately encompass the breadth of domains typically considered in discussions of multiple intelligences and neither captures the even broader range of intelligences discussed in this volume. While both Sternberg's and Gardner's theories are highly regarded, neither would adequately address the broad range of multiple intelligences introduced in this book's chapters. For instance, most of social, emotional, sociopolitical, and cultural intelligence would all be subsumed under two of Gardner's categories: interpersonal and intrapersonal intelligence. Sternberg's three domains likewise seem too limited.

In all likelihood, it is far too early in research on multiple intelligences to expect an integrated framework or theory. In fact, within domains of intelligence there is little agreement among theorists (and sometimes even little overlap). Consider, for example, the different definitions and conceptualizations of social intelligence presented by Zaccaro in this volume, by Sternberg (1988), by Cantor and Kihlstrom (1987), and earlier definitions (Ford & Tisak, 1983; Marlowe, 1986). The same is true for emotional intelligence.

Another reason that an integrating framework for multiple intelligences may be premature is the fact that a great deal of important work is being done that has direct implications for multiple intelligences research, but it is not recognized as such. We are most familiar with work that may constitute some of the components of emotional intelligence. For example, researchers in nonverbal communication have for decades attempted to define, isolate, and measure particular nonverbal and emotional communication skills (e.g., Friedman, 1979; Riggio, 1992; Rosenthal, 1979). These nonverbal and emotional skills are important components of the "ability model" of emotional intelligence presented in this volume and elsewhere (Caruso, Mayer, & Salovey, Chap. 4, this volume; Mayer & Salovey, 1997). Likewise, emotion researchers have focused on emotion regulation, also a presumed component of emotional intelligence (Eisenberg & Fabes, 1992; Gross, 1998). In addition, personality and social psychologists have conducted extensive work on empathic accuracy (e.g., Ickes, 1997), which overlaps with both emotional and social intelligence, as does Aditya and House's concept of interpersonal acumen described in this volume. Similarly, Snyder's construct of self-monitoring (Snyder, 1974, 1987)—the ability to monitor and control one's social behavior—seems applicable to the social intelligence-based role-playing skill required of effective leaders (with Chemers, Zaccaro, and other chapter authors recognizing the relevance of self-monitoring). It seems productive to incorporate much of this work into definitions and conceptualizations of both social and emotional intelligence if we are to truly understand the complexity of this domain of intelligence.

Third, measurement of non-IQ domains of intelligence presents a challenge. Psychologists have labored for more than a century developing methods for measuring intelligence. The notion of the Intelligence Quotient is itself over 80 years old (Terman, 1916). Although attempts to measure social intelligence date back to the 1920s (e.g., Moss, Hunt, Omwake, & Ronning, 1927; Thorndike, 1936), this work was soon abandoned. Only in the last two decades have there been dedicated programs designed to measure social intelligence and related constructs, such as practical intelligence and tacit knowledge. The construct of emotional intelligence, and attempts to measure it, is only a decade old. As might be expected, the measurement of non-IQ domains of intelligence is thus in its very early and primitive stages. Moreover, the measurement of social and emotional intelligences are hampered by their sheer complexity, by the abstract nature of these constructs, and by reliance on methods (e.g., verbal and written reports) that are heavily "contaminated" by academic intelligence. Indeed, it was the inability to distinguish social intelligence from academic intelligence that led to the abandonment of social intelligence research in the 1930s (Thorndike & Stein, 1937).

The contributions to this volume provide a sampling of both the breadth and variety of multiple intelligence constructs, and the number of ways these constructs have been operationalized. For example, in examining aspects of leader social intelligence, Sternberg focuses on tacit knowledge, using his and Wagner's *Tacit Knowledge Inventory for Managers* (Wagner & Sternberg, 1991). This measure, which Sternberg refers to as a "situational-judgment test," asks respondents to read a managerial scenario and rate various courses of action. Comparison to various expert ratings is then used to determine an individual's tacit knowledge. Aditya and House use a somewhat similar technique to assess interpersonal acumen, which they believe to be a critical component of social intelligence. Zacarro operationalizes social intelligence by using a variety of self-report measures, including measures of social insight, and self-monitoring. Likewise, the Hogans use self-report personality measures to assess their construct of sociopolitical intelligence.

Self-report measures of personality-like constructs are also used by some of our authors to operationalize emotional intelligence. For instance, Bass suggests that emotional intelligence is represented by possession of traits such as "emotional maturity," "conscientiousness," and lack of neuroticism, anxiety, and depression (p. 106). Murphy uses Riggio's self-report Social Skills Inventory (SSI; Riggio, 1989) to measure both emotional and social intelligence. Moreover, recent research has made use of personality measures such as self-report instruments of empathy, emotion and mood regulation, and trait affect to assess emotional intelligence (e.g., Fox & Spector, 2000), or researchers have created trait-like self-report measures specifically to measure emotional intelligence (e.g., Bar-On, 1997; Schutte, et al. 1998). Although there are advantages to such self-report measures, including their ease of use, cost effectiveness, and established principles for demonstrating their psychometric soundness, social and emotional intelligence are presumably constellations of competencies or abilities, some dimensions of which may be best measured through performance-based ability tests, such as measures developed by Mayer, Salovey, and Caruso (1997, 1999). The issue of self-report versus performance-based measures is an important one in the assessment of emotional communication skills (see Riggio & Riggio, 2001).

In summary, there are a variety of ways of operationalizing non-IQ domains of intelligence, including self-report personality instruments, scenario-based tests, and performance-based measures. Although there have been a large number of different types of measures used to assess social and emotional intelligence, there is concern about whether these various instruments do a good job of capturing these complex constructs, and there is little agreement among researchers regarding the best ways to measure these types of intelligence.

Fourth, incorporating multiple intelligence constructs into leadership research will help elaborate and expand existing leadership theories, and will lead to greater predictive power for those theories. The leadership theorists who contributed to this volume had no difficulty incorporating multiple intelligences constructs into their respective theories and/or conceptualizations of leadership. Bass views multiple intelligences—cognitive intelligence, social intelligence, and emotional intelligence—as core elements of transformational leadership. Winter suggests that multiple types of intelligence interact with motives to influence leadership. Chemers believes that intelligences represent some of the personal resources available to leaders, and that multiple intelligences assist a leader in image management and relationship development. The theorist who made intelligence a core component of his Cognitive Resources Theory, Fred Fiedler, has already explored the complex interaction between cognitive/academic intelligence, experience, situational characteristics and effective leadership, and he hints that other forms of intelligence may also be involved. In her chapter, Susan Murphy suggests that social and emotional intelligence help illustrate how leaders overcome self-or other-imposed situational variables to enact the leadership role. In all likelihood, these represent just the tip of the iceberg in applying multiple intelligences to leadership theory.

There are a number of important leadership theories that are not represented in this volume that could be enhanced by incorporation of multiple intelligences constructs. For example, some leadership theories, such as the Leader-Member Exchange Theory (LMX; Dansereau, Graen, & Haga, 1975; Graen, 1976), emphasize that effective leadership is determined by the quality of the relationship between leaders and followers. Clearly, social and emotional intelligence are constructs that could contribute to leader-follower relationship quality (and it would be important to look at both leader's and follower's possession of social and emotional intelligences).

Charismatic leadership theory would also benefit from consideration of the role that social and especially emotional intelligences play in contributing to a leader's charisma. For instance, Conger and Kanungo (1998) claim that charismatic leaders are particularly sensitive both to followers' needs and to changes in the social environment—abilities that seem closely linked to emotional and social intelligence, respectively. The charismatic leader's ability to arouse and inspire followers also seems connected to a leader's emotional intelligence. In fact, it has been suggested that both social and emotional intelligences are core, necessary components of a leader's personal charisma (Riggio, 1987, 1998).

As non-IQ domains of intelligence become better understood and refined, and with improved measurement of these complex constructs, we anticipate a great impact on leadership research and theory. Earlier attempts to capture the complexity of leadership via personality traits, or through various leadership "styles," were not very successful. Already we are seeing the development of techniques to assess multiple intelligences that recognize both the complexity of these constructs and their multidimensionality.

Finally, research on multiple intelligences has important implications for both the selection and training/development of leaders. Some of the contributors to this volume discussed directly the implications of their research on multiple intelligences to leader selection and training. For instance, the personality-based approach to sociopolitical intelligence presented by Robert and Joyce Hogan, and the measure they have developed to assess it, argue that this may be a critical dimension for selecting potential leaders. Indeed, the Hogans have created measurement tools, and a company (Hogan Assessment Systems), to assist organizations in improving managerial and leader selection. Bass might also argue for a selection-based approach, using multiple intelligence constructs—operationalized as related personality dimensions—to select potential leaders.

In actual managerial selection, multiple intelligences probably play an important although unstated role. In other words, in hiring, informal assessments are made of an individual's intelligence (likely a combination of both academic and social intelligence), of the applicant's interpersonal competence, and perhaps emotional maturity/intelligence. Research on hiring decisions, particularly decisions made primarily on the basis of hiring interview performance, suggest that social intelligence/competence does indeed have an important effect on the judged "hirability" of applicants, as evidence by more favorable evaluations given to persons who possess social, practical, and emotional intelligence (Fox & Spector, 2000; Riggio & Throckmorton, 1988).

Multiple intelligences also play a part in leadership training and development. For example, Offermann and Phan state explicitly that cultural intelligence can be developed in leaders, although they also recognize how important the organization's culture is in promoting positive attitudes toward diverse cultures. Caruso, Mayer, and Salovey believe that many components of emotional intelligence can be trained, but they are cautious in this regard, citing that much of the evidence for the effectiveness of such training is anecdotal. This suggests that the recent explosion in different types of emotional intelligence training programs should be approached cautiously. Although many of these programs may indeed be effective in developing leadership, there has been little evidence evaluating their effectiveness, and we know little about what constitutes "best practices" for increasing emotional intelligence.

Despite this caution, the editors (Riggio, Murphy, and Pirozzolo) have incorporated multiple intelligences as elements of leadership development programs. Riggio and Murphy have used feedback concerning possession of social and emotional communication skills (presumed components of social and emotional intelligence) as a starting point for developing better emotional and interpersonal communication. Pirozzolo has relied on Gardner's Multiple Intelligences Theory in helping guide his leadership development work with athletes, coaches, and executives. Consistent with Gardner's (1995) work, this approach relies heavily on an Eriksonian construct of a "life story" as the centerpiece of a leader's development.

When considering the role of multiple intelligences in leadership training and development, it is imperative that we also recognize the importance of situational factors in effective leadership. Fiedler emphasizes this in his chapter, but nearly all authors caution against focusing too narrowly on leader characteristics or qualities.

Clearly theories of multiple intelligences and leadership theories that take a comprehensive view of the role of leader (looking at the leader's skills, personality, personal history, as well as considering the leadership situation, and the followers) has much to offer the training and development of today's and of future leaders. The research in this volume can do much to inform leadership trainers, although the training may have leapt ahead of the research. When trainers talk about emotional and social intelligence, it hits home because we recognize that IQ alone is not sufficient to ensure effective leadership in business, government, and elsewhere. Successful leadership is extraordinarily complex, and we are only beginning to understand the implications of multiple intelligences for research on leadership, and for leadership selection, training, and development.

REFERENCES

Bar-On, R. (1997). *Bar-On Emotional Quotient Inventory: Technical manual.* Toronto, ON: Multi-Health Systems.

Cantor, N., & Kihlstrom, J. F. (1987). *Personality and social intelligence.* Englewood Cliffs, NJ: Prentice Hall.

Chemers, M. M. (1997). *An integrative theory of leadership.* Mahwah, NJ: Lawrence Erlbaum Associates.

Conger, J. A., & Kanungo, R. N. (1998). Charismatic leadership in organizations. Thousand Oaks, CA: Sage.

Dansererau, F., Graen, G., & Haga, B. (1975). A vertical dyad linkage approach to leadership within formal organizations: A longitudinal investigation of the role-making process. *Organizational Behavior and Human Performance, 13,* 46–78.

Eisenberg, N., & Fabes, R. A. (1992). Emotion, regulation, and the development of social competence. *Review of Personality and Social Psychology, 12,* 119–150.

Ford, M., & Tisak, M. S. (1983). A further search for social intelligence. *Journal of Educational Psychology, 75,* 197–206.

Fox, S., & Spector, P. E. (2000). Relations of emotional intelligence, practical intelligence, general intelligence, and trait affectivity with interview outcomes: It's not all just 'G.' *Journal of Organizational Behavior, 21,* 203–220.

Friedman, H. S. (1979). The concept of skill in nonverbal communication: Implications for understanding social interaction. In R. Rosenthal (Ed.), *Skill in nonverbal communication* (pp. 2–27). Cambridge, MA: Oelgeschlager, Gunn & Hain.

Gardner, H. (1983). *Frames of mind: The theory of multiple intelligences.* New York: Basic Books.

Gardner, H. (1995). *Leading minds: An anatomy of leadership.* New York: Basic Books.

Gardner, H. (1999). *Intelligence reframed: Multiple intelligences for the 21st century.* New York: Basic Books.

Goleman, D. (1995). *Emotional intelligence: Why it can matter more than IQ.* New York: Bantam.

Goleman, D. (1998). *Working with emotional intelligence.* New York: Bantam.

Graen, G. (1976). Role-making processes within complex organizations. In M. D. Dunnette (Ed.), *Handbook of industrial and organizational psychology,* (pp. 1201–1245). Chicago: Rand McNally.

Gross, J. J. (1998). The emerging field of emotion regulation: An integrative review. *Review of General Psychology, 2,* 271–299.

Guilford, J. P. (1967). *The nature of human intelligence.* New York: McGraw-Hill.

Ickes, W. (Ed.). (1997). *Empathic accuracy.* New York: Guilford.

Marlowe, H. A. (1986). Social intelligence: Evidence for multidimensionality and construct independence. *Journal of Educational Psychology, 78,* 52–58.

Mayer, J. D., & Salovey, P. (1997). What is emotional intelligence? In P. Salovey & D. Sluyter (Eds.). *Emotional development and emotional intelligence: Implications for educators.* (pp. 3–31). New York: Basic Books.

Mayer, J. D., Salovey, P., & Caruso, D. R. (1997). *The Multifactor Emotional Intelligence Test (MEIS).* Available from the authors.

Mayer, J. D., Salovey, P., & Caruso, D. R. (1999). *The Mayor-Salovey-Caruso Emotional Intelligence Test (MSCEIT).* Toronto, ON: Multi-Health Systems.

Moss, F. A., Hunt, Omwake, K. T., & Ronning, M. M. (1927). *Social intelligence test.* Washington, DC: George Washington University.

Riggio, R. E. (1987). *The charisma quotient.* New York: Dodd, Mead.

Riggio, R. E. (1989). *Manual for the Social Skills Inventory.* Palo Alto, CA: Consulting Psychologists Press.

Riggio, R. E. (1992). Social interaction skills and nonverbal behavior. In R. S. Feldman (Ed.), *Applications of nonverbal behavioral theories and research.* (pp. 3–30). Hillsdale, NJ: Lawrence Erlbaum Associates.

Riggio, R. E. (1998). Charisma. In H. S. Friedman (Ed.), *Encyclopedia of mental health.* (pp. 387–396). San Diego, CA: Academic Press.

Riggio, R. E., & Riggio, H. R. (2001). Self-report measurement of interpersonal sensitivity. In J. A. Hall, & F. Bernieri (Eds.), *Measurement of interpersonal sensitivity.* Mahwah, NJ: Lawrence Erlbaum Associates.

Riggio, R. E., & Throckmorton, B. (1988). The relative effects of verbal and nonverbal behavior, appearance, and social skills on evaluations made in hiring interviews. *Journal of Applied Social Psychology, 18,* 331–348.

Rosenthal, R. (Ed.), (1979). *Skill in nonverbal communication.* Cambridge, MA: Oelgeschlager, Gunn & Hain.

Schutte, N. S., Malouff, J. M., Hall, L. E., Haggerty, D. J., Cooper, J. T., Golden, C. J., Dornheim, L. (1998). Development and validation of a measure of emotional intelligence. *Personality and Individual Differences, 25,* 167–177.

Snyder, M. (1974). The self-monitoring of expressive behavior. *Journal of Personality and Social Psychology, 30,* 526–537.

Snyder, M. (1987). *Public appearances/private realities: The psychology of self-monitoring.* New York: W. H. Freeman.

Sternberg, R. J. (1985). *Beyond IQ: A triarchic theory of human intelligence.* Cambridge: Cambridge University Press.

Sternberg, R. J. (1988). *The triarchic mind: A new theory of human intelligence.* New York: Viking.

Sternberg, R. J., & Wagner, R. K. (1986). *Practical intelligence: Nature and origins of competence in the everyday world.* Cambridge: Cambridge University Press.

Terman, L. M. (1916). *The measurement of intelligence.* Boston: Houghton Mifflin.

Thorndike, R. L. (1936). Factor analysis of social and abstract intelligence. *Journal of Educational Psychology, 27,* 231–233.

Thorndike, R. L., & Stein, S. (1937). An evaluation of the attempts to measure social intelligence. *Psychological Bulletin, 34,* 275–285.

Wagner, R. K., & Sternberg, R. J. (1991). *Tacit knowledge inventory for managers.* San Antonio, TX: Psychological Corporation.

Author Index

X, Y

Z

Subject Index

D

E

F

G

H

I

J

K

L

Q, R

S

T

U

V

W

X, Y, Z